WHY IN THE WORLD *NOT*?

AN INTRODUCTION TO DASEINANALYSIS

MILES GROTH

First published in 2024 by
Free Association Books

Copyright © 2024 Miles Groth

The author's rights are fully asserted. The rights of
Miles Groth to be identified as the author of this work
has been asserted by him in accordance with the
Copyright, Designs and Patents Act 1988

A CIP Catalogue of this book is available from
the British Library

ISBN: 978-1-91138-392-5

All rights reserved; no part of this publication may be reproduced, stored in a retrieval system, or transmitted, in any form or by any means, electronic, mechanical, photocopying, recording or otherwise, without the prior written permission of the publisher. Nor be circulated in any form of binding or cover other than that in which it is published and a similar condition including this condition being imposed on the subsequent purchaser.

Typeset by
Typo•glyphix
www.typoglyphix.co.uk

Cover design by
Candescent

Printed in the UK

Virtually everything remains unpredictable about psychotherapy.
Medard Boss

**For
E.S.**

Table of Contents

Preface   vii
Introduction   xi

PART I   BACKGROUND AND THEORY   1

Chapter One
The Term 'Daseinanalysis'   3

Chapter Two
What Daseinanalysis Is Not   7

    (1) Psychoanalysis   7
    (2) Psychiatry   8
    (3) Psychotherapy   19
    (4) Pastoral Care   20

Chapter Three
Daseinanalysis and Psychoanalysis   23

Chapter Four
Theory and Basic Principles   27

    (1) Dasein and Temporality   27
    (2) The Existentives (Existentials)   28
    (3) Language   31
    (4) Person and Other   32
    (5) Caring about Things [Sorge] and Caring about the Other [Fürsorge]   32

PART II   PRACTICE AND PREPARATION   35

Chapter Five
Fundamentals   37

    (1) The Couch   37
    (2) The Fundamental Rule   39

(3) Encounter   *41*
(4) The Art of Conversation   *46*
(5) The Psychotherapeutic Eros   *50*
(6) Dreaming Life   *54*
(7) 'Why?' and 'Why in the world not?'   *60*

Chapter Six
Preparation   61

Introduction   *61*
American Daseinsanalytic Institute (ADI)   *61*
    (1) Program Curriculum   *62*
    (2) The Teaching Analysis   *64*
    (3) Supervision   *64*
    (4) The Control Analysis   *65*

PART III   AN ANNOTATED REVIEW OF SELECTED WRITINGS OF MEDARD BOSS   67

Introductory Note   *69*
Chronological Listing of Publications (1929-2003)   *73*
Biographical and Scientific Texts   *78*
(I) Biographical Texts   *79*
    Interlude   *112*
(II) Publications on Selected Themes   *113*
    (A) The Theory and Practice of Daseinanalysis (1947-1988)   *113*
    (B) The Eastern Influence (1959-2003)   *167*
    (C) Martin Heidegger (1959-2003)   *174*
Concluding Note   *201*

Acknowledgements   *205*
Bibliography   *207*
Appendix   *229*
Notes   *231*
Index   *285*

Preface

Psychiatry and psychotherapy are at a critical point in their parallel and sometimes shared paths. The former had a tradition of a little over a century when an Austrian neurologist offered it a form of psychotherapy that came to be known as psychoanalysis. In Europe, Freud's psychotherapy was readily taken up by psychiatrists working in asylums for the insane and sanitariums for the wealthy to try out as an alternative to the often barbaric ways of management of individuals incarcerated in the former and to the genteel, solicitous care of those residing in the latter. In the States, psychoanalysis was heartily embraced, but psychoanalytic training institutes were from the start open only to psychiatrists, who, as psychoanalysts usually then did, worked in institutions and clinics but soon also practiced out of their homes, much as physicians had since medicine gained scientific respectability.

Psychotherapy for the many had not yet become popular in Europe or the States when, in the 1940s, psychiatry and psychoanalysis came under the influence of the fundamental ontology and analytics of existence of Martin Heidegger (1889-1976), thanks to the response to his work, first by the Swiss hospital psychiatrist, Ludwig Binswanger (1881-1966), and soon after by Medard Boss (1903-1990), a psychiatrist and psychoanalyst who in his early career also worked in institutions but later, like most psychoanalysts, for the most part only saw patients in a consulting room located in his home overlooking Lake Zurich.

The initially close tie between psychotherapy and psychiatry has weakened and most psychiatrists engage very little in conversation with their patients, talking with them only long enough to justify making a diagnosis based on criteria named in the regularly revised *Diagnostic and Statistical Manual of Psychological Disorders* (currently, edition *5-TR*, 2022).[1] The heyday of psychotherapy began in the 1970s and 1980s, but only recently has it been acknowledged to have had a very poor success rate from the start. This has also been the case with pharmacotherapy, which lacks scientific justification based on neurophysiological studies of the kind demanded by general medical practice. Meanwhile, human beings continue to seek out other human beings to meet exclusively to talk about what troubles them when a medical cause for their symptoms has been ruled out.

Daseinanalysis offers an alternative to both psychiatry and psychotherapy. As we will see, daseinanalysis has as little to do with psychotherapy as psychotherapy has to do with psychiatry. While the approach originated among psychiatrists, going forward, however, most candidates for preparation as daseinanalysts will come from academic backgrounds other than medicine. In the not too distant future these other areas will increasingly be philosophy and the humanities, as was the case in the early days of psychoanalysis. Just why we can expect that trend will become clear in what follows.

The disentangling of daseinanalysis from its origins among psychiatrists and psychoanalysts and its later affair with clinical psychology and the full range of the mental illness-care professions, including existential analysis, is already under way in earnest.[2] It is a challenging liberation. This book is part of the radical declaration of independence of daseinanalysis from the medical mode and a response to an unexpected renaissance of interest in the approach during the last decade. While some claim that, having had a brief golden age, daseinanalysis is now over and done with, it is my belief that it has not yet gotten fully under way and holds promise for providing a genuinely human therapy, a therapy of the human being as other that has eluded previous attempts to address the existential hindrances and turning points that are inevitable in everyday life when possibilities are constricted and freedom is at stake for an individual.

Just how radical daseinanalysis is in our era of the hegemony of natural science, including medicine, has also not yet been fully appreciated. Acknowledging the ongoing professional use of and popular familiarity with the language of psychopathology, daseinanalysis is systematically deconstructing both, replacing the medical jargon of signs, symptoms, diagnosis, prognosis and treatment plans with the language of the phenomena of immediate experience. Especially since it eschews the mindset of psychopathology, daseinanalysis does not claim that it is appropriate for one given diagnostic category or spectrum of so-called psychological disorders and not for others.

Daseinanalysis provides an opportunity to recover and explore possibilities of which one has lost sight but which are there to be open to, given a situation in which such possibilities may emerge without prejudice and be explored. Only the degree of freedom to which an individual is attuned determines whether or not daseinanalysis is suitable for him at a given moment in his life. Often a period of preparation is required before one can risk giving up the securities of meeting *vis-à-vis* that he may for a time require so that daseinanalysis can have its full effect in its setting, with the analysand reclining and the analyst sitting beside or behind him and out of view.

Daseinanalysis is the result of an unlikely meeting between contemporary Continental philosophy and that small group of human beings who have felt called upon to respond to fellow beings in a way that is oriented first of all to the common humanity of both analyst and analysand. It plays out for the analyst as an intentionally non-interventional, way-making caring about the other and is committed first and foremost to the freedom of the other. Daseinanalysis is a helping profession only in the sense that it calls on the analysand to help himself, first by as fully as possible recovering his commitment to care about things in general. The latter is understood to be every human being's inherent tendency, around which a number of other equally fundamental tendencies are structured. Daseinanalysis is a calling that makes it possible for the analyst to be there for the other in a partnership with him. It creates the situation for a unique relationship in which the other is afforded sovereign priority, often for the first time in his life.

The goal of this introduction to daseinanalysis is to express in plain language what daseinanalysis is and is not, with special attention to how it is practiced. I begin by contrasting it in detail with psychiatry and the many modalities of psychotherapy and psychological intervention (including forms of existential analysis) that have come to be available to the public since the first modern form of psychotherapy, Freud's psychoanalysis, was deployed. While it is true that daseinanalysis had its origins in psychoanalysis, it is important to emphasize from the outset that it is radically different from the latter in having abandoned the notion of an entity known as the *psyche* as well as the metapsychology that attempts to describe the structure of and understand the functioning of the former.

Daseinanalysis does not claim to replace the great variety of therapeutic modalities known to the public. For some, for example, who are genetically damaged or have suffered terrible neurological assaults *in utero*, perinatally, or during the early months and years of infancy and childhood, compassionate management of behavior must in most cases be the treatment of choice, with the judicious use of medications in some cases to mollify experience in general. Therapeutic interventions in these cases are the province of medicine in general and psychiatry in particular. In addition, training (behavior modification and 'shaping' of behavior), education or re-education, social work and any of a great number of kinds of aid and support that are available from individuals, institutional parental and familial surrogates such as group homes and support groups, are indicated to help such individuals. We must admit that, after a great fall, sometimes Humpty-Dumpty cannot be made whole again and, if he has been damaged such that he cannot even first sit on a wall, we must care for him as well we can, perhaps for the duration of his life.

It has become common to invoke hypothetical physiological dysfunction as causal explanations of the failure of individuals to recognize, embrace, and act out of their freedom. It has become the quest of neuroscience to explain human experience and behavior at the level of the cell and understand the influences of hormones and other substances circulating in the bloodstream and other circuits within the organism on cellular processes However, such explanatory models, including the now popular attempt at a neurological revision of psychoanalysis and disciplines within medicine such as psychoneuroendocrinology, fail to consider that the human being is endowed with the freedom to choose to do otherwise than he has, even for decades, and to act on the basis of such choices with a recognition, however dim at first, of the responsibility that is also part of his being free. In the end, the topic of daseinanalysis is freedom, that irrational feature of beings that are human.

In Part I, I explain what daseinanalysis is not, recount its origins and present its basic principles. In Part II, I describe its practice and how individuals are prepared for such practice. In Part III, I conclude with a survey of the work of Medard Boss, who may be credited with having founded *therapeutic* daseinanalysis. In that review, we will reprise what was outlined in Part I.[3]

Introduction

In a prefatory note to an essay first published in 1980 in *Commentary*, 'Analysis Terminable,' Frederick Crews observed that 'the aggregate curative record was dismal' for psychoanalysis, recalling that, for Freud, 'unique therapeutic efficacy was an indispensable warrant' for his metapsychology.[4] Given Freud's own caveat, if psychoanalysis failed to produce therapeutically viable results, the credibility of its metapsychology had to be called into question. That turned out to be the case. Medard Boss knew this even before psychoanalysis had begun to lose its *caché* and offered a re-envisioning of it that is not underwritten by Freud's philosophy. It was his intention to save what was therapeutically valuable in psychoanalysis while jettisoning its theoretic dross. The result was daseinanalysis.

But not only has orthodox psychoanalysis failed to provide what Freud and his followers had promised. At the present time, in the States, the rate of efficacy of 'psychodynamic psychotherapy' in general is judged to be at about 5 percent.[5] This is an astonishing statistic. If a procedure in medicine or surgery had had such a poor success rate over even a fairly short period of time, it would have been abandoned. Since its widespread use since the last quarter of the twentieth century, psychotherapy broadly defined and in its many iterations can be expected to have that same fate. It is for this reason that it has become incumbent upon us to ask whether there is something better to offer our fellow human beings.

Crews was outspoken in designating psychotherapists as 'hired friends.' And so, in a sense, they are.[6] Here it is appropriate to once again compare the psychotherapist with the psychiatrist, who is in the first place a physician bound by his oath to do no harm and to protect his patient. One does not consult a physician to find a friend. Instead, one wants a skilled scientist and technician, albeit a compassionate one.[7] So-called 'bedside manner' counts for a great deal, but the effectiveness of the physician lies in the quality of the advice offered to the patient and his power to convince the patient to trust his clinical judgment and follow his recommendations. Doctors write orders and prescribe treatments and regimens. Of course, the patient is under no obligation to follow the orders given, as he must when told to do or desist from doing something by, say, an officer of the law. By contrast, a psychotherapist is sought out as a 'friend' of a special sort. He is a surrogate for a trusted 'real' friend. As the first psychotherapists made clear, outside of the consulting room contact with the patient was to be avoided. And yet, during the analytic hour, a powerful closeness was dynamically in play. The patient told the analyst things he might not tell even his best friend.

Introduction

There came a time in recent history when it was more and more frequently the case that a family member was not available to an individual to discuss a sensitive issue, and 'real' friends with whom one could speak openly seemed to have become rarer. At the turn of the twentieth century, this achieved critical mass and a special form of relationship was invented to stand in for one of the former. This was provided by the psychotherapist as 'hired friend.' As we will see, however, the daseinanalyst differs from the psychotherapist in the most fundamental way. Instead of providing a friendship (which often has been purchased at great expense in the world of psychotherapy), the daseinanalyst offers a *partnership* that is more intimate than a relationship with a 'hired friend.' This partnership is described in detail in the following pages. It is important to keep in mind that, although he does not function under the seal of the Hippocratic oath (as the psychiatrist does), the psychotherapist nonetheless functions on the basis of the medical model and in practice is indistinguishable from the psychiatrist in most ways, with the exception of not having access to the prescription pad. That is not the case for the daseinanalyst.

H. C. Rümke (1893-1967), a Dutch psychiatrist and psychotherapist, defined psychotherapy as 'the art of conversation.'[8] He was correct, but the conversation in which daseinanalysts engage with their analysands is quite different from that observed between a psychotherapist and his patient, a doctor and his patient, a priest and a penitent, or an attorney and his client. We will see what is special about the daseinanalyst's linguistic comportment toward his analysand[9] and that it is intimately connected with the very nature of language itself, that utterly baffling phenomenon which is our link with the ineffable.

Understanding the uniqueness of the overall comportment and language of the daseinanalyst depends on familiarity with the notion of *Dasein* introduced by Martin Heidegger in his book *Sein und Zeit* [*Being and Time*] (1927). There we read (and here we greatly simplify) that having already met as *Dasein* and *Dasein* is basic to every human being's experience of and behavior with the other.[10] That is to say, we are all fundamentally already there in relation to each other, existing in the world together, before any particular relationship between any two human beings can develop. This being there together with the other is the origin of the daseinanalytic partnership. Highly nuanced in its development, the partnership will reflect the many individual differences between the two human beings involved in it (sex, age, ethnicity and the rest), but what is most important is that it rests on a prior, immediate *Dasein* to *Dasein* relation, one which knows nothing of such differences.

The closeness of the daseinanalytic meeting or encounter cannot be assessed quantitatively. It cannot be valued at a given number of euros or dollars per forty-five minutes of clock time. What this means for the issue of charging a fee for daseinanalysis is therefore a vexing issue. At the present time, all daseinanalysts charge a fee, just as psychotherapists and medical doctors do. On occasion, some offer their being present in conversation *pro bono* to certain individuals, again just as psychotherapists and doctors sometimes do. And yet, if daseinanalysis is not a service or a profession, but rather a calling, how are we to understand the financial arrangement between daseinanalyst and daseinanalysand?[11]

Introduction

The daseinanalyst, who understands his work as the response to a calling, sees his role in the partnership with the analysand as more like that of a priest or pastor mediating a sacrament for another than a physician intervening to provide a service in order to create the conditions most favorable for the body to heal itself. A very real question then arises about how charging a fee for daseinanalysis is to be justified. Some further, although brief, comments are in order to frame this issue from the outset. It is a touchy issue indeed and bound to come up, so we cannot pretend it is not there. That said, what follows will not provide an easy solution to the problems raised by the issue.

We have said that the daseinanalyst answers to a calling, and that is central to the discussion. A clergyman also answers to a calling. Being a priest, rabbi or pastor is not a profession. Yet such individuals must have the means to live somewhere, be clothed, eat and be taken care of should medical problems arise. The Catholic Church as an institution overseeing the great variety of Holy Orders to which an unmarried man or woman may belong by professing vows of chastity, poverty and obedience sees to its members' needs. A Protestant clergyman and his family are supported by the clergyman's congregation who hand over regular offerings (tithes) to be used to pay his bills. Various arrangements of this kind are made for other religious denominations. By contrast, the daseinanalyst lacks such institutional or communal support.

The comparison between the two sorts of calling also breaks down when one realizes that the clergyman serves both a flock or congregation *and* individuals. By contrast, the daseinanalyst, serially, serves only individuals and practices, first, as an individual and not a member of an order.[12] He does not rely on an institution or community of believers or followers to support him. What, then, should his status be if he is to have a place in society? And what should be provided to such individuals by way of some kind of collective mutuality of support and a means to pass along the approach from generation to generation by way of programs of preparation and mentorship as well as meeting the needs of everyday life? As to the financial issue, the most feasible solution at this time and one that I would encourage trying out, is to face the reality that *the daseinanalyst must earn his living doing something else*, for example, working as a psychiatrist or clinical psychologist or teacher but also practice as a daseinanalyst, only not at the same time and without blurring the boundaries between working as a professional and working in response to a calling. Of course, since it is not possible for a psychiatrist to temporarily suspend his oath, it would seem that psychiatrists are precluded from daseinanalytic practice, even if they declared they were for the time being engaged in daseinanalytic practice. As to the matter of preparing the next generation of daseinanalysts, the best model for this is very likely the medieval guild, which provides opportunities to meet and discuss the approach with mentors as well as a framework of formal preparation for passing along the approach. In fact, the several daseinanalytic institutes now in place are quite independent and serve this guild-like function.

There is another angle from which to approach the issue of earning a livelihood and answering to a calling. And that is the example of Medard Boss himself. We had in Boss a person of his generation who was a psychiatrist, psychoanalyst, philosopher, and daseinanalyst. He accepted fees as a physician but practiced as a daseinanalyst. Today this cannot be an acceptable compromise, primarily because the practice of medicine has changed so dramatically from being a physician to being a technician and the issue of the Hippocratic oath's binding character. More important, if it is the case that there are some human activities the value of which cannot be assessed in terms of euros or dollars, how can a fee be expected for doing them? As we have seen, this is the case for the priest who has taken holy vows, but it is also the case for the philosopher and, I would argue, must also be for the daseinanalyst, if he is to be more than a 'hired friend.' Much of Boss's time was spent reading, thinking and writing and, apart from a few Swiss *francs* in royalties for his books, he was never paid for precisely what he spent most of his most valuable time doing in coming to formulate the practice we know as daseinanalysis. Like thinking, daseinanalytic conversation does not have a dollar-per-hour value. Including daseinanalytic work with activities such as thinking and writing makes sense if one considers that for some (perhaps for all) human beings thinking is their principal calling and as such not something one could be compensated for since, like a calling, it cannot be ignored and its value is in any case indeterminable – priceless, as we say. Writing, of course, is a calling only for some, as is the case for entering the religious life. So also, I would argue, is attending to the other as daseinanalyst. The same inestimable value of any of the callings named implies that the whole matter of financial arrangement must be put to one side, unless a calling is mistaken for a profession. Teach or do what you like to earn a living -- but consider that for the daseinanalyst time is not money.

We must try to come to terms with all this in the coming years. I have only pointed out the issue and it is daunting. At this point, I can only say that a necessary start will be to disentangle daseinanalysis from all connections with the professions *and* with 'third parties' (private insurance payers and governments which reallocate tax money and pay for 'healthcare'), with the clear understanding that whenever such involvement is in the background, the spectral haunting by that third party cannot fail to occur even in the extreme privacy of the consulting room where there should be only the analyst and the analysand.

Even though, like the psychoanalytic situation, the daseinanalytic setting has sometimes been compared to the confessional, I am not suggesting that daseinanalysts are like clergy. In the case of the priest and his penitent, what is spoken through the *Sprachgitter* may not be repeated by the priest to any third person. What is said is known only to the confessor, the penitent – and God. That has not changed. Since he was a medical doctor, what Boss's patients said to him was under the strict seal of privileged communication. But here things have changed. Currently, in the States, by law, medical records (including those of psychiatrists) can be acquired by a court order, subpoenaed *duces tecum*. In most states this is also required of all licensed 'mental health professionals' such as psychotherapists (and teachers in public schools, by the way) who must report to the proper civic authority any patient's talk of suicide or a threat of homicide or terrorist destruction of property. As noted, in most jurisdictions, the license of the mental health professional may be revoked if it is determined that he failed to do so. This has compromised psychiatry (and medicine) and psycho-

Introduction

therapy, however. It would seem that only daseinanalysis remains a therapeutic approach that honors the privacy of the other. This does not, however, entail that it is equivalent to the confessional.

Like doctors, psychotherapists now practice under very different conditions from the confessional, which remains the only reserve of complete confidentiality between two human beings – other than daseinanalysis.[13] It is obvious that the legal requirements imposed on doctors and psychotherapists have compromised the seal of confidentiality which genuine therapy requires. Daseinanalysis can offer a secular equivalent to the priest's sacred seal of absolute confidentiality. As long as it remains caught up in and entangled with psychiatry and psychotherapy, however, this remains problematic for daseinanalysis. There is no more important reason than this for understanding the need for daseinanalysis to declare a full declaration of independence from the illness-care professions.

To be even clearer: Daseinanalys is a not a hybrid – somewhat profession and somewhat calling – as even teaching, for example, has become for many. The latter example is instructive. In the millennia following Socrates and his maieutic encounters with young interlocutors (from whom he did not assess a tuition fee, by the way) and who sat together with him in the agora in dialogue for hours at a stretch, a great many early teachers in the West were also clergy associated with the Roman Catholic Church. Beginning with the first university, which was founded in 1088, in Bologna by a guild of *students*, independent scholars from around the known world were invited to come to that town, join the community of young scholars *at their behest* and form a miniature 'universe' of collegiality with them. Such guests from all over Europe were paid by students to travel to be with them, live with them at their *scholae*, and teach them the liberal arts and, later, also the sciences. Like Socrates, the reward of the *magistri* was answering a calling, but they were also supported at the universities for their work. In another sense, then, the present identity of the daseinanalyst is perhaps best compared to that of the earliest university teachers.[14] We will see how this plays out.

Finally, a word by way of introduction is in order about the term *therapy*. I will often speak about what is therapeutic about daseinanalysis. As well as being related to the earliest university *magistri* the daseinanalyst's calling may be traced back to the ancient Therapeutae. Mentioned by Philo of Alexandria, they were a Jewish sect related to the Essenes and known throughout the Greek world in the first centuries of the Common Era. Their name is based on the Greek verb ϖ , which means 'to attend to,' in order to enhance the conditions of the self-healing powers of the person attended. In this, they shared the understanding of the physicians of the Hippocratic school that the body heals itself. Any 'healer' can only set the best conditions for that to take place. It is worth noting that *ab initio* the service of the Therapeutae was to the gods, however, not to those whom they attended. Only later, in the era of the New Testament, did their service become associated with the care of the other. As in the case of the priest, the effectiveness of the Therapeutae was thought to have been based on their mediation of divine influence and the results of their practice were not explicable in terms of the medical interventions of the Hippocratic school. And, inci-

Introduction

dentally, like Socrates, they did not charge a fee.[15] Dare we attribute to the daseinanalyst a similar sort of mediation? I leave that to others to consider.

I wish to stress that the genuine sense of therapeutic influence remains central to the daseinanalytic approach but has been lost to psychiatry and psychotherapy. As we will see in what follows, the reason for this is that the starting point of the daseinanalyst as therapist is not the psyche but instead the *Dasein* of the other. This mere assertion will be considered with care in what follows.

We have now pointed out some difficult and sensitive issues that daseinanalysis forces us to consider. No claim is made to even having fully elucidated them, let alone found solutions to the problems they raise. But we are not hear to discuss therapy in the age of capitalism. We therefore leave those issues now for later consideration and turn to our topic as such, namely, the background of daseinanalysis as an approach to therapy and its theoretical ground.

PART I
BACKGROUND AND THEORY

Chapter One
The Term 'Daseinanalysis'[16]

Daseinsanalyse is a therapeutic approach that originated in the tradition of Sigmund Freud's (1856-1939) orthodox psychoanalysis. It was introduced into psychiatry by name in the early 1940s by the Swiss psychiatrist Ludwig Binswanger (1881-1966) and took on its most advanced form with the work of the Swiss psychiatrist and psychoanalyst, Medard Boss (1903-1990). According to Gerhard Fichtner, the name *Daseinsanalyse* was suggested by Jakob Wyrsch (1892-1980) at a meeting of the Psychological Society in Bern, Switzerland, on October 23, 1942, where Binswanger read a paper called 'Über Daseinserkenntnis [On Knowledge of Existence].'[17]

A literal translation of the German word *Daseinsanalyse* yields 'analysis of existence,' since the German word '*Daseinsanalyse*' consists of a combination of the possessive form of the noun *Dasein* (that is, *Daseins-*) and the noun *Analyse* (that is, *-analyse*). Daseinanalysis was introduced to English-speaking readers as 'Daseinsanalysis', a word that replicates the German term and merely replaces the German suffix '*-se*' with the English equivalent '*-is*'. Initially, *Daseinsanalyse* was sometimes translated as 'existential analysis', as was *Existenzanalyse*. This left a trail of muddled usage which is still being cleared up. To complicate matters further, a number of psychotherapeutic modalities collectively known as 'existential analysis' are subsumed by the general term 'existential therapy.'[18]

The word 'daseinanalysis' is formed with the German noun '*Dasein*' (existence) and the English noun 'analysis', which is derived from the Greek verb ἀναλύω (*analuō*) and in its primary sense means 'to set loose' or 'free from its mooring.' This is the sense it has for daseinanalysis. A secondary meaning of the verb ἀναλύω, as used, for example, in chemistry and in psychoanalysis, means 'to break apart into constitutive elements.' This is the sense it has in Freud's *Psychoanalyse*.

In its everyday usage, the noun *Dasein* denotes 'existence' or, more commonly, 'life'. In philosophy, it denotes a predicate of a being, indicating that whatever being is under consideration is real (a stone in the road, a human body sitting across from me) by contrast with an imaginary or fanciful being such as a unicorn. An additional sense of existence in everyday usage is that the being in question can be apprehend it with the senses. However, the German word *Dasein*, as used by Binswanger and those who followed in the tradition of daseinanalysis, is a *terminus technicus* introduced by Martin Heidegger in 1927 in his book *Sein und Zeit* [*Being and Time*]. In that work, *Dasein* denotes the ontological condition of the possibility of the ontic actualization of the life [*Existenz*] of a human being.[19] As *Dasein*, the human being is utterly unique and different from all other beings, from the most lowly inorganic thing to the *summum ens*, God.

In his analytics [*Analytik*][20] of *Dasein*, i.e. his *Daseinsanalytik*, Heidegger makes a distinction between what he terms the *ontological* [*ontologisch*] and the *ontic* [*ontisch*]. What is termed *ontological* refers to the structure of human being as existing, as *Dasein*. What is termed *ontic* refers to the actualization of the possibilities inherent to a named *Dasein*. Heidegger's usage of 'ontology' deviates from its traditional sense as that branch of philosophy which is 'the study of what is', distinguished since the mid-eighteenth century from philosophy's other branches: metaphysics, epistemology, ethics and aesthetics. The distinction between the ontological or possible [*das Dasein*] and the ontic or actual [*das Daseiende*] Heidegger terms the 'ontological difference'.

Heidegger warns that such a distinction is only conceptual, however, and potentially misleading, since we know of the ontological only because we have already actualized it to some extent as ontic and can therefore make statements about the ontological and the ontic and their difference. In experience, the human being exists both ontologically and ontically. In the order of the occurrence of matters considered by an outsider, the human being is 'first' ontological (*Dasein*). In the order of experience, however, which is always one's own ontic actuality, the ontic *appears* to take priority.

Heidegger speaks of his project in *Being and Time* as a fundamental ontology, that is, an ontology of human being as existing. Ontology in the traditional sense understands *all* beings according to the classic categories of Aristotle. Heidegger's fundamental ontology, however, is based on a different set of 'categories' which he refers to as existentives or existentials [*Existenziale*].[21]

We read in Heidegger's book: '*Das Wesen des Daseins liegt in seiner Existenz.*'[22] This can be translated: 'The essence of existence is in its existing.' What does this short assertion mean to say? It is perhaps best understood if we consider a bit more carefully the phenomenon of existence [*Dasein*] in terms of the ontological difference, that is, the different between what is given as our *Dasein* (the ontological) and the playing out or actualization of any given existence in everyday life (the ontic).

Understood ontologically, at conception a human being's existence is pure possibility. It is ontically nothing since none of its existential possibilities has yet unfolded. It is an animal being. As embryologists have learned, the zygote is at first undifferentiated as to sex and the primitive embryo is without any anatomically distinguishing features, although what is to become of it during gestation regarding the determination of its sex and other 'givens' is contained in its genetic make-up in the very first cell created at conception. In one sense, then, every zygote is the same as every other zygote, but it is also utterly different genetically from the rest. Ontologically, we are fated to be the same; ontically, we are bound to be different.

The Term 'Daseinanalysis'

Ontically, *Dasein's* history then begins, the range of actualizations of its possibilities circumscribed by implicit (genetic) givens such as its sex, circumstantial givens such as the state of the intrauterine environment, and after roughly nine months its place and time of birth. After birth, the actualizations of an existence are constrained by all manner of happenstance, including the physical environment (*Umwelt*), parenting style, and cultural influences evoked in reaction to accidents of a body's anatomical features (genitalia, skin pigmentation and other genetically determined details). The final actualization of existence is its dying. At that point, possibility no longer ranges over actuality.

With these considerations in mind, we may speak of beings other than the human being using the relative pronoun 'what' (and 'something') and reserve 'who' (and 'someone') for *Dasein*. At its death, the *who* of existence cannot realize further possibilities. The human being *is* for the first time. It no longer exists and has become a *what*.[23]

Chapter Two
What Daseinanalysis Is Not

Recalling the two components of the term 'daseinanalysis',[24] we may characterize the goal of the therapeutic approach so named as the freeing up of a given *Dasein* for its possibilities. To be clear about what daseinanalysis is, we must first consider what it is not.

(1) Psychoanalysis

Daseinanalysis is not psychoanalysis, although it had its origins in this, the best known of the earliest forms of psychotherapy in the modern sense.[25] We will have a great deal more to say about the *commonalities* as well as the *differences* between the two modalities of therapy in Chapter Three. For now, we briefly present in broad strokes a sketch of psychoanalysis as the background for daseinanalysis.

A clinical discipline that grew up in the context of the model of natural science at a time when modern medicine was just evolving, psychoanalysis differed from psychiatry with its physical interventions such as restraint, brain surgery, electroshock (ECT) and somatic treatments. These would be complemented by pharmacotherapy. By Freud's own account, however, psychoanalysis was an exploration of man's soul [*Seele*], not his brain. Its theoretical rationale was a metapsychology grounded in the philosophy of natural science established by Isaac Newton (1643-1727) and others at the turn of the eighteenth century. It was inevitable, Freud thought, that in the future his metapsychology (and psychoanalysis) would be replaced by a physiological (neuroscientific) explanation of the activity of the psyche.[26] Like any discipline that regards itself as a science of whatever sort (natural, social, or human [*Geisteswissenschaft*]), what it studied had to be quantifiable and measurable, governed overall by the principle of causality, and have in view the prospect of predictability about how it would subsequently function. The claims of psychoanalysis to be a science first aspired to this, but failed on philosophical grounds in that its fundamental hypotheses, in particular the Unconscious, are not falsifiable.[27]

The two major figures in the history of daseinanalysis, Ludwig Binswanger and Medard Boss, were personally acquainted with Freud, the latter having been an analysand of Freud's for a brief period of time when he was twenty-two years old. Binswanger and Freud were contemporaries who carried on a mutually satisfying correspondence for thirty years (1908-1938). Both Binswanger and Boss were hospital psychiatrists by early experience, but only Boss went on to train and work as a psychoanalyst in private practice. Binswanger would visit and sometimes dine with his mostly well-heeled wards.

Psychoanalysis came to be of great interest to people outside of medicine, which had co-opted it, in areas in which it was applied such as education, social work, nursing and pastoral care, and it attracted individuals from these professions to prepare as lay (that is, non-medical) psychoanalysts. After its heyday in the middle and end of the twentieth century, orthodox psychoanalysis has all but disappeared. There are few candidates in big-city psychoanalytic institutes, medical and lay.[28] The number of psychoanalytic psychotherapists is still large but also diminishing, having been replaced for the most part by those who practice forms of cognitive-behavioral therapy. The number of daseinanalysts is increasing.

(2) Psychiatry

It may come as a surprise to most readers that daseinanalysis is no stranger to American psychiatrists, having been introduced to the profession in the late 1950s. Usually equated with existential analysis, however, its differences from the latter were not made clear at the time the term 'Daseinsanalysis' first showed up in the psychiatric literature.[29] Given the ever greater prominence of psychiatry in everyday life, which was a major part of the medicalization of everyday life in the technological West, this section on what daseinanalysis is not will be given somewhat more extensive treatment, in particular regarding its earliest presentation to the psychiatric establishment.

'Daseinsanalysis' was introduced to American psychiatrists in a substantial fifty-page, two-part article by Eugen Kahn (1887-1973) in the *Psychiatric Quarterly*.[30] Subsequent understanding of daseinanalysis among medical psychologists may in large measure be attributed to how Kahn characterized it there, since the *Quarterly* was one of the two most important journals in the field at that time and was widely read.

An introductory note to Kahn's 'Appraisal of Existential Analysis' announces it as 'Part I of a two-part discussion of *Daseinsanalysis* appearing in successive issues of *The Psychiatric Quarterly*.'[31] That the word 'Daseinsanalysis' does not appear in the title of the article is telling. Having omitted it there may have been an editorial decision intended to avoid putting off readers unacquainted with an unfamiliar German word, much as *Gestalt* had challenged readers in the areas of psychology and psychiatry when it first appeared in the titles of books in English beginning in the late 1920s. Nor would readers have found help by looking for the word in a dictionary of psychiatric terms or even a standard dictionary. How even to pronounce this strange word?[32]

In his essay, Kahn reviews seven books and ten articles by Binswanger, Boss, and Roland Kuhn (1912-2005) published between 1947 and 1957.[33] The 'appraisal' begins with the sentence: 'If one plans a discussion of *Daseinsanalysis*, it is necessary to go back to Existentialism.' We are off to a bad start, since Heidegger, who is the central figure in the background of daseinanalysis, was quite clear that he never thought of himself as an existentialist and had little interest in the movement. Kahn continues:

'Mentioning Existentialism makes it inevitable that one say something of its founder, Søren Kierkegaard (1813-1855).' As a religious thinker, Kierkegaard would have been surprised to have been given this distinction. Nonetheless, since the publication the previous year of a very influential book edited by Walter Kaufmann, Kierkegaard had been so identified.[34]

There is a brief synopsis of Kierkegaard's life, followed by a short review of the work of the psychiatrist and philosopher Karl Jaspers (1883-1969), who was both a psychiatrist and a philosopher, and then a much more extensive discussion of Martin Heidegger (1889-1976), both of whom are said to have been unusual in taking notice of the Danish writer's work.[35] Both thinkers, says Kahn, were 'profoundly influenced' by Kierkegaard 'and incidentally by Nietzsche's thought.' The implication is that the primary source of daseinanalysis is Existentialism, the somewhat dark, brooding figure of the Danish writer, and perhaps the fiery writer on the *Übermensch*, Friedrich Nietzsche (1844-1900).

In the section on Heidegger, we are told that he 'is considered the godfather of *Daseinsanalyse* (existential analysis)'. Since this 'appraisal' may have been many psychiatrists' first encounter with the philosopher's name, it is worth revisiting just what Kahn said about Heidegger.

> [Heidegger] had been professor of philosophy in Marburg an der Lahn before he was called to Freiburg to succeed [Edmund] Husserl [1859-1938] in 1929. He had been educated as a Jesuit novice, but obviously became estranged from the Roman Catholic church. He appeared for a time to be wholeheartedly Nazi, as rector of the University of Freiburg, with the consequence that he was dismissed in 1945. He is now again lecturing at that university.[36]

The brief sketch required more detail and some of it was misleading. At the time of the writing of the 'appraisal', Heidegger still had twenty more years of life ahead of him, and the circumstances surrounding his early life were not well known except to his family and close friends. His relation to Catholicism was more complicated than his very short-lived novitiate, which was discontinued because of some sort of cardiac ailment and evidently a crisis of faith. Second, Heidegger's nine-month rectorship in 1933-34 at the University of Freiburg during the height of influence of National Socialism in Germany is a far more complex affair than is suggested by Kahn. Some kind of involvement with Germany's Austrian-born *Führer* and his government was unavoidable for all university rectors at the time, so that Heidegger was not exceptional for having spoken in support of National Socialism as the rector of one of Germany's universities. Heidegger soon fell from grace in the eyes of the Nazis and after the defeat of Hitler's regime, Heidegger was forbidden to teach for six years but reinstated after the process of 'denazification', an ordeal to which numerous public intellectuals were submitted.

In connection with Heidegger's reputation, it is worth noting that three years after Kahn's *Quarterly* essay appeared, the American psychoanalyst Leslie Farber broached the topic to his colleagues of bringing Heidegger to the States in 1961 to lecture at the

Washington School of Psychiatry, where Boss was also scheduled to teach. Farber met opposition from his fellow psychiatrists on the basis of 'talk' about Heidegger and National Socialism of the kind found in Kahn's essay. In his correspondence with Farber, who had asked Boss whether Heidegger was yet another 'Nazi man', Boss vigorously defended Heidegger's reputation and spoke of the philosopher as having been a much 'maligned' man. As it turned out, it was reported that the then seventy-one-year-old Heidegger would not able to make the trip in any case because of illness. This was probably not the real reason he did not travel with Boss to the States. We will never know just what his reception might have been among Farber's and Kahn's psychiatrist colleagues.

But to return to the content of the 'appraisal'. With *Dasein* translated as 'human existence', Kahn refers to two passages in Heidegger's *Sein und Zeit* [*Being and Time*]. I have interpolated the German words which correspond to the original text of that book as cited in Kahn's notes:

> [1] *Dasein*, about which more will be said later, always refers to the human individual; it actually means for Heidegger a human mode of individual existence. Hence early in *Sein und Zeit* he writes, 'Human existence [*Dasein*] is a being [*ein Seiendes*] which does not only exist [*vorkommt*] among other beings [*anderen Seienden*]. It is rather characterized as a being that in its Being [*Sein*] is concerned about [*um ... geht*] this Being itself [*Sein selbst*]'.[37] And [2] 'The Being itself [*Sein selbst*] to which human existence can refer in this or that way and to which it always refers in some way is called existence [*Existenz*]'.[38]

Both passages are presented without context and could not have but caused confusion among readers. Worried that such statements might sound 'strange' to his readers (as indeed they do), the German-born Kahn then tried to explain basic terms, but with a less than successful outcome. He summarized what he had said up to that point and then went about presenting a brief grammar lesson:

> This may sound less strange if one tries to clarify some of Heidegger's terminology. It has already been remarked that by *Dasein* he means the individual mode of human existence; *Dasein* will, in the following discussion be rendered, for brevity's sake as human existence; the reference to the individual should always be kept in mind. The German words *sein* [the infinitive 'to be'], *Sein* [the noun 'Being'], *seiend* [the present participle of *sein*] and *Seiendes* [the noun 'being', built on the participle *seiend*] mean: 'to be,' 'Being,' 'being,' and 'existent,' respectively. The word *sein* is the infinitive that corresponds to 'to be'. It is spelled with a small 's' unless it begins a sentence, which will be avoided here. The word *Sein*, always spelled with a capital 'S', is a noun; it means existence per se, the existence due to which all existing things—living and not living—exist; the sentences just quoted 'The Being itself to which human existence can refer in this or that way and to which it always refers in some way is called existence,' may be quite understandable now, although at first sight it may have looked odd.[39]

> The word *seiend* is the present participle of the verb *sein*; *seiend* is related to *sein* as 'being' with a small 'b', is related to 'to be'. From the present participle, *seiend*, the noun *Seiend* [sic] is derived. It can be used for people (male and female) and things (neuter); in order to avoid confusion *Seiend* [sic] will be translated as 'the existent'. 'Existent' will be used only as a noun. If an attribute (adjective) is needed, 'being' as well as 'existing' is available. One might now slightly change the sentence quoted first: 'Human existence is an existent which does not only exist among other existents, it is rather characterized as an existent that in its Being it is concerned about this Being itself.' There is no doubt that many a sentence of Heidegger's must be read repeatedly and carefully before one actually 'gets home'.[40]

In my notes I have detailed the difficulties Kahn introduced for the reader. The point is that psychiatrists will not have found a 'home' in Kahn's discussions of the 'godfather's' terminology. Instead, they will have been led, wading, into a muddle. The remaining paragraphs in the section on Heidegger then suffered from Kahn's confusions of terminology. Since this is not a German lesson, we must forego further comments on the problems with Kahn's attempts to get the reader to be comfortable with Heidegger's language. Suffice to say that most readers likely will have become even more bewildered after reading Kahn's attempts at clarification and explanation. Their interest in reading further about 'Daseinsanalysis' may well have been dampened.

Immediately following his digression on terminology, Kahn claimed that for Heidegger 'human existence, as he wants to have it understood, is '*geistig*'.' In a note, he translated *geistig* with 'spiritual'. It is not made clear to which texts he was referring, but in *Sein und Zeit* there are only two passages on the *geistig* in 'human existence'. Early on in the book, Heidegger says that the human being [*Mensch*] is 'first a spiritual thing [*geistige Ding*] that is then afterwards transferred [*versetzt*] 'into [*in*] some space [*einige Raum*].'[41] Second, very late in the book, he has something more to say about *Dasein* in this context when he writes that 'because it is 'spiritual' [*geistig*] and only because it is so, can *Dasein* be spatial [*räumlich*] in a way that is essentially impossible for an extended bodily thing [*ausgedehnten Körperding*].'[42]

The second quotation is an essential sentence in Heidegger's text as a whole. What Kahn did not see was that Heidegger is talking about *Dasein's* bodiliness [*Leiblichkeit*], *not* the physical body [*Körper*] that occupies space and can be weighed and measured. Indeed, for Heidegger, as *leiblich Dasein* makes room for things. It is not in space. Ontologically, it is space-making, not space-occupying. *Dasein* does not take up or occupy space. Heidegger's comments on the spiritual and space occupied him at length, forty years later, in the Zollikon seminars, where the basic ideas of daseinanalysis were presented to psychiatrists. The seminars began two years after Kahn's article appeared.[43]

Kahn understood the spiritual in a conventional sense, where spirit is something that is somehow superadded to something physical, as when, for example, Christian theologians speak of human beings as having been blessed with the presence of the

Holy Spirit which has descended into the human body, providing it with a soul. For Heidegger, by contrast, *Dasein* is *geistig* in the sense of being the condition for the possibility of what is bodily [*leiblich*].

Kahn's discussion next took up the topic of time in Heidegger, aptly pointing to the fable 'Cura' (Hyginus CCXX) to which Heidegger refers in *Being and Time* as a 'preontological' account of *Dasein*. There were also brief allusions to several of the other existentives worked out in *Being and Time*. All of it is sketchy, though, and does not add up to an accurate or complete introduction to the foundational ideas of the analytics of *Dasein*.

In section VI of Kahn's 'appraisal', the discussion turned to Ludwig Binswanger's appropriation of Heidegger.[44] Kahn did not grasp the difference between Heidegger's *Daseinsanalytik* (analytics of *Dasein*) and Binswanger's *Daseinsanalyse* (analysis of *Dasein*)[45] and again mystified the reader with sentences such as: 'Binswanger considers love the ontological opposite of [Heidegger's] care [*Sorge*].'[46] Kahn mistakenly believed that Heidegger's existentive 'care [*Sorge*]' refers to cares or woes, negative feelings in contrast to which Binswanger proposes providing positive feelings of love to make up for its omission in life. Binswanger saw Heidegger's thought to be a philosophical 'anthropology'. Heidegger's concern is not with attitudes or feelings, however, but rather with the ontological condition for the possibility of such. In any case, an ontic emotion such as love could not be the 'ontological opposite' of an existentive such as *Sorge*, which for Heidegger is the human being's fundamental structural feature as being-in-the-world. Such a way of misunderstanding Heidegger was based on Kahn's appropriation of Binswanger, who failed to grasp the ontological difference at the heart of *Dasein*.

Kahn was not aware that Binswanger eventually realized he had gotten Heidegger wrong and that the two men had agreed about the psychiatrist's 'fruitful misunderstanding'. Kahn could only point to Binswanger's principal interest in what he took to be an anthropology implicit in Heidegger's analytics of *Dasein*, noting that only 'slowly' did Binswanger come 'to believe that there were psychotherapeutic possibilities in existential analy*sis* [Kahn's emphasis] [*Daseinsanalyse*], namely when some patients seemed to show an understanding of the new manner of being understood; [quoting Binswanger] 'when the experience of insight into their own structure of human existence and the pertinent knottings, bendings and shirkings' seemed to carry a certain therapeutic effect.'[47] Further discussion of Binswanger concluded the first part of Kahn's appraisal in the *Psychiatric Quarterly*.

Of most importance to our revisiting Kahn's message to psychiatrists is his account of the work of Medard Boss. 'Medard Boss,' said Kahn, 'is a writer of fertility equal to Binswanger's. Of all the practicing psychiatrists who have accepted Heidegger's teaching, he appears to be closest to the teacher. Boss writes with a tremendous élan, with an admirable vocabulary and, like Binswanger, with the obviously unswerving conviction of being a prophet of a new, unshakable truth.'[48]

Kahn often liked to refer to Boss as a sort of disciple of the master, which is a charge that runs through Kahn's discussion of *Sinn und Gehalt sexueller Perversionen* [Meaning and Content of Sexual Perversions] (1947), *Der Traum und seine Auslegung*

[*The Analysis of Dreams*] (1953d), and *Einführung in die psychosomatische Medizin* [*Introduction to Psychosomatic Medicine*] (1954a).[49] In general, Kahn's review of Boss's three early books was fair.

Apparently referring to Boss's book on psychosomatics, Kahn reprised his reference to the *geistig* in the early Heidegger, quoting Boss, that 'human existence is 'spiritual', it is 'carried out' in the body, its organs and its functions: 'the body is bodying [*Der Leib leibt*]'.' Kahn said 'this is a point of particular interest' which he took as an opportunity to criticize Boss. Kahn, however, misrepresented what Boss wrote, namely, that 'the body [just] happens'. In the end, bodiliness [*Leiblichkeit*] is not understood and will likely always remain inexplicable. For all that we may have learned about physiology and the overall functioning of the organism, we do not understand it. Being honest and candid, the best we can say is that it 'does its thing'.[50] What is spiritual in human being is inherent to this mystery. Finally, on Boss's account, neither spirit [*Geist*] nor body [*Leib*] is reducible to the other.

The passage quoted reflects the tone of much of Kahn's discussion of Boss's 'existential analysis': 'In his great enthusiasm, Boss does not seem to see that he is doing what many psychotherapists do; but he does it with the ample use of resounding words and with all the convert's fervor.'[51] Kahn concluded that 'although Boss's writing not only sounds – but is – fantastic, there is something appealing in it which is missed in Binswanger's, and still more in Kuhn's, publications. The writer cannot help assuming this is due to several factors, among which Boss's sense of humor and his undeniable, if often hidden, common sense are as relevant as his style and his convert's fervor.'[52] Which brings us to Kahn's remarks on Roland Kuhn, who is discussed next.

As early as 1946 Roland Kuhn (1912-2005) had published a case history of a patient diagnosed with schizophrenia whom he treated daseinanalytically.[53] Oddly enough, Kahn did not include this paper and several others by Kuhn among the contributions of the Swiss psychiatrist he reviews in his 'appraisal'. He did comment on five papers published by Kuhn between 1948 and 1955.[54]

Quite apart from his participation in the development of therapeutic *Daseinsanalyse*, Kuhn is an important figure in the history of psychiatry. In 1956, at the psychiatric hospital in Münsterlingen, Switzerland, which he directed, Kuhn began to treat patients diagnosed as schizophrenic with the antihistamine imipramine hydrochloride. The drug had been synthesized in 1951, its sedative and antipsychotic properties having been observed by the French psychiatrists Pierre Deniker (1917-1998) and Jean Delay (1907-1987) a bit later in the 1950s. The use of the drug, branded and marketed in the States as Tofranil, followed on the introduction of the use of chlorpromazine (Thorazine or Largactil), which Deniker and Delay had also used with their patients, in this case as an antipsychotic. Because of its expense, however, something cheaper than chlorpromazine had to be found that could be used with a large number of patients in hospital settings. This motivated Kuhn's experimenting with imipramine. Originally manufactured by the Geigy Chemical Corporation in Switzerland, imipramine was eventually abandoned as an antipsychotic and came to be widely used as the first nominally *antidepressive* medication.[55]

Kahn said of Kuhn that 'one may best consider him as a devoted son–pupil of Binswanger and an adoring grandson–pupil of Heidegger.... Despite all his courtesy, once in a while he seems to be unable – or unwilling – to suppress a certain hostility against non-adherents to his creed. The 'it is so' of the psychiatric existential analysts is very outspoken in Kuhn.... Like Binswanger and Boss, he realizes that not every individual is accessible to, and apt to go through, a deeper reaching psychotherapy. He writes 'In psychotherapy, the attempt is made to extricate the patient from the bane of his past. To the degree to which this attempt succeeds, the patient becomes free, open to the new, and able to unfold his creative faculties." Kahn added: 'This is, one conjectures, likely to reduce the number of candidates for such therapy to a rather modest figure.'[56] The implication is that the only remaining treatment option would be pharmacotherapy.

Following his review of Kuhn's case report on a 'depressive fetishist and sodomite', Kahn admitted that 'Kuhn's case has been presented at some length, as the writer presumes that his method and its shortcomings become visible step by step.'[57] Kahn's generally negative appraisal of 'existential analysis' then became even more explicit. His concern was that in *Daseinsanalyse* 'there is the tendency to complicate matters which in all likelihood are not so complicated at all ... and to use a flood of words where only a few words would be more telling. Who thought and who experienced this or that – the intuiting doctor or the patient under treatment – is often not discernible.'[58] We might conclude that Kahn's personal acquaintance over a period of years with Boss, Kuhn and the others had left him with a rather negative impression. Whatever the case on that score may be, in the end he could not approve of 'existential analysis' as a therapeutic modality.

Kahn's evaluation of Kuhn was quite brief and he returned to Heidegger, whose influence on all three psychiatrists was summarized. He quoted the Hungarian-born philosopher Wilhelm [Vilmos] Szilasi (1889-1966), who had studied with Heidegger: 'Szilasi... strikingly and briefly expressed what I have been trying to present in so many words; Szilasi says that Binswanger dwells 'in his own intermediate territory between psychoanalysis and existential analysis.'[59] Here his assessment was correct, since Binswanger was not a therapeutic daseinanalyst. Credit for that is reserved for Boss.

When Kahn said that Boss 'accepted Heidegger's philosophy as his metaphysics or *Weltanschauung* [world view],' he was mistaken. Heidegger's *Daseinsanalytik* in *Being and Time* is preliminary to a dismantling of metaphysics. His accomplishment is therefore not a new metaphysics that someone (such as Boss) could accept on which to base a world view. It is rather the procedure of his fundamental ontology, accomplished by a hermeneutic phenomenology that attempts to bring to light a different view of humanity, that and nothing more.

Kahn then said that 'to the present writer, Boss appears to be a genuine psychotherapist. His familiarity with Heidegger's work is complete, and his devotion to it is perfect.'[60] Kahn's praise was brief, however. Clearly, he experienced a deep ambivalence toward Boss and daseinanalysis. This is seen in his concluding remarks: 'From his *Glaubenshaltung* [system of belief], Boss admonishes physicians to remember they are 'descendants of ancient priest-physicians [*Priester-Ärzte*]'. He asks the rhetorical question, 'Did not a division of the healers of mankind into priests and physicians then occur, the priests wanting to bring man only salvation, the physicians wanting to bring him nothing but healing?'"[61]

Kahn detected in Boss a sensitivity to the spiritual element in the life of his analysands which was indeed a hallmark of Boss's approach (as it is for nearly all daseinanalysts who have followed him), but Kahn was mistaken in suggesting that Boss's own religious faith somehow played a part in the therapeutic process. For Boss, he wrote, 'if the physician is devoted to his faith and is practicing this faith in his work, his patients will fall in line and share his faith. He is able to transfer his faith to his patient. It does not matter what faith it is. What matters is the doctor.'[62] Kahn suggested that working with Boss could produce in his analysands a deepening of their religious faith. That may be happen, but Boss was clear that the therapist's system of belief was not to intrude into the therapeutic setting.[63]

Kahn concluded his appraisal with some general comments on 'existential analysis,' a few of which were prescient, observing that 'it may not always have been easy for the psychiatrists to keep step with Heidegger's thought.... The [existential] doctors have discarded Freudian theory, but remained faithful to psychoanalytical technique. What will happen to their adherence to Heideggerian theory and its use in their interpretations remains to be seen. What worries the writer is the notion of these colleagues that, with the introduction of the concept of *Dasein*, everything becomes or can be made meaningful – everything that happens to or is experienced by patients; and that every interpretation is looked at as valid which expounds this in pertinent vocabulary and shows how *Dasein* sets body and soul to work.'[64]

As already noted, Kahn had spent several years in the company of Binswanger, Boss and Kuhn in Switzerland. In general, his 'appraisal' of their 'existential analysis' was at best lukewarm: 'The writer wants to express personal gratitude to the three colleagues from whom he has learned much.' But –– the certainty with which they write – 'no doubt', 'because it is so', 'of course', 'naturally'– cannot conceal the fact that concepts, or even worse, words, are often gaily tossed around' by them. The ponderousness of the older, the alacrity of the younger, priest and the assiduity of the deacon, though occasionally irritating, show the manner in which each of them goes after his business. It is the writer's impression that our existential-analytic friends have overdone it philosophically.... Did they try to be revolutionists?'[65]

Kahn then reprised his opening background survey of Kierkegaard and Heidegger, and offered some general impressions of the three 'existential analysts' he had considered. 'It is noteworthy that Binswanger brings brighter colors into the picture' against the background of Kierkegaard, 'an unhappy, gloomy man' with his pessimism, and Heidegger, whose 'existence, eksistence and world are not joyous' but do not fail to be 'consistently beclouded'. The 'picture ... becomes ever brighter the more that existential analy*sis* (Binswanger, Kuhn) and existential analy*tics* (Boss) are brought into closer contact with people – particularly if this contact is a therapeutic one. Here, it is Boss, above all, whose optimism is unmistakable.'[66]

In a 'Postscript', Kahn briefly considered two book-length publications that appeared during the period when his 'appraisal' was under consideration for publication in the *Psychiatric Quarterly*. Given the time frame of publication, the reading required for the 'Postscript' seems to have been done in a bit of a hurry.

The first book reviewed was Binswanger's *Drei Formen mißglückten Daseins* [*Three Forms of Existential Failure*] in which Binswanger identifies three 'unsuccessful' or 'failed' forms of existence: *Verstiegenheit* (eccentricity), *Verschrobenheit* (quirkiness or, for Kahn, 'queerness'), and *Manieriertheit* (manneredness or, for Kahn, 'stiltedness'). All three seem to be disturbances of *Dasein's* relation to verticality or being upright, both in posture and moral performance. For Binswanger, said Kahn, 'unsuccessful' forms of existence are 'facets of one comprehensive rigidity of existence – rigid in the existential sense.' The point seems to be that existence should be flexible, not rigid. It 'fails' when it is disoriented with respect to above and below or has gone off-balance and may have become fixed in that position, 'leaning' one way or another. Of course, *Dasein* is not something positioned in space subject to determination in terms of geophysical coordinates. Binswanger was therefore speaking figuratively of *Dasein's* being, as it were, out of plumb and not in line with ordinary everyday proprieties. More important, *Dasein* is not subject to deformation. Its structural nature is fixed. Being eccentric, being quirky, and being mannered are characterizations of *Existenz*, not *Dasein*. Kahn was therefore not correct in concluding that what 'Binswanger has performed here is a *tour de force* from schizophrenia to schizophrenia, using his particular vocabulary against the background of Heidegger's *Being and Time*.' The 'background' is what the philosopher had to say about the spatiality of *Dasein*.[67] An ontological structure cannot 'fail [*mißglücken*]' just as it cannot succeed.

Boss's *Psychoanalyse und Daseinsanalytik* was reviewed next.[68] Kahn was still not especially kind, remarking that 'Boss stands, in his most recent dissertation, without reservation on the ground of Heidegger's existential analytic and later philosophical concepts, which he accepts and propagates with all the enthusiasm of the fanatically devoted pupil.'[69] He pointed out what for Boss were central observations about psychoanalysis, namely, that Freud's 'practical method' is 'as acceptable and useful as ever' and that as a therapist Freud's 'understanding [*Verstehen*]' was 'always existential-analytical', so that one can speak of Freud as in practice a daseinanalyst, demonstrating the intrinsic 'harmony of psychoanalytic practice and existential-analytic understanding'.[70] On the other hand, Kahn claimed, 'Boss does not see, or does not want to see, that his explication is thoroughly arbitrary, according to the deplorable fact that one can read anything into and out of anything that one cares to read anything into and out of. Boss seems to be ignoring the fact that he is constantly interpreting. He appears to be imbued with the conviction that, where one talks about existence, there are facts.'[71] Kahn did not tire of accusing Boss of what he perceived to be Boss's 'uncritical fanaticism' with regard to Heidegger and the 'dogmatic pomposity' of the acolyte's rhetoric. For Kahn the psychiatrist, 'Boss appears to feel that whatever Heidegger says is the last word concerning existence and related and unrelated problems. One may be glad to leave the pertinent discussion to the philosophers.'[72] Of course, it would be Heidegger's task in the Zollikon seminars to enjoin psychiatrists to think philosophically.[73]

Apart from Kahn's article, the *Psychiatric Quarterly* also contributed to making daseinanalysis known to American psychiatrists by reviewing two of Medard Boss's books: *Meaning and Content of Sexual Perversions* (1949), in 1950,[74] and *Psychoanalyse und Daseinsanalytik* (1957a), in 1957, in the same volume as Kahn's 'appraisal' appeared.[75] In 1960 the journal published an article by the American psychiatrist, Thomas Hora, 'The Process of Existential Psychotherapy', in which we find a detailed discussion of Heidegger and psychotherapy in general.[76] Finally, in 1967, the *Quarterly* reviewed Joseph J. Kockelmans' *Martin Heidegger: A First Introduction to His Philosophy* (1965), in which much background material was presented to help psychiatrists understand the philosophical underpinnings of daseinanalysis.[77]

The other most important journal for psychiatrists at the time was the *American Journal of Psychiatry*, which, however, only reviewed Boss's magnum opus *Existential Foundations of Medicine and Psychology* (1971a) in 1980.[78]

Kahn's essay was reprinted five years later, this time directed to an audience of psychoanalysts.[79] Its influence can therefore be said to have been extensive among psychodynamic psychiatrists. What is lost on Khan is that it required the sensibility of a Boss to communicate the richness of a given human being's often 'unspeakable' existence. Daseinanalysis focuses on that being's complexity, allowing it to slowly show up in all its detail and nuance in the sense of what one sees happening when a photographic negative is being developed or 'brought up' in the dark room. This is in stark contrast to the tendency of the diagnostic approach, the goal of which is to simplify a human life to the barest possible outline. What makes daseinanalysis different from other therapeutic approaches, which look for answers based on causal explanations, is the daseinanalyst's patiently waiting for a richer understanding of the other, allowing time for more and better questions to arise and what there is to appear in its own good time. This reflects its phenomenological well-spring.

Here we have focused on what was available to *psychiatrists* about daseinanalysis, but clearly a survey of literature on the topic in *academic psychology* is also in order. So also is a study of the relation between psychology and psychiatry. We may briefly comment on the often uneasy alliance between non-medical and medical psychotherapists. This is reflected especially in the contents of the *Review of Existential Psychology and Psychiatry*.[80] Given its title, we must include it among the journals published for psychiatrists, even though it welcomed contributions from clinical psychologists of all stripes, as well as philosophers, theologians, and even literary figures.

Unique among journals in this respect, the *Review* was initially the organ of the Association of Existential Psychology and Psychiatry, co-founded in 1960 by Leslie Farber (1912-1981) and Rollo May (1909-1994) at the Washington School of Psychiatry. First published as *Existential Inquiries* (1959-1960), the *Review* took on its final name beginning in 1961 when it was edited by Adrian van Kaam. Thomas Lynaugh later took over editorship and, beginning with volume 16 (1978-79), Keith Hoeller succeeded him in that post. Reflecting the wide interest in and appeal of 'existential analysis', which tacitly included daseinanalysis, the *Review* was remarkable in having published contributions by Binswanger and Boss as well as Albert Ellis, Michel Foucault, Viktor

Frankl, Julia Kristeva, Jacques Lacan, R.D. Laing, Rollo May, Maurice Merleau-Ponty, Joyce Carol Oates, William J. Richardson, Carl Rogers, Thomas Szasz, Paul Tillich and Jan van den Berg. It effectively ceased publishing with volume 27 (2002/2003) and remains in the hands of its final editor.[81]

Before concluding our look at the earliest presentation of daseinanalysis to the psychiatric community, I should remind readers that Kahn's appraisal appeared the year before *Existence*,[82] the anthology that presented 'a new dimension in psychiatry and psychology' and may be said to háve had the widest influence on psychiatrists previously unfamiliar with existential analysis – and daseinanalysis. Dedicated to Ludwig Binswanger and Eugène Minkowski (1885-1972), the book introduced readers to an essay and two case studies ('Ellen West' and 'Ilse') by Binswanger and a case study by Kuhn ('Rudolf', a depressive fetishist and sodomite). Since Kahn had mentioned 'Ellen West' and 'Rudolf' in his 'appraisal', these cases may have rung a bell with some readers who were familiar with it. If they had read even the preface,[83] they would have run across the word *Dasein*. *Daseinsanalyse*, however, was mentioned by name only a few times[84] where it was associated with Binswanger's approach and glossed with 'existential analysis'. Oddly enough, Boss's work is missing from the anthology, even though two of his books and several papers had been translated into English before 1958. Given that samples of work by Binswanger and Kuhn (as well papers by Viktor von Gebsattel, Erwin Straus and Minkowski) had been translated for the volume, a number of important papers by Boss might have been included but for some reason were not.

It is worth taking a brief look at the book *Existence* as a source for psychiatrists on daseinanalysis. The context of the first appearance of the word *Dasein* in the book was as follows: 'But no sooner had we [the editors] commenced work than we found ourselves up against grave difficulties. How could one render into English the key terms and concepts of this way of understanding man, beginning with even such a basic word as *Dasein*?' Again we find spokesmen for daseinanalysis shying away from the term, motivated by anticipated difficulties of readers with the foreign term. For May, Binswanger was the 'chief spokesman' for 'the *Daseinsanalyse*, or existential-analytic movement'.[85] The two expressions are presented as equivalent throughout *Existence*. As a result, daseinanalysis, as distinct from forms of existential psychology, existential psychotherapy, existential analysis and existential psychiatry, was lost in the discussion.

Neuroscience now dominates the field as it does academic psychology. Even though its findings are far from having been well established and the prospect of 'mapping' the brain and localizing psychological functions is still only a promise, understanding the connections between behavior and neurological events is assumed to be the only recourse available to psychiatry and psychology in their attempt to understand and treat human beings. Psychiatric studies increasingly refer to images of brain events (fMRI and PET scans) and treatment nearly always consists of introducing chemical agents into the blood-stream in order to interrupt what is assumed to be the cause of undesirable experiential and behavioral effects of a malfunctioning brain and nervous system. Such substances, known as psychotropic drugs, are said to modify experience and behavior by *acting* on the brain and nervous system. But inert compounds cannot act. Only human beings can act. These compounds are measurable, but nothing human is measurable. To talk in this way, an uncanny pre-established harmony is assumed between series of events in 'the body' and a parallel series of events in 'the psyche'. The mysterious leap from 'the body' to 'the mind' has never been explained.

It should be clear by now that daseinanalysis is not remotely related to contemporary psychiatry, even given the historical closeness of psychoanalysis to psychiatry and the fact that psychiatrists and psychoanalysts were the central figures in the early days of daseinanalysis. This is an especially important consideration when assessing the work of Medard Boss, who is the central figure in the development of therapeutic daseinanalysis.[86]

Finally, it is important to take into consideration that, given the importance of Heidegger for the development of daseinanalysis, one should realize that his understanding of psychiatry, psychoanalysis and psychotherapy was that of any layman. When Heidegger told Boss that he hoped his analytics of *Dasein* might contribute to 'helping' people who seek professional medical or psychological care, the sentiment emanated from a genuine motive of goodwill but a naïve understanding of psychiatric and general 'mental illness-care' professional practice. He was an astute observer, however and, as a telling footnote, it is amusing to recall that, after having met the famous French psychiatrist, Jacques Lacan, Heidegger is reported to have quipped that 'perhaps the psychiatrist needs a psychiatrist'.

(3) Psychotherapy

It should already be clear that daseinanalysis is not a form of *psycho*therapy as this endeavor is generally understood. The term says, loud and clear, that psychotherapy is therapy directed toward the psyche. The problem is that no such entity has ever been found. An heir to the notion of the mind (as somewhat *Geist* and somewhat *Gemüt*), the psyche of the natural, social and human sciences is a presupposition. The psyche of psychology, psychiatry, psychoanalysis and psychotherapy was invented, not discovered. And yet entire fields of study have been built around it.[87]

Passages in the daseinanalytic literature abound on the problem of the psyche, but its clearest presentation is found in the *Zollikon Seminars*. '*Psyche* and psychology are attempts to objectify the human being.'[88] For Heidegger, 'from the perspective of the analytics of *Dasein*, all conventional, objectifying representations of an encapsulated-like psyche, subject [*Subjekt*], person [*Person*], ego [*Ich*], or consciousness [*Bewußtsein*] [as found] in psychology and psychopathology must be abandoned in favor of an entirely different understanding.'[89]

The modern psyche originates with the distinction between physical *materia* and psychic *materia* introduced by René Descartes.[90] In his famous thought experiment recounted in the *Meditations*, the French Catholic had his *Körper* in mind when he attempted to imagine away this *materia* after having done so with the things occupying space around him – his table and pen, his clothing and the rest. Understood phenomenologically, however, the lived body [*Leib*] body is something altogether different from such physical *materia* as the *Körper* (physical organism). It always *comports* itself in a situation. It is never a static something that somehow moves itself through space or is moved by outside forces to change position. The lived body does not respond to cues provided by an environment it finds itself placed in and detects using the five senses, as, for example, B.F. Skinner's theory of operant conditioning postulated. In a sense it is its environment (*Umwelt*). To speak of *embodied existence* is oxymoronic and misleading, since there is no occasion for existing that is not bodily [*leiblich*].[91]

What remained for Descartes after imagining away physical *materia* was the psychic *materia* that went on to constitute the psyche of natural science. But what was left was not observable by Descartes, since ostensibly he was both the observer and the observed. The object of psychology, then, was and remains a mysterious non-entity to which any number of equally hypothetical functions have been adduced.

From the early days of his work, Medard Boss was occupied with so-called psychosomatic disorders. His interest in them, however, was to expose the distinction between psyche and soma as untenable. As he observed, the 'unfortunate term'[92] has lingered despite Heidegger's clear understanding that 'the term 'psychosomatic medicine' endeavors to synthesize two things which simply do not exist' separately.[93]

It is important to keep in mind that psychotherapy as a widespread service known to most people is quite new, having dramatically increased in popularity only in the 1970s and 1980s. Now the numbers of such professionals are legion. As a profession, it arose in response to broad sociocultural changes, especially those that saw populations in Europe and especially the States moving from small-town, rural settings to larger cities where factory work was the principal source of labor and eventually 'office work' became the most common job. Psychotherapy is very much a phenomenon of big cities and their suburbs. It is also a phenomenon secondary to the medicalization of Western society that began in the twentieth century, supplementing and replacing to a great extent the management of psychological disorders by asylum directors and healers of all sorts, ranging from physicians and clergymen to outright charlatans. Attended for the most part by psychiatrists, the first congress of the International Federation of (Medical) Psychotherapy was held only in 1948.[94]

The demand for psychotherapy is now great in the West but, as we have seen, its success rate is alarmingly small. It is in response to this situation that daseinanalysis provides an approach that both helps us understand why psychotherapy is ineffective and, more important, offers an alternative sort of care for the other that is therapeutic.

(4) Pastoral Care

Nor, finally, is daseinanalysis pastoral care. The latter may be best appreciated by recalling the history of the relation of pastoral care to psychiatry and psychoanalysis as well as to organized religion in the States. The connection can be traced back to the American psychiatrist Smiley Jordan Blanton (1882-1966), who was in analysis with Freud irregularly over a period of nine months from 1929 to 1930. Soon after returning to the States, Blanton established the American Foundation of Religion and Psychiatry[95] with Norman Vincent Peale (1898-1993), an ordained minister in the Reformed Church in America, who beginning in 1932 was for fifty-two years pastor of the Marble Collegiate Church in New York.[96] A clinic was established next door to the church where Peale and Blanton took a cooperative approach to working with 'psychologically disturbed persons'. The Blanton-Peale Institute continues to offer a *psychoanalytic* training program, one that retains links to pastoral counseling. It has membership in Division 17 (Counseling Psychology) of the American Psychological Association.

Like all other forms of psychotherapy and counseling psychology, pastoral care is grounded in the medical model. Graduates of approved institute programs in pastoral counseling are hired by churches to work with priests and pastors, and if they are not clergy they are paid by insurance providers much like any other 'mental health practitioner'. Pastoral psychologists who are priests are not paid directly, since their vows include poverty. Protestant and Jewish clergy may work independently as counselors as well as meeting their ministerial duties and may charge a fee.

Providers of pastoral care and psychotherapists continue to vie for the belief of individuals in their respective kinds of power, one emanating from mediated divine intervention, the other granted by government-monitored licensure to practice as experts in psychiatry or as clinical psychologists in psychotherapy. Only psychiatrists, however, have the government-monitored authority to prescribe drugs and set in motion the necessary steps required to hospitalize someone (sometimes involuntarily) for a designated period of observation. In either case, individuals are authorized by a governing body – the Church or the State – to carry out their respective procedures. Thus only an ordained priest may exorcise demons or provide psychoanalytic psychotherapy (if he has been trained how to do that) and only a state-licensed medical doctor (preferably, but not necessarily, a psychiatrist) may lawfully prescribe psychotropic drugs.[97] The vast majority function as psychotherapists, counseling psychologists, and social workers who practice as psychotherapists. Having rejected these authorizing bodies, the daseinanalyst is left only with everyday language.

Chapter Three
Daseinanalysis and Psychoanalysis

Having said what daseinanalysis is *not*, it remains to characterize in broad strokes what it is as a therapeutic modality. The theory and basic principles of daseinanalysis are discussed in Chapter Four and the first chapter of Part Two, which covers the fundamentals of its theory and practice. One can get a sense of its uniqueness by comparing it to psychoanalysis, where it had its origins.

The two major influences on Medard Boss that led to his transformation of psychoanalysis were the fundamental ontology of Martin Heidegger and elements of Hindu philosophy.[98] The impact of Heidegger's thought began in the mid-1940s. It was only in the late 1950s that Boss experienced first-hand the mysticism in which Vedanta philosophy is embedded and which Boss brought into the consulting room, chiefly in his understanding of therapeutic encounter [*Begegnung*]. He had already had an interest in the Eastern tradition (especially Hindu philosophy), some of it likely inspired by his contacts with his early mentor, Carl Gustav Jung (1875-1961).

Daseinanalysis is psychoanalysis that has been 'refined' or further developed [*weiterentwickelt*] in such a way that Freud's metapsychology and the variety of reworkings of his theory of a mental apparatus and psychic forces have been eliminated. In a word, daseinanalysis is psychoanalysis without the psyche. Daseinanalysis is the therapeutic approach the goal of which is the freeing up of the *Dasein* of an individual for the fullest possible realization of its possibilities, subject to limitation by the givens with which the actualizing individual is endowed and the influences of his upbringing and education. By contrast, psychoanalysis is the dissection of the contents of a given personality understood as a psyche driven by instinct-like forces controlled by the operation of the unconscious portion of the hypothesized psychic apparatus.

Some of the 'technical' recommendations of Freud are retained by Boss, especially the analysis of resistance [*Widerstand*], which is understood differently, however, from Freud's version of the phenomenon. Freud's characterization of the analyst's overall relational comportment as mediated by an 'evenly suspended hovering' is also retained, as is the abstinence of the analyst from 'personal' involvement with the analysand. Along with the notion of a dynamic Unconscious, Freud's idea that analysis is mediated by transference and countertransference is also rejected. Dreaming life is taken to be of essential importance for daseinanalysis, is the case for psychoanalysis, but a daseinanalytically informed understanding of dreaming life differs fundamentally from Freud's interpretive approach to dreams.

Daseinanalysis rejects the concept of *mental contents* such as thoughts and affects. Another major difference of daseinanalysis as contrasted with psychoanalysis is its emphasis on a kind of caring about the other in the therapeutic setting that is to the greatest extent possible non-interventional. Interpretations and reconstructions, which are made by the psychoanalyst, are understood instead to be the work of the analysand in daseinananlysis. Rather than searching for the causes of current behavior and experience, the daseinanalyst is concerned with making way for the conditions of motivation that will make it more likely that the analysand will try out possibilities of experience that he has overlooked or has become accustomed to look away from, which he may then choose or not choose to embrace. This is the daseinanalytic understanding of resisting. 'Acting out' is not considered to be a defense, but is encouraged when it occurs as indicating that something new is being tried out by the analysand.

It is part of the function of the daseinanalyst to protect the analysand as well as himself and others from impulsive behavior that the latter would later regret or be penalized for. Actions being 'tried out' might be those of the analysand who at the time is making up for missed childhood experiences – albeit now as a physically mature and legally responsible adult. While certain kinds of such behavior are incongruous for an adult, they must nonetheless be supported, albeit while the analyst protects the analytic *setting* in which such behavior erupts. While it is encouraged to erupt, it may not disrupt the setting. Boss recounts instances when he took seriously the infantile or childlike needs of an analysand, going so far in one case as bottle-feeding a patient who for a period of time was experiencing needs that had not been adequately met as a baby. Finally, for the daseinanalyst, the spiritual life of the analysand is taken to be as important as is his increased capacity for work and for love, which, for Freud, was thought to be perhaps the most important outcome of psychoanalysis.

The relationship between analyst and analysand is not understood as the repetition of earlier relationships, that is, as transference. The feelings the analysand experiences for the analyst are real. Borrowing a phrase from Carlos Alberto Seguín, Boss speaks of what Seguín termed the 'psychotherapeutic eros', which differs fundamentally from feelings found in a romantic or sexual relationship. As in psychoanalysis, of course, physical intimacies are to be avoided between daseinanalyst and daseinanalysand. As we will see, the love the analyst feels for his analysand, who is seen as yet another struggling human being like the analysand, is unidirectional. Nothing is expected in return. This is the hallmark of the therapeutic eros. The phenomenon nearest to this in human experience is probably the love felt by a mother for her infant.

The starting point for daseinanalysis is not an isolated, monadic ego ('I' or 'me') but, rather, *Dasein*. A fundamental ontological *relation* [*Beziehung*] of one existence [*Dasein*] (that of the analysand) and another existence [*Dasein*] (that of the analyst) is the given on which everything else follows. This implies that ontological togetherness

[*Mitsein*] is the *sine qua non* of any therapeutic *relationship* [*Verhältnis*] that follows in the course of an analysis. Were such a *relation* not given, no occasion for even initiating such a *relationship* could eventuate. Therefore it is correct to say that no contact with an other must first be *established* between analyst and analysand since it is in each instance a given of *Dasein*.

For daseinanalysis, the medium of the course of treatment is language, which includes both vocables and silence. Important nonverbal expressions of existence such as crying and laughing also occur in every analysis. Since the analyst does not see the analysand *vis-à-vis*, 'body language' and the expressiveness of the eyes do not come into play. While the analyst may observe movements of the analysand's body as he is reclining on the couch, all that really matters is what is 'spoken', whether it is uttered out loud or withheld in silence.

While psychoanalysis is concerned about the past as a source of causes for current behavior, in daseinanalysis existing is understood as the *concurrence* of (a) what has happened (as remembered) and (b) what is anticipated (the future) in (c) the immediacy of the present moment [*Gegenwart*]. Even though they may be conceptually distinguished, in existence there is no separation of the temporal dimensions. The shared 'present' moment of daseinanalysis is for the analyst 'where' all of the associations of the analysand gather. 'In' this present even things that are not real have a place. Similarly, what is absent or missing [*nicht vorhanden*] for the analysand is also very much *there*.

The context of the therapeutic relationship, grounded as it is in the *Dasein-Dasein* relation, is the 'playground' (Freud's term, adopted by Boss) for the analysand's exploration of his possibilities. It is a place where the analysand may choose to try out or not try out a given possibility that 'comes to mind'. The ontological anonymity of the analyst, his being nothing or nobody in particular to the other to the greatest extent possible, is the source of his becoming what he needs to be for the analysand for the time being. What he is for the analysand is not a revenant or replica of someone from the analysand's past, as in the Freudian account of transference. The analysand will very often be occupied with reporting memories and expressing expectations, all of which distract him from the immediacy of the therapeutic encounter. While memories are the currency of psychoanalysis and plans for the future are the focus of most helping therapies, in particular cognitive-behavioral therapy, the currency of daseinanalysis is the flowing unfolding of existing in the shared world of analyst and analysand.

Chapter Four
Theory and Basic Principles

We turn now to elaborating five basic themes of daseinanalysis: the temporality of existence [*Dasein*], the ontological structural of existence, language in the therapeutic setting, the analysand as other to the analyst, and daseinanalytic caring about the other [*Fürsorge*].

(1) Dasein and Temporality

'What then *is* time? If no one asks me, I know; if I want to explain it to a questioner, I do not know.' So wrote Augustine of Hippo near the turn of the fifth century AD in his *Confessions* (Book XI). About 600 years earlier, Aristotle had said with confidence that time is 'a number of motion with respect to the before and after' (*Physics* 219b1-2). Augustine is as sure as Aristotle had been about what time is, but finds it impossible, when asked, to put into words what he 'knows'. Why did Augustine hesitate where Aristotle had boldly asserted? More important, how can one know what something is and yet not be able to say what it is?

Heidegger realized that his distinguished predecessors were talking about two very different things. For Aristotle, time is a quantity that is measurable, a succession of units that can be counted backwards and forwards from a given point 'in' time depicted as a linear display, and an individual life is a measurable span along that time line. For Augustine, however, time is not visualized. It cannot be represented spatially, in this case as the one-dimensional line of geometry (Euclid's γραμμή). For Heidegger, time is a problem in the way it had been for Augustine, but he does say something about the 'in' of time: 'time is in us'.[99] We *make time for*... (things). To talk about time is to talk about existence, but not about what is. We cannot count moments [*Augenblicke*] in existing, but we can describe experiencing events as passing 'quickly' or 'slowly', not in terms of velocity, but as determined by qualities such as satisfaction, longing or fear, that is, in terms of the mood [*Stimmung*] of existence. We can meaningfully talk about time as *lived*.[100]

Since the invention of the first clocks in the twelfth century, chronometric time (clock time) has come to take precedence over lived time. Clocks first imposed regular units of counting that were meant to be applicable to everyone. The lived time unique to each individual's experiences was lost sight of. Time came to be passed in seconds, minutes, hours and the rest.[101] Lived time was presumably measured in units of chronometric time. The relevance of this for natural science, with its emphasis on accuracy as well as precision, is obvious. Lived time, however, remains entirely uniquely unaccountable and cannot be measured. With the quantification of relatively short or small units of time (seconds, minutes, hours), day, night and the seasons were superseded in importance, and with them so also was everyday life which is ordered by the rising and setting of the sun. The spatialization of time had confounded its essential nature.

To provide a simple example of lived time: a one-half-hour span of chronometric time waiting for the dentist to invite me in for an examination and a one-half-hour span of chronometric time with a friend whom I am about to say 'good-bye' to and may not ever see again are the same time. The lived time, however, of the former is *very long*, while the latter *goes by ever so quickly*. The 'speed' of these experiences cannot be expressed in terms of velocity, but rather of meaningfulness, which cannot be quantified. Experience can be appreciated only in terms of the attunement or mood [*Stimmung*] of the individual and the atmosphere in which he finds himself which determine the meaning for him of the lived time. This is not measurable in minutes.

(2) The Existentives (Existentials)

While the temporality of existence is the horizon against which it can appear, Heidegger described its structural features, all of which taken together are co-constitutive of *Dasein*. He termed these structural features *Existenziale*, which has usually been translated as 'existentials'. They contrast with the ten *categories* worked out by Aristotle in terms of which all beings other than human beings may be understood.[102] Thinking of existence as a structure like a house, the existentives (as I prefer for *Existenziale*) are all the structural features which are necessary so that the house will stand and can be occupied, that is, so that it can house: foundation, walls, roof, windows and the rest, all of which are necessary to make it subsist and function as a house – that is, to repeat, so that it can house and provide a human being with a dwelling place. The structure of existence differs from the example of a building in that its features refer not to something static, but to an unfolding, historical process of ongoing formation: existing [*Existieren*].

Not all of the existentives are described in *Being and Time*, and Medard Boss has added one – dreaming. I briefly review them here in the context of their importance for daseinanalytic theory without any pretense of having treated them as adequately as would be required in an overview of Heidegger's thought, and I consider them roughly in order of their importance for daseinanalytic practice. Although Heidegger gives *prominence* to one above all of the others (caring about things [*Sorge*]), what is essential is that none takes *precedence* over any of the others, nor can any one existentive be fully appreciated without considering it in its relation to all of the others. Beginning with an account of any one of the existentives will necessarily require saying something about all of the others – but one must begin somewhere. That starting point is *Sorge*, that the human being cares about things – if I may express it this way, that he gives a damn about things. As far as we know, we are the only beings that do so. Caring about things is realized in work, whether the work be farming or writing or anything in between. It is distinguished from taking care of things (*Besorgen*) such as my body, my clothing, my living quarters.

Bearing in mind that there is still no consensus about what a complete list of the existentives would include, here is a sketch in broad strokes of those existentives to which we will refer in what follows. Existence [*Dasein*] is tantamount to being-in-the-world [*In-der-Welt-sein*] since the existing human being is always already in-the-world, otherwise there would not have been a starting point for a discussion of any sort about anything, including existing. It is a fact that we are here in the world, a fact that cannot be explained or contested, although, famously (as for Descartes), it may be doubted. Considering existence as 'being-in-the-world', worldliness [*Weltlichkeit*] is also an existentive, as is being-in [*In-sein*], understood not as being contained or encompassed by a limiting membrane or force of some sort, but rather as dwelling, tarrying, sojourning, inhabiting, or staying a while.[103]

Existence implies a sense [*Sinn*] of the be[-ing] [*Sein*] of that existence or being there [*Da-sein*] as well as an understanding [*Verstehen*] at a pre-reflective level of what is going on (including *that* it is going on). Existence understands that dwelling is limited, that is, that the human being is mortal. Existence is therefore being-towards-death [*Sein zum Tode*], which gives existence its sense of urgency and highlights the importance of everything that happens. The human being understands that 'things' may stop happening at any moment, in the 'twinkling of an eye [*Augenblick*]' of death.

The existence of at least one other *Dasein* (existence) gives existence its feature of being-with [*Mitsein*] others or togetherness. This other will be the mother at conception. Such being-with is immediately inclusive of all *Daseins*, now living, dead, and to come. Existing is always self-referential, one's own; that is, it has the feature of being uniquely *my* own [*Jemeinigkeit*] and not interchangeable with that of any other *Dasein*. Each *Dasein* has appeared on the scene without precedence and with certain characteristics, taken together, never seen before and never to be repeated. These include what we term the named *Dasein*'s sex, place and era of origin, accidental physical features and the rest. This is our givenness [*Geworfenheit*], the result of probability or the toss of the dice. One has no choice about this givenness. One may move to another town and die yet somewhere else, but he has always been born in a certain place at a certain time. One may disguise his appearance and act a certain part (perform one's adopted gender), but what he has appeared as, which includes his biological sex, cannot be changed.

At any given moment existence finds itself both disposed and attuned in a certain way, for example, well, ill, curious, joyous, bored. These are its *Befindlichkeit* and *Gestimmtheit*, respectively. Disposition and attunement 'color' everything that is taken in of what is given to existence as discovered in the world.

The existing human being cares about things in general [*Sorge*] but it also cares about other human beings. Such *Fürsorge* is related primarily to *Dasein*'s understanding of the other as being like itself in caring about things, including others. As noted earlier, caring about others is not merely looking after them or taking care of them [*Besorgen*], as when we take care of a sick person, a child or our body.

Others, taken as a whole, constitute the impersonal collective power and influence that is termed 'people' or 'they' or 'one' [*das Man*]. Popular opinion insinuates itself as *das Man* in existence, its power being such that it brings about the lapsing [*Verfallen*] away of existence from being centered on its own uniqueness and instead following the crowd. Given this tendency to lapse, 'what people [*das Man*] might think' distracts *Dasein* from what is most its own [*eigen*], its authenticity' [*Eigentlichkeit*].

Existence has its unique spatiality [*Räumlichkeit*], which is understood not as an occupying of space but rather as a making room for... (things). Given this bodiliness [*Leiblichkeit*],[104] the human being exists *as* its body, not in it. This spatiality and the temporality of existence constitute a single manifold, such that it is only possible to consider one without the other *in abstracto*.

Human beings are implicated in language [*Sprache*] such that they talk [*Rede*]. The implication of this existentive is that they do not principally and in the first place (only) emit signals or (only) communicate information. This is an especially important existentive since the medium of daseinanalysis is language. Heidegger will say that 'language speaks, not the one who utters' phonemes. Silence is part of language understood in this way.

Given its mortality and its caring about things (and the other), existence is always on edge or anxious [*Angst*], which shows itself as being in anticipation of things in general. As such, it is always just somewhat ahead of itself. It is temporally ek-static. It stands out into the future in realizing its present. Existence is also always indebted [*Schuld*] to itself, inasmuch as, having chosen to do one thing, everything else that could have been done remains undone and therefore *Dasein* is always in arrears, in debt to its existence. Reminding itself of its indebtedness is expressed by existence having (a) conscience [*Gewissen*] which 'calls' to it as what we term conscientiousness. The implicit knowledge it has of things as well as what it does not yet know are in this way called to account along with what is consciously in awareness, that is, explicit to it in its present [*Gegenwart*]. Here is the temporal horizon of *Dasein* to which Heidegger directed his attention in the second part of *Being and Time*.

Finally, there is for Heidegger the existentive truth [*Wahrheit*]. Existence is 'in' the truth, where truth is understood as *alētheia* or unconcealment, that openness which is precisely what existence is about as the clearing [*Lichtung*] or availability for what comes to encounter it in the world. All openness or disclosure of this or that implies concomitant closure of the rest. Where there is unconcealment [*Unverborgenheit*], there is always also concealment [*Verborgenheit*].

Boss adds a further existentive which is not taken up explicitly by Heidegger: dreaming life [*Träumen*]. Continuous with waking life and yet different from it, dreaming life is especially important for the therapeutic situation, since dreaming life is often open to possibilities which in waking life one has not espied or tends to look away from (resists).

These existentives will be referred to throughout the discussion of the theory and practice of daseinanalysis. There will be more to say about most of them in the following pages, for example, in the discussion of language which follows and is closely related to the existentive talk [*Rede*].

(3) Language

Among the existentives, talk [*Rede*] is of special importance for daseinanalysis. Like psychoanalysis, the 'talking cure' on which it is based, daseinanalysis is mediated by words alone. The therapeutic setting is one in which analyst and analysand converse, listening to each other. We will consider the details of the setting in which this occurs below and show how it gives priority to the auditory realm over the other 'higher' sense, vision.

Talk is mediated by language [*Sprache*], which distinguishes human beings from other living creatures. The latter only signal and 'message' each other, communicating information. Electronic devices, which receive, store, transmute and transmit (pass along) information, are modeled after such emission and reception of signals. Conversation between two human beings *vis-à-vis* is a unique form of encounter [*Begegnung*]. The question whether so-called 'virtual reality' contacts are equivalent to the immediate presence with each of two human being is open for serious consideration, especially given the ubiquity of 'virtual appointments' and 'tele-medical visits', including those for psychotherapy.

Perhaps the most telling difference between the human being and other beings is that, in addition to speaking out loud, producing vocables, we write. Here language speaks silently as the hand scrawls or taps words onto some medium that retains images of them. In both cases, language has initiated speaking, whether as vocables or script. It is often said that we learn a language much as we learn to throw a ball or play the piano. It is rather the case that we exist in-the-world, one existentive feature of which is talk and that we are therefore open to language. As Heidegger wrote, 'Language speaks, not the speaker.'[105] We do not use language; language uses us. Its source remains a mystery and this mystery is the medium of daseinanalytic encounter.

In the daseinanalytic setting speech is left for the most part to the analysand. For the daseinanalyst, speaking is generally limited to acknowledging that the analysand has been heard, asking for clarification of what has been said, inviting the analysand to go into greater detail about a particular utterance, and offering an occasional hint that will encourage the analysand to 'free associate' further. In the orthodox psychoanalytic tradition, it is well understood that following the fundamental rule is difficult. The extensive time required for a psychoanalysis to be 'completed' is in part due to analysis of the resistance to free associating. In one sense, a psychoanalysis is terminable when the analysand is fully free to make associations, that is, to speak openly.

By contrast, in daseinanalysis, resisting [*Widerstehen*] is considered to be something positive in the sense that it alerts both analyst and analysand to the latter's ongoing attempt to continue to exist as he has without realizing that he is free to choose to attend to different things. Since we are all limited to a certain extent to choose freely, for daseinanalysis resistance is a phenomenon of existence, not an artefact of the therapeutic setting.[106] According to Freud, the analysand resists instead of remembering and speaking, and this 'acting out' is said to be an impediment to the analytic process. For daseinanalysis, however, 'acting out' is a positive step in the direction of self-determination, choice, the liberation of possibilities, and freedom.

(4) Person and Other

As already noted, early in the Zollikon seminars Heidegger said that 'conventional, objectifying representations' such as 'the person . . . in psychology and psychopathology must be abandoned'.[107] Yet, at the center of psychology and psychiatry is the concept of the person. The model for the latter is the early notion of the rational animal (*animal rationale*), which was further abstracted as the subject, and in the early history of psychology as a science; the subject was conceived in terms of the person (literally, a *persona* or mask created by the subject to fit his role as an actor in the drama of a given culture). The trait–theory personology, worked out by the American psychologist Gordon Allport (1897-1967), became the benchmark of this view and still lies at the conceptual heart of psychiatric theory, the relation buried deep in the text of every iteration of the *DSM*.

The idea of the subject and so also of the person is modeled on the object as a self-contained, isolated entity. It is assumed that connections are established between monadic subjects, including the intersubjective or interpersonal relationship between therapist and client. Daseinanalysis points out, however, that there is never a single, isolated individual or person who can be understood on his own terms alone and serially forms ties or bonds with other persons. Instead, there is in each case first, the *Dasein* of a given instance of human being which is from the start in relation with at least one other *Dasein*. Many *Dasein-Dasein* relations unfold from this dual unity or matrix. One such relation is the daseinanalytic partnership between therapist and *other* which is understood as a phenomenon of their being-with [*Mitsein*] one another. So understood, the relation is not fundamentally an interpersonal relationship although it may be construed as such by a third-person observer. In the tradition of psychiatry and clinical psychology, this ontic relationship has been the starting point of descriptions of therapeutic interaction, rather than the ontological relation between the *Dasein* of the analyst and the *Dasein* of the analysand as other to him on which therapeutic encounter is grounded.

Habits of usage are difficult to modify, but to appreciate the essential difference between daseinanalysis and psychotherapy, it is important to become accustomed to think and speak in terms of existence [*Dasein*] or existing [*Existieren*] and the *other*, which is shorthand for *other Dasein*, and leave behind talk of subject, person, psyche, ego and self. It will be a long haul of effort to disabuse everyday discourse of these artefacts of the science of psychology and its medical cousin, psychiatry.

(5) Caring about Things [Sorge] and Caring about the Other [Fürsorge]

A passage in Heidegger's *Sein und Zeit* is basic to daseinanalysis.[108] Often cited in the daseinanalytic literature, it discusses the existentive *Fürsorge* (caring about the other), which is presented by Heidegger in the context of the existentive being-with [*Mitsein*]. Linguistically, its close relation to the predominant existentive *Sorge* (caring about things), 'as which the be[-ing] of existence is to be determined', is evident. As noted earlier, caring *about* the other is contrasted with taking care *of* or looking after

[*Besorgen*] someone, as we find in self-care, parenting, being a good neighbor and, of course, doctoring and nursing.

Heidegger identifies two sorts of *positive* caring about the other: interventional [*einspringend*] and way-making [*vorausspringend*] caring about the other. He distinguishes both from what he terms a deficient [*defizient*] mode of *Fürsorge*, which is indifference toward the other. The latter may seem to be a surprising way of talking about caring about the other, but this becomes understandable when one realizes that *not* paying attention to an other who is present or treating him as though he were a thing requires effort.

Non-interventional or way-making caring about the other is the hallmark of daseinanalysis. Such caring about the other entails providing him with an opportunity to choose or not choose to care about things. This restores to him his *Sorge*. Way-making caring about the other differs fundamentally from those modalities of psychotherapy based on behavioral models such as rational-emotive behavior therapy (REBT) and the cognitive-behavioral therapy (CBT). These modalities are based on the other sort of *Fürsorge*, which is interventional and steps in [*einspringt*] for the other, expressly taking away from the analysand the opportunity to choose or not choose to care about what there is. In 'doing things' for the other, it seems to benefit him by helping him. While helping others is obviously much to be desired and sometimes in the early stages of daseinanalysis is unavoidable, in the end the point of daseinanalytic nonintervention is to make it possible for the other to help himself, first in the safety of the therapeutic play space and then in the world with others to who are not his analyst.

Of course, from time to time the goal of daseinanalysis must be compromised and it will be necessary to intervene. Boss describes one such instance, recounted in his *Existential Foundations of Medicine and Psychology* (1971a), in which Boss visited the analysand's home and helped bottle-feed the other during a period in which she was for the first time allowing herself complete abandonment to the primitive, pleasurable experience of being nourished as an infant. The question comes up about just how to decide when intervention is called for. Are there any principles to follow? Says Boss: 'You try to give or do no more for a patient than is absolutely necessary: the *patient* has to be responsible the whole way, if possible, *if possible*. But not all patients are able to be as adult or mature as is necessary in order to handle a really orthodox' daseinanalytic partnership.[109]

The way-making stance is consistent with what has been termed the daseinanalyst's *Gelassenheit* or leaving things as they are, in this case the things of the analysand's world. Such composure (as *Gelassenheit* has also been translated), is often characterized as light-hearted [*heiter*]. Indeed, leaving things as they are is light years away from the indifference associated with the deficient form of caring about the other described earlier. Sad to say, the psychoanalyst's studied neutrality is often experienced by analysands in precisely that way, however. Claims that complete abstinence encourages greater involvement of the analysand in the analytic process have not been possible to defend. Clearly, everything depends on the comportment of the analyst in the therapeutic encounter. Later, we will describe this in more detail, including its close connection with listening and language. For now it must suffice to say that the therapeutic setting of daseinanalysis, where the analysand reclines, minimizes the intrusion of visible features of the analyst, including his appearance, changes in posture and facial expression, and body language, that will invariably distract the analysand. Minimal talk by the analyst is intended to further the cause of such *therapeutic anonymity*. One can express the total effort as that of attempting to *not be anyone or anything in particular to the other*. This is an ideal, of course, but one to be aspired to.

There is without doubt a Taoist tone about the way-making caring about the other. This entered daseinanalysis as a result of Boss's encounter with one guru with whom he worked while in India, Govind Kaul, an individual with whom Boss could not communicate in a common natural language. As I understand this, what happened between them came to be for Boss a model for how therapeutic encounter works and leads to therapeutic liberation.[110]

This preceding sketch of the main features of the theoretical foundations of daseinanalysis will be elucidated in detail in Part III when we take a closer look at key texts by Boss. The next part is devoted to a discussion of therapeutic practice and the formation or preparation of the daseinanalyst.

PART II
PRACTICE AND PREPARATION

Chapter Five
Fundamentals

(1) The Couch

Use of the couch is unique to daseinanalysis, as it was to psychoanalysis. Freud's employment of the couch was not his idea. About 1890, one of his patients, a certain Madame Benvenisti, suggested that, given problems with back pain, she might be more comfortable during sessions semi-reclined on a Victorian daybed. At this time, Freud was still employing the 'pressure technique' to the forehead of his patient after they had closed their eyes. As a physician, he was within acceptable bounds of behavior in touching the patient's body. Lying back make this easier. In such a reclining position, hypnosis of the patient was also more easily accomplished.

Madame Benvenisti bought such a daybed for Freud, who covered it with a thick rug and cushions. As he replaced the pressure technique and hypnosis with the psychoanalytic technique, he remained seated, behind all of his analysand. An opportunistic moment in this way became the basis of an essential feature of psychoanalysis and, later, daseinanalysis. As Charlotte Aigner recently described, the position of the daseinanalysand's body reclining places 'head' (thought) and 'heart' (in the Pascalian sense) on the same level.[111] As Freud learned, the reclining analysand was inclined to spontaneously close his eyes, although that was not a requirement as it had been for the pressure technique and hypnosis. Today, a daseinanalyst will often find the use of a recliner a convenient substitute for the couch.

The psychoanalyst, too, often closed his eyes, the better to listen with 'the third ear'.[112] It is possible to do this facing the other, but the analytic setting makes doing so less problematic. Facing one another, eyes closed, may be a suitable starting point for eventual use of the recliner or couch. Recumbent, the circumambient auditory realm becomes primary. Being positioned on the couch and chair, respectively, social encounter *vis-à-vis* between analyst and analysand, which is so powerfully mediated by the human gaze and compels speech, gives way to therapeutic encounter which allows for long silences without the customary awkwardness that typically ensues when two human beings are facing one other. Positioning on the couch and chair also discourages ordinary social intimacy while promoting therapeutic closeness [*Nähe*].

As Aigner also points out, such a position eliminates the perception of visual clues provided by facial expression, postural changes and gestures, which together play an extremely important part in everyday human interactions from the most casual to the most intimate. In mothering, for example, there is the well-known smiling response which mediates much early preverbal rapport between mother and infant. In romantic relationships, as William Butler Yeats said, 'love comes in at the eye'. In the absence of eye *contact* (which as the expression suggests has a tactile quality about it), the acoustic realm regains primacy once again, as was the case prenatally for months before the open eyes of a newborn are exposed to the light of day and during the days or weeks before the infant is able to focus his gaze. The acoustic ambience is more primitive and fundamental than the visual. In the absence of visual clues, what is spoken gains in importance. The existential Heidegger termed *Rede* (talk) comes into prominence along with our being-with each other [*Mitsein*], *Dasein*-to-*Dasein*. As the German nicely makes clear, what we hear (*hören*) is what we come to belong to (*gehören*), that is, what we have heard (*gehören*).

Not everyone can tolerate being put in this position at the outset. For some, the gaze as a means for establishing *rapport* and insuring *rapprochement* cannot be dispensed with without risk of failing to maintain attachment. That is, of course, as it is in most day-to-day relationships. We look to the eyes for tacit agreement or disapproval. We look to the smile for assurance against fear. The sneer stops us in our tracks. The silent nod of a 'No' discourages further action or involvement.[113] In short, some individuals need visual support, much as children do. They need to be seen by the other as much as they need to see the other, and trust is possible only when the other is in view. Like the infant, who at first believes that when its mother is no longer in view she no longer exists, such individuals need to 'see' that the analyst is there.

In daseinanalysis, however, as soon as possible, the analytic arrangement is established. Lying back on the couch or a recliner encourages the transition from waking experience to a recovery of dreaming life. On occasion, it even allows for a brief 'absence' from wakeful attention, ranging from reverie to even a brief episode of sleep. At the very least, the reclining position reminds the analysand of the essential continuity between waking life and dreaming life, a feature of existence stressed by Boss. Such continuity had escaped Freud, who saw the two states as radically different from each other and, in fact, representing two realities. For daseinanalysts, however, existence does not serially occupy two different realities, one to which waking life belongs and the other to which dreaming life belongs. The world of *Dasein* – our being-in-*the*-world – is seamless and one of whole cloth.

Finally, in the reclining position compliance with the fundamental rule is easier. The other feels freer to utter thoughts or express feelings that positioning *vis-à-vis* may discourage, limit, or in some cases preclude in anticipation of the expression on the other's face being read as discouraging certain utterances.[114]

Use of the recliner or couch is one of the two features of orthodox psychoanalytic practice retained in daseinanalysis. The second is the invocation of the 'fundamental rule'.

(2) The Fundamental Rule

In daseinanalysis the analyst invokes the 'fundamental rule [*Grundregel*]' basic to Freud's psychoanalysis, inviting the analysand to begin to speak when he wishes and to continue to do so as long as he wants to, without stopping, censoring or withholding what comes to mind, no matter how odd or irrelevant, offensive or irreverent, or embarrassing it may prospectively seem to him to be. The application of valuing criteria such as this or that is 'unimportant' or 'nonsensical' or 'unseemly' is to be suspended. What holds in everyday life, which demands that one talk in such a way so as to preserve the social graces, politeness, political correctness, sex-appropriate speech, and the rest, is put on hold.

Invoking the rule and concluding a session at a predetermined time are among the few times when the analyst takes the initiative in daseinanalysis; otherwise, the 'timing' of a session is left entirely to the analysand. The decision to end the analysis itself is also in the hands of the analysand, who ideally initiates the theme of concluding the work. Of course, there will be occasions, usually early on, when the analyst realizes that a partnership is not feasible and will suggest that the analysand consider exploring other possibilities, including choosing another analyst or another form of treatment.[115]

Some individuals are not able to follow the fundamental rule, since, as Boss suggests, they are not at home in the realm of ideas and images. For this reason daseinanalysis is not suitable for them. This must be reckoned with if after several sessions it has reasonably been established by the analyst. As Boss said, such individuals 'can exist only in the form [*Gestalt*] of very much more hands-on world relations'.[116] Other treatment approaches will be required for them. Boss even recommends group therapies for some such individuals. A caveat was that the latter are likely to be a lifelong requirement for them. When psychotherapy was becoming more and more popular in the 1970s and 1980s, Boss saw that 'recovery groups' especially would be more and more common. He also accurately guessed that former 'patients' were likely to go on to be the 'leaders' or 'therapists' of such groups.

The fundamental rule encourages 'free association', which Freud understood as the medium for revealing what is hidden in the Unconscious. For daseinanalysis, however, 'free association' is something different. It is the means for allowing for a greater openness on the part of the analysand.

Two comments about this understanding of free association are in order.

> [First,] it is not a matter of speaking about everything that is observable, *even though* it seems to be irrelevant, senseless, embarrassing, etc., but of saying how everything shows up, so to speak, namely *as* what is irrelevant, *as* what is senseless, *as* what is embarrassing, etc. This means that the irrelevance, senselessness or embarrassment belongs to the phenomenon as well, [and] is essentially part of it.[117]

Thus, 'only when everything that comes to mind [*einfällt*], as it comes to mind, is taken seriously, is that openness reached which brings the analysand without reserve before himself, that is to say, at the same time before his hitherto concealed way of perceiving as well as before his hitherto concealed, distinctive possibilities of perceiving and behaving.'[118]

Second, free association leads one

> to take seriously that which shows itself, as it shows itself, [to] admit something as threatening, as shaming, as passionately loved or hated. The moods, feelings and passions are not at all separate from the 'matter'.[119] Psychoanalytic theory is mistaken if it believes that, on the one hand, there are so-called ideas as such and, on the other hand, there are only affects that are connected with them, whereby it understands by the latter nothing else than subjective manifestations of energy tension.[120]

In this text, Boss points to something not developed in much detail elsewhere and that is the tradition in academic psychology and psychoanalysis of once having posited such entities as ideas and affects to separate ideas (the products of judging and knowing) and affects (the products of feeling) into two different kinds of content found in the psyche, where feelings are seen as secondary to ideas, which dominate psychic life, and may produces delusions so that he is unable to think clearly. Psychoanalytic theory also explained 'hysteria' as the dominance of affects over ideas. Here feelings overwhelm thinking.

By contrast with the psychology of affects, Heidegger pointed to the moods [Stimmungen] of existence as determinative of experience, where the prevailing mood tints or tones every so-called function of psychological life. Mood also tints conversation, which is, of course, the medium of therapy. Finally, it determines the extent of openness of existence to what is encountering existence. The degree to which an analysand is open to talking about himself and, so, to observing the fundamental rule, is understood to be determined by his attunement in the therapeutic situation and encounter.

According to Boss, Freud and his followers failed to inquire about what exactly an association is. Understood phenomenologically, an association is said to occur 'when something given has ... gotten closer [genähert] to us from out of the open realm of our world'. Such closeness does not refer to physical proximity but, rather, to the meaningfulness or significance something given has for existence. It refers to its 'nearness [Nähe], familiarity and intimacy. We can therefore say of something that 'it has gotten to us [Sie ist uns angegangen]. Something has spoken to us [zugesprochen] from there [the open realm of our world] as something of this or that significance, no matter how vaguely this may have happened at first.'[121]

> In an analytic hour what has thus favored our world usually does not have the character of [the kind of] presence of what is sensually perceivable at the moment, but rather shows itself in the mode of presence of a bringing to mind [or envisioning as presently occurring] of something that is of today [Heutigem], [or of something] that has been [Gewesenen], or [of something] that is

to come [Zukünfigem]. This is not anything that has occurred intrasubjectively. In the taking in of associating, the one taking in always already abides 'outside' *at* what is given in his world openness, that is, in his being related to it and in his being claimed by it. All this has to be kept in mind, whenever... we talk about 'associating'.[122]

The very different understanding of resistance in daseinanalysis already mentioned is relevant here:

> [R]esistance against associations is... always a behavior towards what is given that wants to appear out of the open world of an analysand, the coming to light of which he tries to prevent by foreseeing and *looking away from it* [emphasis added]. He behaves this way because he is only able to perceive what is associating [itself] as something threatening and that should not be.

In general, 'in the form of an association, the possibility of a greater openness to the world shows itself. Resisting is a very specific way of relating to this possibility.'[123] The usefulness of resistance for daseinanalysts then lies in its indication of the analysand's *possibly* being more open to what is encountering it in the world.

Here language as a uniquely human phenomenon once again comes into view. We may add to what has already been said about language that, while for animals an intended signal comes out more or less the same each time it is produced and with the same intended meaning (a bird's mating call, for example), the human being never really knows what he will have said until he has spoken. Spoken language has a 'mind' of its own. The same holds for writing. It is possible to rehearse in thought what one wants to speak or write and then repeat it or write it down as recalled, but most of the time one begins to speak (or to write) not knowing where the to-be-spoken has originated or what will have been expressed when the utterance or composition [Dichten] has been completed. This has special value in the daseinanalytic setting.

The positioning of analyst and analysand and their conversation depend upon and are sustained by the original relation between them. This *Dasein* to *Dasein* relation is perhaps best understood in terms of therapeutic encounter [*Begegnung*].

(3) Encounter

The dynamics of daseinanalysis as experience and practice are based on encounter [*Begegnung*]. One of the most eloquent expressions of the phenomenon is found in a text by Boss, presented on May 1, 1964, at a roundtable of the Milan Group for the Advancement of Psychotherapy. There he said:

> By encounter we mean something uniquely human [*jenes spezifisch Menschliche*] that happens when two or more people confront each other or meet face to face. Therefore, an encounter does *not* take place, for example, when two pebbles bump into each other at the bottom of a stream. Nor is there

encounter when a geologist examines such a pebble to discover its chemical and physical composition. Whether we are justified in speaking of encounter when two dogs run towards each other in the street and sniff each other no cautious scientist will dare to decide.[124]

Boss then credited Freud with 'the courage to break the silence about the emotional phenomena inherent in the doctor-patient relationship that belongs to all therapy, in particular to psychotherapy. [Freud] even made clear that they are the authentic foundation of all psychotherapy.' Here encounter is described in terms of everyday in-person meeting. Such body with body presence is essential to the auditory atmosphere and ambience of the daseinanalytic setting.

Boss rejects Freud's operationalization of human experience. In this text, he is concerned to show that Freud tried to 'explain away' the very 'encounter phenomenon' he had focused on in the psychoanalytic situation by having recourse to the notions of transference and countertransference, themes to which Boss returned frequently.

> The phenomenon [of encounter] immediately showing itself was robbed of its qualities of authenticity and truth, was literally condemned as a 'sham bond [falsche Verknüpfung]', as a 'deception [Täuschung]', as something 'unreal, bogus [Unreales, Unechtes]', as something to be understood as an illusion [Illusion] by the patient and by the doctor, and to be overcome in the treatment.[125]

Boss examines Freud's statements that contradict his belief in the presumed illusory character of real encounter in psychotherapy. In fact, they assert the contrary of what Freud claims in other, theoretical writings. For example, Freud says that 'one has no right to deny the character of 'true love' to the infatuation brought to light in the analytic situation'. Therefore what Freud takes to be the inauthenticity of the feelings of the analysand caught up in transference is belied by the fact that, as he says, 'the analytic situation itself motivates emotions of love and hate directed towards the analyst that are as strong as they would be in a child-parent relationship'. Finally, Freud emphasized, there is no 'other such interpersonal situation in which one adult human being is as steadfastly and intensively there for the other as the analyst is for the analysand in analysis'. All three assertions speak to the reality of the feelings experienced by the analysand toward his analyst, which are not sham replicas of earlier experiences with people such as the analysand's mother or father.

The daseinanalytic partnership is also not to be confused with the Ich-du (I-Thou) relationship described by Martin Buber, which Boss contrasts with genuine therapeutic encounter, noting in Buber's well-known formulation of authentic human relating

> a worrisome fuzziness and lack of clarity about these new basic concepts. A totality and unity is merely assigned to the human being [menschlichen Wesen] represented in this way – so also an awareness, a freedom of will, and a sense

Fundamentals

of responsibility. But the so-called totality and unity remains a purely formal expression and says nothing about the nature [*Natur*] and essence [*Wesen*] of this human totality and unity that lets us see how it could in fact make awareness, freedom and responsibility understandable. Moreover, we learn nothing about how consciousness ought to be correlated with the subject, the person; nor do we hear anything decisive about what human freedom consists of and with respect to whom the responsibility should be applicable.[126]

Boss then raises the critical question:

> How can we say something adequate and meaningful enough about the encounter of two beings as long as insight into their nature [*Natur*] remains so obscure? {This is almost impossible, and therefore the premise of every sensible discussion about this and about encounter in psychotherapy as well must be an essential deepening of our knowledge of the specific nature of what is human. Basically, this consideration alone may lead to a clarification of *the vague bases of our psychological science and our practical psychotherapeutic work* [emphasis added], and I have always sought this, whether in ancient Asian [oriental] philosophies or in modern existential analysis.}[127]

Other authorities are subjected to critique, including Daniel Lagache (1903-1972), the French psychoanalyst and colleague of Jacques Lacan (1901-1981), who, Boss claims, failed to see the 'preconceived prejudicial notions about the essence [*Wesen*] of man, concepts such as subject [*Subjekt*], person [*Person*], psyche [*Psyche*], I [*Ich*] and Thou [*Du*]'. What Lagache overlooked is that 'the nearest, indisputable, essential [*wesensmäßig*], immediately given manifestation [*Erscheinung*] of human existing [*menschlichen Existierens*] is its being-in-the world. There is not a single human being [*Wesen*] (who rightly merits such a name) who does not before all else experience himself as *be*-ing [*seiend*] in a world.' Thus

> everything depends on seeing the immediate, perceptibly emergent nature of being-in-the-world, in other words, the quality [*Qualität*] of what is meant by this initial statement about man. That is why already in the introduction to Martin Heidegger's epoch-making *Sein und Zeit* [*Being and Time*] it is said with utmost clarity that the entire work is oriented solely and entirely to the qualitative determination of human being-in-the-world and has nothing else in mind.[128]

The relevance of this critique is its understanding of the nature of human existence as it determines therapeutic encounter.

> Qualitatively, however, human existence, human being-in-the-world, is to be understood in its decisive feature as fundamentally nothing other than a seeing [*Vernehmen*] and understanding [*Verstehen*], an enabling of the opening out to

and illuminating of what is encountering it [*Aufgehenlassen- und Lichten-können des ihm Begegnende*]. If one only looks at things with eyes wide open, human existing always appears [*ereignet sich*] from the start as nothing other than essentially a standing out [*Hinaus Stehen*], an extare [ex-sisting], existing [*Existieren*] in a perspicuous area of openness [*gelichteten Offenheitsbereich*] within which the phenomena of the world can immediately [*ganz unmittelbar*] come to emerge without any mediation and show up as what they are. Such being-in-the-world, such an existing [*Existieren*] is the fundamental essence of each of our wholly concrete ways of behaving in relation to the things we encounter which are constituent of our nature. How else could we relate to something at all if it had not already come to be known in its meaning for us as what it is in the light [*Lichte*] of an openness [*Offenheit*] in one way or another determinate of our existence [*Dasein*], and thanks to this of its essential drift [*Wesenszug*].[129]

Encounter with an other is understood in the context of the ontological feature being-with [*Mitsein*] that Heidegger included among the existentives of *Dasein*.

All encounter is grounded in this wholly original, essential being-with [*Mitsein*], likewise all encounter in psychotherapy. In their being with one another [*Miteinandersein*] with the same things in a shared world appearing in the open [*Offene*] of their existing, this essential being with others of all human beings, founding and enabling all encounter, sets human encountering [*Begegnen*] apart from every mere running into each other of merely extant things [*vorhandener Sachen*]. In comparison with the momentary [*augenblick-lich*] world-openness of the patient, *what is therapeutically effective in the therapeutic situation is the greater openness and freedom of the therapist to all spheres of the shared world showing itself* [emphasis added]. This essential being in the world with others makes it possible from the outset for the one who is ill [*Kranken*] to participate in the greater expansive openness and freedom of the therapist.[130]

Were it not for the ontological being with the other of analyst and analysand, there would be no possibility of a daseinanalytic partnership at all. The only difference between the two *Daseins* that encounter one another is 'the greater openness [*Offenheit*] and freedom [*Freiheit*] of the therapist', which are the result of his preparation as a daseinanalyst.

It is important to understand that Boss does not conceive of the daseinanalytic partnership as somehow like that of parent and child, even though mention is made of that relationship. In the parent-child relationship, Boss explains, one (the child) *at first* lives in the world of the other (the parent) and only gradually comes to see more of his own world. Something similar happens in daseinanalysis, however, in which the world of the analyst is more open to what is to be disclosed than is the world of the analysand. Since the analysand *at first* lives in part in that more open world of the analyst, the later must never attempt to urge the analysand to see the world as he does, for example with regard to religious beliefs, political ideology, gender identity and the rest. As daseinanalyst, one's concern is only that the analysand see more of the possibilities *open* and *opening up* to him and that he be freer to actualize them (or refuse them). 'Encounter in psychotherapy and its therapeutic effectiveness is just that simple,' says Boss in conclusion, no matter how serious the situation is for the analysand.

Boss concluded his formal presentation at the Milan roundtable referred to with another reference to the somewhat parent-like (in this illustration paternal) 'feel' of the daseinanalyst for the analysand in his therapeutic partnership with the analyst. The analysand

> does not at all have his anxiously determined and childishly reduced capacity to act, but instead *is* it; he exists in such a narrowed down [*verengter*] way and only in such a way. It thus happens that everything that turns up in the particular light [*Lichtstrahl*] of this so narrowed down way of life [*Existenz*], including the analyst, cannot fail to light up [*aufleuchten*] in a way corresponding [to it] in just this light, that is, [in this case] with threatening paternal meaning. A relation so colored by him is no less real, however. It is [a relation] with the patient himself and entirely so, and on this account it is far from being a false connection. To pass this relationship off as bogus [*unecht*] amounts to an unjust pathologizing [*Kränkung*] of the ill person that unnecessarily makes him ever more insecure and is in itself crazy [*irre*].[131]

The analyst is paternal, then, but not a revenant of the analysand's father. There is nothing of psychoanalytic transference in this. In the example, the analyst is not a representative of the analysand's father; he is, however, for a time *paternal*, but this is because the analysand sees *everyone* (certainly everyone who is male) as paternal. For Boss, to suggest that the therapeutic encounter is an ersatz relationship, as the idea of transference would have it, is itself pathologizing in the sense that it makes the analysand 'sicker' and more 'insecure'. Suggesting to the analysand that the therapeutic relationship is 'bogus', 'pretend', 'fake', that is, transferential, is itself therefore a 'crazy' thing to do.

Boss's response to his colleagues' comments at the roundtable added nuance to his reflections on encounter. It concluded with an important note on closeness [*vicinanza*] and distance [*distanza*] in psychotherapy.[132] 'I do not believe that one can make a distinction of this type; in other words, that the doctor must shut himself off from the closeness of a friend or a relative,' as one of his critics had suggested. The partners in the analytic relationship must *always* be close [*vicino*] in the way a friend is close, but with a difference.

> I think the psychotherapist must always be very close to the analysand; however, *there are a thousand kinds of closeness* [emphasis added]. There is the forced closeness of dependency and submission. There is the closeness

created by falling in love, and this is a kind of closeness that should be examined in depth by the analyst. There is [also], for example, the closeness of a free relationship, of an open freedom with respect to the analyst, in which he is extremely close to the analysand. However, despite this closeness, the analyst must retain his own personality and freedom.[133]

The daseinanalyst is first and foremost a model of freedom and openness for the daseinanalysand. For him to be less than maximally free in their encounter is tantamount to sacrificing his therapeutic value to the other. In sum, therapeutic encounter is essentially linguistic. Perhaps more than in any other meeting between two human beings, in the daseinanalytic therapeutic encounter, words matter. This brings us to the next topic, which is therapy as 'the art of conversation'.

(4) The Art of Conversation

A therapist directly influenced by Heidegger, whom he visited in Todtnauberg, was Jan Hendrik van den Berg (1914-2012). His mentor, Henricus Cornelius Rümke (1893-1967), as we have noted referred to therapy as 'the art of conversation'.[134] There are echoes here of lines from Friedrich Hölderlin's 'Celebration of Peace' (to which Heidegger often made reference), in which we find the expression '... for we are a conversation [Gespräch], and hear from one another...'[135]

Perhaps the best of what Boss has left us on the topic of conversation in the therapeutic encounter in terms of its comprehensiveness appears in the following text. Once again, the importance of the daseinanalytic arrangement and setting is stressed. Boss is clear about the times when the desired setting is not feasible or might even be counter-therapeutic.

> What is the essence of this conversation?... The topic [Thema], i.e., whatever is discussed, [i.e., the content] is in fact tied to the analysand's experiential manner. In principle, everything can become a topic, but *only that and how the analysand experiences something and why he experiences it in this way is of interest* [emphasis added]. The form [of whatever is discussed] seems even more troublesome: the analyst and the analysand participate in the conversation in quite different ways, something which becomes physically clear in the 'setting':[136] the lying down of the analysand and the sitting behind [him] of the analyst. In view of these peculiarities, it is overlooked that the analytic conversation is not fundamentally different from any other conversation. Like any other, it presupposes a common ground of understanding. If this ground is too narrow and brittle, as can be the case with schizophrenics, an analytic conversation is neither possible nor appropriate. Conversely, every conversation is exposed to the danger of 'untruthful talk' [lying], [and to] the dangers of lack of understanding, misunderstanding, and [only] appearing to understand. But here there nonetheless lies a difference. Generally, when people talk to each other, the ability and willingness of the participants to resolve misunderstand-

ings is presupposed, rightly or wrongly. The analytical conversation [however] presupposes nothing of the sort . . . . In [the analytic conversation], the analysand becomes able to put into play what he thinks of things, to put it [all] on the line and thus become open to the experience that things can be different than what he has so far thought [they were].[137] Therein lies the sense and justification of the seemingly artificial form of the conversation. Any adaptation to what is customary of the sort other therapeutic approaches have made ignores or obscures the conditions of the analytic conversation. *The analyst's task is to keep open some play space [Spielraum] for possible change.* This play space is kept open by the analyst's unfailing attention to the communications of the analysand. We again characterize this attention as 'phenomenological'. It corresponds to [the communications] – better, it fulfills that openness which is intended by the fundamental rule but is not something that can be made good on by the analysand.[138]

To be sure, the therapists in Boss' presence at the roundtable (mostly psychiatrists and psychoanalysts) naturally wondered: How does the conversation described 'prepare the ground [*Boden*] for the analytic event [*analytische Geschehen*]'? And just what is 'the analytic event'? He replied:

Staying with the phenomenon, dwelling on it, not only rejects the tendency to pass over what is revealed in favor of what is hidden behind it. It is also an instruction about how the analysand's messages should be received by the analyst; namely, with deference and respect. Such understanding is not about a mere enrichment of knowledge, about seeing through what was previously incomprehensible. At the very least, knowledge for knowledge's sake always has the mark of distancing itself from what is revealed. In the phenomenological sense, to dwell on the thing [*Sache*] [what matters] means to accept it as something that has a claim to human understanding to be allowed to unfold in this understanding in all its particularity. The being-together of analyst and analysand is not primarily based on the will to jointly gain knowledge about the analysand, to make the 'Unconscious conscious', but to give him *acceptance* as who he is. The analysand is not so much an unknowing person as one who is unable to accept himself in a wide range of areas of his ability to perceive and behave. Thanks to the phenomenological attitude of the analyst, a 'play space for acceptance' is opened for the analysand in which the associations that have so far been looked down upon as irrelevant, senseless, embarrassing, etc., and suppressed can find a place. In analysis attention is something mutual. What is more, from the very beginning, the analysand has entered into a relationship with his analyst by communicating his associations to him. What the analysand communicates and how he communicates it, as well as how he takes in what the analyst says – in this he carries out his specific relationship to the analyst. *The type of conversation and the type of relationship cannot be separated from each other* [emphasis added]. The relationship between the analysand and the analyst is the scene of the analytic event; the problem of resistance, which has so far been related [only] to the openness demanded by the basic rule, is at the same time the problem of the relationship between patient and therapist [*Therapeut*]. Given their basis in the individual life-historical experiences and impressions of the analysand, no matter how diverse the forms [*Formen*] which the analyst mistakenly takes on, they always have something in common. Analysands perceive the analyst as someone who accepts them only under certain conditions of their being such and such [*Sosein*] or even under certain circumstances classifies them as not worthy of acceptance at all. In their view, the analyst always assumes an attitude that denies them the right to be themselves, to develop their own possibilities. Whether they respond to this by trying to gain acceptance through conformist behavior or by rebelling against supposed pressure to conform or by withdrawing into indifference, they are always under the spell of this denial that shapes them and from which they cannot free themselves.[139]

Talk about mistaking the analyst for someone else would have turned the attention of psychoanalysts listening to Boss to thoughts of transference. Anticipating this, Boss asked: 'Is the analytic relation then merely a repetition?'

'It would be,' he replies,

if the analyst were actually to behave according to the expectations of the analysand because of his own unsolved problems. But if the analyst is able not to be disturbed by the behavioral expectations of the analysand but retains his open accepting attitude, no matter how much the analysand may misjudge it, the situation is a different one, a new one, because his expectations do not find fulfillment in the behavior of the analyst. Having entered into a relationship with the analyst, the patient cannot simply escape the experience that the analyst behaves differently than expected. In the accepting atmosphere of the analytic conversation, his persistence in old ways becomes questionable, loses its legitimacy, so to speak. This makes it possible to suspend the previously held criteria of speech and behavior, to communicate in a new way. *Whether the analysand grasps this possibility and how far he grasps it ultimately lies in his freedom and not in the power of the analyst* [emphasis added]. The analyst can only suggest the possibility of the analysand's more open speech and behavior, and this in two ways: on the one hand, through his own phenomenological attitude, he can give the analysand the sense that he is accepted as being *other* [emphasis added] in a way hitherto quite unknown to him; on the other hand, he can encourage him, the analysand, to give up his own approving attitude toward himself.[140]

We then come to the question that implicitly informs Boss's therapeutic approach in general. The phenomenological dimension of daseinanalysis is reflected in a question, which fits hand-in-glove with the way-making caring about the other makes daseinanalysis distinctive.

In response to the analysand's having proposed to try something out for the first time – the question, for example, 'I wonder if I might give her a call?' – Boss proposes offering the 'question': 'Actually, why *not* [*Warum eigentlich nicht*]?'[141] He refers to this expression as the 'therapeutically most important words of the therapist acting in accordance with existence' and as the 'actual heart' of daseinanalytic therapy.[142] As we have translated this expression for the title of this volume: "Why in the world *not*"?

Boss is wisely careful to add wittily: 'Of course, this is not to be read as a technical instruction to the analyst to use these words at every possible and impossible opportunity. The question contains, on the one hand, the analyst's demand on the analysand that consists in the preservation [by him] of a degree of acceptance of everything that comes to mind, and, on the other hand, the task of the analysand, which ultimately no one, neither the analyst nor anyone else can take away from him, to accept himself such as he is [*Sosein*].'

What happens to the analysand is a 'getting to know, making oneself familiar with and trying things out': 'The space opened up by being together with the analyst becomes a world of rehearsal [*Probewelt*]. Given the setting's limiting, containing boundaries, the boundaries of the existing person can be explored.' Boss mentions new possibilities of 'recollecting, fantasizing, wishing, wanting, and behaving'. The art of daseinanalysis lies in a combination of great intimacy and a necessary 'distance' from the analysand. Only under these circumstances can the analysand 'try out' the new possibilities that have come to light 'as if they had a claim on him to be accomplished solely because they are his possibilities' and have nothing to do with the analyst. 'We know this to be what is called the claim [*Anspruch*] of so-called self-actualization [*Selbstverwirklichung*].'[143]

> The analysand then demands unconditional acceptance of these possibilities. [Thus] the possibilities are not brought out into the open and examined for their worthiness for acceptance but are regarded indiscriminately as accepted. But accepted by whom? Accepting also means taking responsibility for. Since the analysand questions his possibilities too little, he takes little responsibility for them. He tries them out within the scope of acceptance opened up by the analyst and thus sees them as the analyst's responsibility. The relationship to the analyst is also characterized by this, that the analyst is completely 'fit into [*eingefügt*]' the newly discovered world of the analysand; he is 'at his disposal [*zur Verfügung*]'; with him, through him, grounded in him, the analysand creates respect for and finds validity for his suppressed possibilities. The analyst's being used by the analysand manifests itself to outsiders as the often criticized dependence of the analysand. It becomes apparent here as inevitable, even if only temporary. This dependence or, better this undelimited [*unabgegrenzte*] relationship to the analyst does not have to express itself as a clinging, overly strong being related to him. Since the analyst is hardly allowed to fool around [and] is hardly allowed to make his presence felt, even in a relationship that seems to be very loose [*lose*], he is fit in, used in a way necessary for the analysand's testing of his [own] possibilities.[144]

At work on this verbal playground, the daseinanalyst must always be mindful that 'the daseinsanalyst's relationship to the analysand is indeed 'selfless', not in the sense of self-sacrifice, but only in the sense that he does not misuse the analysand, i.e. does not depend on him for the satisfaction of any of his own, otherwise unsatisfied wishes, be it for his own security, recognition, power or love.'[145]

Use of the couch, invocation of the fundamental rule, encounter and therapeutic conversation are the principal elements of daseinanalysis. There is, however, more at work in it. Boss described this as what the Peruvian psychiatrist Carlos Alberto Seguín (1907-1995) called the psychotherapeutic eros.

(5) The Psychotherapeutic Eros

In 1962, Boss published what is perhaps his most important monograph on daseinanalysis as practice. Although he speaks of 'psychotherapy', he very much has in mind therapeutic daseinanalysis in contrast with the modalities of psychotherapy then popular. It is important to keep in mind that the Zollikon seminars had not yet begun in earnest and that Boss hoped to reach as wide an audience of psychiatrists and psychotherapists as possible, albeit to convert them to daseinanalysis.

'The highest aim [*Ziel*] of all psychotherapy,' wrote Boss, 'is and remains the opening up [*Eröffnung*] of our patients to an ability to love and to trust [*Lieben- und Vertrauen-Können*] which permits all oppression by anxiety and guilt to be surmounted as mere misunderstandings [*Mißverständnisse*]. Such trust can and may be fittingly called the most mature [*tiefste*] form of human love.'[146] Here is the essence of daseinanalysis. It is fitting that that same year Boss also wrote an introduction to the German translation of a book by the Peruvian psychiatrist Carlos Alberto Seguín, which had appeared the previous year.[147] Boss's 'Introduction' is important for highlighting the dearth of candid discussions among psychotherapists of 'the actual curative factor in their treatment methods, that is, their own affective relationship to their patients. Rather, they have increasingly regarded the investigation of this phenomenon as peripheral.'[148] Given the 'sad circumstances' of there being little in the literature on psychotherapy on the therapist's way of working that is 'curative', Boss writes, 'our science should consider itself fortunate in being presented, at last, with *a study of the love of the psychotherapist for his patients* [emphasis added], a study which thinks out the core problem of psychotherapy, the doctor–patient relationship, in a radically new fashion. It seeks to replace the long outmoded concepts of transference and counter-transference by a designation more adequate to the phenomenon.' In his 'Introduction' to the book, Boss wrote:

> Seguín first established a broad scientific basis [for psychotherapy] by an extensive examination of interpersonal human possibilities of relationship as a whole.... [He] proceeds to isolate the special and unique relationship of the psychotherapist to his neurotic and psychotic patients from all the forms of human love open to other doctors and to people in general. The doctor–patient relationship in psychotherapy, as Seguín presents it, is so special, so

instructive, and paradigmatic for all forms of human relations as well as for all other doctor–patient relationships, that the author gives it a distinctive name: *the psychotherapeutic eros*. His admirable designation refers to the desired ideal structure of a doctor–patient relationship, perhaps, rather than to any love that can ever be lived out entirely in the doctor–patient relationship by the average doctor or even by the average psychotherapist. A study of this work is, then, for this very reason, most warmly recommended not only to all doctors and psychotherapists but to all those who in any way have fellow human beings in their care.[149]

This speaks directly to the daseinanalysis and Seguín's felicitous term 'psychotherapeutic eros' best describes the sort of love Boss has in mind in his discussion of 'the highest aim' of daseinanalysis.[150] As Seguín says in his book, the psychotherapeutic eros is a 'feeling ... that leads us away from the concept of sexual love and brings us close to the Platonic 'pedagogic Eros', which can bear a certain relationship to our notion .... The psychotherapeutic Eros must be free from (a) authority or any tendency to possession; (b) identification; (c) dogma; (d) the imposition of values, rules, or knowledge; and (e) sexual attraction.'[151]

Introducing Seguín's expression in his monograph, Boss wrote that

there is a special kind [*ein besondere Art*] of attending [*Zuwendung*] of the psychotherapist to his analysands which cannot be found anywhere in the world outside the psychoanalytic setting. This *specific 'psychotherapeutic eros'* [emphasis added] is as different from the love of parents for their children, different from the love between two friends, different from the love of the pastor for his flock, *quite decidedly different from the extremely variable love between the sexes* [emphasis added], as it is from the objectifying indifference [*versachlichenden Gleichgültigkeit*] of purely conventional kindness [*bloß Liebenswürdigkeit*].[152]

Addressing a wide audience of psychoanalysts and psychotherapists, he is advocating for daseinanalysis. There has hardly been a clearer expression of what motivates the daseinanalyst in his work than what we find in these sentences on therapeutic liberation.

Boss adds: 'Genuine psychotherapeutic eros ... has to distinguish itself by an otherwise never practiced [*sonst nie geübte*] [in everyday life] selflessness [*Selbstlosigkeit*], self-restraint [*Selbstzucht*] and reverence [*Ehrfurcht*] before the partner's [*Partner*] unique essence [*Eigenwesen*].'

Perhaps of greatest importance, the therapeutic eros is free from power. One of the central features of the daseinanalytic partnership is the striving on the part of the analyst to level the playing field – the therapeutic playground or play space – by minimizing to the greatest extent possible the hierarchy implicit in the medical model of doctor and patient. It is readily open to observation that not only in psychiatry but also in contemporary psychotherapies in general, especially when practiced in in-patient and clinical settings, the relationship between patient and provider is hierarchical. The therapist is assumed to be the expert, sometimes representing the authority of the theory or technique he is said to represent, but sometimes also the institution in which he practices, which adds a dimension of corporate power to his status as an expert on the experience and behavior of the patient. Sometimes the contemporary psychotherapist is a surrogate for a referring entity (parent or spouse, legal or rehabilitative agency), the power of which authorizes the duties he is paid to carry out. Ultimately, each of these entities also represents a social norm. This is anathema to daseinanalysis. As Thomas Szasz pointed out again and again, norms are enforced by the invocation of such moral authority masquerading as scientific savvy.[153] By contrast with every model of psychotherapeutic intervention, the daseinanalytic stance disavows any power differential between the partners in a therapeutic relationship. Psychotherapeutic eros is an expression of the daseinanalyst's understanding of a way of being encountered by (and, what comes to the same thing, encountering) the other with the greatest humbleness he can muster.[154]

Talk of love and therapy is, of course, a veritable hot potato. Therapy is, after all, a sober undertaking, is it not? It is a coolly rational discussion of the patient's symptoms, wishes, alarming behavior ('acting out'), wild ideas ('delusions'), fantasies, and, of course, extreme, often excessive, affect ('feelings') and behavior within and outside of the therapeutic setting. And so there may be *talk* of love, but surely it is 'all talk'. There is no place for 'real love' in therapy, certainly not any expression of love emanating from the analyst, and when it originates with the analysand, it is said to have its source in a confusion of mistaken identity and misattributed feelings (transference). How are we, then, to understand this 'real love' Seguín and Boss speak of?

A text of Heidegger sheds light on the matter. In his 'Letter on 'Humanism', Heidegger plays on the connection between favoring [*Mögen*] the other and enabling [*Vermögen*] him. There are intimations here of precisely what we see in the therapeutic eros, which is understood as a gift or favor. Heidegger's text is challenging and the vocabulary does not immediately resonate with well-known English equivalents, but it serves us well in pointing out the connection between enabling and loving that is implicit in Boss's understanding of the therapeutic eros. As Heidegger writes:

> To embrace [*annehmen*] a 'matter [*Sache*]' *or a 'person* [*Person*]' [emphasis added] *in their essence* [*Wesen*] means to love them, to favor [*mögen*] them. Thought in a more original way, such favoring [*Mögen*] means to bestow their essence [*die Wesen schenken*] [as a gift]. Such favoring is the proper essence of enabling [*Vermögen*], which can not only accomplish [*leisen*] this or that but can also let something 'come to pass [*wesen*]' in its coming-forth [*Her-kunft*], that is, can let it be [*sein lassen kann*]. It is on the 'strength [*kraft*]' of enabling by favoring that something is actually able be what is authentically its own [*etwas eigentlich zu sein vermag*]. This enabling is the actually 'possible' [*das eigentlich 'Möglich'*], that whose essence resides in favoring.[155]

Such 'gifting' is at the heart of therapeutic eros. Of course, not all gifts can be accepted. In fact, they may be refused, even violently rejected or destroyed by the one offered them, as the literature on so-called 'borderline' psychopathology notes. This does not deter the daseinanalyst, however, and he persists in offering the kind of 'conventional kindness' that is basic to the therapeutic eros.

But what about the person who is aggressive verbally and sometimes even threatening and belligerent in his behavior toward the therapist? Not only does he wave off a therapist's offer of therapeutic eros, but he will do whatever he can to interpret the gift of love as an attack on him by the therapist. Here the famous 'borderline' personality will do whatever he can to sabotage even the expression of good will by the therapist. Such individuals were first said to suffer. As the 'borderline' personality, his success is in seeing to it that everything fails and everyone fails him. Readers with long experience will bring to mind angry, even violent patients of this 'type'. Boss anticipates their worries, noting that allowing the living out of an 'otherwise never practiced' way of being with others in the therapeutic setting might involve a powerful behavioral assertiveness that had only been fantasized by the analysand up to that time. Nonetheless, Boss writes, the daseinanalyst 'must not be shaken and perturbed either by compliant [*entgegenkommendes*], or by indifferent [*gleichgültiges*], or by hostile [*feindseliges*] behavior on the part of the patient.'[156] This is a tall order but, as we will often have the occasion to observe, taking the daseinanalytic approach is challenging and not for everyone. Taking the other seriously and taking seriously what the analysand is capable of doing are equally important considerations. Maintaining composure [*Gelassenheit*] while doing both is very challenging. As it turns out, behind such equanimity is a certain courage and the courage has its source in the selflessness of the analyst.

Thus Boss therefore emphasizes that only if the daseinanalyst is able to assume an attitude of selflessness 'will the openness [*Offenheit*] of a human space [*mitmenschlichen Raumes*] allow our patients to reach the point where they can put out their feelers [*ihre Fülhörner*] again and *with autonomous responsibility* get involved in ever freer and more extensive world relations [*Weltbezüge*].'[157] These 'feelers' may be grotesque, but they must be welcomed.

Boss has no 'fix' to provide, no manualized technique to implement. There is only the 'playground [*Tummelplatz*]' on which the other is at liberty to *regain his freedom*. Such a play space is the place for a game, the rules of which the analyst and analysand together make up as they go along. It is not a competitive playing field. There is no winner, unless one may speak of the analysand winning back his freedom as a goal.

We have now outlined the features of daseinanalysis. It remains to briefly discuss an element of the approach that, once again, hearkens back to its origins in psychoanalysis, but which in the practice of daseinanalysis takes on a very different form. That is dreaming life and the laying out [*Auglegung*] in the therapeutic setting of what it offers the analysand.

(6) Dreaming Life

Dreaming life holds a place of great importance in daseinanalysis. In his first book on the theme, *The Dream and Its Interpretation* (1953d), Boss speaks of the phenomenon of dreaming as 'an admonition to modern man to stop his constant attempts at explaining the mysterious background of all existing things in terms of familiar ideas borrowed from the world of technology, and instead to respect it in all its mystery and inexplicability.'[158] Dreaming life reminds us of the irrational, the uncanny, the mysterious, and even the ineffable. It points to the unique nature of each existence.

With psychoanalytic dream theory in mind, Boss makes a distinction between 'the dream [*der Traum*]' and 'dreaming [*das Träumen*]':

> All the so-called depth psychologies still refer to *the* dream as if it were something that could be had or possessed ... Thus dreaming, a definite mode of human existing, is reified, is made into an objectifiable thing – which it certainly is not. In fact, there is no dream [that is] had, or made, that is an object which can be grasped or possessed. There is always only the dreaming human being. At one time he exists as a dreaming being, at another as a waking being. Waking and dreaming are two autochthonous, though different possibilities or modes of existing of an always integral and whole human being. For this reason, an adequate understanding of the basic constitution of human existing is a prerequisite for any serious theory of dreaming.[159]

Being awake and dreaming are grounded in our 'integral and whole' being-in-the-world. As to just how waking life and dreaming life are said to differ, Boss confesses that philosophers and sages alike are at a loss. All we know is that they are continuous as the one unitary existence unfolds. Waking and dreaming life are not allochthonous worlds.

Dreaming life is overlooked by the Heidegger of *Being and Time* as an existentive. Boss suggests that it belongs among them. The most relevant of the other existentives to the discussion of dreaming life is the spatiality [*Räumlichkeit*] of existence. With regard to the latter, the human being does not find himself *in* the world as a self-enclosed entity inside a container. The 'in' of being *in* the world is not related to the spatial coordinates describe by geometry; 'rather, we span the world openness from which we are addressed by beings *as* a realm of openness, a realm of seeing and perceiving, extended as far as the most distant beings that address us. One is *throughout* the world.' This expansiveness is important since 'at times while dreaming, we experience most vividly this basic fundamental constitution of the human being.'

At such times, of course, 'we may also be seen and handled as bodies [*Körper*] present at a point in space.' This does not, however, change the ontological status of our bodiliness [*Leiblichkeit*]. It is precisely the human body as *Leib* that is common to our waking being and dreaming life, and it is continuous throughout them. Our *Körper* (the body we have) shows up only as we wake up and persists concurrently in waking life [*Wachen*] with our bodiliness [*Leiblichkeit*]. Awake or sleeping, however, as *Leib*

Fundamentals

'we are always 'outside' [out there] by the beings of our world at those places of the world where they are present. This is so even when their mode of being present [*Anwesenheit*] is that of being visualized, remembered, planned, fantasied or hallucinated, and not that of being sensually perceptible' or dreamed.

How do we know this? What confirms that, existing, we are always 'out there'? Boss replies: 'Only as such can we, while dreaming, believe that we are fully awake.' Conversely, while fully awake we may believe that we are dreaming. All that gainsays the belief that we are asleep is that we wake up. It is equally true, however, that we may dream we are awake. The bottom line is that 'any momentary state in which our dreaming as well as our waking existence appears is to be defined by exactly the same criteria.' This is the evidence for their continuity as our being in the world.[160]

Boss finds an echo of this view of dreaming life in Blaise Pascal's (1623-1662) observation that 'we would be unable to distinguish waking from dreaming if the events of the latter observed the strict regular sequence of happenings.' Only because they do *not* do so, however, can we distinguish between dreaming life and waking life. And that is because we wake up and find ourselves among familiar things. For further confirmation of his view, Boss invokes Arthur Schopenhauer (1788-1860), for whom 'the sole distinction he could discover [between dreaming life and waking life] was the empirical experience of awaking. Awaking, however, is not a characteristic of dreaming as such. He could only conclude: 'If both waking [life] and dreaming [life] are judged from an objective viewpoint, then there is no difference to be found [between them]. We have no choice but to admit the poets are right when they say that life is but a long dream.'[161]

While it would seem that the things encountered in dreaming life are 'more fleeting and mutable' than those 'by which we dwell in our waking state . . . in fact, the reverse is true,' Boss claims. Instead, 'waking, we are able to choose the existential relationships in which we dwell, exist.' No such choice is possible in dreaming life. Our nearness to and intimacy with or distance from things now sensually perceived, as well as things 'visualized 'in our thoughts' and 'that which still has to come to be present from the future' are extremely variable and change from moment to moment. By contrast

> what appears to us out of the openness of our dream world appears predominantly – *not exclusively, but to an incomparably greater degree than in waking* [life] [emphasis added] – in that mode of being present of an immediately sensual, optically, auditively perceptible, temporally present presence, as distinct from visualized presences, remembered presences, or expected presences. This is so even when those presences of our dream world are of a more mutable character than are those of our waking life.[162]

In other words, 'the openness of dreaming existence is largely limited to admitting only the sensually perceptible presence of what is encountered as being temporally present.' What appears in dreaming life is nearly always limited to concrete, sensually perceivable realities, not abstractions.[163]

What appears in a dream is not something remembered, as Freud believed. Only while awake do we remember things. But what is remembered is created anew. In dreaming, by contrast, there is a new presentation of experience. Therefore a dream could not be a repetition, say, of a traumatic event. It is a newly being injured, not a memory of a particular incident with which it has striking similarities. It is yet another damaging experience. If it were a memory, it would be of only intellectual interest, as though one were reading a story of the injury. That is not to say our reaction may not be strong, but so are our reactions to reading a murder mystery or salacious text or watching a video while we are awake. There is, however, no willed suspension of disbelief in dreaming life, as, in effect, there is when we see and hear a performance in the theatre or while watching an offering on Netflix. The dreamed event is as new and alive as any given event in the life of a person experienced while awake.

Boss emphasizes an important difference between 'the significations of the encountered as existed [lived out] by the waking being and those of the one dreaming.' The dreaming world is for the most part visual and what is seen tends to 'come impressively and at times uncomfortably close to us. Waking, insights vie for attention with what is sensually perceived. We do not reflect in dreaming life. Everything is immediate presentation. Everyone in a dream in a sense violates the customs of social distancing and what is miles away on a landscape seen in a dream is within reach.' This entails another distinctive feature of dreaming life. The 'significations and referential context' of the dream world 'address us predominantly from 'external' beings, which we ourselves are not.' If the one dreaming makes an appearance, it is usually as an other, as a stranger.

The therapeutic value of examining dreaming life lies in the fact that it frequently allows for the admission into existence for consideration of what is unusual, new and unaccustomed which can be considered while awake. On the other hand, waking life is far richer in content, and therefore more of one's possibilities come to light there than in dreaming life. This gives waking life priority, while granting to dreaming life a special place where what usually does not grab our attention finds a way into existence. This difference is made clear by 'the startling fact that we can awaken (*erwachen*) from a dream state into waking [life] existence but can never in an analogous way say that we *erträumen* – that we 'adream".'

The transition from wakeful alertness to sleep functions as providing an opportunity for dreaming life to occur. Waking up functions as bringing us into alertness and possible interaction with a far more extensive range of things and others. 'Accordingly, it is our awakening [Er*wachen*] and only this awakening which leads out into the full unfolding of being, out of the unfree dimensions of a dreaming being-in-the-world, up to the greatest possible freedom of our most waking mode of existing, and so to the attainment of the proper meaning and purpose of our '*Da-sein*'.'[164]

For Freud, there were *dreams*, self-contained entities that were subject to interpretation [*Deutung*], a procedure that amounted to decoding disguised manifest, remembered content in order to discover the latent dream thoughts that were seeking admission into consciousness disguised by elements of the manifest content. The laying out [*Auslegung*] of dreaming life content in daseinanalysis is something quite different.

[*Auslegung*] first of all starts by *not* interpreting [the dream content] in the psychoanalytical way and not educing a given thing to a mere intrapsychic image, but by letting it be in its own right as the being as which it shows itself to be within a dreamer's world. Daseinsanalytic laying out 'only' takes place in order to unfold and differentiate more and more succinctly the essence of a dream thing, [its] meaningfulness and the significances of the thing itself which address a dreamer's understanding. Thus in the light of daseinsanalysis dream contents never hide or cover up something in a 'symbolical' way – whatever the term 'symbol' is supposed to mean. To the contrary, all dream things are always and from the outset of and as themselves revealing, disclosing their proper meaningfulness to everyone who lingers with them, dwells with them, and carefully looks at them.[165]

A thing in a dream is not a symbol for another thing. A snake, for example, is not a symbol for a penis. Instead, the many characteristics of the dreamed snake as 'the thing itself' are explored in terms of its physical and behavioral features. The point is that 'all those beings shining forth into the world-wide expanded openness or clearance of understanding as which man exists neither "mean" nor are they "in reality" anything other than what they directly reveal themselves to be.' Boss then asks: 'If there is no "hide-and-seek" connection to be found between the worlds of dreaming and of waking, is there any other relation existing between the two states as the necessary prerequisite for a therapeutic application of the daseinsanalytic understanding of dreaming?'[166] In reply, he points out that 'the existence modus of the dreamer is in general more constricted than that of the waking person.' It is 'less open and free', but precisely for that reason its contents stand out and are highlighted. Therein lie their therapeutic value, since 'it often happens that previously unknown significations and referential contexts address the human being and become existent for the first time during dreaming.' They are so poignant 'in' dreaming life because they are new to the person. Their impact, says Boss, is therefore potentially 'massive and ineluctable'.

As reported in the analytic setting, the 'things' presented in dreaming life can in the hands of the practiced analyst be a means of 'appealing to the clearer sightedness of the waking existence of the former dreamer ... [and lead] toward a clarification of his own waking existential state.' Thus,

> the daseinsanalyst has first 'only' to ask his patient over and over again to describe the phenomena which had addressed him during his dreaming state.... The dreamer must continue this phenomenological endeavor until he and the analysand have become fully aware of all of the whereabouts making up the dreamer's worldly dwelling place..... The patient must also describe the general mood [*Stimmung*] he found himself in when perceiving all the dream 'givens [*Gegebenheiten*]', as well as all the particular kinds of emotional relationships to them in which his existence was engaged while he was dreaming, because the attunement of an existence is a sure indicator of the existential freedom a human being has already gained.[167]

The point is for the dreamer to 'become fully aware of the structure of his dreaming state of existence'. Having identified his mood while dreaming, the person may then be asked: 'Do you now, in the more clear-sighted waking state, become aware of one or another as yet not fully realized unobjectifiable, immaterial, 'mental' possibilities of relating to something – a possibility which shows in its basic features an analogy, even a sameness with the essential meaningfulness and signification of one of the sensually perceptible, material objects which addressed you during the dreaming state of the past night?' Of course, no therapist would speak to an analysand in that way. He would say or ask along lines such as the following: 'Well, now that you're awake and here, can you think of some *thing* in your life *here and now* that you saw while dreaming and can now conceive of relating to differently than you ever have before? Since anything goes, what's the first *thing* from your dream that grabs you now?' The point is that what was a 'sensually perceptible, [and] material' thing in the dreaming state that is now present in one's waking life might be seen and related to differently, a possibility for doing so having been *pre*-sent in the dream. What was full-blooded and real in the dream that made the dreamer feel strongly about it – attraction, repulsion, fascination – appeared there as a possible way of relating to it. Now in waking life, where and when actions have consequences, the analysand is asked to say out loud what that thing means to him. The emphasis is on the given thing as a 'place' around which meanings and significances are configured.

Of course, it may happen, says Boss, that an analysand 'still remains blind' to what has come to him in his dreaming life. In other words, nothing stands out for him. Let us say, for example, that someone reports having dreamed about a heavy steamer trunk with big locks. Assuming, as Boss does, that 'the therapist may be more waking [*Wachen*] and see more than the patient,' he 'may dare to make some suggestions in the form of questions such as: 'Does not that big old chest of your dreaming, with its heavy iron ledges and its huge lock, speak to you, whenever you let it address itself to you in its full character, about the meaningfulness of being closed and walled in? Could it be that now, in your waking state, you become more aware than you were while dreaming of a corresponding being walled in of your own existence, and not merely of being walled in by a chest and iron material locks outside yourself but rather by your own neurotic immaterial attitudes?' Or, 'Is it not remarkable that of all possibilities [among the] things of this world it was just and exclusively an old chest with extremely thick wooden walls and heavy locks *which stared at you* [emphasis added] during the dream state?'

Boss does not look, as Freud might have, at the trunk as a symbol.[168] He takes the details provided in the description of the thing as it presents itself as a *phenomena* of the analysand's dreaming life that is of equivalent status to any phenomena of waking life. A thing sensually perceived in dreaming life presents the existential condition of the dreamer (whether he is awake or asleep) and, if reflected on in its details while awake, reveals something fundamental about that condition. And so the dreamer may have reported dreaming of standing in his living room where there were a couch, a few chairs, cabinets, pictures on the walls, a cat, a table with a vase on it that held a bunch of tulips – and a huge, wooden chest locked up tight with multiple locks, as if a

Fundamentals

Houdini were inside it and expected to make a miraculous escape from it. Had the cat 'spoken' to the dreamer instead of the trunk, a very different hint about the existence of the person would have been forthcoming.

Boss believed that all of those who seek therapy share the feature of keeping at a distance what they want to be close to, expressing a lack of courage in the face of what approaches them both in dreaming life and in waking life, and, above all, a lack of freedom to risk being claimed by what approaches the dreamer while dreaming. The bottom line is a want of freedom to try out possibilities that have offered themselves but have been turned away from up to that point. But there is more.

'On the other hand,' Boss adds, 'the patient's attention has also to be drawn to those dream elements of his which are characterized in themselves, and as themselves, by a feature of coercion, of walling in, of hiding, protecting or destructiveness, of animal life in its aggressive form.' All of the latter refer to things in a dream that are violent. They require attention, Boss believes, because social life is disrupted by such behavior. We recall that the freedom Boss always has in mind is not freedom from the constraints that make social life possible but rather the freedom to encounter the possible in one's existence existence. In daseinanalysis, the 'art' of dream *Auslegung* consists in the therapist taking 'care that he choose only those questions among all the possible ones that he is sure the present mental condition of his patient and the actual quality of his patient's emotional relationship with him can well bear.'[169]

Some general conclusions may be adduced from the foregoing:

(1) There is 'dreaming' and 'dreaming life' but there are no such entities as 'dreams';
(2) 'In the course of an analysis, it is usually necessary that the analysand be 'shaken to his roots', that his predominant, rigid, stagnant and, for him, matter-of-course, current ways of seeing, thinking, feeling and behaving be shattered, that is, that resistance and defensive attitudes be dissolved';
(3) The analyst is never represented in a dream disguised as someone else. He is not a 'transference' representative of a figure in the dreaming life of the analysand as little as he is such a figure in the waking life of the analysand;
(4) The *Auslegungen* are always framed as questions, not statements. Daseinanalytic laying out does not includes assertions about the meanings or significances of a dream or its elements. The questions asked about dreaming are always tentative, providing only hints for the analysand to do with as he pleases. "Is it possible that you ...?" The goal is to bring to light the things that approach the dreamer most vividly, that step out of the shadows as it were. For example, if the dreamer reports having been at a certain place while dreaming, Boss will ask him such questions as: 'How did you get to be there?' 'Where were you exactly?' 'Why were you there?';
(5) The now awake, erstwhile dreamer is encouraged to visualize again what he saw in the dream and to allow the feelings experienced in dreaming to occur again;
(6) When it seems clear to the analyst that certain things are being 'evaded, warded off', the analyst is advised not to draw attention to them too early. The analyst

may, however, suggest that, based on what he has heard, the analysand seems not to have said much (if anything at all) about something or someone who made an appearance in the dream reported;
(7) The analyst should invite the analysand to ask himself whether certain features of a given something or someone from dreaming life are also part of the analysand's waking life;
(8) The analyst should emphasize the 'positive aspects' of the analysand's dreaming, which is to say those which suggest new possibilities to be considered in waking life; and
(9) The analyst may want to point out to the analysand that in dreaming life he is more childlike than he is in the waking life of the analytic session or that he is more adult-like while dreaming. The suggestion of being more childlike in dreaming life is not tantamount to being more 'childish', foolish and irresponsible.

(7) 'Why?' and 'Why in the world not?'[170]

In the section on conversation, we ran across what I take to be the motto of daseinanalysis: *Warum denn eigentlich nicht?*[171] The expression serves as the title of the present volume: 'Why in the world *not*?' As we have seen, it can be translated otherwise, as 'Actually, why *not*?' To this we might add the following renderings: 'Why, after all, *not*?' or 'Honestly, why *not*?' or 'Why, after all, *not*?' or simply 'Why *not*?' In German, it is a common expression, a richly idiomatic expression. In part a rhetorical question, in part an utterance in the imperative mood, implicit in it is the suggestion to try out something, to 'give it a go'. Given its interrogative mood, no directive is implied. It is a welcoming to the analysand to take a chance and allow the fluency of life, with all its unexpected twists and turns, to flow more freely. It is, of course, the alternative to the psychoanalytic question 'Why?' which looks for causal explanations of experience and behavior in the person's past, usually his early childhood.

One rendering emphasizes the German word *eigenlich* in the expression. Used as an adverb, *eigenlich* means 'actually', but it can also convey the more serious tone of 'in fact'. As an adjective, *eigenlich* means 'actual', but it can also mean 'authentic'. The latter reminds us of the *Eigentlichkiet* (authenticity) of Heidegger's analytics of existence in *Being and Time*. I would suggest that this allusion was not lost on Boss in giving voice to the spirit of daseinanalysis in the expression and pointing to what he sees as the goal of therapeutic encounter.

Attempting new experiences and risking unaccustomed behavior, the world of possibility is seen to stand 'higher' or 'above' actuality, and in that position it indicates the way back to authenticity and the fullest possibilities of being human available to a given individual. For daseinanalysis, the question 'Why in the world *not*?' is an invitation to the analysand to deploy that most irrational feature of being human, his freedom.

Chapter Six
Preparation

Introduction

Every daseinanalytic institute has its own curriculum, which is based on a general model that has been in place since a training institute and the Medard Boss Foundation associated with it were established in 1970-1971. The American Daseinsanalytic Institute (ADI) is no exception. It offers a certificate that reflects an individual's having completed the requirements of a demanding program. In addition to the Institute's preparation program, a Study Committee affiliated with it meets regularly. The work of the Committee is to build an archive of texts, taped classes, and interviews with members of the ADI faculty, and to make them more readily available to a wider audience of prospective candidates.

What follows is a brief account of ADI's curriculum for the preparation of a daseinanalyst. It differs in a few details from other programs in place world-wide in Austria, Brazil, the Czech Republic, France, Greece, Hungary and Switzerland.[172] Its rigor, however, is at the same level as the older institutes.

A review of the ADI program provides an opportunity to discuss the elements of formation as a daseinanalyst. The program requires a part-time commitment usually taking four to five years. Most applicants for certification are working full-time in a clinic or hospital, in higher education, or in private practice as a psychotherapist or psychiatrist. During the first two years of the program, certificate candidates must commit to about six hours a month of online course work and additional hours of online supervision and in-person personal analysis amounting to another three to four hours per month. During the last two years of the program, individuals will devote four to six or more hours of additional time monthly providing supervised daseinanalysis.

American Daseinsanalytic Institute (ADI)

ADI is not a legally incorporated entity and does not offer a license. It is governed by a mission statement and by-laws. The Institute's faculty is an international group of experienced daseinanalysts, scholars and teachers whose goal is to make daseinanalysis known to both experienced therapists and beginning students. Certificate candidates are seen as key participants in passing along the tradition of practice of therapeutic daseinanalysis. Mentored, they will in turn mentor others as they attain senior status as a result of having practiced extensively as daseinanalyst and often have written papers and participated in webinars and conferences throughout the world.

The entrance requirements for the ADI certificate program include a graduate degree at the doctoral level or its equivalent in clinical psychology, psychoanalysis, psychoanalytic psychotherapy, social work, marriage and family counseling, nursing, or medicine (usually with a specialization in psychiatry). All applicants have had a fair amount of 'clinical' experience when admitted into the program.

After an individual has expressed interest in the Institute's certificate program he or she is interviewed by two members of the Institute's faculty who confer and reach a decision about the appropriateness of the program for the interested individual. A plan for completing the program is worked out, tailored to the individual, based on his or her previous academic and practical experience.

The Institute's certificate does not carry with it any legal privileges since its certificands live and work in many different countries, each of which has its own specific laws governing the practice of psychotherapy broadly defined, medicine, and other professions subject to licensure. Daseinanalysts practice independently under the aegis of the general guidelines of the International Federation of Daseinsanalysis (IFDA).

Given the international representation of ADI certificands, lectures, seminars, tutorials and independent studies are given online. The Preliminary Teaching Analysis (described below) is always experienced in person.

(1) Program Curriculum

The program curriculum as presented next may be modified for certain individuals given their previous experience. This applies especially to the externship and private or institutional clinical practice elements of the program. It is expected that all candidates will attend all seminars, experience the teaching analysis for the suggested minimum of hours (both the preliminary analysis and its continuing period), and meet the other minimum requirements of supervision and a control analysis. All candidates must pass a preliminary oral examination, usually administered after the second year of course work has been completed and the preliminary personal analysis of 50 hours has been completed. A final oral examination must be passed. At the conclusion of the program, the candidate must present a case to the ADI faculty and write a paper suitable for publication.

Year One
- preliminary teaching analysis (50 hours);
- attendance at lectures/seminars/tutorials and independent studies (100 hours); and
- supervision (50 hours).

Preparation

Year Two and Year Three
- oral examination at the end of the second year, given after the completion of the first-year requirements;
- continuation of the teaching analysis (to a total of a minimum of 100 hours by the end of the program);
- attendance at lectures/seminars/tutorials and independent studies (to a total of a minimum of 200 hours);
- supervision (to a total of a minimum of 100 hours); and
- an externship beginning during the third year (usually about 200 hours). Previous clinical experience at a hospital, clinic or school may be credited for advanced applicants up to 100 hours to meet this requirement.

Year Four and Year Five
- continuation of the externship (up to about 200 hours);
- private clinical experience in daseinanalytic practice (about 400 hours);
- supervision of analyses being conducted (about 100 hours), with one hour of supervision for every 10-20 hours of daseinanalysis provided;
- continuing teaching analysis (to a minimum total 100 hours);
- final oral examination;
- oral case presentation; and
- presentation of a theoretical paper suitable for publication.

Curriculum Summary: Courses and Seminars

A. History and Theory (lectures, seminars, tutorials and independent studies)

   1. Introduction to Daseinanalysis
   2. Phenomenology (Edmund Husserl)
   3. Fundamental Ontology and Hermeneutic Phenomenology (Martin Heidegger)
   4. Review of Other Current Modalities of Psychotherapy

C. Praxis (seminars, tutorials and independent studies)

   1. Heidegger for Therapists
   2. The Therapeutic Partnership
   3. Psychosomatics
   4. Dream Analysis
   5. Psychoanalysis and Daseinanalysis

D. Capstone Experiences (faculty seminar for the case presentation and an article for publication)

(2) The Teaching Analysis

The teaching analysis is the core of the certificate program. The term 'teaching analysis' [*Lehranalyse*] is borrowed from psychoanalysis.[173] One learns the art of daseinanalysis by first experiencing it. Daseinanalysis is *demonstrated* by being experienced in the teaching analysis. A tradition of practice is passed along. The teaching analysis is both therapeutic in the traditional sense and the basis of a mentorship relationship between the candidate the teaching analyst. The self-exploration of the candidate as analysand as experienced by him on the couch affords the candidate the opportunity to *see* through his or her experience what his or her own analysands will experience.[174] Daseinanalysis is not a technique, but rather a therapeutic approach based on the phenomenological method.[175]

Like the length of any daseinanalysis, the length of a teaching analysis depends on both the analysand and the analyst. It is determined by the individual candidate's previous experience, his familiarity with the theoretical foundations of daseinanalysis, and the availability of a teaching analyst. One difference between a teaching analysis and a purely therapeutic analysis is that, in the latter, the analysand always determines when the analysis has accomplished what it set out to do for him. In the case of a teaching analysis, however, the teaching analyst must decide whether the candidate has acquired an understanding of daseinanalysis as a practice. The two-part teaching analysis consists of a preliminary analysis of fifty hours, after which the teaching analyst determines whether the candidate is prepared to go on with further formation. A basic understanding of theoretical and practical principles must be demonstrated during the preliminary teaching analysis. It may happen that the teaching analyst will recommend that the candidate wait for a while before resuming and continuing his work in the program. The remaining hours of the personal analysis continue through the duration of the program (as outlined above).

In general, experience during the roughly half-century of its existence has shown that two years in all of teaching analysis proper are optimal for the preparation of a daseinanalyst. However, ongoing analysis throughout the duration of the program is recommended. Daseinanalysis differs from psychoanalysis in not insisting on 'interminable' analysis without interruption and on analysis being experienced a given number of days of the week (now usually three times weekly for psychoanalysis) over a period of many years. The teaching analysis in either of its phases may take place during a concentrated series of meetings over a short period of time, even twice daily meetings for several days.

(3) Supervision

A regular part of the curriculum of preparation for the practice of daseinanalysis is ongoing supervision with an experienced practitioner while the candidate is working with individuals in whatever setting in which the candidate is currently working while in preparation for practice as a daseinanalyst. After beginning course work, which is the Introduction to Daseinanalysis seminar, a candidate arranges with one of the faculty of the Institute to begin supervision of his practice. This continues throughout his or her time of the program. The candidate's later control analysis is often supervised by the same analyst.

The candidate meets at suitable intervals with the supervising analyst who guides him in his understanding and determines the direction of his work with analysands. This element of preparation is designed to aid the candidate's grasp of those aspects of daseinanalytic therapy that distinguish it from other modes of therapeutic practice. Together, the candidate and supervisor monitor and discuss the actions and reactions of the candidate while practicing as well as discussing the behavior of those who are in the candidate's care. It is understood that there will be a learning curve which leads the candidate from approaching the other in therapy as he has been accustomed to doing, given his earlier training, to working with the other from a daseinanalytic perspective.

(4) The Control Analysis

The notion of a control or supervised daseinanalysis as part of preparation to work as a daseinanalyst has its origin in psychoanalysis. Someone beginning to carry out daseinanalysis will have many questions about his work with the first person with whom he works exclusively as a daseinanalyst. These are directed to the senior analyst supervising the control analysis being conducted by the candidate. Such therapeutic work will be the candidate's first experience in conducting a daseinanalysis in its classic form and as different from any earlier modalities of treatment which the candidate has provided.

A schedule of meetings (weekly or monthly) is arranged for supervision of the control daseinanalysis. Early on, it is likely that more frequent meetings will be indicated. Since the candidate is also in his teaching analysis and perhaps also seeing individuals from a perspective other than daseinanalysis, limitations of time for supervision of the control analysis are reckoned with to provide the candidate with the most consistent program of supervision and guided study that focuses on daseinanalytic practice.

A report of the control analysis serves to meet another requirement of the preparation program, namely, the presentation of a case to the Institute faculty and other candidates. The case presentation of the control analysis may also be the basis for the required paper worthy of publication.

Ideally, the teaching analyst and supervising analyst should be different people, since this provides the candidate with a wider range of exposure to practicing daseinanalysts. In principle, however, there is no reason that the same individual may not function in both roles for a candidate, especially during the later stages of the teaching analysis.

PART III

AN ANNOTATED REVIEW OF SELECTED WRITINGS OF MEDARD BOSS

Introductory Note

The work of Ludwig Binswanger marked a first awareness of Martin Heidegger among psychiatrists, but his psychiatric *Daseinsanalyse* was the elaboration of an anthropology and considerations of psychopathology still firmly rooted in natural science were of major importance to Binswanger.[176] By contrast, Medard Boss was the pioneer spokesman for therapeutic daseinanalysis.[177] His work stands as the foundation of that unique modification of psychoanalysis which took shape during his close study of the work of Heidegger and their collaboration on the Zollikon seminars. Daseinanalysis was also in part the result of his experience with Eastern practices, chiefly those based on Hindu Vedanta philosophy.

Important contributions by his colleagues and students, especially Gion Condrau (1919-2006), merit our close attention but, for the purposes of this introduction, I limit a review of the daseinanalytic literature for the most part to Boss's publications.[178] I have done so since so little of what he published has been translated into English and this review may therefore also serve as an introduction to many key texts which are still available only in German. Moreover, some are very difficult to come by even in German. A few have remained inaccessible to the author.

Boss's *Nachlaß* is held by the Swiss National Library, in Bern. Correspondence, manuscripts and other materials that would be essential to writing a full-length biography are therefore not yet available to the public.[179] A number of sources taken together, however, enable us to create a sketch of the major events in the life of this remarkable and creative human being.

Swiss necrology records (available online) provide the following biographical sketch of Boss's life by Gion Condrau:

> Professor Dr. Medard Boss (October 4, 1903) to (December 21, 1990). Shortly before Christmas 1990, the world-famous psychiatrist and psychotherapist Medard Boss died. Born in 1903 in St. Gallen, he grew up in Zürich as the son of the hospital administrator Fridolin Medardus Boss and Klara Schmid and the oldest of three siblings. From his first marriage in 1930 to Gertrud Wissler there were two sons, Martin and Urs Christian and a daughter, Maja [Maia] Dorothea. His second marriage was to Marianne Linsmayer. The deceased's professional career began with studying medicine in Zürich, which was supplemented by

semesters abroad in Paris and Vienna from 1925 to 1927. Already at that time there was a decisive meeting with Sigmund Freud, who allowed him a few hours on his analyst couch. After completing his medical training at the University of Zürich, Boss worked as an assistant doctor at the Burghölzli Psychiatric University Clinic under Prof. Eugen Bleuler and Prof. H. W. Maier. Following a three-year training analysis with Dr. H. Behn-Eschenburg he went to London and Berlin for postgraduate training in neurology and psychoanalysis. After a further period at the Psychiatric Polyclinic in Zürich, he worked as chief physician at the private sanatorium Schloss Knonau from 1934 to 1939; from 1935 onwards he also maintained a private psychiatric and psychoanalytical practice in Zürich. A working group with C. G. Jung enriched his psychotherapeutic knowledge for almost ten years from 1939 on. Later, from 1955 on, he and the psychoanalyst Gustav Bally taught future psychiatrists at the Institute for Medical Psychotherapy in Zürich. Medard Boss completed his habilitation in the field of psychotherapy at the Medical Faculty of the University of Zürich. Guest lectureships took him to various universities in India, Indonesia and the USA, where he lectured for several semesters at the Harvard Medical School in Cambridge, Massachusetts. A significant change in scientific understanding and therapeutic orientation began for Medard Boss with the beginning of his personal acquaintance with the German philosopher Martin Heidegger shortly after the Second World War. Prepared by Ludwig Binswanger's systematizing and scientifically shaped psychiatry Boss turned to a phenomenological view of the essence of people and their being sick. Reading *Being and Time*, Heidegger's monumental philosophical work, Boss was increasingly motivated to radically reject his theory of illness which had hitherto been interpreted psychoanalytically and to place himself entirely at the service of Daseinsanalysis. After a few earlier publications even his first books make this clear. His *Habilitation* thesis *Meaning and Content of Sexual Perversions* {1947} and above all his *Introduction to Psychosomatic Medicine* {1954b} and the *Analysis of Dreams* {1953d} opened up completely new possibilities for understanding human existence, both healthy and sick. Finally, in a comprehensive attack, the book *Psychoanalysis and Daseinsanalysis* {1957a}, Boss settled accounts with almost all previously known directions in psychotherapy: first, with Freud's psychoanalysis, then with C. G. Jung, and finally with the German anthropologists and even with the psychiatric analysis of the existence of Ludwig Binswanger. This led to a split within Daseinsanalysis, a term that Boss later wanted to be understood exclusively for his cause. The relationship with Heidegger intensified. From 1959 onwards, for almost ten years, the German scholar held seminars a number of times a year for residents in psychiatry, in which both philosophical-anthropological and therapeutic issues in the field of psychosomatics and psychotherapy were discussed. The minutes of these seminars were published by Boss after Heidegger's death under the title *Zollikon Seminars* {1987a}. The collaboration with Heidegger, which resulted in a lifelong friendship between the two men, had already borne fruit in the past. Medard Boss's main work,

Introductory Note

Outline of Medicine and Psychology: Approaches to Phenomenological Physiology, Psychology, Pathology, Therapy and Appropriate Preventive Medicine in Modern Industrial Society (1971a), which was created under the influence of and with the participation of Heidegger, became a confrontation with the traditional medical and scientific approach and an 'appropriate' interpretation of human behavior, which is noted in the title. It is obvious that this work did not trigger joy everywhere and it by no means met with undivided approval. After all, it sparked discussions that no one could avoid who really wanted a holistic understanding of human illness. However, Boss received honors from around the world. From 1967 he was Honorary President of the International Federation for Medical Psychotherapy, and in 1971 he received the 'Great Therapist Award' from the American Psychological Association, to name just a few of many awards. When the Swiss Society for Daseinsanalysis was founded in 1970 and the Daseinsanalytic Institute for Psychotherapy and Psychosomatics in Zürich (the latter as the Medard Boss Foundation) in 1971, he was a lifelong president and board member. Apart from a large number of scientific publications and books that have been translated into all the major world languages, it should not be overlooked that Medard Boss was a dedicated psychotherapist who was rightly said to be a particularly sensitive, kind and wise physician, helpful to patients, a role model for his students, and respected even by those who could not fully share his views. He will be remembered forever by all those who owe him a lot. In the meantime, a synopsis of the most important of his contributions to the fields of psychiatry and psychotherapy and his books and papers on daseinanalysis should be a useful complement to the first two parts of this introduction to the approach.[180]

Boss contributed to international conferences on psychiatry and psychotherapy and lectured at universities in Europe, the Americas, and Asia (India, Indonesia, China and Japan).[181] His literary output consisted of thirteen books,[182] two co-edited volumes, thirty-one contributions to edited volumes, ninety-eight journal articles,[183] thirteen co-authored essays, and Boss's edition of Martin Heidegger's *Zollikon Seminars*. Boss published primarily in German, but he also wrote for publication in English, French and Portuguese. He was at home in Italian and had learned some Hindi. Boss has been translated into all the languages named except Hindi as well as into Croatian, Czech, Dutch, Japanese, Korean, Russian and Swedish. As noted earlier, many of the works to be reviewed below have not yet been translated into English. For that reason, I have paid more attention to these texts. I have also been guided in selecting which texts to review by Boss's decisions about which of them he wished to see to republication in his two collections of essays.[184]

In a section in the full Annotated Bibliography headed 'Miscellaneous' found at the end of Part III, I have included (A) two letters not included in the *Zollikon Seminars*:[185] a letter to Martin Heidegger from 1960, and correspondence with his colleague, Erna Hoch, also from 1960.[186] Two other letters were published as texts: an open letter to Heidegger, first published in a newspaper on October 5, 1969, which became the

Introductory Note

'Afterword' to the 2001 English translation of the *Zollikon Seminars*, and a letter to J. M. Kayande of November 23, 1970, the 'Foreword' to Govind Kaul's *Govind Amrit*, published in 1975.[187] Part (B) lists audiovisual materials. The last section (C) contains information about five unpublished papers of which I have become aware.

Not including the *Zollikon Seminars*, only seven of Boss's books and fewer than thirty of his papers or contributions to books, including five texts that were co-authored, have been translated into English. In general, apart from his pioneering *Psychoanalyse und Daseinsanalytik* [*Psychoanalysis and Daseinsanalysis*] {1957a} and the sweeping overview of the *Grundriß der Medizin [und Psychologie]. Ansätze zu einer phänomenologischen Physiologie, Psychologie, Pathologie, Therapie und zu einer daseinsgemäßen Präventiv-Medizin in der modernen Industrie-Gesellschaft* [*Existential Foundations of Medicine and Psychology*] {1971a}, the two books on dreaming life ((1953d), {1975b}) merit special attention,[188] as does his monograph *Lebensangst, Schuldgefühle und psychotherapeutische Befreiung* [*Anxiety, Guilt and Therapeutic Liberation*] {1962c}. His most important paper for therapists is perhaps 'Begegnung in der Psychotherapie [Encounter in Psychotherapy]' {1965d}.

The most unique among Boss's texts is his *Indienfahrt eines Psychiaters* [*A Psychiatrist Discovers India*] {1959a}, which Boss evidently thought of as his favorite book.[189] It is also his most personal publication and may be read in conjunction with the biographical works presented below. In these texts we find a picture of someone of remarkable intelligence and wit who had been lucky enough to know and work with some of the most important figures in twentieth-century philosophy, psychiatry and psychotherapy, but also someone who in late middle age experienced a major transformation in his life and approach to working in the therapeutic setting, namely, his encounter with Indian philosophy. This experience was of as great significance to the creation of daseinanalysis as his work with Martin Heidegger.

Five of Boss's papers, including two that had not been previously published, were included in an anthology he co-edited with his colleagues Gion Condrau and Alois Hicklin in 1977, *Leiben und Leben. Beiträge zur Psychosomatik und Psychotherapie* [*Being Alive and Living Life. Contributions to Psychosomatics and Psychotherapy*] {1977f}. In 1979, Boss selected what he took to be his twenty-five most important papers from 1937 to 1978 and published them as *Von der Psychoanalyse zur Daseinsanalyse. Wege zu einem neuen Selbstverständnis* [*From Psychoanalysis to Daseinsanalysis. Paths to a New Self-Understanding*] {1979c}. A few years later, a second anthology, which brought together thirteen papers written between 1974 and 1981, was published as *Von der Spannweite der Seele. Ausgewählte Vorträge und Aufsätze aus den Anwendungsbereichen des daseinsanalytischen Menschenverständnisses* [*On the Wingspan of the Soul. Selected Presentations and Essays from Areas of Application of the Existential Analytic Understanding of Man*] {1982b}. The title nicely reflects Boss's poetic sensibility, which is evident in all of his writing. He is never pedantic and, although sometimes a bit tart and sharply direct, Boss is never impolite or dismissive.

Chronological Listing of Publications (1929-2003)

{1929} [On the question of the evolutionary biological significance of alcohol]

{1931} [Psychological and characterological investigations of antisocial psychopaths using the Rorschach Inkblot Test]
{1933} [Hallucinations in process of formation]
{1935a} [Psychic energy displacements in the course of a schizophrenic episode]
{1935b} [The psychodynamics of the sleep cure in schizophrenics]
{1936} [Indications [for] and effects of the 'sleep cure'] [In French]
{1937} [Historical review of the fundamental principles of the therapy of schizophrenia]
{1938a} [Preparation of individuals with severe chronic schizophrenia for group occupational therapy]
{1938b} **[The psychopathology of dreams in schizophrenia and organic psychoses]**
{1939} [On three categories of avoidable failures in general medical practice]

{1940a} [Brief and intensive psychotherapy]
{1940b} [On the hidden challenges to psychological well-being and their mitigation]
{1940c} [*Physical illness as a result of psychological imbalance*]
{1941a} [Functional disturbances of sleep in schizophrenia]
{1941b} [Food rationing and popular psychology]
{1941c} [Psychological health on the front lines (military psychiatry)]
{1941d} [Early and recent electroshock therapies and electroshock therapists]
{1943} [*The significance of psychology for human relationships and community life*]
{1944a} [The function of the psychiatric counseling center in independent army units]
{1944b} [*The character of marriage and its forms of disintegration. A contribution to the psychopathology of the formation of human community life*]
{1945} [Bed-wetting]
{1947} [Meaning and content of sexual perversions. A daseinsanalytic approach to the psychopathology of the phenomenon of love]
{1948a} [The method and goal of depth-psychological therapy]
{1948b} [The possibilities and limits of psychotherapy]
{1949a} [Blood pressure ailments as a human problem]
{1949b} [Fundamentals of psychosomatic medicine]

{1950a} [Reply to the report on my presentation at the 66th gathering of Southwest German psychiatrists and neurologists held in Badenweiler [June 2-3, 1950]]
{1950b} [Latest advances in the field of psychoanalysis]
{1951a} [Closing remarks on the survey on the report of my paper given at the 66th gathering of Southwest German psychiatrists and neurologists held in Badenweiler]

{1951b}   [Contribution on the existential analytic foundation of psychiatric thinking]
{1951c}   [Experiences with the hypnotic Plexonal [Scopolamine] (Sandoz)]
{1952a}   **[Mechanistic and holistic thinking in modern medicine]**
{1952b}   [The significance of daseinanalysis for psychology and psychiatry]
{1953a}   [On the origin and essence of the depth-psychological concept of the archetype]
{1953b}   [Reply to: How should frigidity be evaluated and treated in practice?]
{1953c}   [Regulation of the activity of non-medical psychologists]
{1953d}   [The analysis of dreams]
{1953e}   [Origin and nature of the concept of the archetype. A discussion] With H. Fierz and A. Maeder.
{1953f}   **[Psychoanalysis of a sadist]** With G. Benedetti.
{1954a}   [*Introduction to psychosomatic medicine*] See {1978c}.
{1954b}   [Basics of the scientific nature of dream interpretation]
{1955a}   [*Third international congress of [medical] psychotherapy*] (ed.) With H. Fierz and B. Stokvis.
{1955b}   [Psychosomatic medicine in distress]
{1955c}   [Summary and closing remarks] [Schlußsitzung (closing session), July 24, 1954]
{1956a}   **[Moreno's 'Existentialism, daseinsanalyse and psychodrama': A discussion]**
{1956b}   **['Daseinsanalysis' and psychotherapy]**
{1957a}   [Psychoanalysis and Daseinsanalysis]
{1957b}   [The mechanism of action and indications for psychotherapy]
{1957c}   [Psychotherapeutic contribution to the theory of schizophrenia]
{1957d}   [Summary and closing remarks at the international symposium on the psychotherapy of schizophrenia (Lausanne 1956)]
{1958}   **[The role of psychotherapy in schizophrenia]**
{1958a}   [La psychoanalyse de Freud et l'analyse existentielle de Heidegger] [Unpublished paper read at the International Congress of Psychotherapy, September 1-7, 1958, in Barcelona. Cited by Thomas Hora, in 'The Process of Existential Psychotherapy,' in *Psychiatric Quarterly* **34**(3), 1960, 495.]
{1959a}   [A psychiatrist discovers India] See 2002/2003b.
{1959b}   [Martin Heidegger and the doctors]
{1959c}   [Psychotherapy for the practicing physician]
{1959d}   [Brief and intensive psychotherapy for essential hypertension]
{1959e}   [Psychoanalysis and the analysis of 'dasein'] [In Spanish]

{1960a}   [The intensive psychotherapy of psychosomatic diseases]
{1960b}   **[Ego? Motivation?] [The ego? Human motivation?]**
{1960c}   **[Letters to Erna M. Hoch]**
{1960/1961a}   [Existential analytic remarks on Freud's concept of the 'unconscious']
{1960/1961b}   [The significance of existential analysis for psychoanalytic practice]
{1961a}   **[Psychosomatics and existentialism]**

Chronological Listing of Publications (1929-2003)

{1961b} [What makes us behave at all socially?]
{1962a} [Outline of the analysis of dasein]
{1962b} [The conception of man in natural science and daseinsanalysis]
{1962c} [Anxiety, guilt and psychotherapeutic liberation] (The 'Foreword' to the German was the presidential opening address to the Vth International Congress on Psychotherapy, August 21, 1962, in Vienna. It was not included in the translation. The journal evidently had gone to press before the book.)
{1963}   [Thoughts on a schizophrenic hallucination]
{1965a} [Presidential address at the opening session [of the VIth International Congress of Medical Psychotherapy, August 24-29, 1964]
{1965b} [Presidential address at the closing session [of the VIth International Congress of Medical Psychotherapy, August 24-29, 1964]
{1965c} [Discussion of paper by J. Ruesch]
{1965d} [Encounter in psychotherapy]
{1965e} ["Introduction" to Carlos Alberto Seguín, *Love and psychotherapy. The psychotherapeutic eros*]
{1966a} [Five introductory lectures on the analytics of existence]
{1966b} [Examples of the influence of psychotherapy on the religious attitude of the analysand]
{1967a} [Demythologization of psychosomatic medicine]
{1967b} [Model and countermodel in psychosomatic medicine]
{1967c} [Existential psychoanalysis] With G. Condrau.
{1967d} [Psychosomatic disorders and organ neuroses – findings of contemporary psychotherapy]
{1967}   [Man–object of scientific research. Contribution to the series 'L'Homme – Objet de la recherche scientifique' of the main Romanian newspaper *Scinteia* [*The Spark*], Bucharest, 1967]. Cited in Boss's self-portrait. Not attested.
{1968a} [A conversation with Medard Boss, or the evolution of psychoanalysis]
{1968b} [Existential analysis] With G. Condrau.
{1968/1969} [Man – an object of science]
{1969}   [Afterword [to Martin Heidegger, Zollikon Seminars – Protocols – Conversations – Letters]]

{1970a} [A needed revolution in medical thinking]
{1970b} [Daseinsanalysis] With G. Condrau.
{1970c} [Medard Boss [Tribute to Martin Heidegger]]
{1971a} [Existential foundations of medicine and psychology]
{1971b} [A needed revolution in worldview]
{1971c} [Daseinsanalyse] With A. Hicklin.
{1972a} [The training of the future psychotherapist. Improvement of psychiatric services and teaching programs]

Chronological Listing of Publications (1929-2003)

{1972b} [Warning signs of a storm in psychology and psychiatry. Epilogue to a revolutionary international congress on psychotherapy]
{1972c} [The physician and death. An existential analytic investigation]
{1973a} **[Medard Boss]**
{1973b} [The significance of daseinanalysis for psychiatry illustrated by the treatment of a schizophrenic psychosis]
{1973c} [Sigmund Freud and the natural scientific method of thinking]
{1973d} [Daseinsanalysis in today's psychiatry in Zürich] With G. Condrau.
{1974} [Psycho-somatic medicine and the principle of causality]
{1975a} [Solitude and community] [In French]
{1975b} ['I dreamt last night...'. A new approach to the revelations of dreaming – and its uses in psychotherapy]
{1975c} [The schizophrenic's 'being ill' understood in terms of existential analysis]
{1975d} [Existential analysis (Daseinsanalysis)] With G. Condrau.
{1975e} [Foreword to *Govind Amrit*. Letter to J. M. Kayande, November 23, 1970]
{1976a} **[Dreams and the dreamed in the daseinsanalytic way of seeing]**
{1976b} **[Flight from death – mere survival; and flight into death –suicide]**
{1976c} [Culture and psychotherapy]
{1976d} [A new understanding of dreams and its possibilities in practical therapeutic application] (audio recording)
{1976e} [The mind-body problem in light of daseinsanalysis]
{1977a} [The ontogenesis of man ... from the perspective of the daseinsanalyst]
{1977b} [The existential approach and psychotherapeutic suggestibility in human physical ailments]
{1977c} [The psychotherapeutic process]
{1977d} **[Martin Heidegger's Zollikon seminars]**
{1977e} **[Existential analysis (Daseinsanalyse)]**
{1977f} [*Being alive and living life. Contributions to psychosomatics and psychotherapy*]
{1977g} [Education – Yes or no?]
{1977h} [Envy triggers terror. The phenomenon of human violence]
{1977i} [Living with terror]
{1977j} [Corresponding changes in the quality of social life and forms of neurosis in the twentieth century]
{1977k} [Contribution to 2nd Zürcher Gespräche, July 1-7, 1977, on the theme 'Der Herrschaftsanspruch der Wissenschaft auf Welterklärung [The Claim to Power of Science to Explain the World]'.] [No MS. Unpublished]
{1978a} [Contradiction contradicted]
{1978b} [Current changes in the identification of the neuroses in psychotherapy]
{1978c} [*Practice of psychosomatics. Illness and Personal fate*] See 1954a.
{1978d} **[Phenomenological or existential analytic approach [to dreams]]** With B. Kenny.
{1978e} ' The Dream and Its Meaning. Two Dream Images.' Contribution to 3rd Zürcher Gespräche, January 20-23, 1978, on the theme 'Rationale und bildhafte Sprache [Rational and Figurative Speech].' [Unpublished]

Chronological Listing of Publications (1929-2003)

{1979a} [Being-towards-death from the perspective of depth psychology]
{1979b} **[Is psychotherapy rational or rationalistic?]**
{1979c} [*From psychoanalysis to daseinsanalysis. Paths to a new self-understanding*]
{1979d} [Sexuality and psychotherapy]
{1979e} [Psychotherapy and science]

{1980a} [Martin Heidegger and his significance for the evolution of society]
{1980b} [Dreaming. A great healing]
{1980c} [The further development of Ludwig Binswanger's daseinsanalysis] With G. Condrau.
{1981a} [Dreams. Our second life]
{1981b} **[The unconscious – What it is?]**
{1981c} [The phenomenon of resistance in daseinsanalysis] With A. Holzhey-Kunz.
{1981d} [Encounter and self-confrontation in guilt and in conscience]
{1981e} [The world of drives and personalization]
{1981f} [Anxiety and composure from the existential analytic perspective]
{1981g} [The development of psychotherapy in the twentieth century]
{1982a} [Normal anxiety]
{1982b} [*On the wingspan of the soul. Selected presentations and essays from areas of application of the existential analytic understanding of man*]
{1982c} [Actuality as the self-revelation of what there is]. [Contribution to the seventh Zürcher Gespräche, May 9-11, 1980, on the theme 'Rationales Denken – der einzige (wissenschaftliche) Zugang zur Wirklichkeit [Rational Thinking – the Only (Scientific) Approach to Actuality]']
{1982d} **[A phenomenological approach to sexual perversions]**
{1982e} [The existential analytic interpretation of dreams]
{1982f} [Permitting and abstaining in psychotherapy]
{1982g} [The magic of psychosomatic medicine]
{1982h} [The introduction of the analytics of *Dasein* into the thinking of the physician] With G. Condrau.
{1982i} [Outline of the development of psychotherapy in the twentieth century]
{1982j} [The significance of Martin Heidegger for work with suffering people and for the self-understanding of psychotherapy]
{1982k} [Language and anxiety in an engineered world]. Given as 'On the Spirit of Technicity' as a contribution to the ninth Zürcher Gespräche, June 6-8, 1981, on the theme 'Sprache und Angst in einer technifizierten Welt [Language and Anxiety in an Engineered World].']
[1982 'Wo bleibt Gott in der Psychotherapie? Wo bleibt die Psychotherapie in Gott? [Where Is God in Psychotherapy? Where Is Psychotherapy in God?]' Contribution to the twelfth Zürcher Gespräche, October 22-24, 1982, on the theme 'Verlorene Natur, Religion, Persönlichkeit – der Mensch von Heute [Abandoned Nature, Religion, Personhood – the Man of Today?] [No MS. Unpublished]]

{1983}   [The question of so-called 'stress']
{1984a} [Thoughts on Valerie Gamper's presentation, 'By their language shall you know them']
{1984b} [The pressure of existence]
         [1984 [Is human guilt curable with psychotherapy?] ['Ist menschliche Schuld psychotherapeutisch heilbar?' Presented at the Katholische Akademie Freiburg, June 3, 1984.] [Unpublished]]
{1985}   [Psychosomatic medicine. Science or magic?]
         [1985 ['*Daseinsanalyse* and the encounter between East and West'] [Lecture given at thirteenth annual congress, International Federation for Psychotherapy, Opatija, Yugoslavia (Croatia), 'Health for All by the Year 2000.'] [Unpublished]]
{1987a} [**Martin Heidegger, *Zollikon Seminars: Protocols – Conversations – Letters***]
{1988a} [**Recent considerations in daseinsanalysis**]
{1988b} [**An encounter with Medard Boss**]
{1988c} [**What does a human being consist in when he dreams, and where is he then?**]
{1988d} [Daseinsanalysis] [video]

{1990}   [Daseinsanalytic remarks on the essence of Freudian psychoanalysis]
{1991}   [Martin Heidegger's initiatives for a different kind of psychiatry]
{1996}   [**Dialogue between Prof. Medard Boss and Prof. Dongshick Rhee**]

{2001}   [**Preface** [to Martin Heidegger, *Zollikon Seminars. Protocols—Conversations—Letters*]] See {1969} and {1987a}.
{2002/2003a}   [**Letter to Heidegger** [of January 12, 1960]]
{2002/2003b}   [**After thirty years** [Preface to *A Psychiatrist Discover India* (4th Edition, 1987)]] See {1959a}.
{2002/2003c}   [**Martin Heidegger applied to psychiatry and the modern world**]

Biographical and Scientific Texts

Before turning to his scientific publications, I present three texts that bring to life the sojourn of the founder of therapeutic daseinanalysis, the first of which is reprinted in its entirety.[190] Following an 'interlude' of dialogue with the Korean psychiatrist, Dongshick Rhee, I review selected publications on major themes to which Boss frequently returned, including the theory and practice of daseinanalysis, the influence of Eastern philosophy on daseinanalysis, and the impact of Boss's relationship with Martin Heidegger, with whom he collaborated and enjoyed a close friendship.

I review works in chronological order of publication. Throughout the review, I have **bolded** the title of the work under discussion as it appears in the Chronological

Listing, even if it was not published in English. In the case of titles published in English translation, I have used that title, even if it does not well represent the original title.

(I) Biographical Texts

'Medard Boss' (1973a)[191] is the only full-length published autobiographical account we have from Boss. The memoir was written when he was approaching his seventieth birthday. It reveals a man of wide interests ranging from art to neurology, Western philosophy to Eastern religious practices.

Official papers testify that I saw the light of day on 4 October, 1903, in St. Gallen [Switzerland]. My parents later added that the event had taken place on an auspicious Sunday morning when the bells of the nearby monastery church summoned people to mass. It may be that this pious welcome was one that aroused a secret but never quite silenced desire for monastic life. I came close to fulfilling it half a century later when I was granted refuge in a Hindu ashram in northern India. However, just as the transfer of my parents from St. Gallen to Zürich at the beginning of my life quickly spirited me away from the monastery, I also had to leave the stillness of the Indian ashram after only a few weeks and returned to my post in the West at the behest of its abbot. Meanwhile, however, the intervening time has not passed without the appearance of god-like beings.

Of course, instead of gods, demons first came my way. But their work was not just evil. Only because of their intervention in my life when I was four years old do I know from my own experience that I exist at all. They were the source of a long period of often recurring anxiety that made me fear for my very life. They seized me every time I had completed smaller or larger 'business' when, in a single rush, the mass of water from the tank above crashed with an overwhelming din into the toilet bowl below and dragged everything it found there to some ghastly depth. Only a swift escape to my mother could appease my horror at the possibility of being yanked down into the darkness of some unknown gaping maw. At the same time, however, these fears also revealed to me early on with dramatic urgency that I was something unto myself independent of everything else around me. Luckily, my mother came in handy when I confessed my concerns to her. It is true, she said, that man was actually created from dirty earth. But he was also given a guardian angel who, all one's life, pulled us up toward heaven. Therefore, what one actually is can never just decay into mere earth. Such clarification was immediately followed by salvation. Even today, such early maternal psychotherapy seems to have been much more appropriate help at the time for the great power of my fears than were the interpretations much later of my training analyst, who could see in them only symptoms of unconscious fear of castration. In any case, from that point on, over the years only the bright areas of my world have preoccupied me.

My parents went to Zürich when I was two years old because they had been appointed to administrative posts at the University Children's Hospital. With almost submissive respect my parents met their new boss, the medical director of the clinic, Professor [Peter] Fehr, who at that time had already become world famous. His stature in the eyes of their sensitive four- to five-year-old firstborn was heightened by reverential veneration of such a demigod. Looking down the long corridors of the hospital I could see his radiance reflected by the white-coated flock of assistant doctors and nurses who made their daily visit, following their boss like the tail of a comet. Going to school, however, put the boy hitherto well-protected and pampered by a tenderly loving mother into the rough atmosphere of a gang of local street kids. In their world, there was no more of the respect and awe my humble parents showed the great ones of the world. Rather, the opposite was the case. The urchins were left with nothing but rebellion and confusion about adults. Their influence soon changed my view of the hospital director and his doctors from being at an unattainable distance to being more down to earth. My reverence for the latter's supernatural nature made me decide to become one of them myself.

From that point on my decision prompted me to gain as much insight as possible into the wards, operating rooms, and medical and surgical polyclinics of the children's hospital, in both permissible and less permissible ways. The boy's premature 'scientific' curiosity could not be satisfied by anything else. Even harsh punishments failed. Over time, my interest in the medical facilities gained me the outright and enduring goodwill of the medical director. Much later this also benefited me in my state medical examinations.

My father was visibly impressed by my early career choice and supported it whenever he could. Among such endeavors, one day – I may have been ten years old – he took me by the hand and led me to the clinic's morgue. There lay the pale corpse of a girl about my age who had died. Today, I know that leukemia had probably brought her to that end. At the time, I was shaken not only by the peculiar whiteness of the face and folded hands, but above all by the uncanny stillness of the figure. Both gave the dead child a supernatural magnitude and heavenly purity. 'This too,' said my father, referring to the death of the child, 'belongs to life, and all of us face it.' He then took me back outside into the warm sunshine of a bright spring morning. This first physical encounter with death strengthened my determination to become a doctor. At the same time, it called forth a flood of questions about the origin, journey, meaning and purpose of man. I realized that a doctor, who would hour after hour be in close proximity to the challenges and finitude of human life, should not be embarrassed to answer these questions.

I began to assert myself with questions of this kind, not only with doctors but with everyone I thought wise. My father's best friend, who regularly took part in our family's Sunday walks which had now grown to include five members, suffered the most. This was a man who had once joined the Foreign Legion because of a youthful love affair and had therefore seen more of the world and its inhabitants than anyone else around me. And yet he, too, was obviously stumped for answers. He retaliated by giving me the nickname 'philosopher'. Soon my sister and schoolmates had also adopted it. However, since I had no idea what a philosopher was and the word might just as well have referred to something evil as to something good, the gibe didn't bother me at all.

Biographical and Scientific Texts

My steps toward a career in medicine advanced with my entrance into Zürich's high school. But they were soon seriously caused to falter. The minimal requirements of middle school then gave me more than enough time to indulge in 'stupid thoughts'. Soon the idea that dawned on me of becoming an artist instead of a doctor was noticed by my parents and, with a single exception, by all my teachers. The exception not only broke ranks with respect to his colleagues. He was the real reason for the change of career I now envisaged. The drawing teacher of our school had put the 'stupid idea' in my head. He evidently believed I had unusual artistic talent. So, one day, he dragged me to the studio of one of his painter friends. The scholastically most gifted one had been betrayed by his drawing teacher. His friend the able maestro immediately took me on as an apprentice. From that time on, I spent every spare minute in the midst of the indescribable disorder of a painter's workshop. I sized dozens and dozens of canvases for him. From time to time he let me at the paint and brushes. The 'works of art' I created at the time seemed to show him and me that my painterly talent was worth the trouble of sacrificing my whole life. My hope became a certainty when one of my paintings was included in an exhibition at our art gallery. Clever as he was and unaffected by such an honor, my father continued to hold to the opposite view. When due to lack of time and interest my scholastic achievements were affected because of painting, my father resorted to therapy. Rather than saying anything, I traveled with him to Munich. There he took me to the museums and for days let me see the paintings on display there. Above all, I saw the pictures of Rembrandt, Cézanne, Monnet [sic] and Renoir. Their presence moved me to vivid delight. At the same time, however, they also inflicted on me a gloomy anguish that made my father's drastic treatment a full and lasting success. Faced with such inspired masters, the overestimation of my own talent and all my previous bumbling attempts at painting were no longer hidden from me. After returning home, to this day I have never again touched a brush. For better or worse, my former master had to prepare his own canvases again. All the more eagerly did I immerse myself in the works of true painters. I believe that over time I have acquired a considerable degree of 'appreciation for art'. The art historian [Joseph] Zemp [1869-1942], whose lectures I attended regularly and enthusiastically during the first semester of my medical studies, helped me a lot.

More and more, however, I was fascinated by science. This was due not least to my incredible and undeservedly good luck, which started at the beginning of my medical studies and has remained faithful to me to this day. It bestowed on me extraordinarily many and extraordinarily outstanding teachers, each of whom for some unknown reason took utmost care of me and sought to promote me in every way. Hans Schinz [1858-1941], the rowdily distinguished botanist, and Paul Karrer [1889-1971], the chemist and Nobel laureate, were the first. They were followed by W. R. Hess [1881-1973], later also a Nobel laureate in physiology. From the very beginning his teaching captivated me to such an extent that I immediately asked him to save an assistant's position for me in his institute for the time after my state examinations. With obvious joy, he readily agreed. But then came the time for instruction in psychiatry afforded me by Eugen Bleuler [1857-1939]. He was the first of the four men with shining eyes – as I silently try to find a name for them – whom I would encounter during my lifetime.

The other three were Sigmund Freud [1856-1939], Martin Heidegger [1889-1976] and an Indian sage who lived high up in the Kashmir Mountains. All four presented an almost shy demeanor in their outward behavior. At the same time, however, each of them radiated a spiritual fire almost perceptible to the senses that came from deep within and often seemed to erupt from even greater depths.

When I first heard Eugen Bleuler's lectures, he was close to retirement. As is often the case with first-rate scientists, the aging Eugen Bleuler had been increasingly seized by an urge for philosophical reflection. It met my own inclination so much that our conversations filled hours and hours of a small private seminar. The theme was mostly the essence of the 'mneme [memory trace]'. Eugen Bleuler could not be dissuaded from using [Richard] Semon's [1859-1918] engram theory as an adequate explanation for memory phenomena in man and indeed for the development of the entire animal kingdom. On the other hand, it was even then incomprehensible to me how a mental reality [*Gegebenheit*] of the sort which has the capacity for memory of what were significant events could ever be produced by chemical-physical processes that take place within brain cells.

Meantime, in my military career I had made it to medical corporal. In this capacity I faithfully took the refresher course prescribed by the state. My supervisor, the captain, had a book on his desk in the infirmary. It bore the at first incomprehensible title *Introductory Lectures on Psychoanalysis*. Its author was a certain Sigmund Freud. I sneakily started to snoop around in the book. Soon, however, I could not put the book down. I wanted to borrow it but came up against a certain contrariness on the part of its owner. The grounds for his refusal were that one should first undergo his own training analysis [*Lehranalyse*] and only then read psychoanalytic books. Of course, one was unable to interrupt the reading one had begun. Freud's writing opened an incredibly new, fascinating world of which I had not been given even the slightest idea during my previous medical studies. All the riddles of the human soul and many of the body found plausible explanation in this book with its simple, catchy drive formulas. These were so much like the chemical-physical laws of nature I had just learned that I considered Freud's 'metapsychology', which was so logically consistent and self-contained, no less correct and true than those laws. The questionable nature of their premises was to remain hidden from me for quite some time.

Not long after the military refresher course that was so memorable thanks to Freud, I was lucky enough to meet Sigmund Freud face to face. The impressive power of suggestion that emanated from this brilliant man was all that was needed to secure my belief in the truth of psychoanalytic theories. My father's generosity had enabled me to spend the summer semester of 1925 and summer holidays in Vienna. Long before my arrival in Vienna I had intended to visit the famous Freud. Only during the second half of my time in Vienna, however, did I actually gather enough courage to put my intention into action. Of course, my visit to Berggasse 19 had to be done in secret. The whole circle of my Viennese colleagues had nothing but ridicule for Freud. They called everything that was connected with his psychoanalysis one big mess.

Even today I do not quite know how it happened to me then, but suddenly I lay on the couch [*Couch*] in Freud's office and got to hear from his own mouth the only basic rule of his psychoanalytic treatment. It obligated me to unrestrained truthfulness, but also ruthless honesty towards myself and Freud. On the basis of my so-called free associations, I quickly sensed in my body the full force of Freud's power at unmasking. Nothing was any longer what it seemed to be. Everything was just a euphemistic façade [*Fassade*] that would always conceal unfamiliar bad things. That was confusing enough. But even more amazing was the fact that during the entire period of analysis I was to go through with him Freud was completely different than he was supposed to have been according to his own deterministic instinctual theory and his representation of the analyst as a blank screen. For example, at no time did he deal with me as a bundle of drives. In addition, as soon as he heard I had been forced to starve because of him he did not hesitate to reduce to a minimum the fee he was to be paid. More than once he even gave me ten shillings [about $75.00] out of his pocket. Who can say whether this first obvious contradiction between what Freud wrote and theoretically proclaimed and his actual therapeutic behavior was the kernel for all my many later doubts about his theory?

For the time being, however, I innocently followed the entire educational path established by the International Psychoanalytic Association. After my return from Vienna, I continued my training analysis in Zürich for another three years with Hans Behn-Eschenburg [1919-1955]. I went through the stage of permanent guest of the Swiss Society for Psychoanalysis, then the period of associate membership, until I was finally accepted as a full member of the association and eventually even held a post on its board.

Bearing in mind their very strict admission conditions, all of this is worth mentioning because it may be enough evidence that I know what I am talking about when discussing my later experiences with Freud's psychology and psychotherapy. On the other hand, I also take note of these details with a certain amount of pride about my membership in the International Psychoanalytic Association, which I still maintain. It therefore means a great deal to me, since I am well aware that without Freud, without his work, and without his followers I would not have been able to become an even reasonably competent existential analytic therapist [*daseinsanalytischer Therapeut*]. My Zürich training analyst [*Lehranalytiker*] adhered to psychoanalytic theory much more rigorously than its creator had. Nevertheless, if I may trust my own experience, this second bit of analysis, too, managed to bring about decisive and liberating advancement of my maturation as a human being, although I had found neither myself nor my environment to be particularly in need of treatment before the commencement of my analysis. That's how I learned that at its most beneficial psychoanalysis is for the healthy.

Hans Behn-Eschenburg was not only a psychoanalyst. He was also an expert in the administration of the Rorschach Inkblot Test. For many years he had been a student of [Hermann] Rorschach [1884-1922] himself. So, I owe to him the impetus for my own extensive Rorschach studies. However, the more numerous the test protocols that I worked up, the more difficult their proper interpretation seemed to me to be, and above all the more suspicious I became of the increasingly finely tuned mathematization of the findings that began to emerge in the literature.

At the end of my medical studies, the then senior physician of the Psychiatric University Clinic in Zürich and later Professor of Psychiatry at Basel, John Staehelin [1891-1969], approached me. He himself and on behalf of his supervisor asked me whether I was ready to enter the Burghölzli [Hospital] as an assistant after taking the state examination.

From earlier on, however, W. R. Hess [1881-1973] still kept open a position for me at the Physiological Institute. Gradually, however, Eugen Bleuler gained the upper hand over Hess in my thoughts and aspirations. Now more and more psychiatry seemed to me to be able to gain far more of what was essential for man than any ingenious physiology. Still, W. R. Hess's brain stimulus experiments in which he knew how to put cats into different moods still committed me to his subject. Nevertheless, the final decision for psychiatry was not difficult for me. The five-year residency at the Zürich Psychiatric University Hospital and Polyclinic flew by for two reasons: in the first place, even though he had already handed over his post as its director to H[ans]. W[olfgang]. Maier [1882-1945] a half-year earlier, it was still overseen by Eugen Bleuler, whose conception of one's duties kept the assistants busy day and night without a single moment of boredom. On the other hand, I was granted a one-and-a-half-year stay abroad. The first six months of this holiday I spent at the National Hospital for Nervous Diseases in London because I wanted to add some neurology to my psychiatry.

There I was fortunate enough to report directly to the outstanding scientists [W. J.] Adie [1886-1935] and [S. K.] Wilson [1878-1937]. At the same time, I enrolled as a training candidate at the London Institute for Psychoanalysis. There I was given the privilege of being allowed to accompany Ernest Jones [1879-1958], its stern director and later Freud biographer, when he examined patients and decided on their suitability for psychoanalytic treatment. The improbable speed and precision with which his gaze apprehended the ill at their core bordered on magic for me.

I moved from London to Berlin for another year. The change of location meant a change in climate of a very special kind. In London, people knew how to deal with each other in a natural, tactful, amiable and obliging manner, as if everything were self-explanatory. By contrast, Berlin conversation felt like an icy shower. Its brusqueness and mocking hardness initially felt like knife stabs, until I discovered that there could be good-naturedness even under a rough shell.

I was readily accepted as a training candidate at the Eitington Psychoanalytic Institute in Berlin. I was immediately assigned to five patients whom I had to treat analytically under the regular supervision of Karen Horney [1885-1952], [Otto] Fenichel [1897-1946] and [Harald] Schultz-Henke [1892-1953]. In addition, I was permitted to attend the seminars of Hanns Sachs [1881-1947], Wilhelm Reich [1897-1957] and [Siegfried] Bernfeld [1892-1953]. I marveled at Hanns Sachs's supreme ease in giving his lectures. He did not need the least written help. He presented his finely differentiated material in print-ready, form-perfect sentences without any faltering in the flow of his speech. Wilhelm Reich possessed an ingeniously exciting style of presentation. To this day, some of his statements made at the time have remained therapeutic for me. This applies in particular to his statement that in psychoanalytic therapy chaos can be avoided only if one always addresses and questions the resistance behavior of the patient; by contrast, the id content is self-evident. Fenichel had a phenomenal memory. For every word that Freud had ever written, he knew instantly where to find it in the collected works as well as the time of its publication. Bernfeld's stubborn endeavor, with which he was obsessed at the time of my stay in Berlin, seemed rather bizarre to me. It was about measuring quantities of libido. Karen Horney seemed to me the most humane of all the Berlin psychoanalysts. It made a great impression on me how she started out from a myriad of constituents of the human psyche but always spoke of man as a whole person.

In addition to my work at the Berlin Psychoanalytic Institute, I was also engaged as a guest student at the Neurological Department of Kurt Goldstein's [1878-1965] Moabiter Hospital. However, there prevailed there (it was now 1932, and the Nazi Reich was advancing powerfully) too intense a nervousness and doom-and-gloom for the greatness of the master to be able to really surmount. One sentence from Goldstein's lecture has especially stuck with me. The human brain (so I heard him say in a side note) is a structure that far surpasses all man-made works in terms of beauty and efficiency.

After my one-and-a-half year stay abroad, I remained only one more year at Zürich's Burghölzli. Then the management of the private sanatorium Schloss Knonau fell into my lap. It had gained world fame through its then director, Jakob Kläsi [1883-1980]. As the only doctor in the house, I was able to form a very close partnership with ten nurses and a maximum of twenty patients. I owe most of my insights into the nature of schizophrenia to this period. Compared to the routine examinations and usual brief visits the doctors at large psychiatric clinics have to carry out, living together continuously with many different sorts of patients from the time they get up, through their mealtimes, working and playing hours, until bedtime lets one see what is decisive that until then has remained hidden. On the basis of what I was able to see and given my psychoanalytic training, I soon ventured to undertake actual attempts at psychotherapy with schizophrenic patients. As a 1938 paper on 'Preparatory individual treatment for group occupational therapy with severe, chronic schizophrenics' testifies, I had pretty much used the same procedure that was later to be given the name *réalisation symbolique*' by Ms. Sechehay [sic] [Marguerite-Albert Sechehaye (1887-1964)]. Some rather considerable successes completely contradicted Freud's opinion, which he had made known to me in a letter of 5 August, 1936. In it he says: 'It is true that I have seen little success in the analytic treatment of schizophrenia. My advice not to use this method in private practice has practical motives. The failures are written about in accounts of analysis and damage its reputation. Of course, there is nothing wrong with using analysis to study schizophrenia in an institution [Es ist richtig, dass ich von der analytischen Behandlung der Schizophrenien wenig Erfolg gesehen habe. Mein Rat, diese Methode nicht in der Privatpraxis anzuwenden, hat praktische Motive. Die Misserfolge werden auf Rechnung der Analyse geschrieben und schadigen ihren Ruf. Gegen die Verwendung der Analyse zum Studium der Schizophrenie in einer Anstalt ist natürlich nichts einzuwenden]'.

It seemed to me that too much therapeutic pessimism was expressed in these lines. It was he who for the first time shook my blind faith [in psychoanalysis] that I had brought to every statement of the great man. Further disruptions of my confidence in the genuineness of Freudian doctrine followed in rapid succession. I discovered an alarming self-contradiction that gaped between two kinds of Freud's writings. His theoretical treatises on 'metapsychology' represent the strictest determinism. On the other hand, in his writings on technique, which relate to the practical behavior of the psychoanalytic therapist [*psychoanalytischen Therapeuten*], there are at least a half dozen times when there is talk of a being free [*Frei-Sein*] and an even greater freedom that his treatment could bring to the ill. In a conception of man whose psychic life is forced into a seamlessly determined series of causal connections strictly and really scientifically conceived, no place at all is given for any freedom, any more than for 'tactlessness towards the analysand [*Taktlosigkeiten gegenüber den Analysanden*]',[192] which Freud so authoritatively said the therapist was to avoid. Added to this were difficulties of their own in the analytic treatment of neurotic patients. Theoretically, I knew in great detail about Freud's dream theory. In practice, however, its application gave me the biggest headache. Most of my analysands had the disadvantage of being people who were clever and critical well above the average. With none of them did I arrive at Freud's dream explanations. These were flatly rejected by them as highly absurd artefacts for which I had not the slightest evidence to offer. The excuses I made to myself for the peculiar behavior of my patients traced back to the 'resistance' of the patient and to my own inadequate experience never really caught on with me. So I took a closer look at Freud's *Interpretation of Dreams* [1900]. To my astonishment, two peculiar facts came into view at the same time. First, in his numerous examples of interpretation I saw nothing of Freud's analysis until the discovery of the postulated dream core [*Traumkern*]; namely, the actual cause of the dream [*Traumursache*], the infantile dream wish [*Traumwunsch*] that he assumed. Even more serious, however, seemed to be the only 'proof' in favor of his theory of dreams [*Traumlehre*] given in all 500 pages of the work. In fact, it consists of a single reference to so-called undisguised [*unverhüllt*] dreams. In Freud's way of speaking, these are dream images in which the instinctual desire comes to nothing. These undisguised dreams, writes Freud, are not interesting in themselves but only as 'proof [*Beweis*]' that all dreams are constructed the same way. I then wanted and still do not want this 'evidence [*Beweisführung*]' to be as valid as the assertion: since there are white roses, all other-colored roses are basically white, but only a disguised white. The scales fell from my eyes and I realized that present dream phenomena were not the least indication of the factual occurrence of psychic things [*Dinge*] and processes at work presupposed by Freud.

In my perplexity following this discovery, *Freuds Auffassung des Menschen im Lichte der Anthropologie* [*Freud's View of Man in the Light of Anthropology*], which had just been published by Ludwig Binswanger [1881-1966] [in 1936] gave me the help I longed for.[193] On the basis of this excellent critique of Freud, I understood that Freud was forced to invent his whole theory of dreams together with his idea of an 'unconscious' only because a causal connection had to necessitate everything that is present [*Vorhanden*]. Doubt upon doubt about Freud's theoretical metapsychology now assaulted me. Why had Freud resorted to the term 'metapsychology [*Metapsychologie*]', that is, to a beyond [*jenseits*]- or about [*über*]-psychology? 'Meta-' [what]? Apparently because with it he knowingly went beyond factual experience and what is actually present. But whence his justification for the apodictic directive with which he characterizes the basic intention of his entire psychology: 'In our view, perceived phenomena must take a back seat to merely assumed strivings'?[194] Who or what forced on him such an odd 'must'? In any case, Freud himself shot not have the least justification for this 'must' that supports the entirety of psychoanalytic theory. Even more striking, however, seemed to me to be the fact that, on the one hand, Freud declares man's instinctuality to be the actual and only real ground of all psychic phenomena but, at the same time, he characterizes the instincts as fathomless [*bodenlos*] with the words 'vagueness', 'dark' and 'mythic'. Did Freud not contradict himself further and in a dubious manner when, on the one hand, he prescribed the analytic practice of dismantling the prejudices brought by the analysand but under no circumstances replacing them with the analyst's own prejudices, only then to explain the bodily [*Körperliche*] and the instincts that stem directly from it in terms of the actual reality of psychic life [*Wirklichen des Seelenlebens*]? Or is this enthronement of domination by one's physical urges something other than the prejudice of a psychoanalyst?

Being under the burden of these and many other doubts threatened to suffocate my medical work. At just the right time a new great teacher approached me. As he openly admitted, C[arl]. G[ustav]. Jung [1875-1961] was pained that he had been able to gather only a few medical students around him. In Zürich, he was surrounded almost exclusively by a close circle [*dichten Kranz*] of admiring ladies. Certainly this was a wall of protection that might have been vital for his prodigious sensibility. Obviously, that was not enough for him. That is why, in 1938, he summoned half a dozen psychotherapists practicing in the city. One of them was me. He formed a working group with us that lasted for almost ten years. Its abrupt end was my fault. For a while, however, this group of psychotherapists sometimes met weekly, sometimes monthly in Jung's private home in Kusnacht, near Zürich. He tried to make his teaching understandable and acceptable with case discussions. In dire need, he was for me a savior in the truest sense of the word. His opening up of the Freudian prison of the drives and the rehabilitation of the alleged dream façade [*Traumfassade*] by Alphons [sic] [Alphonse] Maeder [1882-1971] and Herbert Silberer [1882-1923] let me breathe again for a while. But soon I also noticed certain discrepancies in C. G. Jung's teaching. I first became suspicious when he called himself a natural scientific phenomenologist [*naturwissenschaftlichen Phänomenologen*]. Shortly before that, I had been informed by L[udwig]. Binswanger about the nature of phenomenology, which is so different from natural science. That is why I now knew that a natural scientific phenomenology is like the nonsense [*Unding*] of wooden iron. There the scientific method, with its rejection of actually present perceptible phenomena in favor of the assumptions of subtle, causal forces; here phenomenological science [*phänomenologische Wissenschaft*], with its interpretive dwelling [*Verweilen*] with what appeals to human beings of the significance of the thing itself [*von den Dinge selbst*] and its renunciation of all inference and causal deduction.

It was my 1947 habilitation thesis [to teach in the university] *Sinn und Gehalt der sexuellen Perversionen*, however, that first caused our working group to break up. For the first time in my work my descriptions were based on the phenomenological approach, but, of course, as I had received it from L. Binswanger. In working this way it was unavoidable that I had to subject to phenomenological critique not only Freud's speculative metapsychology but also C. G. Jung's hypotheses of the archetypes and the 'collective unconscious'. Of course, from such a point of view I could see C. G. Jung's archetypal representation as only an intellectual inference from certain phenomena of human perception of something abstractly logical which could correspond to something factually present and identifiable only with very little probability.

One week after I had given C. G. Jung my book as a gift, his break with me was by that time complete [*perfekt*]; better, half complete. For my part, I maintained bound to C. G. Jung with unchanged gratitude. On the other hand, on his part his response to my gift was a very indignant letter. It is dated 5 August, 1947. Apart from its surly personal tone, it seems to me to be of not insignificant general interest. The text shows in an amazing way the spiritual closeness of C. G. Jung and Sigmund Freud, even though in their later years they both sought to withdraw from one another in such a lively [*lebhaft*] way. In the first place, the letter makes clear the same incapacity for basic philosophical thinking that Freud had always shown. Both sought to compensate for this with an identical contempt for all philosophizing. On the other hand, C. G. Jung's letter shows that, like Freud, he was at times well aware of the purely fictive character of his basic ideas. Again and again, in no time at all both can speak again and again with the greatest degree of self-understanding of the same intellectual constructs [*Gedankengebilden*] as if they were actual facts whose observable occurrence had been long known and proven. For example, as already mentioned, Freud calls the 'impulses' dark, vague, mythic beings [*Wesen*], and called his basic idea of a psychic apparatus [*Apparates*] itself a fiction. On the other hand, every psychic reality [*psychische Wirklichkeit*] and its instinctual energy was for him nothing other than the product of this machine [*Maschine*] which had just been characterized as a fiction. Freud never had a clue that with such statements he spoke as a philosopher (albeit as a bad philosopher), as one, namely, who thoughtlessly transferred the basic philosophical dogma of an allegedly entirely real, thoroughgoing seamless causality of lifeless things to something entirely different – human life [*menschlichen Existenz*].

But C. G. Jung is equally unaware of the philosophy that dominates and supports his ideas. It is obviously the philosophy of the neo-Kantians. Without it, his supposition of a 'collective unconscious' and its archetypes would not have been able to spring from the mind of C. G. Jung at all. Out of such philosophical ignorance Jung was able to write to me: 'Man as an archetype is a purely empirical affair, to which nothing philosophical is attached. The fact that the archetype is causal or conditional is also empirical. If that were not the case, it would never have come to be observed. It's not a theory, but rather a purely factual observation [*Der Mensch als Archetypus ist doch eine rein empirische Angelegenheit, an der nichts Philosophisches haftet. Empirisch* ist auch die Tatsache, dass auch der Archetypus causal oder conditional wirkt. Wenn dem nicht so wäre, so hatte er überhaupt nie beobachtet werden können. Das ist also keine Theorie, sondern rdne Tatsachenbeobachtung]'.

Only C. G. Jung forgot that elsewhere he himself had proclaimed the opposite and also had this opposite confirmed by his crown interpreter, Mrs. Jolanda [sic] [Jolande] Jacobi [1890-1973]. He explicitly stated that the archetypes are never directly observable, but can only be deduced from their effects. Moreover, Jung overlooked the fact that one of the first insights of philosophical reflection is always knowledge of the fundamental impossibility of a 'pure empiricism' or 'pure factuality'. All observation is always 'theory' insofar as it necessarily takes root in some particular earlier, pre-scientific (if for the most part not specifically considered) conception of the basic nature of all facts. Finally, in his letter to me, C. G. Jung does not even consider the possibility that the same factual phenomena he first considered to be the effects of something else, namely psychic causes thought to lie behind them, are archetypes in the sense of general human brain structures or equally ubiquitous intrapsychically organized forces that could be understood quite differently and in a much less complicated way. Why, for example, shouldn't people at different times and diverse places be affected by the same perceptions simply because one and the same thing shows itself to them? When I presented these objections to C. G. Jung, he barely listened and dismissed me with the rather harsh words 'I don't follow you [*Da komme ich nicht mehr nach*]'.

But that, by contrast, in better times while holding so stubbornly to the reality of his basic theoretical concepts, C. G. Jung could also be well aware of their merely fictitious character is clear from a conversation, confirmed to me in writing, that once took place between his former schoolmate, the Basel philosopher Paul Häberlin [1878-1960], and him. To wit, one day Häberlin accused C. G. Jung of being too bright to believe in the reality of his complicated psychological constructions. Jung's startling answer was 'Of course, but *mundus vult decipi* (The world wants to be deceived [*Die Welt will betrogen sein*])'.

From the beginning of the Second World War until its end, each year I had to carry out border guard military service. That was predictable. Just before the outbreak of the war, the prospect of this had prompted me to give up direction of Schloss Knonau Sanitarium in order to be able to dedicate myself to my psychotherapy practice in the city, my scientific research and [my] academic teaching. At first, of course, and for as long I functioned in my military service as the battalion physician for high quality, healthy mountain troops, I was mostly underemployed. With so much free time, time was by now a problem for me. It reminded me that L. Binswanger once mentioned a work on time by Martin Heidegger. I had the book sent high up into the mountains. I wanted to finally find out what had been plaguing [*plagende*] me for too long a time. The disappointment was great. I understood nothing of Heidegger's work *Sein und Zeit* [*Being and Time*] [1927]. At the same time I couldn't get it out of my mind. I vaguely suspected that there was something important about it. I read the book again and again. Here and there, things began to dawn on me. First and foremost, I understood page 122 of the book.[195] I could not believe my eyes when I saw Heidegger writing at that place about two different kinds of caring about [*Fürsorge*] the other. Both paragraphs could well have been taken from one of Freud's *Schriften zur Technik* [*Writings on Technique*][196] in which Freud wanted to characterize how an analytic therapist [*analytischer Therapeut*] should and should not behave. According to Freud, the therapeutic behavior to be avoided at all costs Heidegger calls an 'intervening [*einspringende*]' caring about; [and] that to be carried out, a 'way-making [*vorausspringende*]' looking after.[197] As a matter of fact, that which both Heidegger and Freud warn against is characterized by the philosopher in a way consistent with Freud's, that 'this [intervening] caring about takes over for the other what he is to care about [*Sorge*]. Thus forced from his position, he steps back so that afterwards he can either take over what has been taken care of [for him] as an already done deal, or disburden himself of it completely. In such caring about the other can become one who is dependent and controlled, even though this control may be tacit and remain hidden from him.' Heidegger characterizes the other, 'way-making caring about' [the other], the positively valued caring about in this way: '[It] does not so much intervene on behalf of the other as make way for him in his existential capacity to be, not in order to take away his 'care [*Sorge*]' but instead to restore it to him essentially as such for the first time. This kind of caring about that actually concerns real care, the way of life [*Existenz*] of the Other and not a 'what' that he [the therapist] cares for helps the other in that way to become transparent to himself in his care and to become free for it.' But this characterizes with great conciseness the behavior that Freud described as the analyst's only possible, permissible and fruitful way of dealing with his analysand.

Although I began to understand a little bit of *Sein und Zeit*, it became clear to me that I needed the direct help of the author in order to be able to make much progress in understanding his work. I began to inquire about the man. To my astonishment, the information of all the sources available to me about Heidegger was awful [*miserabel*]. There were rumors of his Nazism, tinged with atrocities committed at the university and toward his former teacher, [Edmund] Husserl [1859-1938]. I did not give up until, immediately after the end of the war I was finally able to look into the files of the university authorities, the command posts of the occupying powers, and the denazification offices. It was not until I had obtained sufficient assurance that Heidegger had become the victim of monstrous slander and abuse [*das Opfer ungeheuerlicher Verleumdungen und Misshandlungen*] that I made direct contact with him. As soon as circumstances allowed, in 1946, I visited him at his cabin [*Hütte*] in Todtnauberg. A mutual good will immediately united us. His physical form was certainly not very impressive. It is even more unsightly than mine. But I was struck by his gaze. His eyes seemed to betray an almost dizzying inscrutability [*eine fast schwindelerregende Abgründigkeit*], and at the same time an unaccustomed sharpness and sureness of thought. A greater contrast between this experience and the encounter with Heidegger that Hans Kunz [1904-1982] recently described in his self-portrait is hard to imagine.[198] It becomes understandable, however, as soon as one remembers that two people can never look at one another exactly the same way. The way in which two people meet is always determined by the nature of both. It depends on whether one partner at least potentially has something to say to the other, and if so how much.

Therefore, depending on the degree of possible harmony between them, seeing and meeting the other runs the gamut for each from meaningful proximity to meaningless distance. My meeting with Heidegger in Todtnauberg was the beginning of a steadfast friendship and intellectual apprenticeship. Soon after our friendship began, however, many strange things were again whispered to me. It was said that I should beware of Heidegger, that he had betrayed [*verraten*] and let down every man soon after he made friends with them.

During a period of more than a quarter of a century, I had not the slightest indication of this. Perhaps it's because I did not overwhelm him personally and respected his human limits. I could succeed in that, however, only because I didn't let myself be blinded by his stupendous intellectual ability, but during our time together was attentive to my habitual, professionally trained observation of human behavior. At the same time, I saw at close range how a tremendous force consumed itself in solitary thought of a kind that is unparalleled in human history. It is not surprising that Heidegger did not have the same amount of strength for maturation and discernment in the area of human relationships. Who should demand of a perfect genius an equal development of all human possibilities for life and be angry with a very great thinker if he is not so very great all around?

The great amount of slander and injustice that had befallen Heidegger made me strive to make amends for it where that was still possible. Heidegger's own complete disinterest in a defense of his personal rights had earned him the bizarre fate of being both suspected and incriminated by the Nazis, and then, after their downfall, being tormented by their counterpart, denazification. Heidegger himself was little moved by my attempts at help. Regardless of his bad luck during hard times, undeterred, he unswervingly stayed on his path of thinking. Insofar as I took him for the man he was and loved him as he was, he thanked me with indescribable patience and helpfulness in philosophical matters. The amount of effort and time that the man's 'Zollikon seminars' cost him really reached the limits of human capacity. For about fifteen years he spared no effort to be a guest in my house in Zollikon for eight to fourteen days each semester where twice (sometimes three) times a day he held seminars on the basic questions of medicine in general and psychiatry and psychotherapy in particular with my young colleagues and earlier on with assistants from the psychiatric clinic. For a good eight to ten years just prior to his physical collapse [*physischen Zusammenbruch*], he also followed the work on my book *Grundriß der Medizin* [1971] with utmost interest. He worked so hard on it that hardly a line of its 600 pages lacked his corrective, supplementary or corroborative comments. At the beginning of our acquaintance, of course, Heidegger had at first been repelled by all psychology. What he had previously known from hearsay about this science seemed to him so bizarre [*skurril*] that he had regretted taking the time to even look into it. With some patience, I persuaded him to read at least a few of Freud's and Jung's writings. On reading them, he no longer appeared to be amazed and shook his head. Obviously, Freud's language did it. Based on the content of their psychological works, however, he could not believe that such intelligent men could be so serious about such abstruse [*abstrusen*] ideas about man. After studying some sections of Freud's three *Abhandlungen zur Sexual-*

theorie [1905], Freud's work *Das Ich und das Es* [1923], and his study *Die Zukunft einer Illusion* [1927], Heidegger said he had never considered it possible for anyone to be able to speculate mechanistically on the peculiarity of human existing [*menschlichen Existierens*]. After reading selections from C. G. Jung's works *Wandlungen und Symbole der Libido* [1967] and *Psychologie des Unbewußten* [1912], Heidegger could only confirm that it was fundamentally the same as Freud, but said less succinctly.

It was not until I spared Heidegger all the psychological theories and began to describe as simply as possible the concrete behavior of my psychoneurotic and psychotic patients that his interest became more and more acute. Soon I could not tell him enough about my professional 'subject matter [*Materie*]'.

For my part, in that way I tried to thank him for his great willingness to help me make serviceable to psychology and medicine his fundamentally new insights into the nature of man, his world and the relationship between the two. But I was never to lose sight of the fact that for Heidegger himself it was never merely about anthropology [*Menschenkunde*]. In fact, all the basic features of human existing which he had worked out in *Sein und Zeit* were important to him only in regard to an appropriate [*rechtes*] question about 'being [*Sein*]' as such. That is why he called his epoch-making work *Sein und Zeit* a 'fundamental ontology [*Fudamentalontologie*]'.

Precisely because Heidegger's philosophy is a fundamental ontology, it seemed to me, his insights into the main features [*Grundzüge*] of human existing did not exclude but rather included the viable theoretical foundation [*Fundament*] of a completely new, more humane [*menschengerechteten*] psychology, psychopathology and psychotherapy, and medicine as a whole. In all probability, such a daseinsanalytic [*daseinsanalytisches*] foundation would far outweigh the viability of previous concepts of psychology and medicine.

So that I could follow this way with some prospect of success but on firm ground, Heidegger first had to disabuse me of the existentialist [*existentialistische*] thinking of J.[-]P. Sartre [1905-1980] and Ludwig Binswanger. In particular, until my personal encounter with Heidegger I considered Sartre, like Binswanger, to be competent interpreters of the analysis of *Dasein* [*Daseinsanalytik*]. But Heidegger now showed me dozens of passages in which both of them back read [*zurück interpretiert*] his discovery of human being-in-the-world into the old subjectivist Cartesianism and only used new terms. For example, in addition to a large number of other errors, Sartre speculated that Heidegger's ontological statements addressed things that were on a completely different level than that of those things belonging to man's ontic behavior which could be explored by psychology. However, such an opinion is so wrong that, to the contrary, the ontic phenomena of human existence of interest to psychology can be what they are only because they are from the very beginning and forever permeated by the fundamental basic features that Heidegger's ontology set forth. These constitute their real nature [*Wesen*]. That is why, from the ground up, neither of them can ever be separated. One is never without the other. For one thing Binswanger had, for example, attributed to manic man a 'hopping existence [*hüpfendes Dasein*]'. Moreover, in his 'daseinsanalytic [*daseinsanalytischem*]' dream interpretations, he also spoke of moving dream figures as symbols of a rising or falling existence [*Dasein*].

Heidegger only needed draw my attention to such formulations and ask me what I made of them in order to let me see to what an alarming extent Binswanger's way of thinking kept man's existence trapped in the old reification [*Verdinglichung*]. Heidegger was even more shocked by Binswanger's misunderstanding of his concept of transcendence. A particularly grave misunderstanding by Binswanger, whose origin was to be found in what was just mentioned, was to be found in his reification of existence as a subject. Binswanger's misunderstanding misjudges Heidegger's central concept of transcendence so thoroughly that he uses the term to describe the subject's alleged rising above [*Überstieg*] his subjectivity toward the things of the world. Through such a representation of transcendence he believed he could overcome the 'malignant evil [*Krebs*übel]' of all human sciences, the subject-object split.

Following warnings of this kind, with unprecedented patience Heidegger prepared me at that time for new opportunities to continue to exercise and sharpen my perception of the genuine being-in-the-world of human existence. He would then add:[199] 'The word transcendence has never meant for me a rising above [*Überstieg*] of man to [*zu*] the things of the world, to individual beings. Rather, by transcendence I have always meant only the relation of human existence to being as such and in the verbal sense of that word [*transcendens*, transcending]. As such, the relation between human existing and being is unique. Human existence is related to being such that it is none other than true existing, a standing out in the most literal sense of the word. The human being *ek-sists* as the abiding of an area of world openness common to all human being that consists in the ability to interrogate the presence of everything that is met and in being responsive to the meaning and referential connections of what is presenting itself. Thanks to the fundamental nature of human existing this constitutes the site of appearance and unfolding of all that is and has to be, that is to say, of everything that arises from being as such, and lets come about the singularity of what there is in an area of world openness formed by human existing. On such a view, the notorious subject-object split is not just apparently bridged by some mysterious subjectivist transcendence; in fact, the Cartesian idea of a gap between a *res cogitans* and the *res extaense* [sic] [*res extensae*] can no longer even come up.[']

Only when we are successful in seeing human existence as such as completely insubstantial [*substanzlos*] and non-objective [*ungegenständliches*] being-in-the-world will it be fully understood why man can behave physically and mentally as he in fact does. To a great extent all previous psychological and medical sciences of man are overwhelmed by the task set for them. It is otherwise if, in place of the philosophy of science which allows only what is measurable to be truly valid, there are philosophical insights into the fundamental theory of the whole study of man, including psychology and medicine [drawn] from the analysis of existence [*Daseinsanalytik*]. At the same time, a necessary 'ethics' are given that can give a well-founded goal and fixed guidelines for therapeutic applications in both sciences. Or is there a more meaningful goal for man than to let himself be used for free and responsible purposes as the manifestation and site of unfolding for all that is and has to be?

To such corrections Heidegger would regularly add the remark: 'As long as you psychologists and physicians have not radically cleared out relics of Descartes' time from your heads, the analytics of existence [*Daseinsanalytik*] will not be able to help you further with your psychotherapy.'

The application to psychotherapy and psychosomatics of daseinsanalytic [*daseinsanalytischen*] insights into the basic features of human existence [*menschlichen Dasein*] brought with it all sort of requirements. First of all, the therapeutic behavior demanded by Freudian psychoanalysis had to be changed where in response to Freud's inhuman theoretical metapsychology it had become unfaithful to its own fundamental rule and the ways of behaving shown by the analysand in the course of treatment no longer let themselves appear as what they obviously are. Disfigurements by Freud's theoretical metapsychology, which incidentally Freud himself called a secondary and replaceable superstructure [*Superstruktur*], had also happened in the area of the cornerstones that support psychoanalytic therapy. These are the field of what is erroneously termed 'transference' phenomena and all dreaming life. The theoretical and practical modifications that more properly humane [*menschengerechterten*] insights necessitated especially in these realms justified, even required, another nomenclature. The term 'psychoanalysis [*Psychoanalyse*]' had to be replaced by 'analysis of existence [*Daseinsanalyse*]'. Like 'psychoanalysis', 'daseinsanalysis' also means two things: as much a science of man [*Menschenkunde*] as a therapeutic treatment [*therapeuticshe Verfahren*].

But not only a name change proved to be unavoidable. My students and their pupils more and more insistently urged me to finally institutionalize the analytics of existence [*Daseinsanalytik*]. Whether it would survive later, they asserted, they could not do without it today. For many years I persistently resisted the suggestion. I would argue that one cannot make a new 'school [*Schule*]' of 'daseinsanalysis [*Daseinsanalyse*]'. It is not an established organization [*Gebilde*] that exists in and of itself, not at all a system of readymade propositions and the like. '*Daseinsanalyse*' can only be an invitation to tirelessly look at things, to take an even better look. The only thing that matters is that the daseinsanalyst [*Daseinsanalytiker*] be able to make the phenomena [*Phänomene*] of his 'objects of investigation [*Untersuchungsgegenst*ände]' and of the patients to be treated more differentiated and more comprehensive.

But these people did not let up. Finally, I gave in. And so in the summer of 1971, a 'Society for Daseinsanalytic Anthropology [*Gesellschaft für daseinsanalytischer Anthropologie*]' based in Zürich was founded. Only nine months later, its offshoot the '[D]aseinsanalytic Institute for Psychotherapy and Psychosomatics [*daseinsanalytische Institut für Psychotherapie und Psychosomatik*]' appeared. It is an educational institution for future practicing medical and non-medical daseinsanalysts and an outpatient treatment center. There even poor patients find a way to be treated daseinsanalytically by candidates in training.

Both institutions, the Daseinsanalytic Society and the Institute, have to some extent replaced the Institute for Medical Psychotherapy [*Institut für ärztliche Psychotherapie*] in Zürich. This emerged from the author's longtime working relationship with Gustav Bally [1893-1966]. As early as 1941, on the initiative of Manfred Bleuler [1903-1994], the son and indirect successor of Eugen Bleuler at the Burghölzli Psychiatric University Hospital, the Zürich government commissioned both of us to take charge of and oversee the psychotherapeutic education [*Ausbildung*] of the assistants. We had a remarkable experience at the beginning of our work. Since no assistant in the clinic had yet completed his own training analysis, we were forced to throw Freud's wise advice to the wind and even give analysands access to unanalyzed young colleagues. However, it did not take a year for all six aspiring analysts whom we first had to supervise [*kontrollieren*] in their work to quite naturally feel an urgent need to undergo their own training analysis. They just didn't get past certain difficulties with their patients. Subsequently, they also unanimously reported to us from their own experience what a tremendous difference it makes in terms of understanding and practical skill whether psychotherapeutic interventions [*Eingriffe*] are based on theoretical knowledge alone or are based on one's own experience. With the death of Gustav Bally, the ground was taken out from under the Institute for Medical Psychotherapy, which had grown out of our collaborative work. There had existed tension and conflict between Bally's more or less psychoanalytic orientation and my new daseinsanalytic [*daseinsanalytische*] view. However, the up-and-coming young colleagues who regrouped had mastered either orthodox psychoanalytic theory or the exclusively daseinsanalytic language, so that fruitful discussions could not come about. As a result, the Institute, once well-known and valued far beyond the country's borders, drifted off into a deep sleep.

My ever active personal contacts with Heidegger were interrupted only once for a two-year period. In 1956 and 1958, I accepted invitations to be a visiting lecturer in India and Indonesia.[200] I surprised myself most of all when out of the blue it occurred to me that my conception of scientific work was much better suited to the superior thinking of the people of the distant Southeast than to American psychology and psychotherapy so long well known by now here. This was done only with the head. However, nothing would appear to be complete to the Indian man without his head and heart being equally involved. It was amazing, then, how easy it was for Indian and Indonesian colleagues to follow my remarks and apply them in their practice. Almost as stunning was the difference that came to light in this regard between my Eastern colleagues and the American aid workers who regularly took part in my local lectures and seminars. Although all of us, Indian and American students, psychologists and physicians alike, were speaking the same English language, understanding was incomparably greater in fact with the Indian people than with the Americans. It is probably more than a mere coincidence that more of my books were translated into Japanese than into Western languages. If I'm not mistaken, gratifying attention will be paid to them there in psychiatry and psychotherapy.[201]

Of course, I had not made the considerable material sacrifice of a long stay in those Far Eastern countries only to hear myself again somewhere else. I hoped to find that there were still true teachers of wisdom there whose insights into the constitution and meaning of man and his world came from past millennia and were passed on only from teacher to student. To my great surprise I often heard about in-depth agreement of their ancient knowledge of man and his world with the findings that had come unexpectedly so much later and from very far away to the mind of a man in the Black Forest of Germany. Neither had my Indian sources ever heard Heidegger's name nor had he heard the least of Indian thought.[202]

With regard to my experience, it might be easily suspected, of course, that it was simply a matter of a misinterpretation of Indian thinking on the basis of my partiality for the daseinsanalytic perspective. That this suspicion is hardly correct is proven by the fact that I'm not blind to critical differences. The essential discrepancy may lie between the ancient Indian conviction about Brahmam, that the coming into the luminant of being [*Gelichtet-Sein*] is possible without the way of life of man [*Existenz des Menschen*]. Heidegger's thinking, on the other hand, requires human existing [*menschliches Existierens*] so that anything can be there at all [*damit überhaupt etwas sein kann*]. Only this is capable of fashioning, opening and keeping open the global [*weltweiten*] ability to take in [*Vernehmenkönnen*][203] things, the actuality of which necessarily requires us in order to be able to be present to [*an-wesen zu können*] them at all. Conversely, of course, that man needs what encounters him is just as indispensable because he can make his sojourn in the world only with interrogating and responding reference to it.

When I later confronted Heidegger with this difference, his answer was that for him 'being [*Sein*]' was experienceable [*erfahrbar*] only in its dependence on human existence [*menschliches Dasein*]. He did not want to go beyond what was factually [*faktisch*] experienceable by himself.

A few years after my return from the Southeast, I received a phone call from America. Presumably, one of my New York friends was right in claiming that the materialistic positivism that prevailed there for many years had aroused great 'ontological hunger' among many psychologists and physicians in the USA. At any rate, more and more invitations to American universities poured in, three of them alone for full-semester stays at Harvard University. Given the extremely strict selection of students who are admitted to this school, lecturers there work only with an intellectual elite, something unknown to us. It is probably thanks to this circumstance that my work there turned into one of my most beautiful teaching experiences. It also happens that American students are used to incomparably harder work and reading than ours are. For this reason alone, one can set his teaching standards very high.[204]

Given such a gathering of so much brilliance, it was proposed that I title one of my Harvard lectures 'Phenomenological Psychology [*Phänomenologische Psychologie*]'. Even there it took a lot of effort to teach the listeners that in principle there can be no such thing. For in the light of a phenomenology, instead of the idea of a psyche as an imagined construct [*vorgestellten Gebilde*] somewhere objectively present (albeit immaterially present) that of the completely different being-in-the-world is always already there. Without a 'psyche', of course, there can be no subject [*Lehre*] about such a thing, that is, no psychology. It is therefore all the more timely that this is itself overcome and a teaching [*Lehre*] about There-being [*Da-Sein*] blossoms forth.

Two of my three children have found their way back to nature from the weird [*versponnen*] world of their father: psychiatry. They became farmers in Brazil. I have heard amazing news from them that for years there has been an extensive Heidegger Circle [*Heidegger-Kreis*] in Rio de Janeiro to which the best minds [*Köpfe*] belong. The prospects are not bad that the daseinsanalytic mindset [*daseinsanalytische Gedank-*

engut] might also prove to be fruitful for South American psychotherapy. Appropriate connections have already been made there. Of course, much will depend on whether I will succeed in adequately mastering the Portuguese language. Anyhow, considering all that I have done, I've by now reached a fairly advanced age. No wonder then that for quite some time the usual occupational symptoms of aging have also begun to set in, in the form of various appointments as corresponding member or even as honorary member of various professional societies. Among the rewards of this kind granted me, my appointment as honorary president of the board of the International Federation of Medical Psychotherapy is the one closest to me since I was one of the obstetricians who helped to bring this creature to life in 1954. Actually, for sixteen years, I even served as its hard-working president. Thankfully, I note, the effort was not in vain. The initially fragile creature has grown into an association of several thousand members. The whole matter of psychotherapy [*Sache der Psychotherapie*] seems to serve this federation superbly because it represents an incomparably wide forum [*Forum*] in which representatives of dozens and dozens of different psychotherapeutic trends have the rare opportunity to talk to each other. It is eagerly utilized year after year.

In recent years, the Zürich faculties of medicine and philosophy, which had hitherto been alienated from each other, have begun to talk. Since then I have stood with one leg in one department, the other one in the other department. This stance has suited me admirably. Most psychologists also seem to take pleasure in it. By contrast, many medical people [*Mediziner*] remain suspicious. Those who have been hardened by a purely scientific, materialistic positivistic way of thinking do so with good reason. The phenomenological approach threatens its claim to absoluteness [*Absolutsanspruch*] regarding man. Moreover, given the trends of our technical age they feel more committed than ever to hold on to them under any circumstances. In any case, I am certainly the last person who would hold their distrust against them. Last but not least, I am among those people who for the benefit of the sick and healthy men and women entrusted to us who have been striving for decades to pull the ground out from under scientists for what they have usurped [*usurpiertern*] – but only what they have usurped. There seems to be no place for mercy. Probably, one thing is more important than anything else: that is, in particular that human beings come back from the homelessness [*Heimatlosigkeit*] of purely natural scientific abstractions to stand on the ground [*Grund*] on which they already fundamentally exist [*existieren*]. For now, I can see such a solid home [*konkret Grund und Boden*] only in the daseinsanalytic understanding of being-in-the-world.

Thus far, Boss' reminiscences. A few years before the publication of his memoir, Boss was interviewed by Mary Harrington Hall for the new popular journal *Psychology Today*, which had been launched the year before. Published as '**A Conversation with Medard Boss; or the Evolution of Psychoanalysis**' (1968a)[205], along with his memoir, sections of the India book (1959a), Boss's preface to the book by Govind Kaul (1970c), and his interview with Erik Craig (1988b), it is among the few sources we have on Boss's life and work. Hall, who was Managing Editor of the periodical, interviewed

Boss in the States when he was on his way to California to see his son, Martin, having come to the States after a visit with his daughter, Maia, in Brazil.

Boss recounted that he had begun to buy paintings during World War II and owned two Picassos (one of which he had sold to buy a cattle ranch for his daughter in South America), and works by Renoir, Degas, Monet and Gaugin. He recalled his meetings in his early twenties with Freud and fondly acknowledged his teachers, Eugen Bleuler and Carl Gustav Jung, whose work he was expected to continue in Zürich.

He was represented by Hall as Martin Heidegger's 'interpreter, close associate and closest friend'. Boss recounted having become acquainted with *Sein und Zeit* while on duty in the Swiss army. He contacted Heidegger in 1946. At that time, Heidegger was under fire and being investigated by government officials about the nature of his involvement in National Socialism before and during World War Two. Hearing that Heidegger and his family were 'starving out there in the Black Forest', he sent them some packages of food.

Boss never ceased defending Heidegger against charges of his having 'supported the Nazi regime': 'The whole thing is a slander. Heidegger is terribly shy and completely unable to defend himself against personal attack. But I investigated the matter thoroughly. I checked all the court files and the university records.'[206] He added that 'some of [Heidegger's] colleagues who were active Nazis had been allowed to return to their posts at the university.' Boss went on: 'I've asked him several times why he doesn't contradict some of these wild statements, but he told me that if he once started there would be no time to do anything constructive. He would spend all his time contradicting, and then contradicting the contradictions.' Heidegger had been forbidden to teach in Germany from to 1945-1951, but was reinstated at the University of Freiburg.

'He is the most splendid man I have ever known,' said Boss. 'And with the same look of genius as Freud, but a very different kind of person. If you saw him you would think he was a vineyard owner from the South of France.' Continuing on Heidegger: 'In his emotions, he always remains a small boy of the Black Forest.... [I]f you understand Heidegger as being this child, he is the most charming and kind-hearted person you could ever know. People often say I am fascinated with Heidegger. I *am* fascinated by him, but I can see his weaknesses. And I have not found any fault in his thinking. We are good friends and he frequently visits me in Zürich. He likes my mountain cottage where we can withdraw and discuss matters in absolute stillness... Heidegger is one of the most religious men of today, only he is too careful a man to talk a lot about unspeakable things. Two or three times each term he comes over to give seminars to my students, both as a psychiatrist and as a philosopher.'[207] These were, of course, the Zollikon seminars, most of which had been completed by the time of the interview. It is interesting that in this interview Boss refers to Heidegger as a psychiatrist.

Harrington suggested that Heidegger's ideas led to Boss's view of dreaming life. 'Yes, I learned to stop regarding dreams as pictures [images], as Freud and all the other theorists always had done. Dreams are real. Dreaming is just a different way of *being* in the world.' Waking life and dreaming life are two different ways of being-in-the-world, and this always means as the illuminating opening for things and fellow human beings to speak to one. Dreams, then, are not replicas of physical objects of the sort one finds in paintings, photographic images, and digitized images. As perceived, dreams are on a par ontologically with things in nature which are the source of stimuli received at the end organs of sensation.'a

Boss repeated a version of his favorite story of the Chinese philosopher, here transliterated and named by Harrington as 'Tschuangtze', on the dream of the butterfly: 'One day he awoke form a dream that he was a butterfly flying from flower to flower. He asked himself, 'Am I actually a man lying in bed wanting to have breakfast, or am I a butterfly who is dreaming that he is a man lying in bed wanting to have breakfast?' To which Hall replied: 'Or am I dreaming that I am sitting here talking to you?' Boss: 'How can you tell? All the philosophers in the world have asked that question. If you are a true phenomenologist you just have to accept that you are existing in this kind of being in the world. And you have to let these dreams remain the things they show themselves to be. In the dreaming state, resistant ways of behavior show themselves, ways that are not yet accepted in the waking state and which have not yet come to the knowledge of the dreamer.' Dreaming life discontinues when one wakes up, but since no one has ever remembered falling asleep, who is to say whether the recollection of a dream is not taking place in an even more fundamental dreaming life or 'stateless' condition? We will know that to be the case only if we wake up from a very long dreaming life. *La vida es sueño* said the Spanish playwright Calderón.

Boss is keenly aware of the etymology of *Bewußtsein* (consciousness) via the verb *wissen* (to know). He rejects, however, the notion of content that could be known but not consciously known, namely, Freud's *Unbewußt*. What has not yet come to be known is coterminous with what is realized of the possibilities of a given *Dasein*. Such realization of a possibility can make an appearance in a dream, where it is then first known. But not all dreams are recalled. Thus the remembered dream is a privileged appearance of possibilities that presumably are being 'realized' while dreaming.

Here we come to the critical matter of memory and its relation to knowledge. What would Boss say about 'dreams' that are not remembered? Since we do not know anything about them and apparently cannot, the question is moot. Studies of verbalizations of experiences while not self-aware of their being uttered – for example, while in so-called altered states of consciousness induced by certain drugs (hallucinogens and drugs with anesthetic properties such as propofol) or perhaps by meditative practices – would have been of interest to Boss. To my knowledge, he did not comment on the topic.

On Boss's thought in general, he told Harrington that 'until I found Heidegger, as a true theoretical psychoanalyst I was just a circus acrobat on a high rope, performing intellectual acrobatics. In Heidegger's thinking, I found at last a good, solid basis.' As for his own work as a doctor and psychotherapist: 'Medicine and psychotherapy lack a basis that can be deduced from natural scientific thinking. You can't deduce therefrom why you practice medicine, or why you try to help people.' In Heidegger's approach, he found another, very different way of thinking and an understanding of his calling as a therapist (keeping in mind the difference between a calling [*Beruf*] and a profession [*Beruf*]), one of the three 'impossible' callings Freud had identified: teaching, healing or therapy, and leading.[208]

There followed an explication of Heidegger's view of the nature of man. Unlike a mechanical device, which has been constructed by human beings and given its meaning and purpose but which does not know it is doing something or what it is doing, the human being is 'capable of understanding the meaning of things' he encounters. Addressing Harrington: '*You* are the understanding, spread out through the world in space and time; because you are already related with the past, the present and the future. And it is as the understanding essence you are that you reach out to the farthest things which show themselves to you.'[209]

Once again, Boss suggested that 'things' (including fellow human beings) confront or encounter us and we respond to or reply to them. 'Man, by his very essence, keeps open such a realm of understanding of and responding to all which makes its appearance in it,' 'the realm of world-openness, into which all that has come to be can come forth, can become present and reveal itself as that which it is.' The question would then follow: 'How could anything appear, become present and be without a 'there [*da*]', if man [as *Da-sein*] were not such a free openness, capable of perceiving [*Wahrnehmen*] things as the things which they are and able to answer them accordingly?'

Dasein is the one and only *there* of and for such openness. 'Existing in such a way, man obviously is primarily with and at the perceived things themselves.' As for knowledge of the so-called 'external world', it is 'not conceivable on the basis of these psychological suppositions . . . an inner psychic box into which the external object would be mirrored and then would have to be projected outside again.'

This led to the question of space and spatiality, in particular the spatiality of the human body. 'Above all man's *Dasein* never means being there at the definite spot where your body is. That's completely wrong.' Daseinanalysis rejects the 'neo-Platonic philosophy which differentiates between a world of 'ideas' and the psychical world we perceive with our senses.'

Harrington picked up on American slang of the time which she believed might reflect the Heideggerian understanding of human existence: 'Our kids say the thing to be is 'where it's at'.' Boss agreed, 'if by 'where it's at' you mean the realm of openness, the realm of lumination which human existence is. Because this is the basis of what we call human freedom, being able to let things reveal themselves to you, *talk to you* of their nature and being able to respond to them, to answer [emphasis added].' Both agreed that 'being where it's at' – another possible rendering of *Da-sein* – expresses well the goal of Boss's 'method of therapy, daseinsanalysis'.

There followed several examples of how constrained freedom is in every case the fundamental problem that brings someone to therapy. 'Neurotic people don't realize how limited their freedom is because *they have never known freedom* [emphasis added]. You have to show them where their freedom as a human being has been limited and give them the first glimpse that there is a greater freedom possible than they have ever known.'

Here a major point of difference between psychoanalysis and daseinanalysis becomes clear. The goal of the former is to make the contents of the Unconscious known to the analysand. It is matter of coming to explicitly know what one has only implicitly known because it was repressed. For Freud, what is repressed is *both* what has been forgotten *and* what is not known to be missing from access to awareness. This is unlike simple forgetting, in which case one knows that something has been forgotten. The goal of daseinanalysis is not the recovery of repressed knowledge but the discovery of potential action. The degree to which freedom for such action is constrained determines the severity of the so-called disorder.

As he does with the neurotic, the daseinanalyst understands the world of the schizophrenic in terms of how things speak to the individual. Boss continued: 'A schizophrenic perceives a chair, and the appeal of the chair is so powerful and the patient so weak in his being that he is compelled to sit down. The healthy man would have the freedom to respond to the challenge of the chair in whatever manner he thinks best.'[210] A chair is for sitting on, but not in every situation. For example, a schizophrenic who enters a dining room in which there are chairs enough to seat fifty people for dinner must sit in each one, in this way acknowledging the nature of each chair in its 'chairness', a description that answers to the question 'What are chairs for?' The 'healthy man,' Boss said, looks for his place at one of the tables or waits to be seated. Every *thing* is, then, a spatiotemporal place, that is, a situation and occasion. The maximally free human being responds to the call of things with specificity and flexibility. He understands the primary meaning of a chair as something that is to be sat upon. Of course, he is able to reinvent its meaning, so that a chair may be stood on to reach something or taken in hand as a tool to break open a window to get out of a fiery room.

The conversation turned to further consideration of the similarities and differences between psychoanalysis and daseinanalysis, which is what would have brought the reader to Harrington's article 'on the evolution of psychoanalysis' in the first place.

'Daseinanalysis is certainly not a new and hostile school of psychotherapy. Psychoanalytic *practice*, with only a few corrections, is the only therapy that can help man to carry out his authentic and wholesome being – help him to be wholly himself,' said Boss. With respect to the way it will appear to an observer, daseinanalysis seems to be just more psychoanalysis. The analysand reclines on a couch and speaks openly. The analyst sits in a chair beside the analysand, close to the head of the couch but out of direct view of the analysand. Each looks at his respective horizon or closes his eyes. The analyst may see something of the analysand's movement, but not his face. For the analysand in his relationship with the analyst, it is an entirely auditory experience. In relation to himself, the analysand hears his own voice and that of the analyst. There are, however, basic differences between the two forms of practice: 'A daseinsanalyst is first of all a phenomenologist, which means he stays with the phenomena themselves.'

Boss also made clear the differences between Husserl's phenomenology of the 'isolated ego into which all things are mirrored and where the impressions of essential facts are combined and give a meaning' and Heidegger's hermeneutic phenomenology as the method of his fundamental ontology of existence. To attend to things phenomenologically is first of all to work at letting them be as they are and not to introduce meanings from the outside. 'A [Heideggerian] phenomenologist just doesn't try to make mental conclusions. He has a respect for things as they are and rather an awe about them. He tries to leave things as they are, accepting what they tell you of themselves.'[211]

For the Heideggerian phenomenologist reality cannot be explained in terms of causality as the natural sciences do. But why not? Boss answered in a way that shows the limits of natural science and makes clear why in principle it is of no relevance to human beings in the therapeutic setting. 'You just can't conceive of reality in this way, because causality doesn't exist. It's just an assumption and can't be proved.' The causal-explanatory method does not apply to human beings, because it depends upon the measurability of what it studies. *But what is human cannot be measured.* One can, for example, measure the liquid produced by lachrymal glands, but one cannot measure tears of grief or happiness. Another way of thinking of the two sorts of reality being distinguished is to consider that reality explained in terms of causality always looks for something that has occurred earlier that produced an observed effect. By contrast, there is nothing 'behind' the reality studied by Heidegger's phenomenology. It is about what is appearing. The emergence as a phenomenon of something or other appearing is ongoing for each *Dasein*. The daseinanalyst's work is to attend the emergence of phenomena for the analysand, much as we say we attend the performance of a musician.

There is mention of Ludwig Binswanger, who is credited with having brought Heidegger to the attention of psychiatrists but who misunderstood him, insisting on the 'inner world' well known to psychiatry. For Boss, there is no inner world distinguishable from an external or outer world. Reality divided into an outside world and an inner world was an invention of René Descartes in the middle of the seventeenth century. There is, however, no inner, isolated, private, subjective world in which a psyche carries out its various functions. We have been told about such a world and have come to believe in it, much as we believe in causality, adjusting our original experience of being-in-the-world. It is, however, a fiction. Causality is said to operate in both worlds: physical events are said to bring about (cause) other physical events in physical reality, and psychological events are said to bring about (cause) other psychological events in psychic reality. For Boss, however, just as there is no cosmos that contains us and creates a life 'out there' for us, there is no psyche which contains the inner life of a subject or ego. If that were the case, we would be 'in' two different worlds. However, being-in-the-world is unitary. There is therefore no question of a need to determine how to toggle back and forth between inner and outside worlds or of explaining why this might be necessary and how it occurs. Attempts to explain such an artificial division of realms of experiences have been fruitless but, more important, they have been superfluous since there is nothing to have to explain.[212]

The discussion then turned to love. In Boss's book on the paraphilias,[213] which he considered to be pathological deformations of love, he had described love as 'the enlargement of yourself with the help of other people'. For example, in sexual intercourse 'a man is able to exist through his partner in feminine ways of relationship to the world.' The converse holds for a woman in her loving a man. He explained: 'Whenever we get a chance to fulfill hitherto unknown or unfulfillable ways of relationship, then we start to love the person who makes this possible.' The paraphilias are 'just crippled and deteriorated forms of love – love hindered by walls that have closed in on people's freedoms.' The sadist and the masochist are exemplary. 'A sadist perceives himself as separated from his fellow human beings by thick walls. When he expresses his sexual feelings by inflicting pain on someone else, he is trying to break through these walls in the only way he can – by violence.'[214]

A discussion of homosexuality followed.[215] For Boss, 'there are many homosexualities' or, rather, many sorts of homosexuals. His examples are of male homosexuality. Lesbianism or female homosexuality is not mentioned. But is it not possible that male same-sex attraction, experience and behavior can also be an enlarging experience? Thus Hall asks Boss: 'And you conceive of homosexuality ... as allowing one to live in additional ways of relating to the world?' 'That's right,' said Boss.[216] It would seem, then, that Boss saw in certain forms of male homosexuality the prospect for a widening of ways of relating to the world, not as a limiting of what a heterosexual relationship promises, namely, the opportunity of seeing the world through the eyes and ears and body of the 'other' sex. That said, Boss's examples of types of homosexuality are traced back to situations in which there has been some limitation of possibilities with respect to the full experience of masculinity. 'For example, there is the neurotic young man who has grown up in a family where there are only women or a very weak, almost non-existent father. In such a family, a young man learns to develop only feminine ways of existing. He must live the masculine ways of existence through another man.'

Hall raised the question about whether this sort of male homosexuality could be eliminated (if that were desirable) and whether psychotherapy might have a role to play. In other words, could daseinanalysis make available to a male homosexual the heterosexual experience of living out the world of the other sex through intimacy with a woman? Boss replied that 'if [the male homosexual] has masculine potentialities ... through psychoanalysis he may accept and develop his masculine ways of behavior. In the course of such an analysis, you watch the [male] partners of these men become less and less masculine and more and more feminine, until at last they can establish [sexual] relationships with women. But there are many [male] homosexuals who just do not have potential masculine ways of relating. They can live the greatest amount of human potentialities through another man.' 'And for them psychoanalysis is no good?' asked Hall. 'No good at all.' Boss added that there is yet another sort of homosexual male who is in a very different situation. Such men, 'after establishing a heterosexual relationship, regress. They deteriorate in a schizophrenic way and have almost no potentialities at all. They can exist as men only through another man.' Such men cannot find any masculinity in themselves but live it vicariously through other males, much as in sexual intercourse heterosexual women seek masculinity, which they wish to experience but cannot find in themselves and must experience vicariously through their male partners.[217] Boss's view of homosexuality is hardly dismissive. On the other hand, he believes that the sexual complementarity of heterosexuality is desirable in that it allows for the fullest experience of the sexual that is possible for a human being.[218]

Harrington led the discussion to LSD. The hallucinogen had been synthesized in Switzerland and was tried out in the treatment of schizophrenia in in-patient settings. Boss was skeptical about any value for the drug as a pharmacotherapeutic agent, since in his experience 'therapeutically, LSD helps in only very, very rare cases, where the so-called resistances are insurmountable. And such artificial ways of surmounting resistance are frequently worthless and, or even damaging. As Freud pointed out,' Boss added, 'effective curing takes place when the person himself overcomes these resistances – not when some external force surmounts them.' On the other hand, Boss acknowledged that 'naturally, LSD is of great scientific interest in the discovery of what human existence is capable of perceiving.'[219] The time of the interview (1968) was marked by the flamboyant proselytizing of LSD by the Harvard psychologist, Timothy Leary, and others. It is not clear what Boss thought about such popularization of research.

The interview concluded with mention of Boss's having been influenced by Eastern (Hindu) philosophy. He repeated his observation about the closeness of some of Heidegger's idea to ancient Indian wisdom and mentioned his travels in India ten years earlier. Harrington observed that Boss had assumed the lotus position on the patio where she was interviewing him.

'What a good observer you are. You can sit like this for hours. You are resting within yourself.'

As for the future: 'I don't miss youth. I wouldn't be young now, nor would I like to go back again. I have a lovely place on the edge of the lake [Zürich] and I'm writing about the meaning of being moral.'[220]

Two years after his interview with Hall, Boss wrote the **'Foreword'** to *Govind [Gobind] Amrit*. Letter to J. M. Kayande, November 23, 1970] {1975e}[221]. It is perhaps Boss's most personal expression of the impact of his experiences in India. It should be read in connection with *A Psychiatrist Discovers India* {1959a} and its sequel, 'After Thirty Years', the preface to the fourth edition (1987) of the book {2002/2003b}. It is a crucial document and worth reproducing in full.

> At the age of about fifty I had reached the stage of a well established and not unsuccessful psychiatrist and academic teacher. People thought of me as a lucky man. Inside, however, the despair had grown to an almost unsupportable degree. Many of the best authorities in my field had been my teachers. Still I lacked any real understanding about the essence and the meaning of human existence. Most of the patients who came to ask for my therapeutic aid complained in a more or less veiled and hidden form of exactly the same failing in knowing about the goal of their lives. Finally, I had to realize that the natural scientific approach to man enabled the modern scientist only to manipulate the human body in an extremely skillful way. Manipulation as such though is by far no proof at all for an adequate understanding of the manipulated matter.

This state of affairs forced me to seek help outside the Western world. I went to India. I had been told the Indian saints and philosophers had searched for the truth about man and his world during an unbroken chain of thousands of years.

I met a great many very learned and saintly Indian men and women. To all of them I shall remain deeply indebted for their help. The turning point of my life, however, only occurred when I was brought before Swami Gobind [Govind] Kaul who had come down from Kashmir just at that time to Goregaon, Bombay.

There was no possibility for him and me to talk to each other directly. All my knowledge of several languages, including my preliminary studies in Hindi, were of no avail. Swamiji only speaks Kashmiri. Nevertheless, *from the very start of our encounter an immediate non-verbal, rather a preverbal understanding between him and me had sprung up* [emphasis added]. In his presence the many torturing questions about man's existence and about beingness as such were instantly stilled. A closeness to godhead at once had opened up. Later on Swamiji showed me through Goregaon friends as interpreters the practice of meditation. Ever since I follow his advice without any break wherever I have to stay in this world. I never could have fulfilled my rather heavy tasks as a psychotherapeutic doctor and as an academic teacher without this fountainhead of mental strength which I was so lucky to find in India.[222]

Boss's interest in Eastern philosophy had begun early, but it was only after what he had read had been brought to life by first-hand experience that it all came home to him. The interplay of influences on Boss of Heidegger and Kaul is complex.[223]

The importance of this letter for the development of daseinanalysis cannot be underestimated, since what Boss describes as having taken place between Kaul and himself on first encountering each other is what he says happens in the immediate relation between analyst and analysand on first encountering one another which makes any subsequent therapeutic partnership possible.

Finally, on August 6 and 19, 1986, the American psychotherapist Erik Craig recorded conversations with Medard Boss at his home in Zollikon. Boss was then eighty-three. The transcript of the recordings remain in the possession of Craig. The publication of the transcript of their meetings, **'An Encounter with Medard Boss'** (1988b)[224], appeared with several other texts in *The Humanistic Psychologist*, including Boss's essay 'Recent Considerations in Daseinsanalysis' (1988a). The context of the interview was 'to acquaint humanistic psychologists in America with [Boss's] own work in psychology and psychotherapy and with the present standing of daseinsanalysis in general.' It was the following year that Martin Heidegger's *Zollikon Seminars* (1987a), edited by Boss, was published, and so we may assume that at the time of the interviews Boss was in the thick of editing the material, reviewing the conversations he had with Heidegger over many years, and selecting excerpts from the letters Heidegger had written to him from 1947 to 1971.[225]

As Craig notes, the following year he met with Boss on four other occasions to go over the manuscript of the transcription, which in the meantime he had seen and corrected in a number of places. The clarifications and interpolations were 'integrated' into the original transcript.[226] I focus especially on what Boss said about the practice of daseinanalysis.

Boss makes clear at the outset that daseinanalysis is not 'human-centered', not a form of humanistic psychology. The 'significances' of things are not understood to be 'manufactured or construed by human beings', which is the view taken by natural science, even in its 'humanistic' form. It is up to the human being to reveal what the meanings of things are, not determine and declare what they are. 'With the daseinsanalytic approach we are staying with the immediately given phenomena which disclose themselves to us. In fact, human existence is thought to be just this: engaged and existing only for giving things room and light so that they can come to their being .... As human beings we are engaged to function ... so that anything can show itself and call upon us.'[227] This is also precisely the 'main aim' of daseinanalysis, namely, 'to try to allow that which appears to us to come into its own best fullness.... And so, as a therapist you are primarily the hearing and seeing, or the openness, which is called forth to allow things to develop.' Thus, 'there is no separateness between persons in daseinsanalysis. There is this unity, inseparable, indivisible.'[228] The relation is initially *Dasein* to *Dasein*, not an interpersonal relationship.

As a daseinanalyst, 'you first have to lend yourself and to be used for the other person to reveal himself.' Boss admits that 'it took me *years* of trying to exercise [his thinking, following the guidance of Heidegger] this way, to turn around in my mind and to see things anew, but once I got it, my therapeutic work seemed to me to be mere holiday.'[229] He dates the beginning of his work with Heidegger to about 1950, when Boss was already in his late forties. Continuing 'exercises' in phenomenological thinking occurred through the especially concentrated years of the Zollikon seminars (1964-1969), which had just been preceded by Boss's travels to India in 1956 and 1958. By way of a further account of the development of daseinanalysis, Boss mentions the influence of his time in India and the remarkable similarities between what he heard about Hindu philosophy from his guru, Govind Kaul, and experienced with him, and what he had heard from and read in Heidegger's publications. 'I was engaged with Heidegger when I went to India,' Boss recounted, adding that his 'India book' was the fruit of those experiences.

In contrast to the natural science perspective, 'that is, the human centeredness of our thinking, starting always from the human mind and the human being,' 'in Heidegger and in India, there is, instead, the light and the openness which is behind and *before* humanity and human existence.'[230] Here Boss has in mind, of course, the luminance [*Lichtung*] and openness [*Offenheit*] that Heidegger himself found so hard to experience as somehow preliminary to that of *Sein* and the being [*seiend*] of what there is [*das Seiende*].[231] When asked to compare the two influences, Boss admits, 'I don't think you can distinguish the two influences. They are much too similar.' It becomes clear from what Boss told Craig that it was not until the mid-1960s that Boss had fully integrated what he learned from Heidegger and his Indian guru. The first therapeutic daseinanalyst had not been fully 'formed' until *he* was in his early to mid-sixties.

Having heard from Boss about his roughly thirty psychoanalytic hours on Freud's couch in 1925,[232] Craig brought up the theme of *Fürsorge* (caring about the other), an existentive named by Heidegger in *Sein und Zeit*. There, as we have heard, Heidegger had distinguished between the two sorts of *positive* caring about the other with whom we are always already implicated and involved as being-with [*Mitsein*] the other: intervening caring about [*einspringende Fürsorge*] and way-making caring about [*vorausspringende Fürsorge*]. While daseinanalysis is characterized by its emphasis on the latter form of positive caring about the other, Craig recalled Boss's example of having intervened in the case of Regula Zürcher, the central figure in his *Grundriß*, whom he visited at her home during a psychotic episode and helped bottle-fed for a period of time as though she were an infant. To a reader in 1988 or 2024, this kind of therapeutic 'caring' was and still is remarkable. It was certainly beyond the pale of even the most extreme psychoanalytic 'parameters'. The only comparable 'case' is that of Marguerite Sèchehaye's treatment of 'Renée'.[233] 'But,' Boss said posthaste, 'these are not [the] usual ways I do psychotherapy. This was an exceptional case. This was not a neurosis, a psychoneurosis, but, rather, a real schizophrenic psychosis and with such individuals you have to take on a completely different method of treatment. But you shouldn't generalize form this – it's unique to these kinds of patients.'[234] Not surprisingly, Boss saluted his analysands, 'who forced me to go beyond what our psychology had taught.'[235]

Understandably, the question came up about just how to decide when intervention is called for in daseinanalysis. Were there any principles to follow? 'Yes: that you can't, let's say, charge or ask more of a patient than he or she can bear and that you have to *feel it in your fingertips* [emphasis added].'[236] That is, 'you try to give or do no more for a patient than is absolutely necessary: the *patient* has to be responsible the whole way, if possible, *if possible*. But not all patients are able to be as adult or mature as is necessary in order to handle a really orthodox patient-doctor [daseinsanalytic] relationship.'

Boss referred to 'psychotic' or 'borderline' cases and 'melancholic' cases (in the terminology of the *DSM-5-TR*, now termed a form of 'major depressive disorder'): 'You can't have a melancholic just lie here (gesturing to his couch) and have the ordinary, orthodox way of treatment. You see I have a couch also! I am not treating patients any more but future analysts. But when I still had many patients, most of them, by *far*, were lying on this couch in a typical, externally seen typical Freudian arrangement.' When asked if Boss allowed his patients to sit up, get up, walk around, and such, Boss replied: 'Yes . . . but patients, they *themselves* try to go back to the couch. I leave this whole room to my patients, at their disposal. Nevertheless, I say the best way for you to come to know yourself and develop what you really are is this way of being there on the couch for yourself, independent of me. There, you're not influenced by my facial expressions, my gestures and so on. But it's not an absolute law. If you feel like lying on the floor or standing on your head, you may do so but what the limits are is my skin.'

Asked about how being harmed physically or embraced affectionately by an analysand are 'outside the limits', Boss was plainly sensible: 'Ja. Ja. I explain to them why: because I'm only a human being too and if I would allow you to handle me physically like this then I would lose my complete freedom in a relationship with you and it would no longer be possible to help you to acquire your own freedom. So these are the limits. Handshakes, nevertheless are not unusual with me. There may be handshakes coming and leaving, but not embracing.'[237] When asked about his consulting room 'being at the disposal' of the analysand and what he would do if someone were to become angry, get up and walk over to his bookcase, say, and start throwing his books around: 'Yes, uh, I try to tell them that they have to pay for any damage.' 'So, they are free – but they must be responsible!' said Craig. 'Yes, so that doesn't happen.'

The conversation returned to Heidegger, whose ideas, Boss said, he has not tried to modify or develop further or to be critical of, but has tried to adapt for therapeutic work. As for Heidegger and psychiatry, said Boss, '*he knew nothing about psychotherapy* [emphasis added]. I had forced him up in the room where he lived and slept and studied, forced him to read some works by Freud. He hadn't read anything of Freud's. So he was shaking [his head] like that'. (Boss 'smirks and mimics Heidegger's head shaking with comical imitation'): 'He couldn't believe that such an intelligent man could write such stupid things, such fantastic hypothetical things, about women and men.'[238]

Boss's own appreciation of Freud was lifelong, even though he entirely rejected his metapsychology. For example, he remained a member of the International Psychoanalytic Association and the Swiss Psychoanalytic Society. 'I have remained true to the society because I am so grateful for what Freud had done for me and because I couldn't have become a daseinsanalyst without what Freud taught me ... And, uh, these people are rather tolerant and so I was never thrown out and am still a member of the national society.'

The interview then turned to the future of daseinanalysis, which is, of course, of central importance to the present book. In 1988, Boss was optimistic that people like Craig 'have been impressed by the width and breadth of this way of approaching things. But I [chuckling] ... I don't think about the future of daseinsanalysis. It's completely stupid because you can't make such a future. If it's something worthwhile it will grow and remain; or it may die. But it depends on the daseinsanalysts and on the recipients. There may come a time when the people will not be open to the meaning of what daseinsanalysis or of what Martin Heidegger has found, has seen, has discovered. Maybe their minds will be closed or maybe they will grow even more open. That doesn't depend on me. I did what I could to tell it, to hand on what I had received from Heidegger, but daseinsanalysis has its own future now, its own fate .... So now daseinsanalysis has to make its own way.'[239] The daseinanalytic outlook was and is of the greatest interest to psychotherapy in general, but Boss also saw that it had also been of value in relation to art, including the work of Paul Klee that was being carried out at the time by one of Boss's students.[240] He also recognized its importance for ecology and sociology.

During their second meeting, the conversation was less structured, organized around the general theme of what daseinanalysis might contribute to humanistic psychology in America. Boss's understanding of 'humanistic' was perhaps different from Craig's, since four days earlier Boss had been careful to say that daseinanalysis was not a 'human-centered' approach. Saying that 'there is no other psychology but humanistic psychology,' he was likely distinguishing between what was originally called 'comparative psychology', which originated at the end of nineteenth century and was represented in the States especially by Conway Lloyd Morgan (1852-1936), an ethologist and contemporary of Freud. 'What we call 'psychology' of the animals and so on [i.e., comparative psychology], that's anthropomorphizing of the animals and has nothing to do with what is psychology.' However, in the States and elsewhere, as Boss well knew, this basic fact had not prevented the founding of laboratories for the study of the behavior of pigeons, mice and rats, with the aim of 'applying' its findings to human beings.

Having addressed the problem of a 'psychology' of the animals', Boss had some further thoughts on the future of daseinanalysis. 'All I can tell you is to repeat that I had to find some other understanding, a different understanding, than what I was taught here by my medical, psychological and psychiatric studies in Europe.'[241]

Boss also dismissed the then popular works of neurophysiologists such as John Eccles (1903-1997), who claimed that research on the structure of the brain was to lead the way in understanding human psychological life. This was, of course, the beginning of the burgeoning world of neuroscience. Citing the search for the engram in the cells of brain tissue as an example of such research in the neurosciences, Boss said: 'I think this is a big error.'[242]

He returned to the dual influence of Heidegger and his experiences in India as crucial and formative for his change of orientation as a therapist and for the origins of therapeutic daseinanalysis. In the context of some comments on *Da-sein*, which made clear that the '*da*' of '*Da-sein*' does *not* mean 'there' as a location but rather 'the world openness, the whole realm we are living in, from the start', he reminded Craig: 'For instance, even the basic reason why you could come out here to me now and have this discussion is that you, from the start as a human being, are an openness into which I came by my books first or by people or disciples of mine. You encountered me and I encountered you in this way. But to encounter something in this way has a presupposition. It means that you have to be an open being, a perceiving being, an understanding being, from the start. It means that you can hear and understand that there is something, some Medard Boss, who is also a human being and who is thinking about human existence and is treating people. But you have to be open in order to be able to understand at all, to have found this place and to have come here, I don't know, either by train or by bus... By just being able to come here you *see*, at the same time, you *see* that you are open, that you are an openness into which I could come and stay.'[243]

An important statement about the spatiality of *Dasein* was included in further comments to Craig: 'You are coming now from St. Moritz. So you were in St. Moritz but at the same time you were already with *me*. You rang me up, for instance, so therefore I would have to be 'in your mind' [i.e., you had me 'in mind']. But you are nothing but a 'mind' fundamentally and therefore *you were, at the same time, both in St. Moritz and with me in Zollikon* [emphasis added]. This is only possible on the basis of the fact that your existence is *expanded* [emphasis added] throughout the world, including St. Moritz and Zollikon at the same time. *That's not a supposition, that's what you experienced. It's what you experienced immediately* [emphasis added]. And otherwise, if you could not experience your openness, your openness including at least St. Moritz and Zollikon, you couldn't have come and found this place. Ja, it's important to know, to state, that this supposition is not a *mental*, a mental artifact; not a mental artifact, but a *fact*, what you experienced.... Usually, one doesn't think of this miraculous fact that this human existence is an expanded understanding, expanded from the start through the whole world, what you call the world. But otherwise it wouldn't be possible for you to come from St. Moritz to this place in this way. That's the *proof*.'[244]

Boss continued: 'So this sight, this seeing, is what the whole of daseinsanalysis, what Heidegger's teaching has taught me: that is, only to open my eyes.' In its application to therapy, 'this is the whole direction that phenomenology or daseinsanalysis can give to a patient: to help him open his eyes and to look at the things themselves and not to build theories beforehand and then to look through the theories to the human being.' Thus 'being a realm of open understanding' is 'primarily our essential way of being... This is nothing physical: it's no object, it can't be objectified. It is an essence [in and] of itself and can't be reduced to anything else.' Finally, further to *Mitsein*, 'human existence means that all human beings are together from the start and are building up together or forming together this openness of the world just as the different rays of the sun are building together the light of day.'[245]

Craig raised the question of the extent of the responsibility of the daseinanalyst himself as a human being to be the open realm Boss had described, which brought the discussion round to the difference between what is a human-centered and a be[-ing]-centered [*Sein*] human therapy. No doubt, Craig had a hard time making this distinction clear to the humanistic psychologists whom he was representing for the journal in which the interview was published. Boss makes it plain, however, that for him 'humanistic means *according to the essence of human existence*' and not based on the principles of Renaissance humanism which puts the human being at the center of things.[246] As understood by daseinanalysis, the human being is not the center of things. Following Heidegger, the center of things is *Sein* (the be[-ing] of beings of whatever sort, including human being or *Dasein*) and the place of *Dasein* is essentially as the guardian or shepherd [*Hirt*] of be[-ing]. *Dasein as* keeping open the question of be[-ing] and *Dasein as* keeping the world open for what can be encountered are the same.[247]

For Boss, the role has about it great dignity. Serving as an openness for what can be encountered is especially important for working with analysands, who, as what is encountered, are served by the analyst in his being open. An appreciation of this is nothing that the analyst can learn from reading about it. It comes of being immersed in such openness. 'If you allow yourself to be soaked, totally, by these insights, then you are changing yourself and this change in yourself as a human being is what most helps your patients. What really *helps* [emphasis added] is not so much what you know intellectually, but your actual being together with your patients in the knowledge of this task of engagement of human be-ing.'[248]

We understand the sense of be[ing] [*Sein*] only if we see 'to be [*sein*]' as an action verb. Such be[ing] ranges over any doing or goings-on in the therapeutic setting. It is not what I do as a therapist that matters, but what and how I *exist* that is therapeutic. Of course, this means that to exist as fully as possible, to be an openness to the greatest extent possible, is to be human to the greatest extent possible. The analyst's greater extensiveness of existing is taken in by the analysand and, with any luck, taken on by him in his own way. The very being together with the analysand is therapeutic if it understood 'in the knowledge of this task of engagement of human be-ing'. Boss added: 'This gives you, the therapist, the freedom in which and into which the patient may develop his potentialities to exist, to communicate with other people and with himself. That's the main factor.' Knowledge of facts from the disciplines of medicine and psychology is not what 'matters most but, rather, it's this basic change in your attitude towards everything that you encounter and that encounters you.'[249] Boss noted that encounter [*Begegnung*] in daseinanalysis is its *sine qua non*[250], repeating that it was to the influence of both Heidegger and the Indian 'saints' with whom he stayed for a period of time that he attributed his having learned to open his eyes as the eyes of Heidegger and above all Govind Kaul had been opened.

Boss reminded Craig that, if he looked around, he would see that the consulting room in which they were meeting 'looks very much like I'm a Freudian.' Indeed: 'In fact, I think I'm more Freudian, a more truly Freudian, a more faithfully Freudian therapist, than Freud was himself. Freud spoiled his insight and his genius by his belief that only natural scientific thinking leads to truth.'[251]

By 1988, the presence of a couch would have been unusual in all but the offices of psychoanalysts. The humanistic psychologists reading the interview would scarcely have had any idea of the importance of the 'furnishings' to daseinanalysis. A return of the couch to the therapist's consulting room would have amounted to a revolution then, since psychotherapists always sat *vis-à-vis* their patients. It marks a revolution now in the first quarter of the 21st century. No doubt part of the resistance to daseinanalysis then and now has had to do precisely with understanding the meaning of using the couch in daseinanalysis.

As the interview continued, a discussion of psychosomatics led to the question about why Heidegger had written so little about the body. 'Heidegger told me that he wrote only a few lines about the body [in *Being and Time*] because this is the most difficult thing. At that time, when he wrote *Sein und Zeit*, he didn't know more about it.'[252] It did, however, become a theme of the Zollikon seminars, especially in the context of the so-called 'psyche'-body relationship,' and most certainly because of the concerns of the psychiatrists who attended the seminars, all of whom had been trained as medical doctors to *see* the body as an object. Boss confirmed Craig's observation that Heidegger had learned much about about the body from his younger Swiss colleague. The remaining moments of the second interview were therefore devoted to a discussion about the phenomenon, including behavior or comportment, and existing as 'a bundle of possibilities of behaving'. Several 'psychosomatic' cases were reviewed.

[111]

The Boss-Craig 'encounter' ended with the appearance of Boss's therapeutic motto. Observing that 'your aim as a therapist is to serve for the patient as a human existence which has become *free*, in the wider sense, *free* to be engaged with what is encountered and to help that which comes to you to develop further. You have only to show your patients where you see they are limited, where they are caught and unable to carry out their own possibilities for perceiving [taking in, *Vernehmen*] and relating to things.' With that Boss reprised the fundamental difference between psychoanalysis and daseinanalysis. Referring to the *Grundriß*, he said: 'I once tried to qualify the difference between psychoanalysis and daseinsanalysis . . . by saying psychoanalysis always asks 'Why?' in a causal way, whereas daseinsanalysis asks 'Why not?' *Why not* try to behave more freely?' Boss continued: 'Daseinsanalysis tries to help patients not to fight against what they are encountering but to love it, to accept it . . . . If you are able to cope with that which encounters you then you needn't defend yourself against it. You can have a party with it or you can love it.'

And, with that and without missing a beat: 'Well, I'm afraid our time is gone.'[253]

Interlude

With these sketches of Boss's life, published over a twenty year period, in the background we will turn in Part (II) to several themes central to daseinanalysis as Boss discussed them in his publications. As a transition, however, Boss's dialogues from 1976 with the Korean psychiatrist, Dongshick Rhee, offer both personal and theoretical material for what I take to be a unifying theme when considering the place of daseinanalysis in contemporary practice, and that is its having a source in Eastern philosophy as well as in Heidegger's thought, with which, as Boss had said in his interview with Craig, there are some remarkable points of congruence.

The exchanges made available as '**Dialogue Between Prof. Medard Boss and Prof. Dongshick Rhee** (1996)'[254] are not well known but were brought to the attention of therapists by Yrjö O. Alanen, Manuel González de Chávez**,** Ann-Louise S. Silver and Brian Martindale.[255] Boss and Dongshick Rhee (1920-2014), a Korean psychiatrist, conversed in German during Rhee's two fifty-minute interviews with Boss in the summer of 1976.[256] The texts are seriously flawed in the form we have them, since they are evidently translations from conversations held in German that were audiotaped and then likely transcribed by Rhee, published in Korean, and then translated into English for their online presentation. I have taken substantial liberties in cleaning up the transcriptions as printed on Rhee's website, which presumably replicates and translates what is found in the Korean journal article referenced.[257] The transcripts are valuable in that they contain comments that may stimulate discussion about Boss the person, his relationship with Heidegger, and the connections between Rhee's 'tao psychotherapy' and daseinanalysis. For the rest, the mix of chattiness and references to serious questions makes for fascinating reading. Unfortunately, limitations of space prevent presenting them in their entirety. A very quick overview must suffice, which it is hoped will encourage the reader to locate the dialogues online.

Perhaps of greatest interest from an historical perspective is Boss's comment to Rhee that all of the Zollikon seminars were audio-taped. The whereabouts of the tapes was not revealed, but they may be among his *Nachlaß*. Just as important is the discussion of 'Western' and 'Eastern' approaches to psychotherapy.

Rhee identifies *Tao* with *Verborgenheit* (hiddenness) and Boss agrees. *Unverborgenheit* (unconcealment), of course, is Heidegger's translation of the Greek *alētheia* (truth). The two sage clinicians consider that in the midst of this hiddenness (the *tao*), existence [*Dasein*] is the place of luminance [*Lichtung*], openness and revelation in the darkness of *lēthe* (forgetfulness), the disappearance of which is *alētheia* (truth).

Heidegger's frequent references to *Weg* (which readily identifies with *tao*) also come to mind, from *Der Feldweg* (*The Country Trail*) [1949] to the titles of his anthologies of papers, *Holzwege* (*Stray Ways*) [1950] and *Wegmarken* (*Waymarkers*) [1967], and the motto of his *Gesamtausgabe*: '*Wege nicht Werke* (Ways not Works)'. The deeper connections between *tao* as hiddenness and way merit exploration.

Talking with Boss, Rhee came to appreciate even more deeply the influence of Eastern philosophy on Boss and, so, on daseinanalysis By the end of the second interview, however, both men had stressed that it is dangerous to simply introduce the practice of either of the approaches – 'Eastern' and 'Western' – into the culture of the other.[258] That said, as I have suggested several times, the extent to which daseinanalysis is indebted to Hindu philosophy has still not been fully appreciated.

(II) Publications on Selected Themes

We turn now to a review of (A) what I take to be Boss' essential contributions to the theory and practice of daseinanalysis as it developed from 1951 to 1988, (B) texts on the influence of Eastern philosophy on his thought and practice and, in turn, on the distinguishing features of daseinanalysis, and (C) several contributions by Boss on Martin Heidegger, whose work and friendship were central to the development of therapeutic daseinanalysis. In this review we will discuss in more detail many of the basic themes of daseinanalysis outlined in Part I.[259]

(A) The Theory and Practice of Daseinanalysis (1947-1988)

Boss's book on the paraphilias (1947), which had already been decisively influenced by Heidegger's thought, was his debut for English-speaking readers.[260] Two years after the English edition of the book appeared (1949), Boss published the first article in which he worked out in detail the sense of the *daseinsanalytisch* (daseinsanalytic) approach. This is his '**Contribution on the Existential Analytic Foundation of Psychiatric Thinking**' (1951b)[261].

Noting that no science approaches its subject matter without presuppositions, Boss points to psychiatry understood as medical psychology as being no exception. With its focus on symptoms – that is, reports of experience – it differs from other areas of specialization in medicine which take observed signs of suspected disease as definitive for diagnosis, albeit without ignoring symptoms. Medicine in general takes the perspective on illness that any manifestation of disease must be explicable causally. The underlying disease process must be identified before any treatment is scientifically justified. However, psychiatry is limited by such 'objectifying and atomizing thinking. For most of the phenomena that occupy it are symptoms of illness [*Krankheitserscheinungen*] that involve [*Mitleidenschaft ziehen*] the human being as human being [*den Menschen als Menschen*]. This way of thinking proves to be particularly inadequate with regard to the specifically [*spezifisch*] human.'[262]

Even when there are observable lesions or documented physiological disturbances, symptoms (for example, in the case of schizophrenia, a delusion of grandeur [*Größenwahn*], or in an affective disturbance such as the manic phase [*manisch-depressiven Irresein*] of what we would now call bi-polar disorder) cannot be understood as effects [*Wirkungen*] of structural changes in brain cells or the functioning of the nervous system. Just as little can dysfunctions of the psychodynamic apparatus postulated by psychoanalytic theory *cause* such symptoms. 'No psychiatrist who talks like this has ever tried to imagine how he actually imagines the 'sitting [*Sitzung*]' of affects [said to be 'seated'] in the brain stem, with much the same problem of imagining how ideas 'lie' in a 'substrate' or 'underlying layer' of the prefrontal cortex.' A mood, for example, is a feature of the existing person, not the manifestation of an organic process. So also for all psychiatric symptoms.

As for the psychoanalytic explanation, Boss asks: 'How could such different things as an id, and ego and a superego emerge from a physical thing [*Körperding*], and how could these objects [*Gegenstände*] together take notice [*Notiz nehmen*] of an outer world [*Außenwelt*] and grasp [*greifen*] it in an understanding way or be stopped in this grasping!' Therefore 'technical thinking in the field of psychiatry leads us from one difficulty of understanding to another. Recently, attempts have been made to remedy this [*Übelstand*] by speaking of the body-soul-spirit unity [*Leib-Seele-Geist-Einheit*] of man. But such talk gets caught in a mere catch phrase, as long as this 'unity' and 'wholeness [*Ganzheit*]' is not specifically and expressly thought of in terms of its being [*Sein*].' This gives Boss the opportunity to express the basic daseinanalytic insight that

> to be a human being does not mean to be any thing or conglomerate of things among other things occurring in this world. For man is neither a body-thing [*Körperding*] nor is he a soul-spirit-thing [*Seelen-Geist-Ding*] in the sense of a primarily worldless subject to which objects in the world outside are made available [*beigestellt*]. For worldless objects that merely appear next to each other can never actually touch [have an effect on] [*berühen*] each other in the sense that one could actually affect [*rühen*] the other and be perceived [*wahrgenommen*], [be] understood [*verstehen*] by him. For this, such a primarily worldless subject thing would first have to climb out of itself over to the things of the world, would have to transcend from out of itself, or the things for their part would have to transcend out of themselves over into the subject thing. Why and how, however, such a subjective or objective *transcendence* [emphasis added] can take place or even be possible in an originally worldless subject

thing is hard to understand [*nicht einzustehen*]. Subjective as well as objective transcendence presuppose an immanence [*Immanenz*] which is never talked about as part of the actuality [*Wirklichkeit*] of man. Rather, being human is from the very beginning a being open [*Offensein*], an understanding 'luminating [*Lichten*]' of the world.... It is an existing [*Existieren*] in the literal sense of the word ek-sistence [*Ek-sistenz*], namely, an original already being out there at the things and together with others [*Schon-immer-draußen-bei-den-Dingen-und-Mitmenschen-Sein*] – better still, a being toward things [*Zu-den-Dingen-Sein*] and a \being toward others [*Zu-den-Mitmenschen-Sein*].[263]

These formulations, which reflect an orientation to Heidegger's analytics of *Dasein*, are also prescient of Heidegger's later essay on *Gelassenheit* and the expression '*Gelassenheit zu den Dinge* (serenity about things)'.[264]

Boss contrasts the psychoanalytic notion of a 'primary total narcissism or complete autoerotism [*Autoerotismus*]' with Heidegger's emphasis on our original togetherness with others [*Mitsein*], at first with only *one* other, the natal mother, as of the very nature of human being. Freud's postulate of a monadic, encapsulated, undifferentiated 'It'-like matrix from which the 'I' differentiates requires a theory of how that given 'I' (for example, a newborn) attaches to another given 'I' (for example, its mother) by somehow escaping the bounds of its insularity and making contact with the other. Much the same problem holds for the theory of intrapsychic objects (self, other) developed in 'object relations theory'. Given the *Mitsein* of human being, the problem of attachment is seen to be a pseudo-problem. It brings into question the theoretical work of, among others, Donald Winnicott and John Bowlby.

This important contribution continues with a discussion of the problem of the subject with reference to both Ludwig Binswanger's and Jean-Paul Sartre's misunderstanding and misappropriation of Heidegger. Boss stresses that the primary and principal concern of a human being understood as *Dasein* is not its subjectivity or 'I-ness [*Ichheit*]'. Instead, 'it is always about being in the world as a whole [*als Ganzes*], about being unto things and others [*Zu-den-Dingen-und-Mitmenschen-Sein*] and being on the lookout for [*Hüten*][265] the truth of being lighting up [*leuchtend*] in human existence.'

Boss concludes the contribution with references to the *Gestimmtheit* or *Stimmung* (ontological tuning or mood) of existence and the kind of spatiality and temporality 'determined by the given mood in which the world is revealed [*entbirgt*] to a human being' in every instance. The metaphor of attunement is borrowed from music. The 'key' to which existence is tuned determines 'the range [*Auswahl*] of references to [what is in the] world and their colorations [*Farbungen*]' from which existence can make its choices of what to attend to.[266] These are elements in harmony with the home key. This attunement is understood as 'the basis for an original efflorescence [*Sich-Erschließen*][267] of the world.' Forming an interval or chord or creating a melody, existence begins 'tuned' to a given key. In his poetic way, Boss writes of the 'melody of existence [*Daseinsmelodie*]' in such cases as being 'tuned to the superabundance of love' but without an outlet for its expression.

An effect of daseinanalysis is that the world begins to 'make' sense to the analysand, a sense that has been there all along but has remained inaccessible. The 'original accessibility to the world in accordance with the given mood can [then] unfold in [our] moving about [*Umgehen*], acting and thinking in the surrounding world.' Most of the time this leads to contact with things and others, but in some instances it eventuates in the self-isolating world of the schizophrenic or, to cite another example Boss gives, in the symptoms of the individual with an 'organ neurosis', whose physical expressiveness is 'dammed up' in the individual's own bodiliness [*Leiblichkeit*]. Boss mentions cases where sexual bodiliness is constrained.

The following year, on February 25, 1952, Boss gave a lecture in West Berlin for RIAS [Broadcasting in the American Sector]. The lecture, '**The Significance of Daseinsanalysis for Psychology and Psychiatry**' (1952b)[268], is perhaps Boss's earliest iteration of therapeutic daseinanalysis for a general audience.

> Daseinsanalyse is neither philosophy, nor is it in itself a psychotherapeutic procedure. It is a new, empirical research method or approach. Its meaningfulness for psychology and psychiatry can hardly be overestimated for two reasons [*Gründe*]. First, it forces us to think about and at the same time enables us to examine the conceptual presuppositions and basic ideas of these sciences for their appropriateness to the nature [*Wesen*] of man. On the other hand, it also gives completely new impulses to concrete psychological and psychiatric research and opens up questions that were previously completely hidden. This double significance is based on its simple demand to leave behind all theoretical abstractions and conceptual constructions and to return to the immediately given phenomena [*Erscheinungen*]. Things and people thus tell us immediately – that is, without the mediation of any internal psychic processes – about their essence from themselves, from their own way of appearing.
>
> But how did the thinking and questions of psychiatry and psychology, which have been decisive up to now, deal with the objects of their investigations, with the mental phenomena [*seelischen Phänomenen*] of man? Obviously, these two sciences started from exactly the same intuitive presuppositions on which the technically so successful natural sciences have already erected their intellectual edifice.
>
> Technical-scientific thinking, however, originates from the belief that the whole world and its mechanisms are nothing else than an accumulation of existing [*vorhandenen*] objects which are able to interact with each other, which stand among themselves in predictable causal relationships. Everything that is, is just represented [*vorgestellt*] as an effecting bringing about [of something] [*als ein wirkend Wirken*]. It is inevitable that the scientific-causal thinking originating from such a pre-scientific basic idea had to shift its weight more and more to the working [*Wirken*] and effecting [*Erwirken*] of something, for the sake of mere effect [*Wirkung*] or performance. The question, however, about what the things, the living beings and the human beings are in themselves, the

question, therefore, about their actual being, from which all their productivity can arise, was completely forgotten.[269]

Four years later, daseinanalysis became more widely known outside of publications for the medical community. **'Daseinsanalysis' and Psychotherapy**' (1956b)[270] was first published in a newspaper founded at the University of Göttingen in 1949. This brief introduction to daseinanalysis was then translated into English for inclusion in the second of a five-volume series published between 1956 and 1960 on new developments in psychotherapy. It was also Boss's first appearance in a major book-length publication for American psychiatrists. Reflecting its importance, five years later (the same year that the English translation of *Sein und Zeit* was published), it was reprinted in Hendrik Ruitenbeek's influential anthology of essays on 'the important influence of existentialism on modern psychoanalysis'. Contributors to the anthology included Binswanger, R. D. Laing, Jan van den Berg, Paul Tillich and Rollo May.

In the reprint, Ruitenbeek writes that 'Medard Boss's essay on *Daseinsanalysis* is a 'wonderfully lucid discussion of Heidegger's influence on existential analysis.'[271] Unfortunately, it is far from lucid and a less than auspicious debut of Boss to a wide audience of psychoanalysts, philosophers and psychotherapists. If Boss translated the text, it is odd that he refers again and again to 'the Daseinsanalysis' and 'the human dasein', and once to 'the daseinsanalytic thinking'. We read of 'Heidegger's Existential Analysis (Daseinsanalysis)', thus conflating two therapeutic approaches, *Daseinsanalyse* and the *Existenzanalyse* (existential analysis) of Viktor Frankl.[272] We recall that, as it became an independent and vigorous movement of its own, for a time Frankl's logotherapy was termed *Existenzanalyse*[273]. *Daseinsanalyse* as 'existential analysis' also became confused with the variety of forms of existential psychotherapy represented in the publication *Existence*.[274] Boss does help the reader, however, by pointing out that 'the term 'existential analysis' has come [already by 1956] to include a variety of philosophical, scientific, psychopathologic and psychotherapeutic schools of thought. Although they differ in their methods and goals, they are all derivatives of Heidegger's Daseinsanalysis.'[275] This is often forgotten in contemporary discussions of 'existential analysis'.

For psychiatrists and psychoanalysts whose first exposure to daseinanalysis was the influential Masserman/Moreno volume, it cannot have been a very helpful beginning. The word 'Dasein' is not defined. Even given an adequate understanding of Heidegger's thought, statements such as the following must have been puzzling to readers: 'Man's special manner of being-in-the-world can ... only be compared to the shining of a light, in the brightness of which the presence of all that is can occur .... Man is fundamentally an essentially spiritual brightness and as such he genuinely exists in the world. As this world-revealing brightness he is claimed by the ultimate be-ness. If a primordial understanding of be-ness were not the very essence of man' nothing would have meaning. Just what 'be-ness' might mean must have been anyone's guess.

Objects and other people, we read, have meaning 'only because man is intrinsically 'brightness' in the sense of being a primordial understanding of be-ness . . . ..

Humanity, as a whole, therefore, is best comparable to the full brightness of the day which also consists of the shining-together of all individual sun rays.'[276] Most would have been baffled by all of the talk of lights, brightness and the sun. Boss was, of course, familiar with Heidegger's notion of luminance [Lichtung], which is referenced here, but it is not metaphoric for the light studied by physicists. Boss is therefore helpful in carefully explaining that 'even physical light cannot appear as light unless it encounters an object and can make it shine,' yet just what this 'brightness' is supposed to denote remains undetermined.

Reading on: 'Because of this being-together-in-the-world the world is always one which I share with others, the world of 'dasein' is a world-of-togetherness.' Boss wants the reader to understand what is unique about daseinanalysis, namely, that it is founded in an understanding of *ontological* being-with [Mitsein], which makes any ontic relationship such as that between analyst and analysand possible. In the sentence just quoted, however, talk of world is not sufficiently nuanced for it to make sense in elucidating the connections between (a) the *Mitsein* (being-with) of every existence [Dasein], (b) the indistinguishability (other than verbal) of *Dasein* and *In-der-Welt-sein* (being-in-the-world), (c) man's existing with others [Mitdasein], and (d) an understanding of (the) world [Welt] as a *Mitwelt* (world with others). All of these terms appear in the passage in *Sein und Zeit* to which Boss refers, which surely should have been presented, but was not.[277]

Boss wanted to communicate to the therapist that insight into Heidegger's view of the nature of man will provide him with

> a more reliable and all-embracing attitude toward his patient and the therapeutic process. If the therapist really understands that man is intrinsically a world-unfolding and world-opening being, in the sense that, in him, as the bright sphere of be-ness comparable to a glade in a forest, all things, plants, animals and fellowmen can show and reveal themselves directly and immediately in all their significance and correlations, then he will have an unceasing reverence for the proper value of each phenomenon he encounters . . . . The daseinsanalytic understanding of man makes the analyst gain so deep a respect for all the phenomena he encounters that it bids him to abide even more fully and more firmly by the chief rule of psychoanalysis than Freud himself could, handicapped as he still was by theoretical prejudices. The therapist will now, according to Freud's technical prescriptions, really be able to accept as equally genuine all the new possibilities for communication which grow 'on the play area of the transference,'[278] without mutilating them through his own intellectual and theoretical prejudices and his personal affective censure.[279]

We have here an early presentation of the fundamental notion that, for daseinanalysis, transference is a mere hypothesis which belies what really goes on in therapy. Reference to a glade would have given the perceptive reader a better idea of the openness to which Boss was referring, namely, a place in the midst of a great density which has been thinned out in which things will have a place to be seen in their individuality and singularity. Boss is also clear here about the importance of 'the divine' in daseinanalysis, which he says will 'reveal itself during psychoanalysis'.[280] Of course, this feature of daseinanalysis sets it apart from psychoanalysis, since, as we know, for Freud, divinity is merely an artefact of childish projection.

The article concludes with further discussion of *Mitsein*, the 'being-together [of analyst and analysand] which is of such intrinsic and essential a nature that no man can in fact perceive another even in the distance, without already – through the mere means of perceiving – being involved in the other's particular world-relatedness in some specific way. Thus, from the very first encounter between the therapist and patient the therapist is already together with his patient's way of existing, just as the patient already partakes in the therapist's manner of living . . . .'[281] If the reader had reached this point in the text, he would with 'knowledge of just this one essential trait of man' understood from the Heideggerian perspective, have a sense of a basic feature of daseinanalytic praxis, namely, the mutual involvement of analyst and analysand in each other's existing [*Existieren*]. Doubts would have remained, however, about the relation of notions such as 'be-ness' to the therapeutic endeavor.

A translation of Boss's first book on dreaming life (1953d) was made available in 1958, followed by the publication in 1959 of the translation of an early paper (1938b) on dreams in schizophrenia and what were then called the 'organic psychoses' for a volume on *Dreams and Personality Dynamics*. The following year, the essay '**Ego? Motivation?**' (1960b)[282] appeared in the newly founded *Journal of Existential Psychiatry* of the American Ontoanalytic Association.[283] (Beginning in 1964, the journal was renamed the *Journal of Existentialism*.) The appearance of his paper in a journal of 'existential psychiatry' may account in part for why Boss came to be connected with the more general movement known as existential psychotherapy as it was developing in the States. But we must never forget that Heidegger was no Existentialist. Nor was Boss.

The origin of the text was a congress in Bonn. Boss participated in many international congresses on psychiatry, psychoanalysis, psychosomatics and psychotherapy, but this seems to represent the only contribution to a congress at which he spoke on *psychology per se*,[284] which accounts for the opening comment about 'my serious ignorance of psychological matters'.[285] It is an important contribution in distancing daseinanalysis from academic psychology and, by association, from the form of applied psychology known as clinical psychology.

Boss is explicit that daseinanalysis has nothing to do with psychology as a science. As his critique claims, if daseinanalysis is taken seriously, 'we shall in time have to give up the notion of the 'psyche' itself, which in an . . . inadmissible way reifies the being of man. In this way, no doubt, psychology would be deprived of the object of its study, the 'psyche' in fact, and could no longer continue as a science bearing this name.'[286] This, he says, would not be 'regrettable'. With respect to the liberation of a genuinely human therapy, it would be an inevitable and necessary break.

The title itself is ironic: 'Ego? Motivation?' These are 'two things . . . the origin and nature of which I, after all, have not the slightest notion.'[287] This must hold for any psychologist, for whom these concepts are introduced and accepted uncritically. Boss presents his already well-known attack on Freud's metapsychology. The term 'instance' which is used in the lecture would have been familiar to his audience, but not perhaps to readers of the standard English translation of Freud. It is Freud's term for an authority [*Instanz*] in the psyche understood as an apparatus. Boss reminds us that Freud's introduction of the term was by analogy with what 'is, after all, a legal concept. It really always refers to an authority, especially to a court, which is empowered to pronounce judgments and make decisions.'[288] The point Boss makes is that such an agency and a 'drive-determined' cause of behavior are 'utterly incompatible notions'. A cause acts blindly, but an ego implies agency. A concept cannot act, as little as can a molecule of serotonin or one of the structural theory's trinity id [*Es*], ego [*Ich*] and superego [*Überich*].

The 'insoluble inner contradiction' of Freud's model was perpetuated by Jung's analytical psychology and by the school of ego psychology, represented here by Heinz Hartmann (1894-1970), Ernst Kris (1900-1957) and Rudolf Lowenstein (1898-1976).[289] There is no possibility of 'an ego instance which decides on something outside of itself'. Rightly understood, talk of a self 'is always merely a human being's reference to relationships with a world, to the way in which a world addresses us and the way in which we belong to a world in which a human being with his fellows finds himself at any precisely given time, has found himself, or will find himself.'[290] Uttering the word 'I' indicates that one has already 'expressly considered and accepted ... the life possibilities belonging to his own existence'.[291] Such behavior does not emanate from some interiority seeking a way out of itself, to transcend itself to meet what there is 'out there' somewhere beyond the confines of our integument. Thus, 'the being of man consists not of psychic entities, not of instances [agencies or systems in operation], but always merely of the possibilities of behavior over against what is encountered, which show themselves at a given time.' That being the case, 'the fundamental nature of the being of man must consist in an entirely primary and immediate capacity to understand and elucidate the earthly and divine things encountering it as the phenomena they are.'[292]

Man acts, but not in response to stimuli whether visual, acoustic, gustatory, olfactory, or tactile emanating from nature. Reference to the five senses introduces the problem of perception, which Boss makes plain can never be understood by resorting to talk that begins with external stimuli and sensory receptors, as modern psychology does. Indeed, perception is assumed before any such problems and questions arise. It is the existing human being who perceives. Neural activity does not perceive. No connection between an 'outside world' and an 'inner world' must be established, since the distinction between inner and outer does not answer to the nature of our experience as existing beings. We are always already in-the-world, which means in meaningful relation to things and other people. Here, following Heidegger, world is not equivalent to external reality or to nature.

There is always the 'primary understanding and 'luminating' of the 'being of man' thanks to which that be[-ing] [*Sein*] has 'always been attracted by what encounters it and engaged by it as if we were addressed and summoned by what appears in the light of our existence.' The 'call and summons' of things entails responding 'on the levels of perceiving, hearing and acting so that the things intended for us can unfold themselves to the utmost fullness of their being.'[293] It is not hard to imagine that Boss's listeners felt challenged by Boss's indictment against psychology as such, although perhaps those who were visiting from the States felt even harder hit.[294] As we saw in Part I, daseinanalysis is not encompassed by the explanatory model of psychology, whether construed as a natural, social or human science, as little as it is by that of medicine and psychiatry. The same can be said about psychology's fellow modern social sciences, anthropology and sociology.

A brief overall synopsis of daseinanalysis was prepared two years later for an Indian journal. It is especially important since it followed on Boss's visits to the subcontinent and nearby Indonesia in 1958 and 1959. Echoes of his experience there can be heard and felt in his '**Outline of the Analysis of Dasein**' (1962a)[295], which appeared in a journal which seems to have had only one volume, perhaps even only one issue. The *Philosophical Bulletin* was published by M. G. Khajanchi in Ahmedabad for the Viśva Tattvajñāna Mandira (International Academy of Philosophy) as a quarterly journal, with co-editors Fritz-Joachim von Rintelen (Mainz) and P. T. Japur (Ahmedabad). Its editorial board included A. Boyce Gibson (an early champion of phenomenology among anglophone readers), Richard Wisser (whose filmed interview with Heidegger from 1969 is unique among such documents, a transcript of which was published in New Delhi by Arnold-Heinemann/Rakesh in a translation by B. Srinirasa Murthy), the philosophers Franklin Edgerton, Richard P. McKeon, Sidney Hook, Ernest Nagle and A. J. Ayer, and Medard Boss. It is not clear why a journal with such a remarkable representation of diverse schools of philosophy did not flourish.

A note to the title of the article says the text 'will also be published as Chapter 5 of the forthcoming book by the author: *Psychoanalysis and Analysis of Dasein*, Basic Books, Inc., publishers, New York, (1962).' The translator is given as Ludwig Lefebre. This suggests that the translation would correspond more or less to the original German Chapter 5, 'Abriß der Daseinsanalytik [Outline of the Analytics of Dasein]'. As we have seen, however, the English book published in 1963 turned out to be a much different text, with the 'Outline of the Analysis of Dasein' appearing as Chapter 2 of the volume. Boss' note also suggests that by the end of 1961, when three other chapters of the book had already been published in German, the given title of the book reflected more accurately the German original, since Heidegger sometimes referred to the *Daseinsanalytik* as a *Daseinsanalyse* or *Analyse des Daseins*.[296] A brief review of this brilliant text will allow us to see the earliest published version of the basic theoretical chapter in *Psychoanalysis and Daseinsanalysis*.

His 'outline', says Boss, 'must necessarily consist mainly of pointers and does not lay claim to completeness.'[297] 'Heidegger urges all those who deal with human beings to start seeing and thinking from the beginning, so that they can remain with what they immediately perceive and do not get lost in 'scientific' abstractions estranged from reality.' To begin with, 'Daseinsanalytic statements differ fundamentally from scientific deductions; they are at all times 'nothing but' pointers to phenomena which can be immediately perceived, but which, as such, can neither be derived from something else nor 'proved' in some way. At best, it is possible to make the essence of these phenomena appear in greater plasticity by illustration, using other phenomena of the same kind.'[298]

Not surprisingly, the starting point of the outline is the problem of perception. The 'magic' of how physical stimuli acting on sensory receptors is translated into visual, auditory, olfactory, gustatory and tactile 'images' (as things seen, things heard, and so on) by the higher centers of the human nervous system (chiefly the organizing areas of the cortex) has eluded psychologists and, in principle, *must remain a mystery*. This includes the account of academic psychology in which consciousness is famously sent out into the world (presumably by the brain) to capture such the objects emitting such stimuli for neural processing.

Although the Zollikon seminars were barely under way, Boss reminds readers of Heidegger's habit of introducing students to phenomenological seeing. Perhaps indirectly echoing an evening of one of the Zollikon seminars, Boss tells us that Heidegger 'usually starts his students' thinking' by asking them to 'tell him what actually takes place if they look out of the window and watch the yellow house across the street.' The students 'begin to realize that they first saw the yellow house immediately as this yellow house. From the beginning, they saw (and understood) that there was a yellow house over there.' Heidegger then asks students where they were 'while they were seeing the yellow house: right here, in the lecture room, perhaps, or within their consciousnesses?' Students realize that 'they were consumed immediately in perception of the house.' 'As human being,' Boss continues,

> our primary dwelling is 'outside' in the space of action constituted by relations to a thing, plant, animal, other human being, ourselves, to heaven or earth in their totality ... [A human being] is at any given moment nothing but in and as this or that perceiving, instinctual, impulsive, emotional, imaginative, dreaming, thinking, acting, willing or wishing relationship towards the things which he encounters.... [M]an is fundamentally 'out in the world' and with the things he encounters; his existence is originally a being-in-the-world.... He is there with the particular beings he encounters.[299]

Problems arise only 'when we start to reflect'. Then we disengage from the immediate, unmediated experience of looking at, listening to, feeling about, wishing for, and so on, and attempt to take the position of a neutral observer of our existence, the fabled 'view from nowhere'.[300] There is, of course, no such position, no such epistemological Archimedean point. Disengaged in such reflection, we are thinking about the experience, which is now no less real existentially than was the looking at the house, but merely in a different, detached mode. Yet we learn nothing about the perceiving of the yellow house in doing so, but instead begin to examine our reflection on what had previously happened. We begin what Jean Piaget called formal operational thinking, that is, thinking about thoughts.[301]

Heidegger is concerned with the ontological situation of the human being with respect to any 'seeing and understanding' in the ontological sense. This is possible only given the 'unique openness of man's existence ... [which is] able to disclose the particular beings which man encounters as the beings they are, with all the context of their meaningful references.' Boss gives the example of a mother encountering her newborn. Her 'emotional attitude' or what is also referred to as her attunement [*Stimmung*] to the newborn is based on an immediate understanding of the neonate she encounters. Something also happens in the newborn who sees and understands its mother. Notions of empathy, instinct and reflex are superfluous here. They imply the encounter and corresponsive openness of newborn and mother as *Dasein* to *Dasein* which has already occurred.

Boss returns to the example of one's taking in [*Vernehmen*] a house, over there across the street. Such *Vernehmen* is not the fabled perception [*Wahrnehmung*] of psychology. The encounter with it implies 'an understanding of the special essence of being, of the being-ness which is common to all possible houses in the world'. In turn, there is an even more primordial 'fundamental understanding that there is something there at all, against the possibility that there might be nothing at all', an 'immediate and primary awareness of 'Being-ness as such [*primäre Seinsverständnis*]". This is an understanding of 'Is-ness', which is not a property of something, one among many that could be included in a list of an entity's features.[302]

We next come across the familiar reference to Dasein, spoken of here as a 'realm of brightness [*Helligkeitsbereich*] of Being-ness'.[303] Boss clarifies the sense of the '*da* [there]' of *Da-sein*, distinguishing *Da-sein's* spatiality from the spatiality familiar to us from geometry and physics. For the latter, the determination *da* says that something is 'here' or 'there' at a particular place in the spatiotemporal manifold. By contrast, the spatiality of nearness [*Nähe*] and distance [*Ferne*] to which the *da* in *Da-sein* refers, is quite different. It is neither 'here' or 'there', nor both. *Da-sein* in its nearness (closeness or intimacy) or distance (alienation from) is 'essentially spatial, *because it is spiritual* [emphasis added]. No extended body-thing is spiritual, and for this reason it cannot be spatial in the way *Da-sein* is spatial. *Da-sein*, qua existent, has always previously found its world-disclosing sphere of activity, because *Da-sein* is essentially world-disclosure.'[304]

The translation of *Da-sein* as 'being-there' is illuminating in referring to *Da-sein's* spatiality as the whole *living room* which shows itself in and is illuminated by *Da-sein's* luminance of the whole system of references belonging to the things disclosed to it. If some special thing in a room is of great interest to me at the moment, if it means a great deal to me, I may want to approach it bodily. I want to *be in touch* with it in some way. In bodily approaching the thing, however, I have merely fulfilled my existential closeness to it in regard to the bodily sphere [*Leiblichkeit*] of my existence, a closeness which is first given. This 'closeness' [*Nähe*] is existential, not objective and measurable in units such as yards or meters. Existential closeness and distance are not quantifiable. Boss provides familiar examples of such 'closeness' (and 'distance'), to which I might add: I may be closer to someone whom I love who is a thousand miles away than to someone pressed up against me inside a subway car, and I may be distant from someone with whom I am entangled in bed having a 'hook-up'.

In the unified spatiotemporal manifold of the world, the attunement [*Stimmung*] of my *Da-sein* determines my taking in [*Nehmen*] of a thing given, its nearness or distance. From the perspective of human bodiliness [*Leiblichkeit*], everything given is different depending on my attunement when it is one, for example, of being-in-pain, being-hungry, or being-aroused.

We see once again that in encounter [*Begegnung*] or meeting, it is not the case that we just encounter things *or* that things just encounter us. Both elements of encounter are always in play together: '[A]s things cannot be without man, man cannot exist as what he is without that which he encounters.' This amounts to seeing the full implication for *Da-sein* as being in-the-world of everything, of 'thing, plant, animal, other human being, ourselves,... heaven or earth in their totality'. In other words,

> if things, plants, animals and fellow-men did not enable man to relate to them, how would he be capable of being in the world in the mode of luminating understanding of Being-ness? Not even so-called physical light can appear as light, unless it encounters things which make it shine forth. This means nothing less than that human being and what appears in the light of human existence are mutually dependent on each other to such an extent, that, for instance, *the questions: What and where were the things before there were men, and what will become of them when men no longer exist? are completely meaningless in the context of the analysis of Dasein* [emphasis added].[305]

In short, the human being and things encountered 'are so immediately integral that Heidegger can say of the relation between Being-ness and man that this relation supports everything, insofar as it brings forth both: the appearance of things and man's Dasein.'[306]

That same year (1962), Boss published a monograph dedicated to his children, Martin, Maya [Maia] and Urs Christian, 'in fatherly love'. An English translation of the small book was published as a journal article entitled '**Anxiety, Guilt and Psychotherapeutic Liberation**' (1962c).[307] It is one of seven important texts to appear in the *Review of Existential Psychology and Psychiatry*[308] and is perhaps Boss's most important statement of therapeutic daseinanalysis. The translation does not include the 'Preface [*Vorwort*]' of the monograph, which, Boss notes, was 'for the most part' his introduction to the Fifth International Congress of Medical Psychotherapy (August 21-26, 1961) in Vienna.[309] The 'Preface' tells us that the monograph is 'a slightly expanded version' of that lecture.

Oversight of the scientific program committee was in the hands of Viktor Frankl. The theme of the conference was 'Psychotherapy and Clinical Medicine', arranged in cooperation with the Österreichische Ärzte Gesellschaft (Austrian Medical Association). Oddly enough, Boss's paper was not published in the proceedings of the conference. In a footnote to the title of the English version, Boss says that the version of the text was first given as a lecture on February 25, 1962, at a meeting in the States of the American Association of Existential Psychology and Psychiatry. There papers were also given by Rollo May and Paul Tillich ('Psychoanalysis and Existentialism').[310]

The impetus for the theme of the congress in Vienna was 'the rapidly growing importance that must be accorded psychotherapy in ever wider areas of clinical medicine'.[311] In the States it was a time when psychiatry was just becoming available to larger numbers of people outside of major cities on an out-patient basis. General practitioners were reading about the usefulness of taking a stance toward their patients that was based, for the most part, on psychoanalytic principles. Books on 'mental health' were being read by more and more of the general population.

Psychotherapy, Boss notes, was 'making claims on a steadily growing number of physical ailments for which, until now, only purely somatic methods of research and treatment were considered competent'. The 'astonishing spread of psychotherapy ... will force us to learn to see more and more clearly the fundamental inseparability of the physical and psychic phenomena of human existence [*Existenz*] in both its healthy and sick days, and to think much more carefully than before about the constitution of the essence [*Wesensverfassung*] and nature [*Natur*] of our unitary capacity for existing [*Existierenskönnen*].'[312]

Boss conjectures that the trend toward the greater utilization of psychotherapy 'is only one of the many testimonies to a decisive change in the whole spiritual situation [*geistige Situation*] of our historical epoch', which suggests 'an imminent overcoming of the centuries-old Cartesian division of the world into a realm of physically extended, sensually perceptible objects [*Gegenstände*] and a radically different sphere [*Sphäre*] of immaterial, unextended and immeasurable spiritual essences [*Wesenheiten*].'[313] In daseinanalytic therapy in particular one sees a dedifferentiation of the psychic and the somatic, comparable to the view of quantum physics that it is not possible to clearly differentiate between matter and energy [*Materie und Energie*].

Boss's title indicates that his topics are 'anxiety about life [*Lebensangst*]' or, more colloquially, 'fear of life as such' (and not anxiety as a disturbance of affect), and 'feelings of guilt [*Schuldgefühle*]', which can more appropriately be rendered as feelings of indebtedness. Such ontological guilt is not based on a moral sense or 'feeling' grounded in remorse, the lack of which is associated with the antisocial personality. Finally, the *Befreiung* he has in mind is perhaps more adequately rendered as 'a freeing up' and loosening of restrictions, as in setting a vessel free from its moorings. This is in every case the goal of dasein*analysis*.

The monograph is Boss's most eloquent presentation of his approach up to that time. He begins by clarifying that the *Angst* and *Schuld* he has in mind are existentives or, as he terms them here, 'basic powers [*Grundmächte*] in the life of the human being'.[314] They are two of the existentives Heidegger had described in his fundamental ontology of human being. Boss compares them to hunger and love, suggesting that anxiety and guilt are in some senses as basic as the latter. This is a large claim but it is essential to his account of the place of therapy in relation to *neurotic* anxiety and feelings of guilt, which are another matter entirely. He suggests that taking a look at the latter *ontic* phenomena and the disorders of which they are generally said to be symptomatic might provide clues as to 'the nature and meaning of human anxiety and guilt in general [as ontological 'powers'], if only we were prepared to hearken to them in the right way.'[315]

From the Freudian perspective, ontic anxiety and feelings of guilt are traceable to events that have set in motion a sequence of processes that led to current experience and behavior. This is the classic psychoanalytic notion of the traumatogenesis of symptoms, based on the view that early childhood events determine present psychopathology. But, stop! says Boss.

> In the reality of psychotherapeutic practice, however, these psychological theories have been far from fulfilling the expectations reposed in them . . . . [A]n increasing number of psychotherapists can be seen abandoning their hypotheses of anxiety and guilt causations as illusions. In point of fact, it has not been possible by psychotherapeutic means to make one single person really free of anxiety and guilt on the basis of these psychological theories in the way they had promised. The hidden anxiety feelings and guilt feelings [*Angst- und Schuldgefühle*] in the modern vacuity or boredom neuroses are particularly stubborn in refusing to yield to a psychotherapeutic procedure aiming at a dismantling of conscience [*Gewissensaufbauverfahren*].[316]

The failure of psychotherapy to reduce or eliminate feelings of guilt can be laid to having approached psychotherapeutic intervention as a matter of weakening the strength of conscience. The failure to make neurotic guilt less poignant is based on a misunderstanding of the nature of both guilt and conscience. Basing their work on either psychodynamic or behaviorist principles, psychotherapists have failed to eliminate two of the most prevalent symptoms that 'present' in the consulting room. Boss is emphatic:

> How could it be otherwise! The psychotherapists themselves after all know nothing of any meaning [*Sinn*] and goal [*Ziel*] because in their own perceptual world, thinking as they do in scientific-technical terms, in so-called dynamic chains of causation, there are only factual and functional interrelationships [*Sach- und Funktionszusammenhänge*] that are meaningless [*sinnfrei*],[317] calculable, and predetermined [*vorbestimmte*] and quite neutral as to meaningful values.[318]

Boss suggests that, given their theoretical orientation, psychotherapists

> are in principle oblivious to the sense or meaning [*Sinn*] of their patient's experience and [therefore] lack a goal [*Ziel*] in their work since they are not oriented to meaning . . . . How should these psychotherapists be in a position to remedy the boring meaninglessness [*Sinnlosigkeit*] from which their patients are suffering? They are at the very most able to console themselves for their therapeutic helplessness with new causal hypotheses. They seek such consolation [*Trost*] perhaps on the assumption of an especially potent death drive or a derivative congenital, primary moral masochism.[319]

Psychotherapists must come to realize that 'the basic principle of the ordinary causal mode of thinking in psychology cannot be justified by anything at all tangible [*Faßbares*] and demonstrable [*Nachweisbares*].'[320] We come, then, to what is Boss's clearest statement of what is at stake:

It cannot be proved by any means of any set of facts [*wie immer gearteten Tatbestand*], no matter how constituted, that [and why] what was appearing earlier in a life history [*das lebensgeschichtlich früher Erscheinende*] should also be the efficient cause [*die bewirkende Ursache*] of everything that follows and actually is [*das eigentlich Wirkliche*] simply because it preceded it in time [*weil es zeitlich vorangeht*].[321]

This holds for events that are said to cause anxiety, feelings of guilt, depression and the rest of the panoply of symptoms that are said to bring people to the office of a psychiatrist or psychotherapist. Nor can present experience be explained as the result of defense mechanisms such as sublimation or reaction formation, classic examples of how Freudian theory claims to account, for example, for the transformation of aggressive drives into an interest in performing surgery or for an extremely kind and caring person's behavior being the result of having staved off anxiety caused by a tendency to harm living things. 'What alone is in actual fact perceivable [*wahrnehmbar*] and detectable [*feststellbar*] is the temporally regular succession of phenomena [*Erscheinungen*]'[322] and nothing more. Hidden forces are in principle not susceptible of being perceived. There are only phenomena and they are 'out there'. We must take them as they come and as they manifest themselves without resorting to explanations based on what caused them to appear just when and as they have. If we do this, experience is degraded and denatured into 'something inauthentic [*etwas Uneigentlichem*], *merely derivative or expressive of something else* [*Ausgedrückten*] [emphasis added]. In this way we have from the outset given up any possibility of grasping things themselves [*Dinge selbst*] in their own unmediated actuality [*unmittelbaran Wirklichkeit*].' As for the purported hidden causes, we remain entirely in the dark about them. Their essence [*Wesen*] remains 'wholly indeterminate'. The entire enterprise is only so much guesswork, while what there is before us is overlooked.[323]

If there is to be an understanding of the ontic feelings of anxiety and guilt feelings as they are seen in the practice of psychotherapy, a fundamentally new understanding of man must be brought to bear or, as the German heading of one section has it, a new 'consideration [*Besinnung*]' of the *who* of the human being must take place.[324] This requires a very different kind of thinking, a different way of thinking about things. This is provided by Heidegger's analytics of *Dasein* and its ontological study of anxiety and guilt.

In a passage added for the 1962 version of the lecture, Boss told his audience:

What we must do is to restore an attitude of due reverence before the actual authenticity of all human phenomena. We must be capable of allowing what appears before us to remain intact and as what it immediately shows itself to be in the whole framework of references inherent in [what appears] itself. We have to learn *to once again just look at the things actually confronting us and let the phenomena themselves which we encounter tell us their meaning and content* [emphasis added]. Here we have in a nutshell, the fundamental discrepancy between the up-to-now available so-called psychodynamic psychologies and the Analysis of Dasein.[325]

Heidegger's ontological existentives, *Angst* and *Schuld*, are then explored by contrast with the ontic symptoms of anxiety and guilt feelings. Ontologically, we are anxious in the face of knowing we will die and guilty given our ever-renewed indebtedness to life. These are not examples of psychopathology. Ontological anxiety moves the human being to do more and *be* more intensively, knowing that his time is limited. 'It is precisely anxiety that opens to man that dimension of *freedom* [emphasis added] into which alone the experiences of love and trust can unfold at all. Like love, anxiety which is freed from subjectivistic pettiness presents the existence [*Dasein*] of man not only with the possibility of what is more intense and richer [*Größerem und Reicherem*] but presents it with the direct possibility of being that which is completely different from everything that *there is* [*Seiendes*] and that as *something* that is there [*etwas* Seiendes] cannot after all be without its ever-limiting limits [*je begrenzendes Grenzen*].' Thus, anxiety confronts man with 'not being [*Nicht-Seins*]', the 'nothing [*Nichts*]', that 'great nothingness … which is precisely the opposite of a nihilistic emptiness and nullity [*Leere und Nichtigkeit*], such that it is able to both conceal and reveal us and the things of our world.'[326]

On the connection between ontological anxiety and love, Boss observes: 'When experienced in its deepest meaning anxiety so little contradicts love as its opposing force [*Gegenmacht*] that it blows apart [*sprengt*] all subjectivistic, psychologistic anxiousness [*Ängstlichkeit*] – ever continually overcoming itself – and opens up [*auftut*] love's way to the encompassing boundlessness [*bergenden Grenzenlosen*] of what no longer merely *is*.'[327] The formulation reflects what might be the watchword of daseinanalysis as found in *Being and Time*: '*Possibility* surpasses actuality.'[328] It bears repeating that, for daseinanalysis, what has come to be – that is, what has happened ('what *is*') – does not matter. What *does* matter is what might and can happen, that is, what is possible for the existing human being. While psychoanalysis is concerned with what has happened and what has been done, daseinanalysis is concerned with what has not happened to him and what he has not yet done.

Then there is ontological guilt or, better translated, indebtedness [*Schuld*].[329] This has nothing to do with feelings of guilt that come and go when one feels he has done something wrong, but is rather a structural feature of *Dasein* that one cannot be relieved of. Ontic feelings of guilt are for the most part a consequence of socialization. Ontological indebtedness, by contrast, refers to the inevitable fact that we are always in arrears to what we could have done or might have done but did not do, given that we have to make choices among possible courses of action. The greater the range and number of choices that are open to one, the less is he bound by the dictates of instinct.[330]

To bring into view the phenomenological account of being human he has been presenting, Boss invites his audience to consider the situation they are in: 'We have to ask ourselves, for example, what am I like, what kind of beings are we here, in order to account for the simple fact that I could see you from the moment I entered this room and could realize that you are my audience of fellow human beings and that you were able to perceive me just as directly as the speaker this evening ... [T]he immediate experience itself shows us that an enigmatic transcending on the part of man from out of the interior of a psyche, a subjectivity of or a person is not needed at all' as science would have us believe. Science has proposed a view of the formation inside us of 'intellectually meaningful contents' somehow produced by the 'conversion of chemical-physical excitation processes in the brain'. But natural science must then explain how these 'entities of unknown nature' somehow get 'over to the objects in the outside world'. It has failed to do so and in principle cannot.

In fact, 'fortunately, immediate experience itself shows us that there is no need at all for such an enigmatic transcending on the part of man from out of the interior of a psyche, subjectivity or the person, because such an interior [*Inneres*] simply does not exist.'[331] How, then, are we to understand what is going on?

> Let us only recollect carefully what actually and really happened when we met here an hour ago! Surely you by no means became aware of yourselves as beings which had been first enclosed inside some kind of bodily organism that had been sealed in by a skin; nor did you exist primarily inside an ego, in a psyche, in a subject of a person, [all] mental-intellectual containers [*seelisch-geistigen Behältern*] you would then have had to climb out of in order to get across to me with your understanding of my personality. Again, I too experienced myself just as little as something initially in my body [*anfänglich in meinem Körper*], something simply present there in myself [*in mir selber drin Vorhandenes*]. Rather, *from the get go, we were all 'outside', together present in the whole free play of this lecture hall, spanning the openness of this illuminated area of the world that was opened up to us with an understanding of what we encountered together in it* [emphasis added].[332]

Being human is existing as 'a luminance [*Lichtung*], needed by the phenomena of our world to enable them to come to light [*zum Vorschein kommen*][333] within it [*in sie hinein*] and be.' Quite simply, the world needs us human beings so that *phenomena* may make an appearance in it.

Other sentient beings (dogs, cats, chimpanzees) do not provide this *Lichtung*. They apprehend objects already present and on hand and interact with them. A dog, for example, smells meat or another dog, and follows the scent. The dog does not have, as we have, a 'comprehending relationship [*verstehende Beziehung*] *within* which something confronting us at any given moment can appear originally as what it is, can unfold and show itself in its contexts of meaning and reference.' The dog smells food, follows the odor, goes to the food and eats it. It does not concern itself with the meaning of the odor, the meat, or eating.

As to *Schuld* as ontological indebtedness, to find meaning in and give sense to what is in the world is the privilege of *Dasein*, but this privilege comes with a price, since it is precisely to this, and nothing other than such a letting oneself be put to use [*Sich-brauchen-Lassen*] that man is in debt [*schuldet*] most deeply for what is and has to be [*was ist und zu sein hat*]. Therefore, *this* bearing the blame [*Schuld-Sein*], if you like, grounds man's existential [*existentiale*] [ontic] guiltiness [*Schuldhaftigkeit*]. Consequently, not a single phenomenon [*Phänomen*] of human conscience [*Gewissens*] might or could be understood fundamentally as other than a summons [*Aufruf*] and exhortation [*Mahnung*] at work, given our human duty [*Amtes*] as caretaker [*Hüters*] and shepherd [*Hirten*] of eyerything that has [the possibility] of showing up [*erscheinen*], to be [*zu sein*] and to unfold [*sich zu entfalten*] in the light [*im Lichte*] of a given life [*Existenz*].[334]

The close connection in Heidegger's thought between ontological *Schuld* and the call of conscience [*Ruf des Gewissens*] needs clarifying. It is easy to mistakenly associate the *moral* notion of conscience (what Heidegger refers to as 'the voice of conscience [*Stimme des Gewissens*]') with the 'call of conscience'.[335] Recalling the discussion of *Schuld*, Boss asserts that the aforementioned 'human bearing the blame loses the oppressive character of an imperfection [*Mangel*]' in the same way that *Angst* did when understood ontologically. Just as ontological *Angst* is far from being a limitation (which is how neurotic anxiety is experienced) but is rather part of the human disposition of our fundamental caring about things [*Sorge*], so also in the case of *Schuld* we see that it is about the realization of possibilities in a world of things to which we are called as conscientious beings. The call of conscience holds existence to the task of being the 'guardian and shepherd of everything that has to show up' in the light of human being as existing. The image is of a watchman who is on permanent duty, without any breaks. An essential part of being human, such obligation is inevitable. Once aware that his essential 'bearing the blame' of existence is a privilege as situated among all other beings, a human being's *Existenz* is experienced as meaningful.

Boss says that we see human being at its best in the child, who *wants* to be at the disposal of 'things'. We see it in the child's 'delightful readiness [*beglückenden Bereitschaft*] to place himself without reservation at the disposal of all phenomena [*Phänomenen*] as the luminating sphere [*lichtender Bereich*] into which they can show up and unfold, and as their caretaker [*Hüter*]'.[336] It should come as no surprise, then, that in his clinical examples Boss often speaks about individuals who are in distress precisely because they have not had the opportunity to fully be a child. For many analysands, the remedy of daseinanalysis is that it provides a place for living out what had been denied them of their childhood.

The text concludes with some of Boss's best writing on therapy. 'The new consideration [*Besinnung*] [of human being] as foundation for the possibility of liberation in psychotherapy [*psychotherapeutischer Befreiungsmöglichkeit*]' amounts to a very different approach to therapy to than that found among the practitioners of its predecessor, psychoanalysis.

As daseinanalysts,

we ought to refrain completely from any self-important imposition on our patients of maxims or dogmas of any sort. We have to content ourselves with clearing away a little stone here and there, any obstacles in the way, so that what is already there [*da*] and has always constituted the essence [*Wesen*] of the patient can emerge [*hervorkommen*] on its own from its previous reserve [*Verschlossenheit*] into the open [*ins Offene*]. The highest goal [*Ziel*] of all psychotherapy is and remains the opening up [*Eröffnung*] of our patients to an ability to love and to trust [*zu einem Lieben- und Vertrauen-Können*] that allows [him] to get over [*überwinden*] any and all oppression by [neurotic] anxiety and guilt as mere misunderstandings [*bloße Mißverständnisse*] .... [T]he first thing is to let the patient make up for the missing but basically indispensable experience of being, [which is] provided by the protective and unshakable caring about and love [*Fürsorge und Liebe*] [shown by the analyst that is] suited to the patient's own distinctive nature [*Eigenwesen*].[337]

At this point, Boss introduces the notion of the 'psychotherapeutic eros'. To repeat: It is 'a special kind of human attention [*Zuwendung*] of the psychotherapist to his analysands which is not to be found anywhere else in the world outside of' the therapeutic setting. It is 'as different from the love of parents for their children, [as] different from the love between two friends, [as] different from the love of the pastor for his congregation, [and as] quite decidedly different from the extremely variable love between the sexes as it is from merely conventional kindness [*konventioneller Liebenswürdigkeit*].'

Short of quoting the remaining paragraphs, it is difficult to adequately summarize Boss's description of the psychotherapeutic eros in practice. Suffice to say, he stresses that it is to be understood only by having experienced it in the teaching analysis [*Lehranalyse*] and not by reading about it in books; it occurs, as it were, 'indiscernibly [*unsichtbar*]' (here following Freud's choice of term), without being driven by the force of therapeutic zeal and in the absence of any interest on the part of the analyst to gain anything from the experience. Boss speaks of a general stance of 'selflessness, self-restraint [or self-discipline] and reverence [*Selbstlosigkeit, Selbstzucht und Ehrfurcht*]' vis-à-vis the uniqueness [*Eigenwesen*] of the partner [*Partner*] in the therapeutic encounter. He invokes a favorite image of Freud's *Tummelplatz* (playground) in which the analysand can try out behavior and expressions (verbal and otherwise) that would ordinarily not be tolerated outside of the therapeutic setting. Freedom to move outside of his usual 'reserve [*Verschlossenheit*]', the analysand may, as it were, rehearse what he might at some later point dare perform on the world's stage, but without any pressure to do so. It is no part of the analyst's work 'to determine in what special *way* such a healing experience [*heilsame Erfahrung*] in the course of psychotherapeutic treatment [*psychotherapeutischen Kur*] occurs [*ereignet*].' Nor when it occurs.[338] That is up to the analysand. Finally, it should not be overlooked that in this text Boss points out that the spiritual life of the other is not to be left out of consideration in therapy.

In 1963, Boss published what would seem to have been an English translation of his *Psychoanalyse und Daseinsanalytik*, the first book to feature the term *Daseins-*

analyse in the title. **Psychoanalysis and Daseinsanalysis** (1957a)[339] is not, however, a translation of the German text.[340] The two volumes have an interesting history. Notes to two papers, 'Daseinsanalytische Bemerkungen zu Freuds Vorstellung des 'Unbewußten' {1960/1961a} and 'Die Bedeutung der Daseinsanalyse für die psychoanalytische Praxis' {1960/1961b}, tell us that the original text of *Psychoanalyse und Daseinsanalytik* was written in English. Boss then translated three chapters (5, 7 and 8) from that manuscript for publication in a single issue of the *Zeitschrift für psychosomatische Medizin*, two years before the English book was published.[341] *Psychoanalysis and Daseinsanalysis* is an entirely different text than *Psychoanalyse und Daseinsanalytik*, written for a very different audience than the latter volume had been penned.

Beginning in 1959, in the years just after the publication of *Psychoanalyse und Daseinsanalytik*, Boss lectured in the States at Harvard, Yale, the Washington School of Psychiatry, the University of Wisconsin (Madison), the University of California and the Langley Porter University Psychiatric Hospital in San Francisco. In the 'Preface' to *Psychoanalysis and Daseinsanalysis* Boss explains that after giving lectures and seminars in 1961 and 1962 in the States, he hoped to write something for readers there. He decided to translate *Psychoanalyse und Daseinsanalytik*, but 'as the work proceeded ... the book grew until in its English version it is three times as long as the German original. The enormous differences between the American and the European ways of dealing with such a subject made longer explanations inevitable.'[342] We are told that his former student, Ludwig Lefebre, 'did most of the translation'.[343] Boss also acknowledges his debt to Jurgen Ruesch, Rollo May and Leslie Farber, who, as we have learned, had wanted Heidegger to present a series of lectures at the Washington School of Psychiatry in 1961, following in the steps of Martin Buber who had spoken there in 1956.[344]

Following the opening chapter on the case of 'Dr. Cobling' is an 'Outline of Analysis of *Dasein*'. 'Martin Heidegger's untiring personal help in compiling' the text of the chapter is acknowledged.[345] It is said to be the result of a cooperative effort with the philosopher, whose involvement with daseinanalysis had formally and publicly begun in 1959 with a lecture at the Burghölzi. This, of course, led to the full decade of the Zollikon seminars and culminated in 1971 with the first German edition of *Existential Foundations of Medicine* {1971a}, which was also closely monitored by Heidegger as the text was being written.

The remaining theoretical chapters of *Psychoanalysis and Daseinsanalysis* are devoted to 'The Most Common Misunderstandings about Analysis of Dasein', 'The Intrinsic Harmony of Psychoanalytic Therapy and Daseinsanalysis', and 'Daseinsanalytic Re-evaluation of the Basic Conceptions of Psychoanalytic Theory'. Only 'The Intrinsic Harmony of Psychoanalytic Therapy and Daseinsanalysis' more or less corresponds to a chapter in the German book, namely, Chapter 6, 'Der Einklang von psychoanalytischer Praxis und daseinsanalytischem Menschenverständnis'.

The last two parts of the book are devoted to a 'Daseinsanalytic Re-evaluation of the Psychoanalytic Doctrine of the Neuroses' ('Conversion Hysteria' and 'Organ Neurosis'; 'A Patient Who Suffered Alternately from Colitis and Migraine'; 'A Patient with Functional and Structural 'Psychosomatic' Disturbances'; 'Anxiety Neurosis'; 'Obsessional Neurosis'; 'The Case History of a Sadistic Pervert'; and 'The 'Narcissistic' Neuroses') and 'The Impact of Daseinsanalysis on Traditional Psychoanalytic Techniques' ('The Daseinsanalyt's Attitude toward his Patients'; 'Daseinsanalytic Handling of 'Transference' and 'Acting Out'; 'The Psychoanalytic 'Why?' and the Daseinsanalytic 'Why not?'; 'Frustration and Permissiveness in the Light of Daseinsanalysis'; 'Daseinsanalytic Handling of 'Countertransference'; 'The Therapeutic Use of Daseinsanalytic Dream Interpretation'; 'Further Daseinsanalytic Corrections in Therapy: The Analysis of 'Guilt Feelings' and the Goal of Psychotherapy'; and 'Daseinsanalytically Modified Treatment of a Modern Neurosis of Dullness and the Patient's Comments on the Modifications'). In this text we find the first mention in English of Boss's *signature question* 'Why in the world *not?*'

In preparing the reader for the chapters on praxis, Boss makes the significant statement that 'the Daseinsanalytic approach to the neuroses is still in its beginnings, and a more systematic and complete portrayal of the Daseinsanalytic theory of neuroses is still to come.' He would provide a further, giant step in this direction in his *magnum opus* eight years later. Meanwhile, 'at present, the most important task is to discuss psychoanalytic *therapy* in terms of the Daseinsanalytic view of man. Only in this way can we determine whether Daseinsanalytic thinking is of immediate and practical value for the therapeutic endeavor.'[346]

Boss's caution then is just as important for the reader now, *sixty* years later, as it was in 1963. Daseinanalysis is still in its beginnings, having remained unknown to most individuals in training programs for psychiatry, psychoanalysis, clinical psychology, counseling psychology, pastoral counseling and social work.

The text makes it clear that daseinanalysis is not about providing a corrective emotional experience or re-living an earlier troubled relationship that reappears in the 'transference'. Instead, the other is allowed, often for the first time, to live a certain way in the therapeutic 'test world', as Boss termed it. Thus, for example, 'Dr. Cobling' was able to be a babbling infant for the first time, early on having been forced by her strict parents to skip that era. 'As a rule,' says Boss,

> neurotically reduced people regard their wretched interpersonal relations as the only ones possible. They do not know that greater freedom is available. If their restrictions are repeatedly questioned, previously non-admitted possibilities of behavior regularly appear, along with perception of things and fellow human beings who belong to these world-disclosing possibilities. The analyst practicing in this fashion will not try to persuade patients that much of what they feel and mean is only a cloak for opposite wishes and tendencies.

The analyst understands that the analysand's often frightening 'possibilities of relating have to be acknowledged' and that they may be 'tried out' in analysis. That will often entail the involvement of the analyst in a very unusual relationship. As a result of the daseinanalyst's preparation, however, 'he is able to accept *all* [emphasis added] the ways in which his analysands begin to relate.'[347]

Once again we read that Boss preserves from psychoanalysis the technical procedure of analysis of resistance, understood differently, however, than Freud had. Here 'the patient is tirelessly confronted with the limitations of his life and wherein these limitations are incessantly questioned, so that the possibility of a richer existence is implied.'[348]

We are again reminded that there is nothing 'behind' present experience and behavior in daseinanalysis. In his discussion of transference and acting out, Boss again formulates his basic position about the untenable psychoanalytic concept.

> Human existence is essentially not a physical process but primarily an historical event. This means that in every actual relation to something or somebody, *Dasein's* whole history is inherent and present, whether the historical unfolding of a certain kind of relationship is remembered explicitly or not. What matters most, therapeutically, is not the recalling of the occasion when a neurotic pattern of relating to fellow men was acquired in childhood, but finding the answers to two questions: Why has the patient remained, right up to the present time, caught within this same, restricted way of communicating? What is keeping him a prisoner of his neurotic behavior patterns right now? The general answer to these all-important questions is that neurotic patients usually cannot even imagine that another way of relating to people is possible. Some may intellectually know of a greater freedom, but they do not trust it sufficiently to dare to try it. Instead, they are most anxious to prove the contrary to themselves, by provoking their environment to continue the neurotically restricted way of communicating with them. For all neurotics, any change of the narrow perspective to which they are accustomed is terrifying, especially if it is a change toward greater freedom.[349]

Psychiatry and clinical psychology no longer use the word 'neurosis', but 'neuroticism' is still found in the pages of *the DSM-5-TR* to describe a feature of individuals diagnosed with psychological disorders. As the title of his monograph indicates, when speaking of 'the neurotic' Boss has in mind the individual bothered by 'fear of life [*Lebensangst*]' and 'feelings of guilt [*Schuldgefühle*]' understood both ontically and ontologically. By contrast, the psychiatric notion of neuroticism suggests what in the early days of psychoanalysis was termed neurasthenia. For psychiatry, neuroticism denotes global psychological weakness rather apprehension in the face of life's untested possibilities.

There is still talk in psychiatry of 'the schizophrenic', now for the most part in the context of a 'spectrum' of disorders, but for both the Boss of sixty years ago and the contemporary practicing psychotherapist, 'the schizophrenic' 'presents' in much the same way. As understood by Boss, such an individual is a special challenge inasmuch as such he remains 'moored' at the level of childhood. In that case, 'the analyst must be mature enough to permit the patient to unfold in an atmosphere of complete security, in a relationship comparable to that of a mother with an unborn child. Actually, the therapist must often maintain such a relationship for as many years as a pregnancy has months.'[350] Nine years is a very long time indeed, but some daseinanalysis continues for such a span. During such a period, the daseinanalyst's role is one of protecting the analysand *as* he lives a very vulnerable existence that eventually gains in strength.

In one case presented, we see Boss spending time outside of the office with his analysand, at the person's home. This is a powerful image which makes it plain that the practice of daseinanalysis, at least for Boss, exceeded the boundaries – physical and emotional – of traditional psychoanalysis, psychiatry and clinical psychology. In 1963, talk about working therapeutically outside of the consulting room would have made most analysts put down the book as unrealistic or an expression of unusual therapeutic zeal. The question would likely also have come up about just how much time a therapist should devote to a single patient over a long period of time, and not only in his consulting room.[351]

The volume introduces the fundamental distinction discussed in Part I between what is here translated as 'intervening care [*einspringende Fürsorge*]' and 'anticipating care [*vorausspringende Fürsorge*]'. It ends with the memorable section on 'the psychoanalytic 'Why?' and the daseinsanalytic 'Why not?': 'The daseinsanalyst often asks his patients, 'Why not?' thereby encouraging them to ever greater tests of daring. 'Why is it that you don't dare to behave in such-and-such a manner during the analytic session?' It is important to add that Boss does not preclude asking 'Why?' of the analysand by inquiring about his personal history, but that he cautions this must not be done 'prematurely'.[352]

In the 'Conclusion', in keeping with his goal of contrasting daseinanalysis and psychoanalysis, Boss offers that

> analysis of *Dasein* makes it possible *to discover what psychoanalytic therapy essentially is* [emphasis added]. In the light of Daseinsanalytic reflection, psychoanalytic endeavor becomes transparent to the fullest possible extent and, most important, the therapeutic potentialities of psychoanalysis become fully accessible. Analysis of *Dasein* is able to render this invaluable service to psychoanalysis because the understanding of man which is explicit in analysis of *Dasein* has been present, if only implicitly, in psychoanalytic *therapy*, and has secretly guided it from the very beginning, in spite of the mechanistic *theory* of psychoanalysis.[353]

Boss hoped his readers would take a fresh look at psychoanalytic theory, abandon it, and take as a different starting point the analytics of *Dasein* provided by Heidegger, since 'with only a few – though decisive – corrections, no other psychotherapeutic procedure but that of psychoanalytic *practice* is capable of helping man to break through to, and to carry out, his authentic and wholesome being-wholly-himself…. [A]nalysis of *Dasein* restores to us, above all, a deep respect for the full, specific, and immediately accessible meaning and content of all immediately perceptible phenomena…. Only analysis of *Dasein* enables us to accept all the encountered things as what they are – foci of referential connections encompassing heaven and earth, the human and divine.'[354] In short, daseinanalysis is very much in the tradition of psychoanalysis, preserving its therapeutic gold but relieving it of its theoretical dross. The book was briefly noted in *The Review of Metaphysics*[355] and reviewed in the *American Sociological Review*,[356] the *British Journal of Psychiatry*,[357] and the *Canadian Journal of Psychiatry*.[358]

Several years after *Psychoanalysis and Daseinsanalysis* appeared, Boss collaborated with Gion Condrau on the first of six texts the two men co-authored between 1967 and 1980. **'Existential Psychoanalysis'** (1967c)[359] is the first of three essays designed to introduce daseinanalysis to American psychoanalysts and psychiatrists. It is therefore regrettable that the chapter is entitled 'Existential Psychoanalysis' rather than 'Daseinsanalysis', since that is how the 'technique' is referred to throughout the body of the chapter. In the prefatory paragraphs Boss is credited with having begun to use the term 'Daseinsanalysis' 'in order to avoid confusion with other so-called existential-psychoanalytical schools'. To say that the 'existential analytic' ('daseinsanalytic') approach is one among a number of 'existential *psycho*analytic' approaches created a bit of confusion, since while daseinanalysis originated with psychoanalysis, it is a radical departure from it from the theoretical ground up. Nor, as we have been at great pains to emphasize, is daseinanalysis to be confused with later forms of 'existential analysis.'

As for 'existential psychoanalysis' the term was Jean-Paul Sartre's, but it was never been intended to be understood as or used as a therapeutic approach.[360] The chapter so titled in Wolman, then, was about a non-existent 'technique'. It is unfortunate therefore that the authors state that 'the term 'existential psychoanalysis' is applied in psychiatry and psychotherapy to all those theoretical and practical deviations from the classic psychoanalysis of Sigmund Freud that replace the 'libido theory' and the 'psychic apparatus' by the immediately apprehensible human *existence*. Existential psychoanalysis bases its knowledge of the nature of man's being on the insights of existential philosophy, particularly on the work of the German philosopher Martin Heidegger, *Sein und Zeit* (which appeared in English under the title 'Being and Time', New York, 1962) and his subsequent works.'[361] That *this* 'existential psychoanalysis' – namely, daseinanalysis -- is based on Heidegger's work and not Sartre's is, of course, correct but, given the title of the 1953 work by Sartre, many might still have associated the term with him. Daseinanalysis might have been off to a better start, then, if the approach had been first known as a Heideggerian 'existential psychoanalysis' and subsequently as the approach based on his analytics of *Dasein* [*Daseinsanalytik*] that came to be known as 'Daseinsanalysis' ten years later in Boss's *Psychoanalysis and Daseinsanalysis*.[362]

The Wolman volume was subtitled *A Handbook for the Practicing Psychoanalyst* ('the diversified techniques of modern psychoanalysis, set forth by twenty-seven eminent clinicians').[363] It is revealed in editorial material that opting for the chapter title 'Existential Psychoanalysis' was in the interest of not 'employing a foreign word that is incapable of being adequately translated in a way that will be generally understood.' That said, at the outset of the chapter itself Boss and Condrau write that 'the key term in the works of Heidegger and his followers is *Dasein*, popularly translated as 'existence''. Although they might have explained the special sense of existence in

Heidegger and retained the English with that qualification in mind, they use the term 'Dasein' throughout. Evidently, there was a breakdown in communications at the editorial level. This is odd, since Wolman and Boss knew each other well. But the handbook is sizable.

The chapter is 'a presentation, partly word-for-word, partly in summary form, of the daseinsanalytic notions that have already been made known in several of the author's [sic] publications. Particular reference is made to the two works *Psychoanalysis and Daseinsanalysis* [1963] . . . and *Daseinsanalytische Psychotherapie* [*Daseinsanalytic Psychotherapy*] by Gion Condrau (Berne and Stuttgart, Hans Huber, 1963).'[364]

Since this was perhaps the first acquaintance with Daseinsanalysis for many American psychoanalysts (except those who had read *Psychoanalysis and Daseinsanalysis*), the text holds a place of special significance and deserves detailed synopsis.[365] The chapter is divided into six sections: 'rationale of the method', 'transference [*Übertragung*]', 'resistance [*Widerstand*]', 'interpretation [*Deutung*] of [the] unconscious [*das Unbewßt*]', 'working through [*Durcharbeitung*]', and 'the concept of cure'.

In daseinanalysis the analyst limits himself only to 'the description and investigation of all the immediately observable modes of human behavior and their equally perceptible underlying moods, and it limits him to speaking of them in everyday language,' not the language of a given theory.

> The discovery that man is essentially one in whose meaning-disclosing relationships [to things and people] the phenomena of our world make their appearance develops in the Daseinsanalytic therapist a basic respect for the intrinsic value of and essential content of everything that shines forth and comes into its being in the light of a Dasein. Without being concerned with the translation of what is occurring in the psyche, the psychotherapist becomes less prejudiced. He can devote himself fully to the analysand in that 'evenly-hovering attention [*gleichschwebende Aufmerksamkeit*]' that Freud always demanded.

Moreover, 'the analyst's behavior rests on the insight that, being human, he is called upon to disclose both things and men. This knowledge increases his sensitivity to all the obstacles which generally reduce the potential relationships of a patient to a few rigid and unauthentic modes of behavior.' The analyst, then, is more aware of what is standing in the way of the analysand's limited repertoire of relationships with things and other human beings. In more general terms, 'daseinsanalytic understanding of man imbues the analyst with a deep respect for everything he encounters . . . [thus making] it possible for him to *take seriously* and to regard without prejudice all behavior and all utterances the patient produces [emphasis added].'[366]

Needing to frame what he sees within the context of the conceptual vocabulary of Freudian metapsychology would amount to the analyst's 'put[ting] in the patient's way new obstacles arising from his personal censorship based on theoretical prejudices.' Here the biggest culprit is the notion of the transference, which 'attempts to reduce . . . a new mode of behavior on the part of the patient to an earlier relationship in the patient's life, a relationship considered primary and causal *because* it took place earlier' in the analysand's life, whether a few weeks earlier or decades before. Assuming that transference is in play, the analysis begins spinning wheels from the outset. But 'it is unlikely that this will happen if the patient's feelings are regarded as actually directed toward the analyst and thus accepted in their full reality, even though the patient's perception of the analyst is still distorted and restricted because of earlier experiences.'[367]

The authors suggest that daseinanalysis is the most radical revision of Freud's approach to therapy that has occurred – and there had been many, from Jung's analytical psychology and Alfred Adler's individual psychology to the recent twist of psychoanalysis known as ego psychology. The daseinanalytic revision is not at the theoretical level, however. Psychoanalytic theory is dropped entirely. Instead, 'Daseinsanalysis gives psychotherapists a better understanding of the meaning of Freud's recommendations for psychoanalytic treatment than does Freud's own theory.' This seemed to preserve continuity with psychoanalysis, but what would have been very new to readers was hearing that 'fundamental insights into human nature . . . explicitly developed since Freud's day in Heidegger's work' are implicit in Freud, 'although unexpressed in psychoanalytic theory'. On the other hand, however, there are 'a few (though important) realms of therapy where Freud's secondary theories have negatively influenced therapeutic procedures . . . . Perhaps the most significant area . . . is in the conception of *transference*.'

For Freud, 'buried and forgotten emotions of love or hate become actual and manifest' in the course of analysis because analysands want to express in action – reproduce in the real-life relationship with the therapist – infantile feelings for their parents, which have been repressed, that is to say, forgotten. *That* such feelings have been forgotten is also not in the awareness of the individual. In other words, these feelings are said to be known [*bewußt*], but not consciously known, that is to say, they are *unbewußt* (unconscious). According to psychoanalytic theory, analysands 'want to 'act out [these feelings]', but they do not see and understand what they are doing, their acting out is an indication that they resist any consciousness of feelings they had for their parents in early life, and these repressed feelings now hide behind the feelings for the analyst.' Thus, Freud thought, the feelings for the analyst are not really about the analyst. Instead, they are about someone the analysand mistakenly takes the analyst to represent, that is 'be', and it is up to the analyst to 'uncover this strategy of acting out. The patient is to be encouraged to remember feelings he had for infantile love objects, but to remember *only*. He is to 'retain (them) within the mental sphere'. In other words, the transference is to be overcome.' The apparently real feelings about the analyst are to be unmasked for what they are. Strong reactions, for example, of love, admiration, anger, hate and the rest toward the analyst are to be seen as illusory. They are there only to be talked about, and the therapeutic strategy is one of 'frustrating the acting out', so that 'the patient can be brought to remember infantile love objects and thus to detach himself gradually from the transference situation.'[368]

The authors want to show that daseinanalysis accomplishes what psychoanalysis cannot, and that this can happen only because the so-called 'transference' is precisely *not* frustrated. Why do this? 'The reason is simple: [the daseinanalyst] does not believe that the theoretical assumptions leading to Freud's suggestions are correct. Nowhere does Freud prove convincingly that the patient's feelings for the analyst do not arise from the present situation' of therapy 'but really [are directed] towards the patient's mother or father'. Indeed, Freud 'even proves the contrary'. He does not 'dispute the genuine nature of the love which makes its appearance in the course of treatment' and admits that 'a correct interpretation of an emotional attachment to the analyst as 'transference' from somewhere else, that is, of acting out as 'transference resistance', does not produce the results we expect from correct interpretations . . . namely, the cessation of it.' Resistance and analysis of resistance then become the justification for the great length of a classic psychoanalysis and the suggestion that psychoanalysis is most likely interminable.

What, then, is one to do? The daseinanalyst 'knows that cures are not effected by months of 'working through', during which the supposed meaning of the patient's relationship to the analyst, his acting out are drilled into him. The Daseinsanalyst believes that 'transference love or hate' is a genuine interpersonal relationship to the analyst as experienced by the analysand.'[369]

Although usually the adult analysand is functional in the affairs of everyday life, emotionally he is often childlike. This is not to be construed pejoratively, however. 'The fact that the analysand behaves in an infantile manner and therefore misjudges the actual situation to a large extent (because of his emotional immaturity, which in turn is due to faulty training in his youth) does not detract from the genuineness of his present feelings. The analysand begins to love the analyst as soon as he becomes aware that he has found someone – possibly for the first time in his life – who really understands him and who accepts him even though he is stunted by his neurosis. He loves him all the more because the analyst permits him to unfold more fully his real and essential being within a safe, interpersonal relationship on the 'playground [*Spielplatz*] of [what Freud called] the transference'.[370]

The analyst's love for the analysand – what Boss, as we have heard, borrowing from Carlos Alberto Seguín, called the 'psychotherapeutic eros' – is the therapeutic agent. For Boss and Condrau, 'as we have said before, all genuine love of one person for another is based on *the possibility* that the loved one offers to the lover *of more fully unfolding his own being-in-the-world with him.*'[371] The psychotherapeutic eros is based on nothing other than the analyst's desire for the possibility of a fuller unfolding of the analysand's existence *with* him in the therapeutic setting. *Amo. Volo ut sis.* In Augustine's words: 'I love you. Now do as you will.' This is all the daseinanalyst 'wants' from the analysand. In turn, 'the attitude of the analyst is taken up by the analysand as a new orientation to life . . . . In each being-together [*Mitsein*], the partners disclose themselves to each other as human beings, that is to say, each as basically the same kind of being as the other,' namely, as *Dasein*. Far from hiding from the analysand behind a mask of anonymity, he discloses himself to the analytic partner *as a human being*. This is not tantamount to chatting to the analysand about his family life, his worries, his aspirations. The disclosure referred to here is *as an existing being*. Being open to the analysand in such a way is in a certain sense indistinguishable from the therapeutic eros.

One should not understand the therapeutic relation in terms of empathy, the 'basic nature of [which] has never been elucidated' in any case, the authors caution. The radical nature of daseinanalysis is perhaps nowhere more evident than in its critique of empathy as the *sine qua non* of effective therapeutic interaction. Accounts of 'effective psychotherapy' are replete with reports of an unearthly capacity for empathy. But just what that means remains entirely unclear. And so, empathy goes the way of transference. Being-in-the-world together, the daseinanalytic partners are in an immediate relation with each other that is a default of being human. No special talent for such 'feeling with' the other is required of the analyst.[372]

The authors add the important qualifier regarding the 'fuller unfolding' of the analysand's being-in-the-world or existence by cautioning that 'we must realize that the primary openness of a human being for the discovery of encountered fellow human beings does not necessarily result in perceptions that do full justice to the one who is encountered.' In other words, there is no guarantee that even given his greater openness the analyst will be seen by the analysand in the fullness of the latter's own ongoing unfolding. Moreover, the analysand's understanding of certain features of the analyst may well be very much 'off'.[373]

It is often of the nature of someone who seeks out a daseinanalyst that he is 'limited to modes of disclosure and behavior similar to a child's. The great variety of mature, full, and free manners of relating are not available to him (as indeed they are not available to the healthy child, but for different reasons). This limitation enables us to understand the phenomena of transference in the narrow sense of the term, namely, the so-called neurotic transference.'[374] It was potentially misleading to use the term 'neurotic transference' here, but the authors' point is that, whatever one calls it, the analysand's less than adequate openness hearkens back to childhood patterns of experience. We now understand that for Boss and Condrau 'neurotic' means 'child-like' (not childish) for a given adult analysand during a given phase of the analysis.

At the outset, the development of a therapeutic partnership is limited by the analysand's possibilities for relating to another human being, which includes the analyst. Given the analysand's expectations, which today are often expressed in the vocabulary of psychopathology and psychiatric diagnosis permeating a medicalized society littered with dubious advertisements for pharmaceuticals, and the analysand's initially constrained capacity for relating to the analyst, the opening hours of analysis are especially important. The authors give an example of such a limitation in the capacity for relating to the analyst in a fully open way by considering an analysand who initially expects the analyst to take on a certain kind of paternal role.

Summarizing the discussion of transference, the authors write: 'Daseinsanalysis regards every analysand-analyst relationship as a genuine relationship *sui generis*. It is genuine despite the fact that the patient is carrying it out in a limited fashion, owing to his mental distortions. It could not be otherwise. The analysand-analyst relationship, like any other, is grounded in the primary being-with [*Mitsein*] of one man with another, which is part of Dasein's primary world-disclosure.' In general, 'fearing that they might be thought unscientific, [psychoanalysts] use this *terminus technicus* ['transference phenomena'] to assuage their uneasiness and to protect themselves against 'real' love or hate directed towards them by their analysands.'

Further elucidation of resistance complements the discussion of transference.

As a rule, neurotically reduced people regard their wretched interpersonal relations as the only ones possible. They do not know that greater freedom is available. If their restrictions are repeatedly questioned, previously non-admitted possibilities of behavior regularly appear, along with perception of the things and fellow human beings who are part of these world-disclosing possibilities. The analyst practicing in this fashion will not try to persuade patients that much of what they feel and mean is only a cloak for opposite wishes and tendencies. He will thus avoid giving the impression of devaluing their experience, thereby confusing them and arousing unnecessary anxiety. However, the Daseinsanalyst's respect for phenomena should not be confused with an exclusive concern with those phenomena of which the patient is already fully aware. He knows that the patient's being, apart from overtly admitted and accepted modes of behavior includes a great many other modes of being, some of which the patient is trying hard not to become aware of, and many of which contrast with the overtly expressed modes. He also knows that these possibilities for relating have to be acknowledged by the patient as his own before he can get well. Nevertheless, all of the patient's modes of behavior – those openly carried out and those far warded off – are considered autonomous by the therapist; he must treat them all as valid. He must never try to deny the reality of a phenomenon. Transference and resistance indisputably refer to actual phenomena of interhuman relationships, although in a veiled way.[375]

In the analysis of resistance understood daseinanalytically 'the patient is tirelessly confronted with the limitations of his life and ... these limitations are incessantly questioned, so that the possibility of a richer existence is implied.'[376] In the course of such exploration, a 'deep attachment of the patient to the analyst develops by itself.' This is not different from the formation of any other human relationship in which the other is taken seriously, valued and respected regardless of his currently dominant behavior. The difference is that this being taken seriously is focal for the therapeutic partnership. Finally, 'the overcoming of these resistances is the essential function of the analysis, that part of its function which alone assures us that we have achieved something for the patient.'[377]

In the next section, on 'interpretation of [the] unconscious [*das Unbewußt*]', we find Boss's well-known critique of the Freudian topographic (conscious, preconscious and unconscious [*das Bewußte, das Vorbewußte, das Unbewußte*]) and structural (I, it, more-than-me [*Ich, Es, Überich*]) models of the dynamic unconscious. The problem of the Unconscious [*das Unbewußte*] is related to the notion of consciousness [*das Bewußtsein*], on which the metapsychology of the Unconscious ultimately rests. The difficulty with the Freudian notion of consciousness (literally, what is *bewußt*, that is to say, known) is *there* for us one minute but (quoting Freud) 'is no longer so a moment later ... [And] what the idea [that is, what is known] [*Vorstellung*] was in the interval [*Zwischenzeit*] we do know. We can only say it was latent [*latent*].'[378]

As part of the conceptual world of psychology and psychoanalysis, the phenomenon of consciousness has been assumed without having been explained.[379] It follows that if one does not grasp what being conscious [*bewußt*] means, one cannot possibly make intelligible what being not-conscious [*unbewußt*] might mean. The notion of *the* Unconscious or *an* Unconscious is therefore be left behind. 'One of the immeasurable advantages of the Daseinsanalytic understanding of man is the fact that it renders superfluous the assumption of an unconscious' and so also all of the theoretical difficulties it introduces. 'The recognition that others have the same ability as I have to understand – or to become 'conscious' of – something is not based on deduction and analogy (as are, according to Freud's own statements, his notions of a consciousness [*Bewußtsein*] and an unconscious [*Unbewußt*]).' They float in the air of speculation.

In the second part of the section on the Unconscious, the authors further clarify the daseinanalytic perspective:

> Analysis of Dasein enables us to become aware that the things and fellow men an individual encounters appear to him – within the meaning-disclosing light of his Dasein – immediately (and *without any subjective processes being involved*) [emphasis added]. They appear as what they are, in accordance with the world-openness of his existence. Because it is the essence of Dasein to light up, illuminate, disclose, and perceive, we always find Dasein primordially *with* what it encounters, similar to so-called physical light. Light, too, is always 'out there', shining *on* the things that appear within its luminous realm. Relating to the things in the way of being-with-them-primordially, of letting them shine forth and appear, Dasein spatializes itself into its relationships with what it encounters, in accordance with its close or distant concern for the encountered in any given case. This given man exists, consumes his time, and fulfills his Dasein. Existing in this fashion, man depends on what he encounters as much as the encountered depends on the disclosing nature of man for its appearance. Daseinsanalysis can grant an immediate and autonomous reality to all kinds of phenomena, which in Freud's view would be degraded from the outset to incorrect deceptions of the unconscious. Daseinsanalysis can grant this reality because it has not prejudged a whole host of phenomena according to an arbitrary decision about the nature of the world and reality. Daseinsanalysis makes it unnecessary to go beyond immediate experience. It can elucidate without difficulty, on the basis of immediate experience alone, all those psychic phenomena that compelled Freud to invent the unconscious.[380]

So-called 'acting out' is, once again, affirmed as something positive. It 'may indicate that something is unfolding for the first time in the analysand's life. He dares to behave in a manner that has never before been permitted him (at least not sufficiently). Acting out in these cases can be neither a remembering nor a repetition.'[381] It follows that 'the only therapeutically effective action by the therapist is *permission* to act out. With this permission it is possible for the patient to experience again and again, to practice, and eventually to acquire modes of behaving that had not been permitted in the relationship to his real parents and educators.' Indeed, it is 'harmful to 'transform' acting out into remembering, especially if the therapist tries to accomplish this by calling the behavior of the analysand 'infantile'.'[382] Permission is the extent of intervention in daseinanalysis. The scenario is one of the analyst not 'correcting' an analysand's behavior, implicitly or explicitly, for example, by suggesting that the analysand is not behaving as adults do. Instead of lying quietly on the couch, the analysand may get up and begin to pace. He may do more. Boss and Condrau give the example of someone who kneels at the side of the couch. More florid behavior (yelling, cursing, threatening the therapist) can be alarming to the analyst, reminding him of the tantrums children 'throw'. These must be permitted – within the limits described by Boss in his interview with Hall (1968a) reviewed earlier.

Most experienced therapists have witnessed gestures that might suggest that the analysand is about to strike out at them. Here, Boss and Condrau say, the analyst must remain calm since

> the childlike modes of behavior that sprout for the first time in the analysand-analyst relationship should be valued as the precious starting points from which all future developments will arise. The analysand's being-himself will mature into ever more differentiated forms of relating, if the more primitive forms of relating are first permitted to unfold themselves fully. If this is allowed, maturer forms of behavior appear spontaneously. Thus the gradual detachment from the analytic situation happens *because* acting out is now permitted; it is not produced by a misinterpretation of acting out as renewal of childhood memories.[383]

Thus, the Freudian notion of strictly verbal 'working through' is a theoretical rationalization that disallows permissiveness in regard to the trying out and practicing of newly admitted ways of behaving in the analyst-analysand relationship.'

Happily, the acting out that is permitted as the analysand opens himself in his relationship to the analyst is mostly verbal. 'With seriously ill people,' however,

> this is seldom [at] the conceptual, intellectual-verbal level. Therefore, the analysand-analyst relationship must often resemble that of an infant to his mother, if the relationship is to be genuine and appropriate to the patient's condition. At times this relationship can grow only if it is confined to the silent language of gestures, sometimes even exclusively to silence, so that Dasein may come to light and grow... [I]n the analysis of adults we have failed to recognize sufficiently that we are dealing with people who have remained small children at the very core of their existence and to whom we can genuinely relate only if we meet them on that same childlike level.[384]

This is an indirect indictment of Freud's notion of the childhood etiology of the psychoneuroses or, in current terms, the source of current problems in early childhood experiences with dysfunctional parents in badly damaged families:

> Nothing that happens to a child, however, is capable of producing and maintaining any pattern of behavior in this causal sense. The experiences of childhood can only *limit* and *distort* the carrying out of [the] innate possibilities [of *Dasein*] of relating to the world. They cannot cause and produce the relationships themselves.... We cannot repeat often enough that no amount whatever of 'blind' energies can ever produce and build a lucid human world consisting of meaning-disclosing relationships with what is encountered. *Human existence is essentially not a physical process but primarily a historical event* [emphasis added]. This means that in every actual relation to something or somebody, Dasein's whole history is inherent and present, whether the historical unfolding of a certain kind of relationship is remembered explicitly or not.... [W]hat matters most, therapeutically, is not the recalling of the occasion when a neurotic pattern of relating to one's fellow men was acquired in childhood but finding the answer to two questions: Why has the patient remained, right up to the present time, caught within this same, restricted way of communicating? What is keeping him a prisoner of his neurotic behavior patterns right now?

And what are the answers to these questions?

> Neurotic patients usually cannot even imagine that another way of relating to people is possible. Some may know intellectually of a greater freedom, but they do not trust it sufficiently to try it out.... [A]ny change of the narrow perspective to which they are accustomed is terrifying, especially if it is a change toward greater freedom.[385]

And so we come once more to the famous 'Why after all *not*?' of daseinanalysis.

> The Daseinsanalyst often asks his patients 'Why not?' thereby encouraging them to ever greater tests of daring. 'Why is it that you don't dare to behave in such-and-such a manner during the analytic session?' is a question often asked in place of the usual analytic 'Why?'[386]

This text comes as close as any to offering what might be construed as a complete 'theory' of daseinanalysis. Adopting the use of the couch and invocation of the fundamental rule, daseinanalysis (1) places the unrealized possibilities of the analysand's existence above the actuality of his personality, concerned not with what the analysand has done but rather with what he has *not* done; (2) focuses on the immediacy of the given *Dasein-Dasein* relation between analyst and analysand and (3) on the freedom of the other; and (4) welcomes the appearance of surprising behavior, seeing in it the emergence or opening out of previously constrained ways of relating to others (in this case the analyst) and to things.

The chapter concludes with a section on 'the concept of cure'. It is important to recall that cure [*Kur*] means a course of treatment and that 'cure' and 'care' have a common source, both etymologically and in terms of praxis. Here the authors raise the perennial question about what constitutes 'effective psychotherapy'. In psychoanalysis, the gold standard is effective interpretations. Some have seen in other modalities the opportunity for a 'corrective emotional experience'. By contrast, daseinanalysis beats an 'urgently required' hasty 'retreat [from theoretical concepts of that sort], as swift and complete a one as possible, to what immediately discloses itself in our dealings with our patients and is to be experienced there.' This, we begin to see, amounts to thinking differently about the experience of both the analysand and the analyst.

Citing a variety of well-known therapeutically effective interventions from popular lore, Boss and Condrau again quote Freud with approval. 'We make available to him [the analysand] the arena in which he is permitted [*gestattet wird*] to unfold [*entfalten*] in almost total freedom.'[387] The procedure is effective, however, 'only to the extent it allows the patient to gain his essential human freedom *vis-à-vis* himself and the world, and his freedom to place himself fully at the service of what he encounters.' Daseinanalysis is effective by 'changing his [the analysand's] basic attunement of anxiety and mistrust to one characterized by a more trusting relationship to the world around him' and is tantamount to the 'transformation of an existence'.[388]

A second overview of daseinanalysis by Boss and Gion Condrau, '**Existential Analysis**' (1968b)[389], was written for a major anthology of articles by psychiatrists, first published in the United Kingdom. The book is divided into two parts: 'scientific' and 'clinical'. The Boss/Condrau contribution appears in the second part, which includes chapters on (1) the contribution of clinical psychology to psychiatry, by H. J. Eysenck, (2) schizophrenia (two chapters), (3) psychoanalysis, (4) Morita therapy, (5) Pavlovian theory in psychiatry, (6) 'learning therapies' (essentially on behavior therapy, by Joseph Wolpe), (7) 'group hypnosis or collective hypnosis in the USSR', (8) the placebo effect (here termed the 'placebo response'), (9) 'clinical perspectives in psycho-pharmacology' (by Jean Delay and Pierre Deniker),[390] (10) family psychiatry, (11) community psychiatry, (12) transcultural psychiatry, and (13) 'general principles of construction of psychiatric hospitals'.

The authors' chapter title is an alternate translation of *Daseinsanalyse* ('analysis of existence'). It presents the reader with problems of how to distinguish what Boss and Condrau present from the *Existenzanalyse* (analysis of existence) of Viktor Frankl, as well as the various forms of psychotherapy that were inspired by the publication in 1958 of *Existence* and came to be known generically as 'existential analysis'.[391]

As in the contribution to the volume on psychoanalytic techniques (1967c), the title avoids the German word *Dasein*. The authors also write of 'analytical psychotherapy' in place of 'psychoanalysis', introducing possible confusion with Carl Gustav Jung's analytical psychology [*analytische Psychologie*], which had also recently come to be well known in English-speaking countries.[392] Heidegger's 'existential-ontological ideas' are mentioned at the outset as having been the source of 'new points of departure' for psychotherapists. The authors stress, however, that 'from the standpoint of the method [to be described], *Freudian psychoanalysis remains the basis of this psychotherapeutic approach* [emphasis added].'

Remarking that 'it is rather astonishing that psychotherapists nowadays are concerned about philosophy, and they are sometimes blamed for doing so,' Boss and Condrau review the influences that led to the natural sciences' hegemony in psychiatry and psychotherapy. They refer to representatives from academic and experimental psychology (most of them from the Gestalt school) that have had an influence on the study of the relation of the body and the mind – Hans Driesch (1867-1941), Felix Krueger (1874-1948), Wolfgang Köhler (1887-1967), Max Wertheimer (1809-1943), Kurt Koffka (1886-1941) and Eduard Spranger (1882-1963) – and were in the background of the development of the field of medicine known as psychosomatics.

They quote Binswanger, who is credited with having clearly seen the issues that are involved in psychotherapy: 'The organism is from the outset always something different and much more than merely organism, the mind is always something more than merely mind. The human being is and remains a unity. It does not split up into body and mind; rather, the body is already mind, and the mind already body.'[393] Insight into the unity of body and mind is attributed to Heidegger, 'one of a group of philosophical thinkers whose works, despite their occasional divergences, are all subsumed under the collective designation of 'Existential Philosophy'. It is not clear who these other folks may be, but they likely have in mind those authors represented in the famous anthology by Walter Kaufmann, *Existentialism from Dostoevsky to Sartre* (1956; expanded edition 1975), referenced above.

The term 'daseinsanalysis' is first used in this section of the text, but here 'the daseinsanalysis, or existential analysis, of Martin Heidegger [which] inquires into the meaning of being as such' the authors have in mind is the analytics of existence [*Daseinsanalytik*] of *Being and Time*, not the approach to psychotherapy known as *Daseinsanalyse* (analysis of *Dasein* [existence]). Hence the definite article. Readers were likely already confused about the difference between the two, one that had been introduced, as we have seen, in 1963 with the publication of Boss's own *Psychoanalysis and Daseinsanalysis*, which had in fact originally been about psychoanalysis and the analytics of *Dasein* [*Daseinsanalytik*].

The preliminary treatment of Heidegger in this section focuses in part on the body, noting that 'man's body is something essentially different from an animal organism.' Citing *Being and Time*, the authors are, however, quoting from the *Letter on Humanism*: 'It could very well be that nature presents only one of its sides for technical manipulation and mastery by man and its essence is completely concealed. No, the essential nature of man does not consist in being an animal organism, nor can this inadequate definition of man's essence be dealt with and compensated by equipping man with an immortal soul or with reason or with a personality. In every case, being (essence), and that on the basis of the same metaphysical scheme, is passed over.' The translation is not good and might have left some readers puzzled as they worked their way through this 'historical' section. What Heidegger, in fact, had said was this: 'It could even be that nature hides its essence [*Wesen*] in the side it turns to technical control by man. As little as the essence of man consists in being an animal organism [*animalischer Organismus*] can this insufficient determination of the essence [*Wesensbestimmung*] of man be eliminated and compensated for by outfitting man with an immortal soul [*unsterblichen Seele*] or with reason or with the character of a person [*Personcharakter*]. In each instance, and that on the basis of the same metaphysical design, the essence is passed over.'[394]

There are similar problems with further discussion of Heidegger that follows, but there is an evocative formulation that summarizes part of it: 'Therefore the question can no longer be: *What* is man, but how *is* man?' Speaking of Heidegger's understanding of *Dasein* as 'standing in the openness of being', we read that this is 'called by Heidegger the ec-sistence of man'. The neologism 'ec-sistence' would likely have made little sense to readers. The authors are picking up on Heidegger's expression of *Existenz*, later expressed as 'ek-sistence' traced back to the Latin *eksistere* (literally, to stand [-*sistere*] out [*ek*-]), having paraphrased Heidegger's well-known sentence from *Sein und Zeit*, which they render: 'The 'essence' of existence (Dasein) lies in its actual existence (Existenz).'[395] Just what the interpolation of 'actual' is meant to convey is not clear but, once again, it likely threw off readers. What could the difference be between 'existence' and 'actual existence'? The point of the discussion is to describe 'opening up and discovering meaning', which is there from the start, as an example of the infant's encounter of and by its mother: 'If understanding of what is encountered were not of the essence of human nature, as Heidegger claims, the importance of the mother could not be explained beyond her being the source of breast milk.'[396]

The authors mention what we have come to know as the Zollikon seminars, which by then had for the most part been completed. 'Psychotherapy has gained from [Heidegger's] writings more than a new outlook on man and an elucidation of our understanding of illness. In personal talks and in seminars in Zürich, in the last few years, he has made himself increasingly acquainted with the endeavors of psychiatrists and psychotherapists and has given them an opportunity to put Daseinsanalysis on a firm scientific basis.'[397]

The third section is on 'analysis of Dasein [*Daseinsanalytik*]' of Heidegger, which 'is more appropriate to an understanding of man than the concepts which natural science has introduced into medicine and psychotherapy.' This is a crucial point, since 'if this kind of approach does come closer to human reality than the approach of natural science, it will be able to give us something we have hitherto not been able to find in psychoanalytic theory: an understanding of what we are doing (and of why we are doing it in just this way) when we treat a patient psychoanalytically, such an understanding being based on insights into the essence of human being. A deeper understanding of our practices could not but have a beneficial effect on them.'[398] By contrast with the view of the natural sciences, the 'analysis of Dasein' 'urges all those who deal with human beings to ... remain in the presence of what they immediately perceive and do not get lost in 'scientific' abstractions, derivations, explanations, and calculations estranged from the immediate reality of the given phenomena .... [T]he *fundamental difference which separates the natural sciences from the Daseins analytic or existential science of man is to be found right at this point.*'[399]

In the context of discussing encounter between analyst and analysand, the authors clarify the spatiality of the human body. The human body [*Leib*] is not in space; instead, it spatializes or, as Heidegger will later say, makes room for [*einräumt*][400] *some* things which disclose themselves in the open provided by *Dasein* while *other* beings conceal themselves. This occurs in the context of always already given meaningful references. Boss and Condrau give the example of the relation between an infant and its mother, who 'can be importantly 'meaningful' to [the infant] in this interpersonal sense only if his initial relation to her is one of opening up and discovering meanings – in this case the meaning of being sheltered or loved by her.'[401] Here the *Dasein-Dasein* relation is understood as the ground for any 'relationship'.

The differences between this 'existential analysis' and psychoanalysis are discussed in the fourth section of the chapter. Here the focus is on the so-called psychosomatic conditions, which have been conceptualized on the faulty assumption of an ontological distinction between physical things and mental things. Boss and Condrau discuss Freud's notion of 'hysterical conversion' as a misconception that is possible only on the basis of making such a false distinction and then having to explain the so-called 'mysterious leap' between the body and the mind: 'Psychic 'things' – conscious and unconscious thoughts, fantasies or emotions, body functions and body organs – do not, in fact, exist as primarily separate phenomena, nor is there such a thing as an illness which exists by itself.' Talk therefore of 'having diabetes' or 'having OCD', for example, is just that, *un façon de parler*. The human being does not 'have' diseases of the body or what came to be known as 'diseases of the mind'.

> *The* stomach and *the* stomach illness, *the* thoughts and *the* general paralysis are unreal abstractions. On the other hand, *my* arm, *my* stomach, *our* instincts, *your* thoughts are real. Mention of my, your, of their *being ill*, refers to reality. The possessive pronouns of the daily language point to an existence which persists and unfolds in a life history. They refer to a human being never exhaustively described by reference to his 'possessions', whether they are thought of as the constantly changing 'substance' of his 'body' or his equally inconstant instincts, feelings, fantasies, and thoughts. Nor is man identical with the sum of all these objectifications.[402]

Were the human being 'an extant [*vorhanden*] object among other mundane objects ... how could such a 'thing' ever encounter a fellow human being and become aware of him as that particular being?' The section is a rich analysis of what were then called organ neuroses such as asthma, ulcers, colitis, contact dermatitis, migraine and the rest. The term 'psychosomatic' has been expunged from official psychiatry. It is perhaps not a loss, since the notion itself was unclarified in the literature and its origins in Cartesian dualism were not made explicit.

The Zollikon Seminars directed by Heidegger and Boss were not published until 1987, but the book that is the fruit of that collaborative effort appeared in 1971.[403] *Existential Foundations of Medicine and Psychology* (1971a)[404], as the book came to be known in English translation, is a textbook for physicians and psychologists that argues for revising the very starting point of their research and practice. *Caveat lector*. The translation is very loose and free, and a very much reduced version of the German original. It would require a monograph of its own to reveal the many misrepresentations of Boss's prose and his meaning. What reviewers said about the book should be considered in view of this.

Boss acknowledges his gratitude to his teachers, who ranged over many disciplines: Walter R. Hess (1881-1973) in physiology; Eugen Bleuler (1857-1939) and Julius Wagner von Jauregg (1857-1940) in psychiatry; Franz Chvostek (1864-1944) and Wilhelm Loeffler (1887-1872) in internal medicine; Freud and Jung, in 'depth psychology'; and, of course, Martin Heidegger.

Although written for medical doctors, the book was not intended to be beyond the reach and grasp of those who lacked medical training. Few doctors, including psychiatrists, living today have heard of this book. That is regrettable for the profession, since the *Outline* [*Grundriß*] is among only a few works that might yet serve as a radical re-envisioning of the professions, especially the subspeciality medicine known as psychiatry. It is also a possible starting point of a declaration of independence of psychotherapy from the medical model.[405]

Although translated as 'outline', a *Grundriß* is more a 'layout' or 'ground plan' or 'floor plan' much like what an architect produces. Heidegger carefully examined the manuscript of Boss' *Grundriß* much as he had the first dream book, but played a much greater role in its genesis and evolution than he had with the earlier book. Heidegger, Boss says quite clearly, 'is responsible for this attempt to lay out a foundation for medicine [and psychology].'[406] Two decades later, echoing an addendum to the preface of the dream book, Boss is openly grateful in acknowledging his indebtedness to Heidegger's involvement in the project. Referring to the text's grounding in the Zollikon seminars, Boss writes that the book 'reflects the countless conversations in which I was privileged to participate over two decades of friendship. For the past fifteen years, Heidegger has held two or three seminars each semester for the benefit of medical students, including mine. The discussions coming out of these 'Zollikon Seminars' also figure significantly in this work. More important, though, is the fact that this work actually evolved under Heidegger's watchful eye. There is not one section of 'philosophical' import which was denied his generous criticism.'[407]

The first edition of the book was published in 1971 as *Grundriß der Medizin*. In the preface to the second, 'enlarged' edition of 1975, Boss wrote: 'The title of the first edition, as it turned out, failed to express the author's original intent; it seemed to indicate that the book could be understood only by physicians. I had assumed with too much haste that everyone would accept a foundation of medicine based on human nature as, necessarily, a foundation of psychology and sociology as well.'[408] And so it became an 'outline of medicine *and* psychology [*Medizin und der Psychologie*]'. This would make it a book for doctors and psychiatrists, but also for clinical psychologists and others grounded in academic psychology.

The book consists of three parts: an outline of medicine as currently understood, a sketch of a contrasting human [*menschengerecht*] medicine, and approaches to an existentially informed [*daseinsgemäße*] pathology (etiology, pathogenesis, and phenomenology of being ill [*Krank-sein*]). In a fourth part Boss offers some pointers or preliminary notes [*Hinweise*] on an existentially informed therapy [*daseinsgemäße Therapie*] and, finally, an approach to preventative medicine from an existential perspective 'in modern industrial society'.

The English title likely reflects Boss's appreciation that people outside of medicine would be attracted by the word 'existential' in the title, linking his book with the tradition of 'existential psychology and psychiatry' that had developed in the 1960s. Rollo May's anthology *Existence* (1958) had only recently brought European psychology and psychiatry (especially Ludwig Binswanger, Erwin Straus and Viktor von Gebsattel) to the attention of American readers. Associations were likely also first made with the tradition of 'humanistic psychology' that originated as the 'Third Force' of American psychology beginning with the work of Gordon Allport and Carl Rogers. In the end, these associations are problematic, however, since daseinanalysis is essentially different not only from medical science – more specifically, medical psychology – but also from 'existentialist' and 'humanistic' approaches.

The English volume was said to be a 'somewhat abridged' version of the second German edition.[409] In fact, it is an extensively reduced text of the second edition of the *Grundriß*, which runs to about 154,000 words. The translation is 28,000 words shy of that. The subtitle was omitted for the English edition. As noted, in it Boss had named (in order) physiology, pathology, psychology, therapy and, in general, an existentially-informed [*daseinsgemäßig*] approach to preventive medicine. Apart from 'psychology', all of the areas mentioned belong to medicine. This raises the question of how Boss then understood the relation between academic psychology and psychiatry. In the volume, 'therapy' refers throughout both to a form of medical treatment and to psychoanalysis as a modality of psychotherapy. His English-speaking readers were reminded that any sort of ground plan for medical practice 'based on human nature' must also be a ground plan for psychology, academic and applied, and sociology. Having made claims for such wide application, it is worth recalling that in the Zollikon seminars the social sciences known as psychology, anthropology and sociology had been rejected as caught up in the premises of natural science. The broad sweep of the *Grundriß* is addressed to all of these 'disciplines' as well as to medicine and psychiatry, but with a highly critical stance toward all of them.

It is not possible to summarize this work here, especially the far richer German text. Suffice to say by way of a general orientation to it, the volume is organized around a 'test case *Testfall*', Regula Zurcher, whose illness is explored, 'symptom' by 'symptom', from the contrasting points of view of traditional psychiatry and Boss's daseinanalytically informed approach. His familiarity with the literature of neuroscience, learning theory, and behaviorism is found in these pages. This is important, since Boss cannot be accused of having overlooked two of the most powerful influences in clinical psychology then prominent at the end of the 1960s. Little attention is paid to pharmacotherapy, however, and this is a significant omission since, as early as 1951, Boss had published a paper on the use of Scopolamine and colleagues were experimenting with the newly synthesized so-called psychotropics such as chlorpromazine (Thorazine), various antipsychotics and antidepressives, and LSD in the treatment of inpatients.

References include publications in English, French and German. We see that Boss was following the work of American psychologists such as Gordon Allport, whose theory of personality provides the philosophical orientation of American psychiatry, and also the highly influential psychiatrist Harry Stack Sullivan. We learn that Boss was familiar with unpublished manuscripts by Heidegger, including the 1936 course on Schelling's *Vom Wesen der menschlichen Freiheit*.[410]

Key sections are devoted to the basics or essentials [*Grundzüge*] of being human [*Mensch-sein*]: *Dasein's* spatiality [*Räumlichkeit*], temporality [*Zeitlichkeit*], corporeality [*Leiblichkeit*], being-with-others [*Miteinandersein*], being-attuned [*Gestimmt-sein*], memory [*Gedächtnis*] and historicity [*Geschichtlichkeit*]. The section on pathology should be read with care, noting that Boss does not understand being ill as attributable to pathogenesis, that is, as caused. Instead, he is concerned solely with the phenomenology of being-ill. Of greatest interest for practice is the concluding part on 'Suggestions for a Daseinsanalytic Therapy'. The topic falls under three headings: the patient to be treated [*der zu behandelnde Patient*], the locus [*Ort*] of therapeutic treatment, and treatment by 'those who are therapeutically active'.

By the late 1970s, psychotherapy was becoming more and more a part of the everyday life of the middle class. Nine international congresses on the topic had been held before the summer of 1976. '**The Psychotherapeutic Process**' (1977c)[411] is the original manuscript of Boss's closing paper for the Tenth International Congress for Psychotherapy, given on July 10, 1976, only a few weeks after Heidegger's death. The theme of the congress was the 'Psychotherapeutic Process'. Following the conference, Boss was interviewed by the Korean psychiatrist Dongshick Rhee at Boss's home in Zurich. As we have seen, an account of the dialogues surfaced in 1996.

The proceedings of the conference are given a brief survey in Boss's concluding comments. He then identifies two definitions of the *process* of psychotherapy: (a) the Freudian notion of 'a sequence of psychic processes' in which *it* [*Id*] becomes *I* [*Ich*], that is, what was unconscious becomes conscious, and (b) 'a dialogue [*Dialog*] between one or more psychotherapists, on the one hand, and one or more individuals being looked after [*Schutzbefohlenen*], on the other, in the course of which the latter are able to attain individuation [*Individuation*] or self-actualization [*Selbstverwirklichung*].' Boss's term *Schutzbefohlenen* is interesting in that he avoids the terms patient, client and analysand, instead characterizing the person in therapy as someone who is not capable of fully or adequately looking after himself and is perhaps a ward of others.

Both definitions of the process of psychotherapy have been applied to all of its forms, from psychoanalysis to group therapy [*Gruppentherapie*], talk therapy [*Gesprächstherapie*] and behavior therapy [*Verhaltenstherapie*]. 'So far so good [*So weit, so gut*],' Boss writes. 'But [*Aber*]...':

> As long as we have not sufficiently thought about it, all our definitions of the psychotherapeutic process remain unfounded [*bodenlos*]. To get to the bottom [*Grund*] of it, we obviously need deeper insight into the specific character [*Eigenart*] of our human existing [*Existieren*]. For it is only from this specific character

that the conditions of the possibility arise for being able to speak about something like a behavior, a conversation, a dialogue, an it-transformation [*Es-Umwandlung*] at all.[412]

As preparation for dealing with new *questions* Boss hopes attendees will consider in the immediate future, he asks them (and us) to consider two events he had only recently caught wind of. He presents an anecdote of a twenty-eight-year-old PhD psychologist who was beginning his 'so-called teaching analysis' with an experienced older analyst. The young man was the supervisor of a number of children's homes. Boss's text is worth repeating verbatim since it presents a scenario that is ubiquitous in our own time.

> All possible relations to the things and fellow men of his world were characterized by an enormous detachment [*Distanzhaltung*]. What the analysand provided consisted almost entirely of objective, scientific observations of what presented itself to him. Nothing, not even the children whose welfare he had to supervise, concerned him, as they say, emotionally [*gefühlsmäßig*]. He did not get involved in anything. Everything there was to know about psychology he knew with his head. He fulfilled his administrative duties perfectly. He was only surprised that all his attempts to deal therapeutically with the individual children failed again and again because the children simply did not want to come back after only a few hours [of treatment] with him. Four weeks after the beginning of his training analysis the analyst noticed for the first time a visible emotional change in him when he entered the treatment room. The psychologist confessed to her that today, for the first time in his life, it had occurred to him to stroke the hair of some children who had gathered around him during one of his visits to the children's home. As a result, the children were transformed. They had not looked at him as before, fearfully shy, but [instead] delighted. The idea of such a first gesture of tenderness had come to him without the analyst having done anything else in the few preceding hours of therapy than to greet him in a benevolent and friendly [*wohlwollend-freundlich*] manner and then to say goodbye again in the same attitude after she had listened to him during the session with constant attentiveness without having verbally expressed herself.'[413]

The second anecdote consisted of the report of two dreams from the analysis of a forty-two-year-old university professor, one from early on in the analysis and the second from two years later. Briefly, the second dreams showed that the analysand's waking relationships with women had become 'humanized [*vermenschlicht*]' of the period of analysis.

 The point of the two anecdotes was that in both cases the therapy consisted of 'co-human dialogue [*mitmenschlich Zwiegespräch*]', bearing in mind that the silent listening [*schweigsam Zuhören*] of the analyst 'is also directly part of the speaking [*Sprechen*] between two people'. The conditions of the possibility of any conversation consist in the pregiven mutuality of relatedness, a common openness to a shared world of things and fellow human beings. Human nature consists in a responsiveness and capacity to act that any given bit of behavior implies. This is, for Boss, the starting point for understanding the content of therapeutic conversation based on the ontological given *Rede* [talk].

The words of the poet Hölderlin were likely very much in mind: 'for we *are* a conversation [*Gespräch*], and hear from one another....' This is why dialogue [*Zwiegespräch*] can take place. Only because existing is being together [*Mitsein*] and being in [*In-sein*] are conversation of that occur in therapy at all possible. We are already conversing (< *conversor*, 'to abide and be engaged with') with one another, so it only appears that the analyst begins a session. The conversation already in play is taken up by both. And, as Boss pointed out, being in conversation includes silences. Genuine *Gespräch* is not only phonemes. Communication of information or data is secondary to our being in conversation.

Therapy, then, occurs at the level of conversation, not the communication of facts, stories, reports of experiences (symptoms, for example), the expression of wishes, ideas, and affects. 'If it is like this,' Boss says, 'then strictly speaking it is misleading to call the psychotherapeutic process dia-logue [*Dia-log*]. For dia-logue is a talking back and forth [*Hin- und Herreden*],' which

> in turn, presupposes at least two primarily self-existing, separate encapsulated subjects or encapsulated consciousnesses. However, it remains forever unclear, and no epistemology has ever been able to clarify it, how encapsulated subjects primarily imagined as immanences [*Immanenzen*] [that is, intramental realities] step out of themselves and over to [*hinübersteigen*] things and fellow human beings, transcend [*transzendieren*] [literally, 'to climb over'] to them.[414] Rather, we experience ourselves in fact [*faktisch*] [or in the reality of everyday experience] in this way, since *from the beginning we are never first given to ourselves alone* [emphasis added]. Rather, we always find ourselves already together with our fellow human beings. Every single one of us always already originally takes part in the open realm of a common world opening which consists of a being able to take in and to be responsive to that which shows itself to us.[415]

Reflecting on his first example: 'Only because of our original togetherness [*Miteinandersein*] was it possible ... that in the togetherness of the patients with their freer [*freier*] therapists the previously untouchable psychologist suddenly became open for stroking the children's hair and the dysfunctional university professor was able to bring the full possibilities of love to fruition.'[416]

Reflecting on the therapeutic process in his two case examples, Boss notes that the behaviors eventually realized by the respective analysands were at first accessible only to one of the partners – the analyst – but given the 'primary' ontological togetherness that characterizes every existing human being, the other partner was able to openly respond within it in such a way that he, as it were, borrowed from the analyst his excess of freedom and over time worked out in his own life – sometimes taking a very long time – a different way of relating to others. In the case of the psychologist, it was to warm up to his juvenile charges and for the university professor it was to express his sexuality. The 'content' of the freedom is in every case nothing more or less than an increase in being open to what was encountering the individual in meaningful ways: the children entrusted to the care of the school psychologist, or females in the life of the university professor.

All this leads to a central question: 'If what happens in the course of psychotherapy can only wrongly be called a dialogue, is it a psychotherapeutic process?' Given the limits imposed on him as the person responsible for wrapping up the conference, Boss focused on the notion of process. In Heideggerian fashion, he looked to the etymology of the word *Prozeß* in the context of what the psychotherapist does – or, he added, 'should do'.

The term 'process' derives from the Latin *procedere* (and the related *processus*), which Boss glossed with *Fortschritt* (which means 'progress', 'headway' or 'advance') and *Vor-sich-Gehen* ('goings-on' in the sense of a happening). A process so understood takes place or 'goes on' 'in time' over a certain span of minutes or hours or weeks. For example, the process of fermentation of grapes to become wine happens in a more or less determinable number of weeks. A given surgical procedure, if done well, usually takes from a half-hour to many hours. Here the 'in' of the process happening 'in time' [*in der Zeit*]' is understood spatially. But 'if we imagine the 'in' of the psychotherapeutic process happening 'in time' in this way,' Boss asked his audience, 'can we even come close to what really happens when the psychotherapist is with one or another person seeking help?': 'What was the time when, in our concrete example, it happened that suddenly, one day, a young psychologist, shortly after the beginning of an analysis, but for the first time in his life, could delicately stroke the hair of the children entrusted to him? What was the time when the other analysand was able to 'progress [*prozedieren*] from being essentially a head [*Kopfwesen*] to being a fully loving partner with a woman?' In each case these time refers to the lived timeliness [*Zeithaftigkeit*] of the individual, which is indistinguishable from the quality of his existing [*Existieren*] in any given instance. It cannot be measured. The time of the psychotherapeutic process is to be understood as a 'having time for . . . [*Zeithaben für* . . .]' and

> there is no psychotherapeutic process [*Prozeß*] – seen from a human point of view – which would take place in a time container [*Zeithälter*] surrounding the human being from the outside, as it were. Rather, the analyst and the analysand only have time for each other [*füreinander haben*], inasmuch as in being together with the same things of their common world they carry out [*austragen*] their time, each carrying out his own existing. The time both spend in the world is well spent when in their togetherness the therapist's greater and freer openness to the world gives the pathologically unfree patient the courage to now have more and more time for things that have always been pressing on him, but for which he had no time [earlier on] because, fearfully unfree or vain, he fled from them to others . . .. No psychotherapeutic happening [*Geschehen*], then, is merely a process [*Prozeß*] in the everyday [*vulgar*] or modern scientific sense of the taking place

[Ablaufen] of proceedings [Vorgangen] and occurrences [Vorkomnisse]. Psychotherapeutic happenings are always in and of themselves timely [zeithaft] in nature, insofar as they give the patient more and more time for the realization of more and more manifold possibilities of behavior in relation to what he encounters in our common world. Psychotherapy is therefore an expansion [Weitung] of the realization of man's original temporality [Zeitlichkeit] and thus of himself as an essentially timely being [zeithaften Wesens] which always consists only in having time for.... For being a human being [Mensch-sein] is essentially and exclusively a timing itself [Sich-zeitigen], i.e. the carrying out of itself [Sich-austragen] and bringing to appearance [Zum-Vorschein-bringen] of [the human being's] given possibilities of existence [Existenzmöglichkeiten].[417]

Since processes occur in time, psychotherapy cannot be a process since it does not take place *in* time. It is rather a making time for ... what the analysand has lost in its fullness but sees in the analyst.

Boss thus concludes his talk and the conference by deconstructing its theme. The questions he asked at the beginning of his talk are directed to the attendees as possibilities for they themselves to realize. He is not dismissive of any psychotherapeutic modality but only wants the wide-ranging representatives of specialist modalities to reconsider the nature of their 'charges', that is, those in their care, but also who they are as therapists. In conclusion, said Boss,

> all psychotherapies have the one common goal, considered by them more or less to be to free the erstwhile neurotic, i.e. to a large extent timeless, ahistorical [zeitlos-ungeschichtlichen] patient for [zu] an ever more comprehensive having time for... [Zeithaben für...], [that is] always keeping to what is past [Gewesene behaltenden], inclusive of the present [Gegenwärtige enthaltenden], and holding out for the future [Zukünftige voraushaltenden]. But if this is the meaning and the essence of all psychotherapy, then like few other people who answer to a calling [Berufsleuten], we psychotherapists in the plying of our trade are given to exist in a human way *par excellence*. Therein lies what is exhilarating about our calling [Beruf].[418]

One of Boss's most important papers was given in April 1977. Considerations of space preclude a full discussion of the lecture, 'Das Irrationale in der psychotherapeutischen Behandlung [The Irrational in Psychotherapeutic Treatment]', which was published two years later and reprinted in Boss's second anthology of papers he considered to be among his best as 'Ist die Psychotherapie rational oder rationell? [Is Psychotherapy Rational or Rationalistic?]' (1979b). Suffice to say, in it, Boss shows that therapy is not a rational phenomenon, given that the motivation for engaging in it and staying with it, its course based on the free associations of the analysand, and its goal, freedom, are themselves not rational.[419]

Approaching his eightieth birthday, Boss sometimes presented more broadly reflective papers as well as clinical and theoretical essays on dreaming life, psychosomatics, the paraphilias, schizophrenia, and encounter [*Begegnung*] in daseinanalysis.[420] As we know, for Boss the therapeutic partnership takes place in the context of encounter on a shared, level playing field. The essay '**Encounter and Self-confrontation in Guilt and in Conscience**' (1981d)[421], a contribution to a *Festschrift* for Boss's student, Gaetano Benedetti, considers the phenomenon of encounter in connection with ontological indebtedness [*Schuld*] and the call of conscience [*Gewissen*]. It is one of twenty-three papers collected in the volume *Challenge and Encounter in Psychiatry*. Other contributors included Manfred Bleuler, Martti Siirla, and the editor of the volume, Raymond Battegay. Both Boss and Jarl Jörstad wrote on the general theme 'Guilt and Conscience'.

The essay opens with a description of Heidegger's existentive *Geworfenheit* (givenness) and its relation to *Schuld* (indebtedness) and related ontic feelings of guilt.

> As far as we know, no human being is to blame for the fact that he came into the world nor as who he was born. Nobody asked him before his sensually perceptible beginning in the womb whether he wanted to become a human being or not. The human being is simply there one day, thrown into the middle of the crowd of all the other givens [*Gegebenheiten*] and among beings of his own kind whose context of meanings [*Bedeutungszusammenhänge*] make up his world. Nevertheless, soon enough man is called to account by a thousand kinds of remorse and guilt for what he does with the unasked-for, not self-chosen and not self-made gift of his human life.[422]

For the psychoanalyst this is relevant since 'no psychoanalyst has ever succeeded in analyzing away the being guilty [*Schuldigsein*] of even a single one of his analysands and in making him a guiltless and conscience-less person through his course of treatment, as Freud's theory was supposed to make possible.' On the other hand,

> the pathologically distorted feelings of guilt of many obsessive-compulsive and melancholic patients can be cured. But even such people, freed from their pathological feelings of guilt, by no means become conscienceless [*gewissenlos*], but remain sensitive to the specifically human 'indebtedness [*Schuld*]'. An understanding of the profound difference between 'healthy' 'being indebted [*Schuldigsein*]' as an essential basic feature of human existence and the pathologically hypertrophied, twisted [*verschoben*] and warped [*verbogen*] feelings of guilt of sick people requires, however, some detailed preparation.

It is Boss's intention in the essay to elucidate the ontological indebtedness that is a feature of human being and explore its implications. Like many of the essays in his second anthology of papers, it is philosophically sophisticated. He surveys the traditional religious responses to feelings of guilt, such as the Catholic priest's administering the sacrament of reconciliation following confession or the zazen master's instruction to meditate ever more deeply 'after having done something unheard of [*ungehörige Tun*]', or a Hindu guru's admonition 'to be more selfless and loving with our fellow human beings in the future when we are guilty about our own actions' in response to such feelings.[423]

The major point made is that the concept and even the word *Schuld* (understood ontically) would never have been assigned to human experience if human beings 'had not already realized beforehand – even if ever so vaguely – the significance of the fact that there is such a thing as evil [*böse*] behavior and good behavior and that he makes himself guilty [*er sich schuldig macht*] if he involves himself in the former.' Boss adds: 'This is not at all contradicted by the fact that concrete ideas about what is good and what is evil in a particular case often change. How should something ever be able to change if it, like conscience [itself], were not already there?'

This view is based on the different way of thinking introduced by Heidegger, 'a thinking of a completely different kind than the calculating of the natural scientist,' but also of theology and its handmaiden, philosophy as metaphysics. Such thinking 'consists of an immediate letting oneself be spoken to [*Sich-zusprechen-lassen*] and hearing of [*Hören*] the essential significances [*Bedeutsamkeiten*] which the givens [*Gegebenheiten*] of our world reveal of themselves to human taking in [of what is given] [*Vernehmen*].' Thus, special attention is given to the 'call of conscience [*Ruf des Gewissens*]', which is the human being's call

> to be open [*Offensein*] and to keep open [*Offenhalten*] one's existence [*Existenz*] to what is granted [*zusprechen*] to him by this open [*Offen*] and perspicuousness [*Gelichteten*] [in relation] to the 'world'. The call that arises from [*Anruf*] this, to respond to the best of one's ability to one's always-being-related-to [*Immer-schon-bezogen-Sein*] what is encountering [him] and responding to it, is the actual conscience. Man hears this call from things and fellow men. In wanting to have a conscience [*Gewissen-Haben-wollen*], conscience is not simply meant as a good [*gut*] conscience, but rather the readiness [*Bereitschaft*] for being called. As the mountain range [*Ge-birge*][424] is the gathering together of mountains, conscience [*Ge-wissen*] is a human being's knowing [*Wissen*] the calls to [*Anrufe*] a full expression of those possibilities of living in a unique way that are given to him.[425]

Ontologically understood, conscience also contains implicit knowledge one has of all that he can choose to actualize for which he is to be ready to called to do. In other words, 'man's essential or 'existential' [ontological] guilt consists in what he 'owes [*schuldet*]' in the way of the expression [*Austrag*] of the possible behaviors towards the givens of his world that appeal to him. At any given moment, he is in arrears to the fulfillment of all the other possibilities of his existence except the one in which he has just engaged and as the fulfillment of which he now exists [*existiert*].'[426] Conscience is therefore evidence of the human being's implicit awareness that he is called to be all that he can be, although this will never be fully realized.

Boss then answered four possible objections to the account of daseinsanalysis he had given[427] and presented two case examples which elucidate the difference between ontic feelings of guilt and *Schuld* as an ontologically structural existentive.

There was only passing reference to the influence of Eastern thought on daseinanalysis when he discussed implications for psychotherapy of what had been said. It is notable nonetheless even if brief.

> Insight into the existential being guilty [*existentiale Schuldigsein*] of man can only impart a much greater healing power to the therapist if it first transforms him in the core of his own being in the sense that he now has a never-ending reverence for everything he encounters, [and] at the same time an unshakable freedom towards it and a constant readiness to let himself be fully taken up by it. Of course, it is not up to the doctor or psychologist to determine in which particular way the healing self-experience of a phenomenologically oriented therapy takes place. In the case of one patient it comes about out of his own essence [*Wesen*] in the form of a newly emerging religious experience. In another, it just as naturally takes the form of a new, completely self-reliant, liberating, philosophical [kind of] thinking and insight. In a third, it requires a long-practiced, liberating philosophical thinking and superhuman and superdivine [*übergöttlich*] great 'arising [*Aufgehen*]', which since ancient times the Indians have called 'BRAHMAN'. Most perhaps attain their recovery according to the old Freudian goal of his psychoanalysis. This is the free ability to work and to enjoy [*Arbeits- und Genüssfähigkeit*], except that people healed by a phenomenologically oriented therapy no longer exercise their abilities in a selfish striving for power and pleasure. They, too, will work and enjoy themselves out of a more or less specifically articulated knowledge that as a being able to take in and to respond their existing [*Existieren*] forms an immediate unity with what is taken in [*Vernommenen*], in which both need each other, because this one needs that [one] and that one needs this one for its capacity to be [*Seinkönnen*].[428]

Like feelings of guilt in contrast to ontological indebtedness, ontological anxiety must always be distinguished from neurotic anxiety. In an effort to make clear the latter distinction, Boss gave a lecture on August 17, 1982, in Rio de Janeiro, which was translated as **'Normal Anxiety'** (1982a)[429]. The occasion was an International Forum on Anxiety. It is remarkable to think that as recently as forty years ago a newspaper would publish a technical paper of such sophistication for a general readership. This had also been the case, we recall, with Boss's **"Daseinsanalysis' and Psychotherapy'** (1956b).

The topic is a recurrent theme in Boss's writings. As published, the title may have struck readers as puzzling. Is there such a thing as 'normal anxiety'? Ordinarily, readers would always have thought of anxiety as a symptom of mental illness. It was a time when psychotherapy was appearing more generally as a topic of everyday conversation among people and media treatment as the word itself gained currency. Not surprisingly, the incidence of reports of anxiety also increased significantly. Today, anxiety is said to be ubiquitous.

Boss begins by making the point that anxiety is not *something*, like a house or a car, and so not something one could 'have' or possess. The phenomenon is better expressed as *being-anxious* and understood as a basic attunement of existing, fundamental in its being associated with knowledge of our mortality. Such anxiety is both 'anxiety about [*um*] existence' (that life will end) and 'anxiety in the face of [*vor*] existence' (life's challenges). Boss observes that 'it is always the same people who are most afraid of [*vor*] dying as well as most afraid of [*vor*] living.' The fears that people had earlier on were specific and included invisibles such as spirits and demons. At the time he gave his lecture, Boss noted, the fear of annihilation by a nuclear bomb (or worldwide pandemic) was perhaps the most intense fear. But such anxiety in the face of the spirit of technicity itself had long since surfaced as more people knew less and less about more and more, a situation that rivalled the European Middle Ages.

Knowledge of our mortality leads to *Angst* of a very different kind. In fact, Boss said, such anxiety is a privilege [*Vorrecht*] of human beings since such knowledge gives importance to life. Such knowledge is absent in other creatures. We cannot be sure about this, of course, and so it is reasonable to admit that we must wait for other creatures such as higher animals to tell us whether they have such knowledge. In the meantime, it seems improbable. For the human being, knowing he is not immortal means that it is not possible that 'everything ever missed could be made up'. Carrying out the activities of everyday life, but especially working on significant projects, therefore becomes something to which we commit ourselves, knowing that there is not 'all the time in the world' to complete them.

The spirit of technology, Boss reminded listeners and readers, is itself nothing technological. Technologies with all their remarkable capabilities have taken on *spiritual* quality. Consider, for example, the incomprehensible power of the internet, a phenomenon with which Boss was only vaguely familiar at the time he gave his lecture. The world-wide web would be launched only in 1990. He refers to Heidegger's observation that given an awareness of the nature of technology should entail being free *not* to use what it has spawned (for example, most electronic telecommunication media). When the claim of technicity is understood in this way, as inviting the possibility of saying 'no' to certain of its elements, 'our relationship to the technological world becomes in a miraculous way simple and calm. We 'let [*lassen*]' technical objects into our daily world and at the same time leave them outside, i.e. on their own, as things that are nothing absolute, but remain themselves dependent on something higher. I would like to call this simultaneous 'Yes' and 'No' to the technical world with an old way of putting it: serenity toward things [*Gelassenheit zu den Dinge*].' This is, of course, Heidegger's expression.

In the midst of all this there is an awareness or sense of 'something higher' lurking in the spirit of technology that is uncanny [*Unheimlich*]. Unlike other forces and other powers, 'a hidden meaning touches us' from out of it. Everything depends on our cultivating 'an attitude by virtue of which we keep ourselves open to' what is hidden in the technical world. Boss (following Heidegger) terms this an 'openness to the mystery [*Offenheit* für den *Geheimnis*]'. Serenity toward things and remaining open to mystery belong together. But what do these have to do with anxiety? 'They afford [*gewähren*] us the possibility of staying [*aufzuhalten*] in the world in a completely different way. They promise us a new ground [*Grund und Boden*] on which we can be [*stehen*] and survive [*bestehen*] unthreatened by it in the technical world .... [S]uch serenity and openness to the hidden meaning of our age are the most primal phenomena of human existence. They are more primordial than anxiety.' This becomes understandable insofar as 'the more original a human phenomenon is, the more clearly it opens the deepest insights into the essence of our existence. The more an existence has been able to mature into the mood of equanimity, the less it knows anxiety [*Angst*] and anxieties [*Aengste*].' But does this not lead to an indifference toward 'things'? On the contrary, Boss anticipated the question, closing the presentation observing that in such an attitude of *Gelassenheit* 'human existence [*Existenz*] allows [*lässt*] everything that it encounters to be what it is according to its nature [*Wesen*] and [so] with wholehearted devotion helps *it* to unfold [*entfalten*] into what it is meant to be [emphasis added].'

The question about 'limits' in psychotherapy has been a source of much discussion since the early days of psychoanalysis when analysts such as Sándor Ferenczi (1973-1933) advocated a more demonstrative response on the part of the analyst. Concern about the analyst searching for a way to meet his unfulfilled needs with hapless patients in the context of the therapeutic setting first led to inquiring whether the analyst's teaching analysis had been thorough enough so that harmful 'countertransference' responses could be avoided. Mild countertransference feelings were taken to be of therapeutic value, alerting the analyst to transferential and relational features of which he had not yet become aware. And yet stories of analysts falling in love with a patient, engaging in sexual relations with him or her, and sometimes even moving past a therapeutic relationship to one in 'real life' are common in the history of psychoanalysis. Therefore complete abstinence was counseled, sometimes leading to extremes such as not shaking the hand of the analysand on his arrival or at the end of a session. The emotionally susceptible individual was apt to misread any physical gesture as having sexual meaning since in many cases the patient was lonely and sexually needy. Boss deals with these issues in several papers, including '**Permitting and Abstaining in Psychotherapy**' {1982f},[430] which is a translation of the text of a lecture given at an annual gathering of the Swiss Medical Society for Psychotherapy, in Bern, on November 11, 1978.

In his lecture Boss was concerned with the allowable limits of the analysand's behavior in therapy and what had come to be known as 'acting out in the transference', a topic we have already met in these pages. Boss frames the issue in terms of 'permitting [*Gewähren*]'[431] and 'abstaining from [*Versagen*]'. Having invoked the fundamental rule, to say anything and everything, no matter how disturbing or offensive it might turn out to be, the analyst should be prepared to hear 'anything and everything' from his analysand, from outrageous accusations to a seductive plaint. Boss diagnoses Freud's official directive that analysis be carried out in complete 'abstinence [*Abstinenz*]' to be the result of Freud's own 'great insecurity [*Unsicherheit*] about spontaneity [*Spontaneität*]' and a need for 'extreme rational control [*Kontroll*]' over the proceedings and not of something inherent in the therapeutic setting. On the other hand, he reports his own experience as Freud's analysand in 1925, when at age twenty-two Boss was in Vienna on his own financially and sacrificing food money in order to pay Freud's fees. 'Because of my great poverty at that time, he accommodated me to an unimaginable extent, even in terms of fees. But even the minimal fee exceeded my financial capacities at that time. What else could I do but often skip lunch or dinner? It happened a dozen times that when he heard my stomach growling too loudly with hunger during the hour of analysis Freud gave me ten or twenty shillings so that I could once again have a proper meal.'

Boss observed that such exceptions to complete abstinence were minor by comparison with what he was then seeing in the popular forms of Gestalt group encounter, 'sensitivity groups' (in English), and even Arthur Janov's 'primal scream therapy': 'I cannot forget, for example, the mass hugs I saw at a meeting of the enormous American Psychological Association in Washington in 1970. There, in an immensely large hotel hall, about 3000 psychotherapists were together, divided into groups of four. All these innumerable groups began to hug each other fiercely at the command of the chairman, ostensibly to feel closeness. At any moment one could expect that the thing would end in a mass coitus [*Massenkoitus*].' If such 'openness' was permissible in a public setting among psychoanalysts, he conjectured, what might have been sanctioned by any of them in private practice with a patient or client?

The rest of the section of the text is very engaging.[432] That the relationship between analyst and analysand is not transferential, as might be expected, was reprised. The warmth and affection felt toward the analysand was to be understood as being as real as those experienced as directed to him by the analysand. But here, again, the irrational nature of therapy must never be lost sight of. This means that *both* partners are free to choose to do or say (or not do or say) what comes to mind. That said, the analyst's 'maturity [*Reife*], [his] steadfastness [*Standfestigkeit*] and autonomy [*Eigenständigkeit*]' are crucial in such a potentially volatile setting.

This is one of the few places where Boss mentioned the importance in some cases of working with the family or important 'others' in the analysand's life. After all, the analysand is not a monadic ego or 'I', but as an existing human being is always to be understood in the context of 'its' *Dasein* being with others, no matter how isolated the individual might appear to be, no matter how lonely he says he is. Boss suggested that protestations of isolation and loneliness very likely were behind the proliferation and popularity of 'group' therapies such as 'family therapy' and encounter groups.

Boss next reported on the changing incidence of 'types' of neurotic disturbance he was seeing and the ways in which a given 'disease entity' had come to manifest itself during the middle of the twentieth century, a theme he had taken up the previous year in 'Der korrespondierende Wandel von Gesellschaftsqualität und Neurosenformer im XX.Jahrhundert [Corresponding Changes in the Quality of Social Life and the Forms of Neurosis in the 20th Century]' (1977j). Hysteria, which had been Freud's major interest, 'gave way to the much more introverted organ neuroses [psychosomatic disorders]. These in turn were supplanted more and more by the depressive states of the so-called psychoneuroses. Not long after that, other forms of neurosis came to the fore and established themselves especially among young people. These neuroses were called the boredom neuroses [*Langweiligkeitsneurosen*] or meaninglessness neuroses [*Sinnlosigkeitneurosen*].' In contrast to the earlier forms, which were characterized by strained and dissatisfying relationships, those now suffering 'are no longer spoken to [*angesprochen*] by anything approaching [*nähere*] them. Accordingly, they lack any ability to engage with their environment and their fellow human beings. 'It doesn't matter [*Ist ja alles egal*]' is their main phrase. For many of them, this is already the basis for slipping into drug addiction. From an etiological point of view, this lack of relationship [*Beziehungslosigkeit*] and homelessness [*Heimatlosigkeit*] may be a consequence of the emptying of our world of meaning [*Bedeutungsentleerung*] under the dictatorship of the spirit of technicity [*Geist der Technik*].'[433]

It is here where daseinanalysis becomes especially relevant in our time since, as Boss suggests, 'those suffering from depression ['depressive states'] or the neurosis of meaninglessness cannot be treated by the classic psychoanalytic course of treatment [*Kur*]. With all of them a much stronger provision [*Gewähren*] of emotional protection [*Geborgenheit*] on the part of the analyst is necessary and at the same time quite different from the attempt to keep everything that comes from the analysand only in the psychic realm of thoughts.' And this is where the topic of permissiveness in the form of 'emotional protection' becomes relevant.

Boss next makes the important point that some individuals are unable to follow the fundamental rule since they are 'not at home' in the world of ideas, images and memories. Much less verbally adept than the typically well-educated psychoanalysand, 'they can exist only in the context of very much more hands-on world relations.' Boss did not hesitate to advise group sessions for such individuals (Alcoholics Anonymous [AA], for example), but cautions quite rightly that attendance at such meetings can be expected to be a lifelong requirement for such individuals. He also saw that many 'recovery group' members later go on to direct such groups. They become 'therapists' of a sort.

The lecture concluded with a charming personal summary of Boss's own life course on the way to developing therapeutic daseinanalysis. The question of just how much permissiveness on the part of the daseinanalyst is to be allowed is the occasion for these reflections.

> To sum up, I would like to say the following: You all know that I refined [*weiterentwickelt*] the classical Freudian method of psychotherapy into the daseinsanalytic course of treatment after twenty years of independent practice. I succeeded in doing this by drawing on the analytics of existence [*Daseinsanalytik*] of Martin Heidegger instead of the Cartesian philosophy which Freud used – albeit unwittingly – as the basic theory of his method. The former's philosophical insights into the basic constitution of man gave me what I saw as an incomparably much more human foundation for my therapeutic work. Thanks to these insights I was able to correct the therapeutic mistakes [*Fehlverhalten*] which could be understood as repercussions [*Rückschl*äge] of Freud's inappropriate natural science-like theory on his practical-therapeutic measures. The new theoretical foundation had very far-reaching consequences in relation to my practical therapeutic procedures [*Eingriffe*], especially in the areas of the so-called handling of the transference, acting out, and the thera-

peutic use of dream phenomena [*Traumph*änomene], but nowhere probably as far-reaching as with regard to the relationship between permitting and abstaining. That is why, in the wake of all my experiences, I consider the daseinsanalytic method to be the method of choice wherever it is important for a person to reach his highest possible development [*Entfaltung*], autonomy [*Eigenständigkeit*] and freedom. The less high the therapeutic goal is set in this relationship – whether for reasons of the patient's defective disposition or for external reasons – the more likely it is that group therapies of one kind or another will suffice. Finally, when I survey my experiences with occasional combinations of group therapies with the two-person therapy of daseinsanalysis, I believe I may say that now and then – though not too often – group therapeutic methods have brought about a certain cathartic opening of walled-off [*vermauert*] patients in a short time, which could not have been expected with a purely two-person relationship of daseinsanalysis, or only after a longer period of time. More often, however, the group-therapeutic intermezzi were recognized after a certain time by the analysands themselves as a resistant behavior in the sense that it was incomparably easier for them to let their relational difficulties resonate in a diluted form among many members of a group than experience them fully in the concentration of the individual relationship with the analyst. In my opinion, the permissive therapies in the sense of the modern Gestalt groups, scream [*Schrei*] groups and hugging [*Umarmung*] groups have their own justification and their own sense [*Sinn*]. It is only necessary to recognize for which people they are indicated and when, but also in which situations they must be considered contraindicated because they keep ill people from a really independent maturation and freedom who would otherwise have attained to the possibilities of maturation.[434]

At the end of his life, Boss summed up what he had learned and what he believed daseinanalysis has to offer as an option to psychoanalysis, psychiatry, clinical psychology, and psychotherapy and counseling in great variety of forms. '**Recent Considerations in Daseinsanalysis**' (1988a)[435] appeared in a special edition of *The Humanistic Psychologist* along with **'An Encounter with Medard Boss'** (1988b), the interview with Erik Craig reviewed earlier in this volume in the section on Biographical Texts. It may be considered to be Boss's most seasoned thoughts on the approach to therapy that had 'refined' or, better, 'further developed' psychoanalysis.[436] According to Craig, these 'considerations' 'grew spontaneously out of audio-taped personal conversations with the editor of this issue' of the journal.

The 'considerations' fall under four headings: (1) Heidegger's understanding of the sense of *be*[-ing] [*Sein*], (2) the meaning of 'mind' or 'soul' in daseinanalysis, (3) possibility, and (4) freedom. We will focus on the last two themes since they are the most important for therapeutic practice.

Possibility 'as *potentiality*, as *ability* or *capacity*' has a unique place in human life. While animals and plants have the capacity, to grow, they do not have the singular capacity 'to understand that it has these possibilities'. This is reserved for human beings. Consequently, we have 'a degree of freedom which does not belong to any other kind of being'. We are able to *choose* the way we relate to something or someone encountering us. We can 'pay attention to it or ignore it; accept it or reject it; approach it or withdraw from it; love it or fear it.' Existing is tantamount to this *'bundle of possibilities* for relating to the world'. Boss spoke of a possibility in terms of what one chooses, 'into which [one] of our [many] possibilities we will allow ourselves to become absorbed'.

Boss quickly added, however: 'I have been careful here *not* to suggest that certain possibilities are 'realized' or 'actualized' while others are not, for, as I have said, every possibility is being and therefore every possibility is 'real' or 'actual'.' The idea of realizing or actualizing a possibility then, is misleading since it implies 'that some possibilities are less real or less actual than others. I therefore prefer to say that *Da-sein exists as a whole assembly of possibilities for being in the world and that in any given moment it may 'carry out' only one of these while each of the others remain simply 'uncarried out'.*'[437] Thus *we are at all times all of our possibilities*, choosing which one to carry out at a given moment. It is not that one is patent while the others are latent. Possibilities are serially equipotent.

The important thing to keep in mind is that, for the daseinanalyst, 'it is the *patients themselves who are responsible* for choosing which of their possibilities they will carry out and which they will leave fallow.' The question 'Why not?', then, is not interrogative. It 'is an invitation to patients to consider the full range of their own possibilities for existing and to assume responsibility for choosing which of these possibilities they will carry out in the present moment [*Gegenwart*] but also in each moment which approaches them from their own future.'[438] But just as important as the choice is the responsibility one has for what one permits himself to become absorbed by at any given moment.

Under the heading 'On the Significance of Freedom in Daseinsanalysis', Boss considers the broader meaning of freedom in daseinanalysis, which concerns the individual's 'fundamental openness [*Lichtung*] as a human being'. Here Boss has translated *Lichtung* with 'openness', suggesting that the *Offenheit* (openness) we have heard about and the human being's luminance [*Lichtung*] as *Dasein* can only formally be teased apart.[439] Boss continued:

> Obviously, freedom to choose can only exist if, prior to this, a number of beings and things and human possibilities for relating to these beings, had already appeared and revealed themselves to you. If nothing or even if only one thing is able to appear to you at any given moment, then you are unable to have any capacity to choose. Always a multiplicity of things must reveal themselves to you before you can employ your free will [*Willensfreiheit*] to choose among them.... It is also only on the basis of this original openness that you can choose *how* you will relate to your chosen concern.... So in any situation, at any time, there may be a number of things that appear to us as well as a number of possibilities for relating to these things....[440]

Thus 'this basic precondition for freedom is the single most significant 'fact' about freedom which daseinsanalysis reveals, for it responds to the question, 'Why is there freedom at all?''. The implications for therapy of this choice of the *what* and *how* of engagement with what reveals itself to the analysand include the following qualifier, that 'in daseinsanalysis we never begin by insisting that patients simply '*exert*' their free will as if it were some kind of independent force somewhere 'within' them,' as the psychology of conation has held.

> On the contrary, daseinsanalysis reveals free will as a 'mere' capacity to choose, a capacity which is best appropriated [in a] particular manner for which individual patients themselves are open and ready at any given moment in their lives. Becoming free does not mean that analysands must strain to discover the so-called 'internal will power' but, rather, it means *growing in the readiness to appropriate* [emphasis added] the freedom of *perception, understanding and response* which is already 'theirs' and which has been 'theirs' from the beginning.

But what does this readiness amount to? For daseinsanalysis, being 'more ready' follows from entertaining the question 'Why in the world not?' And yet

> it must also be said that we definitely are *not* capable of anything like absolute freedom; we are not free to perceive and do *whatever* we wish at any given moment of our lives, to follow continuously our every caprice. Such absolute freedom is never a human possibility, for *our freedom, like human existence itself, is always finite, always limited and bound* [emphasis added], not only by the particular nature of human existence itself *per se*, but also by our own inherent individual constellation of capacities and incapacities, as well as the various material, social, political, and economic circumstances which impinge on us in every moment of our lives.[441]

The lesson is that, 'we are always at once both free and unfree'. Apart from this 'ubiquitous existential [*existentiell*] circumstantial of freedom, the *fundamental unfreedom* of being human, the capacity for freedom is even further circumscribed by and impaired in neurotically troubled individuals.' What Boss meant by *neurotic* unfreedom is 'a privation of what is necessary for carrying out a full and authentic human existence'. He added that 'it is this very privation that becomes the major concern of therapy or analysis. In fact the main goal of psychotherapy ... is to liberate individuals from their unnecessary constraints, from their neurotic *in*capacity to be addressed by a multiplicity of phenomena and to consider a variety of appropriate and wholesome possibilities for responding and relating to these phenomena.'[442]

But how is it that some 'human beings may become so unfree, so neurotically impaired and imprisoned'? Boss's reply was that 'no one, not even the most fortunate among us, encounters a world which is always concerned with preserving the fundamental openness of and freedom of human existence.' Those who are deemed 'neurotic', however, have been especially influenced by their parents, teachers, and other people who have constantly told them what they must or must not do or say. From the time they were very young children they always heard, 'You must not do this' or 'You must not touch that.' When human beings are young children they are especially fragile and vulnerable, and – not having the strength or experience to judge for themselves what is right or wrong, appropriate or inappropriate, dangerous or safe – they are easily influenced in their freedom by the adults in their world. Therefore, as a child one may easily 'fall prey' to the will of other individuals by following *them*, by accepting and fulfilling *their* taboos and prescriptions as if *their* attitudes and convictions were one's own.[443]

Both Heidegger and Freud, said Boss, 'were acknowledging one essential truth... that the human being may so easily lose sight of its own original freedom and openness by falling victim to the verdicts and views of others.' The Heideggerian perspective is more compelling for the daseinanalyst, however, in pointing out the pervasive tendency of the human being to defer to what 'they [*das Man*]' or 'people' would say. 'Privations' of this sort are 'ways by which human beings may lose sight of their original freedom and openness.' There are, of course, accidents and injuries, including brain injuries, ranging from accidents before, during and after birth to long-term damage to the organ by chemicals ingested by an individual such as drugs and alcohol. But, Boss avers, 'regardless of how the privation occurs, we can say that originally *Da-sein* is free to consider and enact (*verfügen*) its capacities and it is only by encountering some privational condition(s) or circumstance(s) that *Da-sein* is no longer able to make use of its original openness and its freedom to dispose of its capacities in its own authentic manner.' Boss thus held out hope even for those whose bodies have been ravaged by long-term assaults on its most sensitive organ, the brain, and the nervous system it subserves.

With respect to practice, where does all this find us? 'Psychotherapy has only one aim: to give back to neurotically crippled men and women their own original openness and freedom, to return to them what was already 'their own', that is, the freedom to dispose of the possibilities of their own existence in a way that accords with their own-most perceptions, judgments and talents. *This is what daseinsanalysis calls health: the free disposing and carrying out of one's own-most possibilities for being in the world* [emphasis added].'

It is one of the hallmarks of daseinanalysis that it begins not with psychopathology but with a notion of health which is indistinguishable from the definition of human being as *freedom*. It explains why the daseinanalyst speaks of 'appropriate and *wholesome* possibilities for responding and relating to these phenomena', that is, to what addresses a human being in the world. As Boss explained, 'this condition may be called 'healthy' only because it corresponds exactly with what human existence is originally, that is, a Be-ing which serves as an open and free sphere of perceiving and answering correspondingly to that which is revealing itself in the clearing of individual existence.' By contrast, 'unhealthiness is nothing but the privation, blocking, impairment or constriction of this original openness and freedom.'[444]

Concluding the section on freedom in daseinanalysis, Boss wrote: 'Naturally, returning the full use of a patient's own original openness and freedom is not a quick and easy task. Depending on the length, extent and depth of 'injury' or privation, the restoration of freedom can take a very long time and many hours of very hard work. But you also see this, on a purely physical level.' Recovering from a serious disabling injury, for example, requires months or even years of physical therapy, perhaps learning to walk again, and even reinventing one's lifestyle. 'This is also the way it is for psychotherapy. The more profound the wound, the privation, the longer and harder will be the work in restoring to individuals what was already theirs originally and from the beginning: that is, their full capacity for openness and freedom, for freely disposing and carrying out their own special and authentic possibilities for being in the world.'[445]

We have now come to the end of our review of selected texts of Boss in which the major themes of daseinanalytic theory and practice were discussed over a period of forty years. While the origin of therapeutic daseinanalysis in the work of Freud and Heidegger has been well documented, the importance of elements of Eastern philosophy to its genesis and development has not been adequately considered. Indeed, part of the impulse to prepare this volume was to make this dimension of daseinanalysis better known. We turn, then, to an aspect of daseinanalysis that has received limited attention so far, but which I believe is of major importance to understanding what is unique about it.

(B) The Eastern Influence (1959-2003)

In a certain respect, it is no exaggeration to say that **A Psychiatrist Discovers India** (1959a)[446] is Medard Boss's most important book for understanding the therapeutic partnership in daseinanalysis as discussed in his papers and books, especially **Existential Foundations of Medicine and Psychology** (1971a).[447] It was the last book Boss revised for publication. A 'Postscript' was added for the third edition (1976) and in 1987 Boss added the text 'Nach dreissig Jahren [After Thirty Years]' (see (1987b)). It is Boss's intellectual biography and offers us a look at the man as well as the therapist and thinker. It should be read along with Boss's autobiographic **'Foreword'** to Govind Kaul, *Govind Amrit* (1975e), with special attention given to the additions Boss made to 'the India book' in the editions of 1976 and 1987, the latter of which is discussed here.

Boss experienced three *Wundere* (miracles) while in India in 1958 that were an answer to his dissatisfaction with the model of psychiatric treatment he had learned in the West. The miracles are neatly summarized in the concluding sentence of the chapter on the third *Wunder*: 'For only because, to my astonishment [*Erstaunen*], the experience of an essential human sameness [*Übereinstimmung*] and an immediate ability to understand [*Verstehenkönnens*] each other was repeated within the much more comprehensive and deeper dimensions [*Dimensionen*] of hour-long and day-long conversations with Indian sages, was I able to perceive [*wahrnehmen*] at all the highest unfolding [*Entfaltung*] in all people of the possibility [*Möglichkeit*] of human perfection [*Vollkommenheit*] and undisturbed happiness [*ungetrübten Glücklichsein*].'[448]

The three 'miracles' led to as many insights. The first is that, given that each of us 'is' *Dasein*, we 'are' the same. This entails the second, that there is an immediate mutual understanding between any two people based on *Dasein's* being-with [*Mitsein*]. Finally, since the nature [*Wesen*] of *Dasein* is the unfolding of its possibilities, the task of the daseinanalyst is to set the conditions that allow for the realization of these possibilities guaranteed by *Dasein's* freedom. The relation of these insights to the basic lineaments of Heidegger's analytics [*Analytik*] of *Dasein* is obvious.

The English translation includes several passages added for that edition that mention the importance of Heidegger to Boss's development.[449] The 'Postscript' to the third edition (1976), published the year of Heidegger's death, tells us that the book had been restored to its full version seventeen years after its first appearance. He notes that in the intervening years he had remained in close contact with his Indian mentor, Govind Kaul. He also acknowledges the important part played by Erna Hoch[450] in his having remained in contact with Kaul. Boss notes that he had continued to practice daily 'meditative exercises [*meditativen Übungen*]' since leaving India, and he makes an all-important comparison between such practices with what he had experienced the previous year (1975) with Zen masters in Japan, where he had gone to lecture: 'It is precisely a comparison with his Indian experiences with Zen Buddhist practices and teachings and what has become outstanding about them that made it possible for the author to confirm just how appropriately the Indian realities [*Gegebenheiten*] mentioned in this book are.'[451] He also mentions Heidegger's ongoing deep influence on him, which had not been stressed in the original edition, adding that including mention of Heidegger there would have interrupted the continuity of his exposition of 'Indian realities and ways of thinking [*Gegebenheiten und Denkweisen*]'.

As noted, for the English version he had added two passages that point to the remarkable coincidence of ideas from ancient Indian practices with elements of Heidegger's thought. Boss answers an unnamed critic who had suggested that his reading of Indian philosophy was tainted, first, by Boss's having worn the 'spectacles' of 'Western' philosophical metaphysics while reading the literature of Hindu philosophy and then, later, having seen the error of his ways, filtering his reading of the Indian masters through the 'lens' of 'the equally Western fundamental ontology' of Heidegger's ideas. Boss denies this. He writes that, although it had begun much earlier (reading *Sein und Zeit* in the mid-1940s), the influence of Heidegger 'had only recently [*kurz zuvor*] impressed him deeply.'

Boss asserts that 'the fundamental difference [*Unterschied*] between the Hindu and daseinsanalytic study of man [*Menschenkunde*] had been internalized [*inne wurde*]' early on in his life. Where they intersect is fundamental to Boss's therapeutic outlook, an outlook that was prepared as much by his reading of Heidegger as by his immersion in Indian Vedanta philosophy.

Boss reminds the reader of the 'sacred space [*Heiligkeitsbereich*]' provided by *Dasein*, where what is encountering a human being can be taken in [*Vernehmenkönnen*]. He then recalls having 'heard from the Mahamahopadyaya [great scholars] of India' about 'the quite different experience... that there is most certainly 'Brahman', the 'great dawning [*Aufgehen*]', 'luminance [*Lichtung*]',[452] 'perspicuity [*Gelichtetheit*]', 'awareness [*Bewußtheit*]' even *without* the human beings [*Menschenwesen*].' This, of course, flatly contested Heidegger's view about the necessity of *Dasein* for there to be anything coming to light of *be-*[ing]. Late in his life, however, Heidegger admitted that he had been shaken by what he had heard from Boss about the arguments of the Indian philosophers. We read that on *first* learning about them, Heidegger averred after a long silence 'that what was just conveyed by the author [Boss] was for him simply not immediately experienceable [*nicht unmittelbar erfahrbar*] and therefore did not count as truth for him [*für ihn nicht als Wahrheit gelten*].' At issue was 'non-human dependent [*menschen-unabhängiges*]' *Lichtung* (Brahman) as 'the most immediate, most certain meditative experience [*meditative Erfahrung*].' At that time, though, it was for Heidegger a question of what he could not experience, namely, the fundamental insight of the Indian Mahamahopadyayas that Boss had encountered.

Boss does not 'side' with either Heidegger or his guru but rather points to the Zen Buddhism of southern Japan that he had experienced in 1975. This evidently was not communicated to Heidegger before his death and, so, not in time for a discussion about the 'original Hindu experience which, on its way to the East' changed into Zen Buddhism. Boss adds that Brahman (*Lichtung*) is not only independent of human being, but also of 'a God [*Gott*], of gods [*Göttern*], or a deity [*Gottheit*]'.[453] Meanwhile, we know that Heidegger had exprienced contact with ideas from Zen Buddhism in his contacts with figures such as Daisetz Suzuki (1870-1966) and Shin'ichi Hisamatsu (1889-1980).

Boss saw fit to publish the final chapter of the 'India book' in 1979 in a collection of previously published essays, many of them from the *Journal of Transpersonal Psychology*, a periodical founded in 1969 to reflect a new approach to psychotherapy very much influenced by the ethos of the Sixties. The anthology, *Meeting of the Ways*, contains works by authors such as Ken Wilbur who popularized ideas said to have been borrowed from 'Eastern' philosophy, meditative practices and lifestyles. Many contributions originated with experiences in a variety of encounter groups at Esalen on the West Coast of the States and the Naropa Institute in Colorado. The movement that grew up around transpersonal psychology has for the most part disappeared, to a great extent because of its association with 'progressive' political positions and the famous trinity of the sixties, 'sex, drugs and rock'n'roll'.

The chapter from the 'India book' published in *Meeting of the Ways* Boss thought worthy of seeing in print long after the book from which it was taken (published in 1959 in London) was readily available. 'Eastern Wisdom and Western Psychotherapy' is his most important statement of the influence of Eastern philosophy in general on daseinanalysis. In the text, Boss notes that, while in the West the 'intellectual investigation of the truth' was the 'ultimate aim' of philosophy, 'Indian philosophies were nothing more than spiritual remedies [*Rezepte*] against human suffering in all its forms.' Therefore, he says, 'we should call them psychotherapies rather than philosophies' were it not for the fact that no such thing as the psyche was ever imagined by Indian philosophy as the source of these 'remedies'. The starting point of this tradition of Indian philosophy was that 'man is in essence a luminous [*essentiell lichthaft*] '*atman*-being [*Atman-Wesen*]' belonging to directly to '*Brahman*', the hidden ground of possibility of all appearing [*verborgenen Ermöglichungsgrund alles Erscheinens*], being [*Sein*], disappearing [*Verschwinden*], and not-being [*Nicht-sein*].'[454]

Boss confesses that 'the *degree* [*Grad*] of illuminating power [*Leuchtkraft*] that the Western psychotherapies are as a rule capable of attaining struck me as so insufficient that I began to look for assistance in the Indian tradition.'[455] He then tells the story of an Indian philosophy professor he knew who had been in Europe for two years to train as a psychotherapist. The mood of the latter had changed dramatically while there. 'He had forgotten how to wait patiently, and had become harder [*härter*] and more loveless [*liebloser*].'[456] In short, says Boss, he had acquired a psyche. It is not revealed what approach this Indian philosopher *cum* psychoanalyst had studied but, Boss observes, the practice of the 'same psychotherapy [as his friend had learned] would have been of the greatest use to many a hardened, ego-obsessed [*verhärteten, ich-besessenen*] European or American.' He regrets to report, however, that the Indian philosopher had 'lost so much of his former Indian wisdom and poised calm [*Gelassenheit*],' the mood which is precisely the goal of daseinanalysis.[457]

Boss writes of eight Europeans and Americans who had gone to India to, as we say, 'have an experience'. They had gone to ashrams, acquired new ascetic habits and eaten a new diet – but had not genuinely changed. Readers can recall any number of celebrities – some famous in the media (for example, the 'Beatle' George Harrison), some having brought back 'Indian wisdom' and even 'Indian wise men' to Europe and the States. Far from having led to enlightenment, however, in several individuals, Boss tells us, the experiences they had had 'unleashed in them a schizophrenic episode [*schizophrenen Prozeß*]'. He saw that these spiritual tourists 'had remained boring, jealous and intolerant Westerners [*einsinnige, eifersüchtige und unduldsame Westler*].' Moreover, the process of playing at becoming enlightened 'Easterners' had 'left them with ungenerous contempt [*enghertzige Verachtung*] for Western culture and Christian beliefs.' In short, now they were entirely adrift spiritually, at home neither in the West nor in the East.

The message of Boss' guru was to 'keep all Indian knowledge about the nature of man far removed from my future therapeutic work.' He nevertheless continued to be influenced by the sages he had studied with, 'each one of them a living example of the possibility of human growth and maturity and of the attainment of an imperturbable inner peace [*unstörbaren inneren Frieden*], a joyous freedom [*glückhaften Freiheit*] from [neurotic] anxiety [*Angst*] and guilt [*Schuld*], and a detached, selfless goodness and calmness [*abgeklärten selbstlosen Güte und Gelassenheit*].'[458] They exemplified the sort of individual who would reform himself in the therapeutic setting of daseinanalysis.

Boss's assessment of Western psychotherapy is direct and harsh in this text. 'The means and aims of our Western psychotherapy struck me as quite inadequate in comparison with the teachings and the *behavior* of these masters [emphasis added].' As for what Western psychologies provide students, they are seen to be 'easily assimilable ... [as] formulas [*Formeln*] and ideas [*Vorstellungen*]. Their obvious handiness [*Handlichkeit*] nourishes our belief that they give us something really solid, something we can rely on. They make us forget that they are for the most part only intellectual reductions of the nature of man to unreal abstractions [*unwirkliche*

Abstraktionen].' He recalls the 'preparation analysis [*Ausbildungsanalyse*]' that has been the essential part of psychoanalytic 'training' from the start but concludes that even the best teaching psychoanalysis [*Lehranalyse*] is only an 'introductory course [*Propaedeutikum*]' compared to the 'purification [*Läuterung*]' undergone by Indian sages. 'Whenever I listened to the Indian sages, I always asked myself whether I would not have to overhaul my whole psychotherapeutic knowledge or give it up entirely.' Here we should recall that people like Govind Kaul were emphatic about Boss *not* applying what he had learned in India in his work as a therapist or 'derive from it a new psychotherapeutic technique . . . . Don't make the slightest change in your psychological technique of free association and in your analysis of resistance,'[459] he was advised.

How, then, should one understand the influence of Eastern wisdom on daseinanalysis as a 'refinement' of psychoanalysis, and not the way some 'new age' modern psychotherapies have come to represent it? He heard from Kaul: 'The outward realities [*sichtbaren Gegebenheiten*] of your work will hardly change. For the best thing you can do as a conscientious doctor is quietly to assimilate your Indian experiences. If these have sunk in [*eingegangen*] deeply enough, everything else will follow of itself.'[460] What will matter is having gained that 'unshakable trust [*unschütterliches Vertrauen*] in what is inconceivable by conceptual understanding, incalculable by all calculations, in which all things are rooted [*gründet*]. Many another precondition of a fruitful psychotherapy will be automatically established if you are prepared to make the effort of tireless [*unablässigen*], open [*offen*], still [*stillen*], and at the same time highly concentrated listening [*höchst konzentrierten Horschen*] to what goes on within, to the undertone of all that is [*Grundton aller Wesen*].'[461]

Psychotherapeutic 'techniques [*Techniken*]', 'artefacts [*Kunstgriffe*]' and 'equipment [*Rüstzeug*]' -- what Rollo May termed 'gimmicks' -- are, like the rest of what has been devised by 'scientific' clinical psychologists, more like toys to be played with [*spielen*]. Only without concern about technicalities can the art of therapy be practiced. The attitude toward therapy should become one of a 'liberating sunniness [*befreiende Heiterkeit*]' of outlook. The sense here is of a serene lightheartedness, a detachment from things, where nothing is of any special importance and so everything is of equal importance. Both come to the same thing. This is the outlook that Kaul recommended to Boss that would enable him to truly listen to his partner in daseinanalysis.

Boss heard Kaul speak of the absence of any barriers between the 'I' and 'Thou', an unmistakable allusion to Martin Buber. 'Then the master was silent,' Boss writes.[462] The rest of the concluding paragraph is perhaps among the most important lessons to be taken away from the 'India book'. It is certainly central as a scenario that might become thoughtfully incorporated in the preparation of daseinanalysts or for that matter any therapist.

> Like my previous Indian teachers, he had also early requested me to look him straight in the eyes [*geradewegs in die Augen zu blicken*], as often and long as possible [*möglichst oft und lange*]. That helped understanding [*Verstehen*], pro-

moted mutual access to the essential human core [*Wesenskern*] in each of us, and let the partners get past adhering to their respective cultural and social roles. Here, too, I overcame my Western shyness [*Scheu*], my fear of offending by such unabashed staring. In this intimate bond [*unmittelbaren Verbundenheit*] with the master I gained for a while the great peace that simply allows things to come to pass [*ganz einfach werden*].[463]

Boss concludes: 'This simple thing [*Einfache*] was the certainty that *what our psychotherapy needs above all is a change in the psychotherapists* [emphasis added],' not a change in approaches or modalities of psychotherapy. 'If our healing of the soul [*Seelenheilkunde*] is to become more curative [*heilkräftiger*], the possession of psychological concepts and psychotherapeutic techniques will have to be balanced by a prudence [*Besonnenheit*] on the part of psychotherapists, who will practice [*übt*] a daily silent being open [*Offensein*] to the promise of the ineffable origin of all that is, of the healthy and the sick, and of all psychotherapeutic measures [*Maßnahmen*] as well. Then psychiatrists will be able to help in their own way to give back to people who in every respect and year by year are more and more sick with homelessness [*Heimatlosigkeit*] that comfort [*Geborgenheit*] which is able to protect and support them more reliably than all of our fragile earth's institutions and venues.'[464] It remained to transpose this encounter to the psychoanalytic setting, which is precisely what Boss did. The result was daseinanalysis.[465]

One of seven important translations of Boss to appear in the *Review of Existential Psychology and Psychiatry* is **'After Thirty Years'** [Preface to *A Psychiatrist Discovers India* (4th Edition, 1987) {2002/2003b}[466], the brief essay Boss added to introduce the third edition (1976) of the India book. That edition also contains the already mentioned important 'Postscript' on the influence on Boss of Heidegger's thought, his reading of Indian philosophy, and the impact of his experiences in India in 1956 and 1958. The issue of the *Review* also contains Boss's letter to Heidegger of January 12, 1960 {2002/2003a}, and his essay **'Martin Heidegger Applied to Psychiatry and the Modern World'** {2002/2003c}.

'After Thirty Years' is dated January 1987, the year in which Boss's edition of the *Zollikon Seminars* was published. In 1959, when the 'India book' was first published, Boss had already hinted at concerns he had about the influence on India of Westernization. Here he again names Erna Hoch, as he had in the 1976 'Postscript', and refers to long conversations he had with her while she was in Switzerland at the end of 1986. What he heard about the situation where Hoch had worked for decades confirmed his worst fears, namely, 'that a sojourn in India [*Indienfahrt*] with approximately the same experiences that one can read about in the earlier editions of this book would no longer be possible.'[467] Fellow therapist, R. D. Laing, had spent time in India in 1970. Even by that time, however, Boss tells us with regret, the purity of his experience only a decade earlier was no longer possible. A variety of gurus [*Weise*] had commercialized their image in India and abroad. Indian doctors who had trained as psychiatrists in Europe and America often remained there. Nevertheless, the number of psychiatrists had proliferated in India, in large part due to an increasing need for their services as a result of major cultural changes, especially the introduction of technology that had disrupted the traditional way of life of Indians of all castes. Boss mentions the great increase in addictions to alcohol and 'modern drugs [*modernen Drogen*]' imported by Western doctors ostensibly to be used to treat newly diagnosed mental illnesses.

Boss also, somewhat wistfully, cites changes in dress and deportment (for example, 'American jeans [*amerikanischen Jeans*]'), the presence of women in the military for the first time in India's history, and above all a change in the facial expressions of people, now 'tighter, greedier [*verbissener, habgrieriger*]', reflecting the Western emphasis placed on 'greed for material [*Gier nach materiellen Erfolg*] and the greatest possible efficiency [*Effizienz*]'. He is saddened by the influence of the 'gray machines [*grauen Maschinen*]' of technology on the 'rootedness [*Verwurzelung*]', provided by India's ancient culture and its 'spiritual tradition'. Of course, in Germany Heidegger was also pointing to the catastrophe of technology's effect on the sense of being at home that fewer and fewer Europeans and Americans were able to experience.

Reference is made to Heidegger, who, Boss recalls, had been central to his comments in the 'Postscript' to the third edition, published the year Heidegger died. Here we learn more about the all-important encounter between Heidegger and the ideas Boss had brought back with him in 1958 and, later, through the mediation of Erna Hoch:

> After the author's return from India, I held countless conversations with Martin Heidegger about my Indian experiences. Previously, Martin Heidegger had known next to nothing [*so gut wie nichts*] about the thinking of ancient India. Until then, he was under the impression that man's meditative thinking [*besinnliche Denken*] had only begun with the pre-Socratic philosophers of ancient Greece. In particular, he had up to that time heard nothing of the fact that thousands of years ago, the ancient Indian sages placed the greatest importance on the single word which also provided Heidegger's thinking with its own foundations.

Here we expect to hear of *Sein*. Instead, we heard of *Lichtung* (Brahman) (luminance), the 'great dawning [*große Aufgehen*]', and the 'primordially luminating [*das von Grund auf Lichtende*]'.[468] Boss reminds us that Heidegger had used the word *Lichtung* as early as *Sein und Zeit*.[469] He focuses on discussions with Heidegger about the evidently ontological necessity of *Dasein* for things to show up at all, namely, that there could be anything at all ('something luminous and open [*Lichtenhaft und Offenen*]') rather than nothing at all 'without the presence [*Anwesenheit*] of human beings'. Boss recalls that 'in the period *preceding* the author's sojourn in India, Martin Heidegger was unable to follow [*folgen*] his Indian fore-thinkers [*Vordenkern*] on precisely this point. But then, many years after the author's return from India' Heidegger wrote a text which makes clear that he had in fact changed his mind about something fundamental.[470]

Boss then quotes from the 1984 publication of the text, edited by Hermann Heidegger, which has received little attention in the literature on Heidegger but which, in my view, is one of the most significant penned by the late Heidegger: 'But it required decades of wandering on stray ways [*Holzwege*] to realize that the sentence in *Being and Time* – 'Man's existence [*Dasein*] is itself the luminance' – has perhaps divined [*geahnt*] the matter of thinking, but it has in no way adequately thought it through, i.e. presented it as a question that has really [*schon*] reached the very matter itself. Existence [*Dasein*] is the luminance [*Lichtung*] for presence [*Anwesenheit*] as such, and at the same time it is not at all this luminance, insofar as the luminance is prior [*erst*] to existence, i.e. allows it to appear as such. The analytics [*Analytik*] of existence does not yet reach luminance in its own right [*das Eigene der Lichtung*] and *a fortiori* it also does not reach that realm [*Bereich*] to which luminance itself belongs.'[471]

Little has been said about this radical revisiting of *Being and Time* that came to Heidegger in his old age, arguably as a result of the influence on him of what he learned from Boss about Hindu philosophy and at that very time when Heidegger was giving the Zollikon seminars that laid the groundwork for daseinanalysis. Boss is not interested in having 'corrected' Heidegger, but only that 'the western thinker Martin Heidegger now also accepts the same thought that the age-old Indian sages had perceived. Now Martin Heidegger as well saw that the luminance of perceptive, perspicuous human existing [*vernehmende, gelichtete menschliche Existieren*] is in itself a being [*ein Seiendes*] and as such requires a prehuman, more all-encompassing [*vormenschlich, umfassenderen*] luminance for it to come to light [*zum Vorschein gelangen*] at all.'[472]

Having pointed to the remarkable coincidence of ancient Hindu philosophy and post-metaphysical thinking, Boss closes his look back expressing the hope that the two ways of thinking can 'work together to overcome the subjectivism of the modern machine and atomic age which dominates the entire globe today.'[473] Given Boss's own principal concern and with passing reference to Leibniz and the 'principles of sufficient reason' (the '*principium grande et nobilissimum* [great and most noble principle]'), it is not surprising to read the concluding sentence of the text, which resonates with the sense of *Lichtung* in its relation to bringing something to light not yet of note: 'Such a change in thinking [that is not grounded in the principles of natural science] could have significant repercussions for medicine, because it could allow the somatic [*Leibliche*] and the spiritual-intellectual [*Seelich-geistige*] as well as their relation to one another to appear [*erscheinen*] in a completely different light [*Licht*] than hitherto.'[474] It was Boss's hope that his therapeutic daseinanalysis would have that effect, not only on medicine and psychiatry but also on contemporary psychotherapy broadly defined.

(C) Martin Heidegger (1959-2003)

I conclude this review of Boss's publications with some reflections on publications in which Boss details Heidegger's influence on medicine, psychiatry and psychotherapy. It was Heidegger's hope that the effect of his thought might be felt by doctors, including psychiatrists and psychotherapists, and affect what they do in such a way as to bring improvement in the lives of human beings. The texts cover a thirty-year period of leading up to the publication of the *Zollikon Seminars*.

'**Martin Heidegger and the Doctors**' (1959b)[475] is one of thirty-three contributions to a *Festschrift* for Heidegger's seventieth birthday, edited by Gunther Neske, one of Heidegger's publishers. Others contributors include Jean Beaufret, Georges Braque, Rudolf Bultmann, René Char, Hans-Georg Gadamer, Werner Heisenberg, Ernst Jünger, Hajime Tanabe and Carl-Friedrich von Weizäcker. The volume includes poems and several color plates. Boss' text would also serve as part of what came to be published as 'Einem Therapeuten wird sein bio-psychologischer Star gestochen [A Psychiatrist Has His Biopsychological Cataracts Removed]' in *Von Psychoanalyse zur Daseinsanalyse* (1979c). The commemorative essay is based on a lecture given in India on **'The Role of Psychotherapy in Schizophrenia'** (1958), which also served as the basis for the first chapter of *Psychoanalysis and Daseinsanalysis* (1957a) published in 1963.

The essay begins with an account of the case of 'Dr. Cobling' with which Boss opened *Psychoanalysis and Daseinsanalysis*. Thrown for a loop by the patient's strident verbal assault, 'the doctor only regained his footing when he found an openness [*Offenheit*] of thought in Martin Heidegger's *Being and Time* that could withstand his psychotic patient's criticism.' The criticism had come from a 'full frontal assault' on Boss by a thirty-six-year-old English psychiatrist who had challenged Boss by anticipating that he would interpret her hallucinations as projections in the traditional psychoanalytic sense, that the images and sounds she heard were nothing by intrapsychic reality: 'What on earth do you psychiatrists know then about reality?, she railed. 'Nothing and once again nothing.' She challenged Boss' distinction between a subjective reality and objective reality. 'How dare you maintain, you silly fool, that you actually know in the least what you are saying by calling something subjective or objective?'[476]

Boss then recounts his reading of *Being and Time*, in particular the early part that focuses on *Dasein*'s initial understanding of the world and the luminance of be[-ing] [*Lichtung des Seins*]. The conclusion reached is that there are not two realities, one psychic and the other physical, one subjective and the other objective. The voices and images experienced by 'Dr. Cobling', Boss realized, were coming at her there in the world, the one world of *Dasein* as being-in-the-world. They showed directly, immediately her unrealized possibilities. The task of the therapist, says Boss, was 'with diligence and love' to allow these voices and images to make their appearance, no matter how disconcerting they might be.[477] In this case, it was images of invading motorcyclists who would arrive during the night and turn into lice. In all, as we learn, they were appearances of the young woman's as yet unrealized sensual-erotic life with 'easy riders' who could make her flesh come alive. The tribute moves on from a discussion of the case to a more general observation about Heidegger and the relevance of his thought for medicine. Once again turning to the passage in *Being and Time* that speaks of two sorts of *Fürsorge*, Boss stresses the importance of non-interventional caring about the other [*vorausspringende Fürsorge*] that is the hallmark of daseinanalytic practice. As individuals informed by Heidegger's view of man as the 'servant and guardian of be[-ing] [*Diener und Hüter des Seins*]', therapists are afforded the 'grace [*Gnade*] to let who comes to therapeutic encounter with them be who they are, without interfering in their lives and trying to change them.'[478]

A decade later another public appreciation of Heidegger appeared. This '**Tribute to Martin Heidegger**' (1970c)[479] should be read along with Boss' 'Letter to a Friend' published in 1969 in the *Neue Zürcher Zeitung*, October 5, 1969 (#606, 5), which was reprinted as the editor's 'Schlußwort' (closing remarks) to the *Zollikoner Seminare* published two decades later.[480] Both texts celebrate Heidegger's eightieth birthday and the friendship between the two men. The tribute appeared in Richard Wisser's book, first published in India, which also contains the transcript of a televised interview with Heidegger filmed on September 17, 1969, for broadcast on ZDF.[481]

Boss writes that 'it was actually a medical concern which brought together the unequal pair, the philosopher and the physician,' a 'concern' 'which still keeps us together today'. This was Heidegger's aforementioned concern that his thought might have application in everyday life medical practice. There is room for speculation that Boss was also Heidegger's doctor in some sense, especially during the years after Heidegger's existential crisis which saw him officially in the care of Viktor von Gebsattel for several months in 1946 at the latter's sanitarium. There may have been a 'medical concern' in Heidegger's own life that is referenced here. This remains to be supported by documentation from unpublished correspondence and other sources not available to us. That said, Boss did write of his efforts to help Heidegger out of the seclusion into which he had been driven from the post-war ordeal he was subjected to. The 'treatment' may have amounted to several vacations taken together, first in Italy and later on the Adriatic and in Greece, as well as the many hours of conversation the men shared while Heidegger was with Boss in Zurich and Lenzerheide. At the same time, however, it is possible that Heidegger had a therapeutic effect on Boss, if we take 'therapeutic' in the fully authentic sense it has in daseinanalysis.

Here Boss writes much as he had in his open letter 'to a friend' of October 9, 1969: 'I, for one, had long been searching for a solid scientific basis for my medical undertakings. I soon realized that my scientific opinions about man could never furnish such a basis. *The basic humanity of our patients is therefore forever fundamentally inaccessible to the scientific method of research* . . . .'[482] He is careful to add that the 'enormous usefulness of scientific research, as long as it concerns itself with the pure manipulation of the human body' is undeniable. But treating the body, intervening in its structures and functions, is quite different than treating the human being. The basic distinction between interventional caring about the other [*Fürsorge*] *Dasein* and way-making (solicitous) caring about him is implicit here. The 'basic traits of human existence expressed in Martin Heidegger's epoch-making work *Being and Time*' as worked out in the analytics of *Dasein* [*Daseinsanalytik*], 'I found to be the most reliable basis ever for a human medicine. And to this day, I have not seen a better basis for it.' Boss concludes: 'Martin Heidegger, the philosopher, and myself, as physician, each according to his capacity – but with *all* his capacity – have been and continue to be engaged in the same task. This is probably the secret of our unshakable friendship.' He praises Heidegger's 'deep benevolence and his unreserved sympathy for the smallest and greatest affairs of others; also, his shy tenderness and the wide-open sensitivity of his heart.'[483] High praise indeed.

In this volume we are concerned for the most part with Heidegger's impact on medicine and therapy, but the broader implications of Heidegger's thought and its relation to daseinanalysis were taken up by Boss in '**Martin Heidegger and His Significance for the Evolution of Society**' {1980a}[484], his contribution to a volume in the series in which *Leiben und Leben* {1977f} appeared: *Diskussion. Menschsein in unserer Zeit* [*Discussion: Being Human in Our Time*]. Other contributors to the anthology included, in addition to the editor, Urs C. Reinhardt, James Schwarzenbach, Peter Atteslander, Max Thürkauf, Helmut Bach and Gion Condrau.

Given recent attacks on Heidegger's apparent indifference to the cruelties of World War II imposed by Germany's National Socialists, the text is a very contemporary response to that discussion. Given a sort of guilt by association, similar accusations had been leveled at daseinanalysis, Boss notes, suggesting that its therapeutic goals seemed not to take into consideration the social realities of analysands such as their sex, class and ideological position, and merely encouraged 'a thoughtless conformity to the respective establishment' in which the analysand lives and works. Some 'managers of big companies... officially forbid their employees to undergo a daseinsanalytic therapy. For them there is the danger that their subordinates will no longer be able to integrate themselves into their company's bureaucratic machinery [or clockwork] [*Räderwerk*] but will start to have their own ideas and behave in a correspondingly self-willed way.'[485] A frightening commentary about the priority of the 'organization man' (William H. Whyte) over the human being, but Boss was entirely correct in his assessment of how the priorities of efficiency of the machinery of the corporate-technological world had were increasingly overrunning the dignity of the individual.

With respect to the application of Heidegger's thought to social change in general, 'any practical meaning for the formation of society [*Gesellschaftsbildung*] cannot be attributed to it.'[486] Thus it might appear that it is solipsistic, 'indifferent to society and its evolution'. Boss counters such a suggestion, pointing to the unacknowledged and unexamined presuppositions of Marxist philosophy itself in relation to socialist sociocultural experiments such as those well under way in the Soviet Union, and, in particular, to Sartre's variations on it in his creative literature and essays, which were thought by some to reflect a position aligned with Heidegger's. Boss's elucidation of Sartre's position in this text redounds to the latter's misapprehension of the analytics of existence, which failed to recall that being-with [*Mitsein*] others is a fundamental existentive of a being-in-the-world. Existing implicitly entails caring about [*Fürsorge*] others. Hardly an isolated 'egoistic' monad, the human being exists *as* 'taking care of [*Schonen*], tending [*Pflegen*] and protecting [*Hüten*]'[487] what encounters it, and the most important examples of that are always others. The human being exists as a 'careful protecting [*Hüten*] and letting unfold [*Sich-entfalten-lassen*] of everything that is encountering [*Begegnenden*] it.' Of course, the problem is that of all that presents itself one can respond in action to only some of it. 'At any given moment he can engage [*einlassen*] only in one of his thousands of possibilities of behavior [*Verhaltensmöglichkeiten*].' Therefore, the human being is essentially a being of what is to come [*Zukunft*], that is, of the future.[488] Something more, such as a socialist or communist retooling of society, is therefore unnecsssary.

Boss briefly discusses the implications of Heidegger's view of ontological indebtedness [*Schuld*] for civil and criminal law.[489] He makes the claim that an understanding of ontological *Schuld* could provide the starting point for a view of the foundations of social life as such and so for the problem of the evolution of society, which was the theme of the congress. Our ontological indebtedness, our being-with others, and the call of conscience [*Gewissen*] considered together provide a fundamental-ontological orientation to certain problems of sociology and to the matter of a 'proportionally just democratic [*demokratik*] structure' for a given society. They also support an ethics based on Heidegger's thought.

It is important to recall that Boss traveled widely outside of Europe and saw firsthand life in both 'developed' and 'underdeveloped' countries. In India, as we have seen, he took a cautionary stance about any zealous programs directed at 'improving' the lives of human beings there and in the so-called 'third world [*dritten Welt*]' by simply introducing an American or European model of medical care which decenters the individual from his community of extended family by introducing major changes 'overnight'. The same held for introducing a new form of government; for example, 'democracy' in an ancient culture built on the caste system. The being-with [*Mitsein*] of existence is more fundamental than any formal arrangements indigenous to a 'people', culture, society or nation, and this is where Heidegger's insight about what being human means could be envisioned as having a major influence on matters of social planning under the general rubric of development and progress. The paper is as 'political' as Boss gets in any of his publications. In the end, Boss is critical of 'well-meaning but impatient Western sociologists and freedom fighters [*Freiheitskämpfer*] who do not know what great demands on human maturity democratic freedoms presuppose.'[490]

Boss closes, 'last but not least', reminding the reader that all *social* behavioral possibilities are grounded in ontological being- with, which requires our closer attention and study, especially by those who are concerned with where 'society' is heading. He asserts that 'daseinsanalytic anthropology [*Menschenkunde*] knows as hardly any other [anthropology] that the fighting of people against each other is absolutely one of the autochthonous existential [*existentiellen*] modes of carrying out [*Vollzugsweisen*] of the existentive [*existential*] 'being with'. It also knows that under certain circumstances individuals and groups of people actually owe their fate to a fight for life or death.' He does not encourage war, but seems to suggest that, paradoxically, conflict between people is grounded in their ontological *Mitsein*. There is the reality to consider, that 'in political practice, the powerful rarely give up their prerogatives freely and of their own accord, even if they have forfeited these prerogatives long ago and no matter to what extent. This is a phenomenon that belongs to the fact that in everyday life all other ways of 'being with' have a difficult stand against the self-seeking striving for power.' And, as one has read in many other places over and over, 'it seems to be a specific feature of mankind that in it the highly developed, free and mature is rather the exception, [while] the deficient and immature, on the other hand, is the rule.'

Heidegger's philosophy is given even stronger support. It 'is not only of inestimable value in its significance for contemporary society. It also gives us decisive hints for our social future.' Here Boss articulates the later Heidegger's understanding that be[-ing] [*Sein*] 'is granted [*zuspricht*] to mankind' differently, in one fashion at the origin of Western philosophy with the Greeks (as 'a revealing itself out of concealment [*Sich-entbergen aus Verborgenheit*]', a 'showing itself [*Sich-zeigen*]', as 'a *phainesthai* of phenomena [*Phänomene*]'), still another to the medieval epoch (as 'being created [*Geschöpflich-sein*]', as 'a being created [*Kreiert-sein*]' by the Christian God), yet otherwise to Western modernity (as 'being represented [*Vorgestellt-sein*]' by a human subject as being 'object-like [*Objekthaftigkeit*]'), and differently at the origin of 'Eastern' Hindu philosophy.[491] The essay concludes with reference to the opening section of the *Old Testament* and an expression of the hope that Heidegger's philosophy will 'penetrate' readers in such a way that by a revised attitude toward the earth, humanity will be open to a still different *Zuspruch* (granting) of be[-ing] [*Sein*] than any of those just enumerated.

Concern with the spiritual dimension of human being has been a part of daseinanalysis from its beginnings even though it is not among the differences from psychoanalysis that have been given most attention. Interest in the theme can be traced once again to the all-important influence of Boss's visits to India. It is evident in Boss' papers on psychotherapy beginning in the late 1960s (see (1966b)), culminating in contributions in the early 1980s, including the unpublished paper 'Where Is God in Psychotherapy? Where is Psychotherapy in God?' This contribution to a 'Zurich Conversation' is likely among his still private and unavailable papers. I have not been able to trace it to other sources, for example, the archives of the Zurcher Gespräche. So also his lecture given at the Catholic Academy of the Archdiocese of Freiburg im Breisgau in 1984, 'Is Human Guilt Curable with Psychotherapy?' We do have, however, **'The Significance of Martin Heidegger for Work with Suffering People and for the Self-understanding of Psychotherapy**' (1982j)[492], which is the text of a lecture read at the conference of the Catholic Academy in commemoration of the fifth anniversary of the death of Martin Heidegger given on February 8, 1981.[493]

This short text is based on material found in earlier lectures by Boss and repeats familiar themes, but its emphasis is on Heidegger's indirect contribution to the care of 'suffering [*leidend*]' human beings by doctors and therapists. Boss stresses the caution such providers must take when trying to understand how the purely ontological insights of Heidegger's analytics of existence are to be 'introduced into [*anzuwenden*]' everyday practice, especially given the pressing ontic concerns of medicine. Jean-Paul Sartre (in his 'existential psychoanalysis') and Ludwig Binswanger (in his 'psychiatric daseinsanalysis') are recalled as two individuals who had misunderstood the implications of the ontological difference and in so doing focused only on the ontic.

Suffering, Boss claims, can only be understood in terms of the 'non-suffering, healthy human being'. One who suffers 'lacks something [*etwas fehlt*]. He lacks something of the well-being [*Wohlbefinden*] and freedom of the healthy [person].' Heidegger's notion of our 'primal [*primär*] being in the world' provides a clue about the meaning of suffering. A correct understanding of the sense of this 'in' is essential. 'The unique 'in' of human being-in-the-world can only be understood if the word for its existing [*Existieren*] is taken much more seriously than before. Heidegger heard [hörte] being [Seiende] in its original Greek-Latin sense as an 'ek-stare [Ek-stare]'. Ek-stare, however, means specifically to hold out [aushalten], to bear up under [ertragen], to put up with [erdulden]. The question remains to what this withstanding [Ausstehen], enduring [Durchstehen], getting through [Durchspannen] refers as which the human being exists [existiert].'[494] The not surprising answer is that his 'basic constitution [Grundverfasssung]', the 'essence of man [Menschenwesen]' is, in the various connotations of the words Boss chooses, to exert himself ontologically in such 'withstanding, enduring and keeping [or holding] open [Offenhalten]', as a 'keeping open of a luminated [gelichtet] area of world openness [Weltoffenständigskeit] in the sense of a capacity for taking in [Vernehmenkönnen] the significances and contexts of reference of everything that speaks to [zuspricht] him from out of the open [Offen] of his world, that presents [vorstellt] itself to him in the most literal sense [of the word] in the sense of standing before him [Sich-vor-ihn-hinstellen].'[495] This disposition is, of course, the condition for the possibility of any 'x-subject', any abstraction such as a 'given' male (XY) or female (XX), an American or a German, a Muslim or a Catholic.

The sense of existing [Existieren] as an ex-tanting [Ek-stare] is formulated in this text in a unique and compelling way. Ontological suffering (bearing up under the ontological demand to da sein, to be there) is something quite different than the ontic sufferings of the symptomatic analysand. Unfortunately, much discussion in 'existential analysis' fails to acknowledge this difference so that physical suffering is distinguished from the metaphoric suffering of those in crisis, to which Boss then turns.

Boss reprises his description of the essentially out-there-bound mutuality of human beings and his critique of the hypothesis of an isolated inner world. 'So far so good', he says.. But what are the implications of all this for those of us who treat suffering people. First, they 'allow us [therapists] to see why we are trying to help the suffering in the first place'; second, they afford us the insight that we have 'the means to determine the health and illness of a person in a humane and rigorous way'; and, finally, such insights 'provide a guiding principle along which all therapeutic measures are to be conducted'. Boss' further comments are, once again, perhaps even more germane today than they were forty years ago:

> The natural-scientific approach to *the suffering human being*, which medical doctors have been solely forced to opt for up to now if they wanted to pass their state examination, cannot provide therapy with a meaning, a goal and a motive. If, however, the philosophical insights of Heidegger are taken as a basis for the theory of healing, then being healthy as well as being sick can be determined in its essence. A human being can be called healthy if he is equipped with the behavioral possibilities constituting human existence, quantitatively and qualitatively, at least on average and if his environment has allowed him to appropriate all his essential behavioral possibilities towards the person encountering him, to assemble them into a being-a-self [Selbstsein] according to his own unique nature and to have them freely at his disposal. In contrast, a person is sick as soon as he lacks something of this freedom. This definition of being healthy and being sick, which is made possible by Heidegger's philosophical

insights into the basic constitution of human existence, is so comprehensive that it is able to provide a solid foundation for all pathology.[496]

The lecture concluded with a clear statement about what daseinanalysis owes to Freud, something Boss never denied. 'On the other hand,' Boss reminded his listeners, given the view of natural science to which Freud was committed, 'which is based on the belief that only that which can be measured is really real ... Freud committed a kind of suicide using his own findings by trying to press them theoretically into the natural scientific world of representation [*Vorstellungswelt*].' But, as we know, commitment to the hegemony of the principle of causality in the natural sciences is a matter of *belief*, not science, since it 'is anything but a scientifically provable law' and that means 'it is and remains a prejudice [*Glaubensatz*],' a matter of belief. Freud's deference to his metapsychology over what he saw amounted to 'a monstrous violation [in the sense of a rape] [*ungeheure Vergewaltigung*] of human phenomena.'

Boss's language is vivid. Had Freud's metapsychology been only a theory to test without any possible harm to human beings, 'one could easily leave the whole thing alone. But it has been shown again and again that in the field of psychotherapy false theories often have devastating effects on the practical therapeutic treatment of those who are suffering.' The 'self-understanding' of psychoanalysis that Boss undertook shows how 'psychoanalytic theory actually misses what is in actual fact the essence of human existing [*Existieren*]. For the same reason, Martin Heidegger's fundamentally new insights into the constitution [*Verfassung*] of human existence are eminently important for *the self-understanding of psychoanalysis* in every respect [emphasis added].'[497]

The textual centerpiece of daseinanalysis is, of course, Martin Heidegger's seminars given for the most part at Boss's home in the Zollikon area of Zurich. It is fitting to save them for last in this review of the literature on therapeutic daseinanalysis and its debt to Heidegger. A first report on the seminars appeared as '**Martin Heidegger's Zollikon Seminars**' (1977d)[498]. This is another one of seven important translations of Boss's papers that appeared in the *Review of Existential Psychology and Psychiatry*. Boss is generously grateful to 'the wonder that is Heidegger – who ... found my very first written communication worthy of an extremely warm response.'[499] Heidegger's reason for his reply is revealed, affirming what we have seen to be Heidegger's reason for establishing close contact with Boss: 'He hoped that through me – a physician and psychotherapist – his thinking would escape the confines of the philosopher's study and become of benefit to wider circles, in particular to a large number of suffering human beings.'[500]

There is then an account of the seminars: 'Up to three times each semester Heidegger spent two weeks as my house guest in Zollikon. For years [from January 24, 1964 to March 21, 1969] he conducted during each visit four evening seminars, each of three hours duration, for a chosen group of fifty to seventy medical students and assistants of the Psychiatric University Clinic of Zürich.'[501] We learn that Heidegger first read Freud only during this period. Boss writes of seventeen years of seminars, but they covered only ten years. Boss may have had in mind the discussions following them in Freiburg that would be synopsized in the 1987 volume as well as ongoing contacts Boss had with Heidegger until his death in 1976.

Apart from the awkward, long silences during at least one meeting, special mention is made of a participant from Australia, someone Boss had in analysis as a candidate. The man, an internist and psychiatrist, 'confided to me,' says Boss: 'Just after the first hour [of his first seminar with Heidegger], I thought, 'So! This is Europe whose intellectual heights and traditions so surpass the miserable pragmatism of my own land.' It was only much later that I realized that even in Europe these Heidegger seminars were a unique bright spot.'[502] To this, Boss added what we know about the genesis of Boss's *Grundriß*: 'No less convincing evidence for the earnestness of Heidegger's '*vor[aus]springende*' caring about his fellow humans is to be seen in his equally patient and painstaking care for my personal scientific works. In particular, Heidegger watched attentively over my *Grundriß der Medizin und Psychologie* [1971; second expanded edition, 1975] (appearing in English under the title, *Existential Foundations of Medicine and Psychology*, Aronson, 1979)[503] during the whole eight years of its development.' Since the first edition appeared in 1971, we can assume from what Boss says that it had been in the works since 1962 or thereabouts, even preceding the bulk of the seminars. 'The magnitude of his care for the work above all else [über äußerte *Sorgfalt*] is vividly illustrated by a facsimile of a page of the manuscript which Heidegger corrected with his own hand.'[504] In fact, this text, on stress, is material that appears in the *Zollikon Seminars* from the May 11, 1965 seminar, not in the *Grundriß*.[505] No matter. It shows the extensive emendations and notes Heidegger evidently made to every page of manuscript Boss sent him.

This reminiscence is also notable for Boss's comments on the status of *Daseinsanalyse* as a therapeutic modality that might be practiced by psychiatrists and other 'psychotherapists'. He recalls having resisted interest in the formation of a training institute for 'daseinsanalytic oriented therapy' on the part of participants in the seminars. 'As the band of medical practitioners trained in Daseinsanalytic oriented therapy had reached considerable proportions [by the time of the last of the seminars] they petitioned that a proper institute might be organized for such training. For a long time, I refused the fulfillment of their wish.' Then comes the surprising revelation that it was under Heidegger's influence that just such an institute was formed. 'As the insistence became ever more vehement, I sought Heidegger's advice. He pondered long over every aspect of the matter. At last, he came to the conclusion that I would do better to give up my resistance to an institutionalization. He considered the danger great that if there were no such institute, the Daseinsanalytic foothold already won in medical circles in Zürich would rapidly be lost after my demise. I yielded.'[506]

As Boss would say on several occasions, he resisted forming an institute because 'I felt too strongly that what Heidegger had taught me did not consist of a framework of special knowledge which could serve as the basis of another 'school' of psychotherapy.' Indeed, he adds, 'had not Heidegger 'merely' helped me expand my field of vision [*die Augen weiter aufzutun*] in that he lanced the cataracts which eliminated all seeing except that in terms of the pre-scientific, philosophical presuppositions concerning the fundamental nature [*Grundnatur*] of what is given [*Gegebenheiten*][507] as such?' Attributing the founding of the first daseinanalytic institute to Heidegger, what matters, Boss says, is that 'today, it is evident how *Heidegger, through this institute, initiated a humanizing not only of psychotherapy, but of medicine as a whole*. The undiminished power of his spirit is to be seen perhaps not least in that branches of our institute have already begun to appear overseas.' The reference is to Brazil, whose group Boss help found in 1974, having been a visitor for many years to the country where two of his children had emigrated.

The volume from which thought we had a sample appeared in 1987 and was translated in 2001 as Martin Heidegger, *Zollikon Seminars: Protocols—Conversations—Letters* (1987a)[508]. In his interview with Dongshick Rhee in 1976 briefly discussed earlier (see (1996)), Boss told the Korean psychiatrist that all of the seminars were tape-recorded and that 'minutes' of the sessions were turned over to the Heidegger-Archiv in Marbach.[509] Boss notes that 'all of the Heidegger seminars cited in this paper took place in the circle of about fifty assistants of the psychiatric clinic of the University [of Zurich] and independently practicing students of M. Boss at his house in Zollikon. They will be kept in the Heidegger Archives in Marbach/Germany. The protocols based on [a] stenographer's [text] were corrected and authorized by Heidegger himself.'[510] By special arrangement with Heidegger's son, Hermann, the book was published as a volume outside of the *Gesamtausgabe* edition and before the deaths of both Heidegger and Boss, that condition of their publication having evidently been agreed to by both men.[511]

As we learn from the preface to the 'American translation', the idea of preparing a translation into English of Heidegger's book came from Franz Mayr and Richard Askay, philosophers teaching at the University of Portland where Boss gave an English version of a paper published as 'Woraus besteht der Mensch, wenn er träumt, und wo ist er dann? [What Is Man Made of When He Dreams, and Where Is He Then?]'[512]

Boss's preface to *Zollikoner Seminare* is worth reviewing in its entirety. It may also be included among the sparse autobiographical material that we have access to for now.

> This book owes its origin to the wonder that Martin Heidegger, who received hundreds of letters from all over the world every year and answered only a few of them, found the first lines I addressed to him worthy of an extremely gracious response. That was shortly after the end of the war in 1947. This event had a history of many years.
>
> Like all Swiss men who were not psychologically or physically impaired, I had to do active military duty throughout the whole war. During these years, I was repeatedly torn away from my civilian work as a university *Dozent* and psychotherapist for months at a time and transferred to a Swiss Army mountain troop as the battalion doctor. As prescribed by Swiss Army military ordinance, no fewer than three assistant doctors were assigned to me. The troops I had to care for were composed of strong mountain countryfolk who were accustomed to doing work. As a result I was nearly unemployed throughout the whole long duration of my military service. For the first time in my life, I was occasionally

gripped by boredom. In the midst of it, what we call 'time' became problematic for me. I began to think specifically about this 'thing'. I sought help in all the pertinent literature available to me. By chance, I came across a newspaper item about Heidegger's book *Being and Time*. I plunged into it, but I discovered that I understood almost none of its content. The book opened up question after question which I had never encountered before in my entire scientifically oriented education. For the most part, these questions were answered in reference to new questions. Disappointed, I laid the book aside only half-read, but strangely it gave me no rest. I would pick it up again and again and begin studying it anew. This first 'conversation' with Heidegger outlasted the war.

Next it extended to research on the [personal historical background] of the author. At first, the information I got was devastating in nature. Serious philosophers I talked with almost always dissuaded me from any further occupation with Heidegger and his work. The recurring argument in these warnings was the characterization of Heidegger as a typical Nazi.

However, this vituperation did not at all fit with what I found in reading *Being and Time*. At first I had more of a hunch than a well-thought out idea that this work articulated fundamentally new, unheard of insights into the human being's way of existing in his world. Being fully packed with psychiatric knowledge my mind of course told me that a human being's social and political behavior need not impair the creativity of his genius. Nonetheless, I did not have the heart to have anything to do with a man who could be proved to have committed specific acts of baseness against other human beings. Therefore, immediately after the end of the war, within the framework of the possibilities available to me at the time, I began to make inquiries about Heidegger through the French occupation authorities and through the highest administrative officials of the University of Freiburg i. Br. [in Breisgau]. Both inquiries finally gave me the certainty that for a short time Heidegger had indeed made some initial 'worldly innocent' misjudgments and mistakes.

In all earnestness, he had initially believed that Hitler and the masses behind him would be able to build a wall against political Communism's encroaching waves of spiritual darkness. In spite of that, nothing came to light regarding any concrete, voluntary act of baseness toward Heidegger's fellow human beings. When I tried to be absolutely honest with myself, *I had to admit that had I been forced to live in environmental conditions such as Heidegger had at the time, I could not swear to avoid falling victim to similar errors* [emphasis added]. In spite of the fact that I had definite anti-Hitler convictions at that time because of my Swiss perspective, this could have been the case. Furthermore, I never had a moment's doubt about being prepared to stand my ground to the very end as a soldier against the German invaders.

On the other hand, in all these inquiries Heidegger very clearly seemed to be the most slandered man I had ever encountered. He had become entangled in a network of lies by his colleagues. Most of the people, who were unable to do serious harm to the substance of Heidegger's thinking, tried to get at Heidegger the man with personal attacks. The only remaining puzzle was why Heidegger did not defend himself against these slanders publicly. The astonishing fact of his defenselessness gave me the incentive to stand up for him to the best of my ability.

In any case, from 1947 on, there was no longer any compelling reason which could have kept me from trying to approach Heidegger for the first time on a personal basis. As a doctor, I wrote a letter to the philosopher and asked for help in [reflective] thinking. I was very surprised when an answer arrived by return mail. In it Martin Heidegger agreed in a friendly way to give me any help he could. At first, there was an exchange of letters, which grew to a collection of 256 letters by the time of the thinker's death. In addition, there were over fifty greeting cards from his trips abroad.

As soon as the border between our countries was somewhat passable, we began to make regular personal visits and return visits to each other's homes. During our first meeting at Martin Heidegger's mountain hut

in Todtnauberg in the summer of 1949, a mutual human sympathy developed between us. It gradually grew into a cordial friendship. Only much later did I discover the most important motive for Heidegger's prompt answer to my first letter. From the very beginning, as he himself once admitted, Heidegger had set great hope on an association with a doctor and had a seemingly extensive understanding of his thought. He saw the possibility that his philosophical insights would not be confined merely to the philosopher's quarters but also might benefit many more people, especially people in need of help.

From the time that the seminars were incorporated into Heidegger's private visits to my home, certainly no one thought to take verbatim protocols or to print up protocols afterward. To begin with, I did not think it proper to be the only person to benefit from frequent meetings with the great thinker. Therefore, each year, beginning in 1959, I invited from fifty to seventy colleagues and psychiatry students to seminars at my home on the occasion of Heidegger's usual two-week visits. His visits to my home in Zollikon took place two to three times each semester. Only occasionally did my stays abroad make longer intervals unavoidable.

Heidegger sacrificed three hours, two evenings a week, to be with the guests. He spent the whole day beforehand preparing carefully for these seminars. In spite of his contempt for the psychological and psychopathological theories which filled our heads, Heidegger deserves great credit for taking on the almost Sisyphean task of giving my friends, colleagues, and students a sound philosophical foundation for their medical practice. He continued this task for a full decade within the framework of the Zollikon Seminars, which in the meantime had gained widespread fame. His untiring, unwavering patience and forbearance in carrying out and completing this undertaking to the limits of his physical abilities provide unshakable proof of the greatness of Heidegger's concern for his fellow human beings. By displaying this attitude toward our Zollikon circle, he proved that he could not only talk and write about the highest level of human fellowship, but that he was also prepared to live it in an exemplary way. *He exemplified selfless, loving solicitude, which leaps ahead of the other [human being], returning to him his own freedom* [emphasis added].

The series of seminars began on September 8, 1959, with Heidegger's lecture in the large auditorium of the University of Zurich psychiatric clinic known as the 'Burghölzli' The choice of this location proved rather inauspicious. The recently renovated auditorium had such a hypermodern, technological appearance that its atmosphere was simply not conducive to Heidegger's thinking. Therefore, the impending second seminar was moved to my house in Zollikon. All subsequent seminars continued there for the entire next decade.

From 1970, my conscience as a doctor no longer allowed me to expect that Heidegger could continue to endure the great strain of the Zollikon Seminars. By then Martin Heidegger's physical powers were quickly declining because of his age. From then on, I asked for his intellectual help only by mail or during my visits to his home in Freiburg.

It was a full four years after the seminars began that I started to see the light and to become aware that it was possible to gain insights directly from Heidegger's words in the seminars, which were impossible to hear

delivered elsewhere. The seminar protocols recorded by the students were unsuccessful, so I took over the recording. Beginning with the next seminar, I recorded Heidegger's every word. I dictated the short protocol

into a tape recorder immediately after the seminar. Then my secretary transcribed it into typewritten form. Next the protocol drafts were immediately sent to Martin Heidegger in Freiburg. He corrected them very carefully, made some minor additions here and there, and occasionally added major additions in his German handwriting. He returned the corrected and supplemented protocols to me. Finally, these fully authorized protocols, corrected by Heidegger himself, were mimeographed in typewritten form so that every seminar participant had a record of them and had a chance to prepare for the next seminar.

Some of the seminars were recorded in a way that must make it obvious to the reader, from the written record, just how exceedingly difficult the seminars were at the beginning. This is clearly evidenced by the fact that the discussions and responses were separated by long silences and pauses and by the fact that these scientifically educated doctors had never encountered most of Heidegger's questions as questions. Many participants seemed to be shocked, even outraged, that such questions would be permitted in the first place. At the start of the seminars in the late 1950s, even I was able to assimilate Heidegger's thinking only as a beginner would. I could provide very little help in overcoming the pauses in the conversations. Quite often the situations in the seminars grew reminiscent of some imaginary scene: it was as if a man from Mars were visiting a group of earth-dwellers in an attempt to communicate with them.

Today, more than twenty years after the first Zollikon Seminars, this analogy seems grossly exaggerated. Certainly, some of Heidegger's characteristic neologisms, such as Being-in-the-world or Care, have become more familiar. One or the other of these terms has found its way into everyday, readable illustrated magazines. Of course, it remains to be seen whether this is the product of a genuine familiarity – in the sense of a deep understanding of its meaning – or whether it is a rather superficial habituation of the ear. In any case, the same question the seminar participants in those days occasionally dared to ask Heidegger directly can frequently still be heard today. The proverbial question used to be why Heidegger did not try to talk about his subject matter in plain understandable German. The thinker's answer was regularly the same: after all, we can only speak as we think and think as we speak. If the essential ground of a subject matter emerges from thinking anew and from seeing different, significant features – even if the subject matter is the human being's being itself – then this demands an appropriate, new discourse. For instance, if we were to define and to speak about the human being as a subject or as an 'I', then what remains totally concealed is the understanding of the essential ground of the human being's being, which endures in a domain of receptive openness to the world.

Considering the enormous difficulties in communication then, the strangest thing about the Zollikon Seminars was that neither Heidegger nor the seminar participants grew tired of them. From the beginning and over the years, the teacher and students worked persistently toward achieving a common ground.

Heidegger and I had many hours to ourselves and plenty of time for conversation on the days between seminars. It finally occurred to me to take down Heidegger's remarks in shorthand on these occasions as well. Understandably, I was able to record only a fraction of what was said during the discussions. This collection of shorthand notes forms part 2 of this book.

In a few cases the handwritten texts which Heidegger jotted down while preparing for the seminars and for the conversations are included here instead of protocols and shorthand notes. These texts are identified in the table of contents and in the text itself. In quoting philosophical and literary texts, Heidegger usually referred to editions that were easily available at the time with a view toward the compositions of the seminar participants. With a few exceptions, these respective editions were not recorded in the protocols. In view of this circumstance, and in consideration of the fact that the Zollikon Seminars are addressed to a wide circle of readers and not just to an exclusive or to a 'specific' philosophically oriented [audience], the philosophical and literary texts are [now] quoted in reference to editions easily available today. This corresponds to Martin Heidegger's method at the time. When Martin Heidegger rendered texts from the writings of Aristotle, he always provided his own translations. Reference to particular translations of Aristotle was therefore unnecessary.

Part 3 of this book includes excerpts from 256 letters which Martin Heidegger had written to me since 1947. Almost half of them can be read in their entirety or in part.

Most of the abbreviations in the letters have been spelled out, and dates have been written in complete form. Punctuation has been adjusted to current practice. A few apparent mistakes in spelling have been corrected, but unique Heideggerian spelling has been retained. Explanatory remarks by the editor, not placed in the footnotes, have been put in brackets.

Numerous proper names were not printed in this book whenever such anonymity did not detract from the content of the particular passage. Nevertheless, some proper names could not be eliminated without making the whole context incomprehensible. In making each of these decisions, I obtained Martin Heidegger's approval during his lifetime.

Of course, this publication does not fully fathom the reach of Heidegger's spiritual radiance. This thinker's new insights into what is – and how it is – have already started to encompass the world. In any case, there is surely no place on earth that remains entirely unaffected by them. Of course, for the most part these insights are kept alive by only a few people. Basically, they are much too simple to be painlessly understood by masses of people so accustomed to the complicated formulas of the technical age. The philosopher himself often spoke about there being a particular blindness to his insights and about how those [people] who were not struck by them could not be helped.

We also cannot disregard the fact that Heidegger's fundamental thinking further dethrones the human being and causes many people to close their minds in desperation. Sigmund Freud had already called his discovery a second Copernican revolution. It was not enough that Copernicus had displaced our earth from the center of the universe, but Freud had been able to show that autocratic human consciousness is driven back and forth by 'Id-forces', as he called them, the origin and nature of which are unknown. Heidegger went even further and recognized that even the human subject could be of little value as a measure and as the starting point for [the knowledge] of all things. Human consciousness is 'merely' something which is. It is a being among thousands of other beings. In its being-ness as such, it depends on and is sustained by the disclosive appropriating Event [*Ereignis*] of being, unconcealment. Nonetheless, the human being has the great honor and distinction of being able to exist as this openness and 'clearing' [*Lichtung*], which, as such, must serve as the unconditional place for the appearance and emergence of everything that is.

Therefore, it can be hoped that Heidegger's fundamental insights – even in any diluted form – may contribute to the humanization of our world in the most positive sense of the word. In no way does this mean a further 'subjectivization' of the human mind as the absolute maker of all [*Alles-Macher*]. Rather, it means yielding oneself [*Sich*-fügen] to a love that is granted to the human being's being in all that discloses itself in its being and in all that addresses the human being from the openness of his world.

The editor is deeply grateful to Dr. Hermann Heidegger, whose father granted him the imprimatur for printing all posthumous works. He has taken extraordinary care with this present book as well. I am no less indebted to Professor F. W. von Herrmann, Dr. Hermann Heidegger's expert collaborator. The editor is especially indebted to him for the preparation of the very detailed table of contents. He was also the one who gave me, Dr. Heidegger, and the publisher, Mr. Michael Klostermann, the idea of publishing the Zollikon Seminars ahead of schedule, although this volume had been planned to come out at a much later time as part of the Collected Works. It is highly improbable that the present editor will be alive in the next decade. At the same time, it is difficult to imagine how someone could arrange and prepare for publication the shorthand seminar notes, the dialogues, and the letter excerpts. In addition, the editor is indebted to Dr. Hartmut Tietjen for his supervision of the bibliographical data. Thanks are also due my wife, Marianne Boss-Linsmayer. Without her expert cooperation in organizing, and selecting from, Heidegger's papers, this book could not have been published. Last but not least, I must thank my student Karin Schoeller von Haslinger for her sacrifice in helping me read the proofs.

Medard Boss
Spring 1987

The fruit of the seminars, as we know, was Boss's *Grundriß* for doctors and psychologists, which predated the publication of the first edition of protocols of the seminars and related material by sixteen years. Both volumes are foundational for understanding the new approach to which Heidegger introduced his seminar participants. Here we can at most survey the general themes of the sessions, which began with a lecture given by Heidegger at the Burghölzi Hospital on September 8, 1959, followed by several seminars at the hospital that year and in 1960. The regular meetings at Boss's office and home began on January 24, 1964 and continued through March 21, 1969, the bulk of the sessions having been held in the years 1964-1966. After a break of two years, sessions were held in 1968 and March 1969.

The early sessions are devoted to disabusing the attendees of their unacknowledged allegiance to the method of natural science. The central place of the principle of causality in the medical model is stressed over and over, as is its inapplicability in any therapy that is oriented to the human being. The next major theme is human temporality, which occupies five sessions. The traditional division between the physical and the psychological (psyche and soma) next comes under scrutiny, especially the nature of human *Leiblichkeit* (bodiliness), which is based on a phenomenology of human spatiality [*Räumlichkeit*]. The concluding seminars are devoted to the differences between daseinanalysis and traditional psychiatric practice and psychoanalysis.

Sections of the protocols are verbatim records of dialogues between Heidegger and participants. The bulk of the text, however, is direct address to the participants as a group. Some of the 'Conversations', which date from November 29, 1961 and thereafter, are also presented as dialogue. The last of these is dated March 3, 1972, and was held at Heidegger's home in the Zähringen suburb of Freiburg. Boss's conversations with Heidegger before and after the seminars as well as on trips the men took with their spouses and the time they spent in Lenzerheide, Boss's alpine retreat, are far-ranging, from Binswanger's appropriation of Heidegger's thought to some of the shibboleths of Freud's psychoanalysis (transference, projection, introduction). More or less self-standing texts dated September 8, 1959 (contested by Trawny), March 8, 1965, November 13, 1966 and September 27, 1968, are interpolated in the protocols and conversations.[513] The Trawny edition, published forty years after Boss's edition, is based on manuscript material to which Trawny had access at the Marbach archive. Notes Heidegger prepared for sessions and sometimes wrote during and after seminars are remarkable for the scope of their references, from a mention of the third century Vedanta philosopher and sage, Shankaracharya (788-820)... to Henry Miller (1891-1980).

A fitting conclusion to a discussion of the book is a review of Boss's preface to the English translation of the seminars and his **'Afterword'** to Martin Heidegger, Zollikon Seminars—Protocols—Conversations—Letters (1969)[514]. The 'Afterword' is a revised version of an open letter to Heidegger published in a Swiss newspaper in 1969. It is a touching and very personal statement by Boss on the nature of the collaboration between the psychiatrist and the philosopher. The letter was written on the occasion of Heidegger's birthday, September 26, 1969. The two men had met for their last times in Zürich on March 18 and July 14, 1969. It is poignant that Boss speaks of it as a 'farewell letter [Abschiedsbrief]'. He tells us that 'the content of virtually all of the letters which Heidegger wrote to me after 1969' as well as other 'signs' 'indicated that my friend had begun to retire more and more into himself and to prepare for dying.' Looking back on their by then quarter-century friendship, Boss remarks yet again on Heidegger's charisma.

> Only twice in my life had I encountered eyes which could look at you in a similar way. The first time was nearly twenty years earlier [than their first meeting at the Hütte in Todtnauberg] when I stood face to face with Sigmund Freud at the Bergstrasse [sic] in Vienna. A good ten years after my first visit with you it happened again in the hermit's cell of probably the greatest sage of present-day India [Govind Kaul].[515]

Boss again reminisces about having helped bring Heidegger out of seclusion following his Lehrverbot in the late 1940s. He credits Heidegger with having changed the course of his thinking and practice as a physician: 'For a long time I had been searching for a sound, scientific foundation [wissenschaftliche Fundament] for my whole medical practice.' Realizing that natural science could not provide a basis for the work of 'dealing with the human body', 'in this distress, afflicting so many of my colleagues and myself, you came to our aid. Thanks to your untiring effort, my originally faint notion of the fundamental importance of your thinking for the realm of medicine too has changed in the course of the years into an increasingly more secure knowledge.' Thus far Heidegger himself. In the next passages, however, Boss makes explicit the other source of therapeutic daseinanalysis as he worked it out. Once again, I would stress that we need to give to Boss's encounter with Eastern philosophy and, in particular, one of its living authorities: 'In the basic structures of the way of human existing [*Wesenzügens des menschliches Existierens*] which you elaborated, I recognized the most reliable outline of an art of healing [*Heilenkunde*], *which I had glimpsed till then during my wanderings through the history of philosophy and medicine and during my expeditions to the Far East* [India and Malaysia in the late 1950s] *and the Far West.*'[516] The complementary synergy of both Heidegger's thought and ancient Hindu philosophy for the development of daseinanalysis has yet to be fully appreciated, but it is worth pointing out that later in his letter Boss elaborates on the East-West theme, noting that Heidegger's 'thinking is just now experiencing such a great breakthrough in Japan and America.' It is well known that Japanese philosophers had been among the first to seriously embrace Heidegger's thought in the 1920s, but the implications for therapy of the sources of Zen in earlier Indian thought were only being made explicit in the late 1960s.[517]

In his letter, we are apprised of Heidegger's motivation for having worked with Boss in Zollikon for the decade that had just ended (1959-1969).

> The joint idea of the Zollikon Seminars originated in your wish to grant the aid of your philosophical thinking to as many suffering people [*leidenden Menschen*] as possible and in my need for a solid support for my medical science [*artzliche Wissenschaft*] ... You never shirked the heavy burden of being my guest one, two, three times per semester in order to bring the best of my students and co-workers closer to a fundamental thinking over which they as one-sided, [natural] scientifically educated psychiatrists had so little command. Today dozens of young Swiss doctors and former seminar participants from abroad are deeply grateful to you for the patience with which you always grappled again and again with the clumsiness of our one-track vision. With these seminars you created numerous and indissoluble bonds connecting you with my hometown and my country. It is quite clear how your decisive and enduring way of teaching the circle of novice psychiatrists and psychotherapists in Zürich influenced the style and form of their medical practice and made them more human in character. Yet, what unending effort you had to expend until you brought these young people to the insight that for them as doctors – and especially for those who are involved with living, human beings – a philosophical reflection on the foundation of their [natural] science is a necessary presupposition for the true, scientific character of the healing art and is not merely a playful, spare-time activity.[518]

As a synopsis of the daseinanalytic perspective, this remains fundamental and invites us to pay close attention to Boss's further explication: 'Later on, we understood that and also why man's constitution [*Verfasssung*] and the meaning of his existing [*Sinn seines Existierens*] cannot be comprehended as long as one takes being human [*Mensch-Sein*][519] itself as the starting point and the goal of the investigation in the manner of the traditional, psychological anthropologies.' As becomes clear, daseinanalysis is *not* a branch of psychology, namely, as applied psychology in areas such as clinical psychology, psychoanalysis, and other forms of psychotherapy based on it, as well as the various forms of counseling psychology, social work and pastoral psychology. 'You demanded from us that we turn to the fundamental question of all philosophy, which wants to know what it really means that something can be, and '*is*' at all and that there is not simply nothing. Thus, you taught us to marvel at this 'is', 'being' [*Sein*], as the greatest wonder there is [*das es gibt*].' In view of the question about be[-ing],

> being human shows itself as something claimed [*in Anspruch genommen wird*] by something much higher than itself. Being human is needed fundamentally as the world-expansive open realm of a being able to see [*Vernehmen-Könnens*] so that the given things making up the world in their significance and referential relationships can emerge in [the world], manifest themselves, in their presencing, in their being. If there were not something like the essence of such a means [*Art*] of open [*offenständig*] being human, how and into what should anything come to presence at all and reveal itself, that is, to be? With these discoveries of your thinking, you let us doctors known the true dignity of man.[520]

Given the close relation between medicine and science that Heidegger's thought exposes as utterly inadequate to human being, it is not surprising that Boss concludes with some general observations about technicity [*Technik*], medicine's inevitable implication in its hegemony, and how Heidegger had been able

> to lead us from a demonic state of being spellbound by technology [*dämonische Gebanntsein in die Technik*] to a free relationship [*freie Verhältnis*] with it. You are teaching us to comprehend the technical relationship to the world in which we people of today must exist as a destiny [*Geschick*] of the history of humanity [*Menschheitsgeschichte*]. With this you let us become aware of its unavoidable character as a mandate, yet at the same time you are removing the fateful character [*Verhängnishafte*] of something absolute and ultimate which has finally befallen us. With such a determination of the relationship 'technicity-nature' you returned again to the domain of the physicianly [*Ärtzlichen*], if only one conceives of the healing art broadly enough.[521]

With the last section of his *Grundriß* clearly in mind, Boss adds: 'By having clarified the spirit of technology, you have also become the founder [*Begründer*] of an effective, preventive medicine.'

This 'letter to a friend' is important as a bridge between the Zollikon seminars and what they bore fruit to in what was effectively Boss's *second* book written in cooperation with Heidegger, the *Grundriß*. Boss's gratitude is expansive but, as the preface to the letter suggests, given Heidegger's age and health, what they had worked on closely together during the final years of seminars was an incomplete, albeit major achievement.

Finally, there is Boss's **'Preface'** to the American Translation of Martin Heidegger's *Zollikon Seminars* (2001)[522]. It is a singular document, both as an introduction to the basic text of daseinanalysis and as the last bit of writing Medard Boss was working on before his death. Completed by his second wife, Marianne Linsmayer-Boss, it is worth reproducing in its entirety in bringing this review of the literature of daseinanalysis to a conclusion.

> This translation was initiated by Dr. Franz Mayr and Dr. Richard Askay, both of whom are philosophy professors at the University of Portland. In September 1989, I was invited to the first Applied Heidegger Conference at Berkeley by its organizers, Dr. Hubert Dreyfus of the University of California, Berkeley, and Dr. Michael Zimmerman of Tulane University. They asked me to deliver the keynote address at this conference concerning my cooperation and work with Martin Heidegger.[523] My discussion of Heidegger's new and alternative way of thinking about the human being and his world was received with great enthusiasm. This also happened in response to my lecture on the new 'phenomenological' understanding of human dreaming that was delivered at the University of Portland, immediately after the Heidegger conference at Berkeley.
>
> I simply did not anticipate that American philosophers like those mentioned above would master the profound insight of *Da-sein-analytical* or phenomenological thinking.
>
> Some thirty years earlier, in the summer of 1963, during my first encounter with my American colleagues as a visiting faculty member at Harvard University, I delivered lectures on Heidegger's alternative way of thinking. Many more obstacles had to be surmounted at that time.
>
> It soon became clear to me that the participants at the Applied Heidegger Conference at Berkeley continue to be great exceptions among American philosophers. Most of my American colleagues in philosophy and psychology encountered greater obstacles during all other discussions of *Da-seinanalysis* themes than I had to overcome in discussions with European, Indian, and South American colleagues.
>
> The Americans experienced problems primarily in accomplishing the 'leap of thought' – which is indispensable, though not always successful – in changing from traditional, causal-genetic, explanatory, and calculative modes of thinking to the entirely different Da-sein-analytical approach of Heidegger's phenomenological thinking.
>
> In this new and alternative view, human existence in its unique way, like everything else in our world, no longer appears as something present as an object within a pregiven world space. Rather, human existence can be viewed as being, which cannot be objectified and which consists of an openness to the world and of the capacity to perceive what it encounters in that world. Through this openness, human existence itself, as well as any other given facts of our world, can come to their presence and unfolding. The proper task of human Dasein is the event of letting-be what emerges into the openness of being. Human existence is necessary for this event, which constitutes its proper and most profound meaning. Thus, it also becomes clear that this meditative, alter-

native, and new way of thinking may also disclose meaning and purpose to the art of healing.

Many people who are initially touched by this new and different way of thinking are stricken with great panic. They fear that if they let themselves really be touched by this thinking they will have to abandon the time-honored definition of the human being as an Ego, as a center of personality, and as a separate bodily organism. They believe they will completely lose themselves thereby. As a result, many of them quickly take refuge in the seemingly secure Freudian view of a 'psychic apparatus'. Yet in doing so they forget that it was Freud himself who called his notion of a 'psychic apparatus' a mere 'fiction' which only pretends to give human thinking a solid foundation.

Heidegger would not have devoted as much time and energy to instructing medical doctors as he did in the Zollikon Seminars had he not thought his new and alternative thinking – meditative thinking – was of essential benefit to all medical therapies. Indeed, if the therapists let themselves be imbued in body and soul with this 'new and alternative' way of thinking, they themselves would experience its benefits, primarily in the form of self-transformation. From then on, they would understand themselves as individuals who are called upon to serve all beings including patients, who in their openness to the world encounter the therapist as a place for self-disclosure.

When they are 'together with' the therapist in *Da-seinanalysis* situations, the patients are allowed to assume and to perform all their pregiven possibilities of behavior in a reflective and responsible way. This is the essential meaning and the inherent goal of all medical therapies, whether they are physical or psychotherapeutic in nature.

The *Zollikon Seminars* presented here are unique. Nowhere else has this philosopher so directly addressed students who had a purely scientific educational background. This required the teacher to proceed with special care and caution.

Medard Boss
Spring 1990

At this point in the preface, in December 1990, illness took the pen from Medard Boss's hand. Therefore, it may be meaningful to quote a few sentences from the preface to the second German edition for the American reader (Frankfurt am Main, 1994):

Today the reader can take this newly reprinted volume in his hand, although both the author and the editor have gone through the door of eternity – Martin Heidegger in 1976 and Medard Boss in 1990.

Unlike the doctor, Medard Boss, the reader does not have to courageously question the foundation of his science and to ask the philosopher for advice regarding a more sustainable platform for his medical thought and practice.

Biographical and Scientific Texts

This publication also addresses a broader circle of readers than just those who are professionally interested in philosophy. The reader gets acquainted with the background of developments which began with Medard Boss's first letter to Martin Heidegger in 1947 – from the packet of chocolate to the subtle struggle for an adequate understanding of Being and of the nature of *Daseinanalysis*. Woven into this fabric of manifold questions and answers – talk and countertalk – is the call for carefulness regarding the originary and proper meaning of phenomena.

The Zollikon Seminars were borne by friendship and were written by two hands, like a spiritual child who found its own life and went abroad by being translated into foreign languages.

Martin Heidegger's name appears prominently on the cover. But whenever one associates Medard Boss with that Chinese customs office and its customs collector one is reminded of the thirteenth stanza of the 'Legend' ['Legend of the Origin of the Book *Tao-te-Ching* by Lao Tzu on His Way to Emigration'] by Bertolt Brecht, which schoolchildren in Medard Boss's hometown of Zurich can still read in their reading book:

> But let us praise not only the sage
> Whose name shines on the book,
> For first of all one has to tear the wisdom from the sage.
> That is why the customs collector should also be thanked.
> He was the one who asked it of him.[524]

Only a few weeks ago the writer became aware of how much Martin Heidegger loved this poem (see Heinrich Wiegand Petzet, *Encounters and Dialogues with Martin Heidegger, 1929-1976*, trans. P. Emad and K. Maly, with an introduction by P. Emad [Chicago: University of Chicago Press, 1993], p. 217, as well as Hannah Arendt and Martin Heidegger, *Briefe* [Frankfurt am Main, 1998], p. 345).

It was not granted to Medard Boss to participate in the progress of this translation and to review the finished text. Fortunately, Professor William J. Richardson (Boston College) undertook this task. To him and to both translators, I express my cordial gratitude.

In memory of Medard Boss and Martin Heidegger, this book is sent on its way in a further foreign language.[525]

Marianne Boss-Linsmayer
Zollikon, Christmas 1998

With the publication of his edition of Heidegger's seminars and Boss's own 'ground plan' for medicine and psychology behind him, Boss's career was drawing to an end. In 1989, about a year before writing the preface to *Zollikon Seminars*, Boss gave two lectures that sum up the influence of Heidegger on medicine, psychiatry and his own life's work. We conclude a brief look at each of these texts.

The first lecture, '**Martin Heidegger's Initiatives for a Different Kind of Psychiatry**' [1989] (1991)[526], was a contribution to a series of lectures given in Meßkirch, Heidegger's home town, marking the centenary of his birth there. It appeared two years later in the first volume published by the Martin-Heidegger-Gesellschaft, *From a Heideggerian Perspective. Impact on Art and Medicine. Meßkirch Lectures*. The volume also contains contributions by Max Müller (1906-1994), Friedrich-Wilhelm von Herrmann (1934-2022), Manfred Riedel (1936-2009), Vincenzo Vitiello (1935-), Ryiôsuke Ohashi (1944-) and Hans Kock (1920-2007).

We hear more about Boss's first conversations with Heidegger in 1947 in Todtnauberg. The discussion had turned to 'Existentialism', that basically French literary and cultural movement that emerged during World War II, the best-known representative of which was Jean-Paul Sartre. 'Of all that Sartre writes there [in *L'Être et le Néant*], not a word is true. Rather, all ontological essences of a thing are always only visible through ontically describable givens [*Gegebenheiten*], as conversely all ontically perceivable [*wahnehmbaren*] givens are founded on their ontological determinations and are – as long as they are – enforced [*ständig*] by them.'[527] The failure to distinguish between Heidegger's fundamental ontology and the ontic concerns of psychology, psychiatry and psychoanalysis had begun with Binswanger and echoed through the Existentialist movement as it spread throughout Europe and eventually made its way to the States in the mid-1950s. It remains a problem in discussions of daseinanalysis, but resolves if Boss's observation is taken to heart, that the ontological is 'visible' only in the ontic and that the ontic can appear only because it is 'founded' on the ontological. One does not have precedence over the other.

Boss also notes in this text that dreaming is not mentioned by Heidegger as an existentive, although, he believes, it belongs there along with being spatial [*Räumlich-sein*], being temporal [*Zeitlich-sein*], being attuned [*Gestimmt-sein*], being-with [*Mit-sein*], being bodily [*Leiblich-sein*], and being mortal [*Sterblich-sein*] as 'phenomena [*Phänomene*] seen by the doctor in his patients', both in health and when they are ill. For Boss, dreaming is an essential part of the ontological structure of *Dasein* and, like the other existentives, belongs to the repertoire of what the therapist sees as essential to every individual he meets. That Heidegger was a 'poor dreamer' may account for the fact that this did not receive his attention from the start in *Being and Time*.

Boss's theme is Heidegger's 'new thinking' as it applies to medicine, challenging the approach of psychiatric nosology and psychopathology, replacing it with one based on Heidegger's analytics of *Dasein*, which focuses 'ways of being ill', for example, (1) 'with marked impairment in the deployment [*Austrag*] of being-bodily', (2) 'with marked impairment in the deployment of settling in [*Sich-einräumens*] and of getting ready for the future [*Sich-zeitigens*]', (3) 'with marked disturbances [*Störungen*] in the accomplishment [*Vollzug*] of being-attuned', and (4) 'with marked impairment in the accomplishment of the fundamental character of being-open [*Öffenständig-seins*] and freedom of existence [*Dasein*]'. This does not amount to a nosology but rather to disturbances of what is common to every existence.

Boss astutely notes that psychiatrists everywhere begin, as medical doctors do, with the question '*Was fehlt Ihnen denn?*': 'What's wrong with you?' The question asks, literally, 'What's *missing* in you?' to which, Boss notes, patients typically reply by telling the doctor about something that he *has*: 'I have a headache'; 'I have a stomach ache'; or, more to the point of psychiatric practice: 'I have a thought that keeps coming back.' 'I have anxiety when I think of speaking in public', etc. Today, prospective patients routinely speak of *having* a named mental illness or psychological disturbance they have heard about from friends or in the media: 'I have OCD'; 'I have bi-polar disorder'; 'I have schizophrenia.' Less sophisticated patients may simply say 'I have a lot of anxiety' or 'I have bouts of depression.' The point, Boss says, is that beginning this way, doctor and patient miss each other, like ships passing in the night. The doctor asks about a presumptive lack of health while the patient answers in terms of a presumptive disease entity that is thought to be causing him to feel ill or be sick. His symptoms are what he has. By contrast with such an approach is the phenomenological investigation of the human being's experience of being ill. The goal of treatment oriented this way cannot be reached by reducing the human being to a corporeal entity subject to a series of events at the somatic level and the possession of intrusive, foreign bodylike inhabitants of their minds that are their result. Instead, what comes first is bodily being [*Leiblichkeit*], a feature of the existence of the patient. For the human being, which 'is alive and lives its life [*leibt und lebt*][528], being-[a]-body [*Leib-sein*] is only sensuously the first, that which first is pressing itself into view.'[529] *Leib-sein* is not all of *Dasein*, but only its first sign.

One of several case examples given by way of illustration is that of a so-called manic-depressive personality in a manic phase. The psychiatric view of health must be scrutinized, Boss claims, since the manic is not in any sense ill. He does not feel that there is something wrong or amiss with him. 'Manic patients claim that they have never felt so healthy, so strong, so happy in their lives as they do now. Life is one big party.' Both the report of expansiveness (a symptom) and the excessive behavior (a sign) are misleading. Everything is too good to be true. 'On closer inspection, however, the happiness of the manic is far removed from the happy sunniness [*glückhafte Heiterkeit*] and open composure [*offenen Gelassenheit*] of those healthy people who have matured into the free, independent deployment of the behavioral possibilities [*Verhaltensmöglichkeiten*] given to them [*herangereift*].'[530] As Boss explains: 'In their manic moodiness [*manische Verstimmtheit*], only an extremely deficient temporal playspace [*Zeit-Spiel-Raum*] is open to these patients as a world. They know no free, open counterpart to what they encounter. They can neither leave alone the things and fellow men they see where they spatiotemporally are, nor are they able to let what is in each case encountering [*Begegnende*] them be and become what it is to appear as. The seeing [*Vernehmen*][531] of these patients is so highly dimmed [*abgeblendet*] that they are addressed in a uniform way by only one and the same significance of that which shows itself of what is given to them. Everything appeals to them only as what is to be snatched up, seized upon, and gobbled up as quickly as possible.'[532] No matter how involved the manic appears to be with everyone, he 'cannot succeed in establishing genuine closeness with anyone present.' Mania 'manifests itself in a boundless, but empty and bottomless, completely self-referential feeling of omnipotence.' This does not qualify as a disease process, however, since there is no diminution of overall functioning. The patient is not less capable of living fully than he was before the manic episode. In this sense, the manic is closely related to the 'melancholic' or depressive. Again, thinking in terms of the currently well-known bi-polar mood disorder, like the manic mood, 'the melancholic mood [*melancholische Verstimmung*] is also a mode of deployment of that essential being attuned [*wesensmäßigen Gestimmt-seins*] of human existing [*Existierens*].' In this case, however, the melancholic 'perceives in himself nothing but inferiority, nothingness and guilt.' He speaks of 'nothing 'going on [*laufe*]'.'

Boss points to the change in the experience of lived time that is at the heart of such existential situations. 'Nothing is going on because their [the depressives'] time stands still [*ihre Zeit stille steht*].' As Boss explains: 'With this, however, they have already turned into an humanly unworthy nothing [*menschenunwürdigen Nichts*].' Such a disturbance of temporality has the effects it has because 'being human [*Mensch-sein*] is [*gibt*] only as the timing [*Zeitigung*] of being there [*Da-sein*] in the expression of one's own innate behavioral possibilities in relation to that which speaks to [*das Zuprechenden*] the human being.'[533] In general, as we have seen, 'the essential sense [*Sinn*] of being human [*Menschseins*] is to answer [*antworten*] to what is encountering [*Begegnende*] with all the existential [*existentiellen*] possibilities inherent in a human being and to allow them [what is encountering] to attain to their unfolding [*Entfaltung*] in their own free realm [*in derem freiem Bereich*].'[534] This is disturbed in the manic and the melancholic. They are not invaded by disturbances as though by foreign bodies. What can be learned from these examples is that existence 'times' what is given to it and has significance for it, that is, signifies something to it or speaks to it, for which existence provides lumination. In melancholic or depressive *Dasein*, attuned as it is, past and future are collapsed into a static present that is entirely 'self-referential'. Others have no place in such a present. There is no 'room' for them.

The discussion turns next to schizophrenia. Patients so diagnosed 'experience disturbances in the consummation [*Vollzug*] of this defining feature [*Grundmerkmals*] of being there [*Da-sein*] ... [namely] its world-disclosing [*welt-erschließen*], free being-open [*Offenständig-seins*].' Here Boss presents what is a remarkable insight, what remains one of the most challenging phenomena that has occupied psychiatry from the outset. 'Schizophrenic being-ill may be called the most human and at the same time the most inhuman of all suffering [*Leiden*] because only human beings, but not animals or other living beings [*Lebewesen*], can fall ill with schizophrenia.' Given the general view that the schizophrenic is not treatable in the way other 'mental disorders' are, seen from a daseinanalytic perspective, schizophrenia is understood as the most striking example of *the failure of being human*, understood as 'primary, openly responsive, addressable [*ansprechbares*], ec-static[535] being-in-the-world [*ek-statisches In-der-Welt-sein*]'. The essential feature of being human is vividly brought to our attention by its absence, much as sound is by silence as the absence of sound. Just as silence is audible, the failure of being human of the schizophrenic draws our attention and brings into relief what is human. To be more precise, the 'schizophrenic patients reveal themselves as people who are no longer capable of 'existing' in the most literal sense of the word, who are no longer capable of enduring [*Ausstehen*] this being-open [*Offenständig-sein*]' which is the essence of being human. Schizophrenic existing

> is incapable of opening itself to the acceptance of the realities of its world, of engaging in such an approach to things with its entire being while yet preserving its own independence. Schizophrenically ill existence . . . is at the mercy of the person encountering it to such a great degree that it is absorbed by him and perishes as an independent being human [*Mensch-sein*] from such overpowering.[536]

This accounts for why the schizophrenic dodges, as it were, what approaches it and stays away from it, especially when what confronts it is another human being. Finally, 'his' time does not want to pass at all because it is not his time at all. He has no time of his own. He only lives the time of others.' What, then, is to be done therapeutically in these cases? 'Unwavering [*unentwegte*], affectionate [*liebevolle*] human attention [*Zuwendung*] would be the most healing therapeutic agent [*heilsamste Therapeutikum*] for even the most severely ill among them.'[537]

After a contrast with so-called obsessive-compulsive patients, by way of an overview of the influence of Heidegger's thought on his work with the sort of client who is seen more and more often, Boss writes:

> Martin Heidegger's ontological insights bring the greatest practical benefit to those patients who, according to their own self-understanding, do not feel sick at all, but for whom only society is impossible. This is today's main harangue of the so-called 'psychoneurotic'. They only complain about boredom and the meaninglessness of their life. *It is precisely to them that a therapy based on the analysis of existence is able to restore both the motive for existing and the goal of psychotherapy.* The prerequisite for this, however, is the therapist's commitment not only to learn by heart from books about the *Da-sein* of man, but to let himself be penetrated by Martin Heidegger's ontological determinations of this *Da-sein* body and soul. This alone effects a radical transformation of therapists themselves. Thanks to Martin Heidegger's insight into the essence of *Da-sein*, practicing daseinsanalysts are pervaded by the ethics[538] immanent in the ontological analytics of *Dasein*. According to this ethics, human *Da-sein* is always concerned about its being itself.[539]

The text concludes with a passage from the essay *Gelassenheit*[540] in which Heidegger describes two fundamental dispositions toward what there is [*das Seiende*]: *Gelassenheit zu den Dinge* (detachment with respect to things) and *Offenheit für das Geheimnis* (openness to the mystery). For Boss, this is the ambience of the therapeutic situation in daseinanalysis, in which the wholesome [*heilsam*] outlook of the therapist offers an alternative to the 'neurotic's abandoned sense of self permeated by boredom [*Langweiligkeit*] and senselessness [*Sinnslosigkeit*]. The 'ontic' 'directives [*Weisungen*]' of the analyst should be understood more as a direction he represents, rather than as suggestions or orders he gives to the analysand as to how he should behave or live his life. The most the analyst can do is exist as what might be emulated by the analysand. He does not encourage or enjoin the latter to act or be different, least of all to do as he, the analyst, does. Lest therapeutic zeal overwhelm the analyst, Boss cautions that 'the detachment with respect to things and openness to the mystery never fall to us by itself. They are not something to be taken for granted. Both thrive only on incessant heartfelt thinking.'[541] What is expected for the analysand must have been attained by the analyst in his own teaching analysis [*Lehranalyse*], which, as we have seen, is the essential component of preparation to work as a daseinanalyst. To be free is to be the source of direction of one's actions and not a pawn moved by others to meet extraneous agendas. This orientation as existing is passed along to the analysand, not in words but by example.

The second lecture was given during Boss' last visit to the States and the Americas at the Applied Heidegger Conference, held September 8-10, 1989, at the University of California, Berkeley. '**Martin Heidegger Applied to Psychiatry and the Modern World**' (2002/2003c)[542] is said to have been translated by Michael Eldred for the Hoeller volume, but was likely given in an English version by Boss. It is, again, one of those seven important translations of Boss's work to appear in the *Review of Existential Psychology and Psychiatry*. The conference had been organized by prominent Heidegger scholars, Hubert Dreyfus (who had been part of a small group who first attempted a translation of *Sein und Zeit*)[543] and Michael Zimmerman.

Apart from the general observations about a re-envisioning of psychology and medicine (psychiatry in particular), this text is important for Boss's comments on Heidegger and ethics, briefly alluded to in the centenary lecture just reviewed. Given the daseinsanalytic perspective of Heidegger's fundamental ontology, a 'necessary *ethics* is also provided which is able to give the therapeutic application of both sciences their meaning, a well-rounded aim, and a firm guideline. Or is there a more fulfilling 'Ethic' for humans than to allow themselves of their own free will and responsibility to be used as the place of appearance and unfolding of everything which is and has to be?'[544] Boss tells us that, when he put the question to Heidegger about why he had not written an ethics, 'he simply used to respond by saying that all those who talked like that had not read his work carefully. 'All my writings,' he would continue, 'are pervaded by ethics. How else could I have repeated over and over again that human existence is used by being [*Sein*] as such to serve as the world-openness into which all that has to be may emerge and shine forth?"[545] The text is also very important in yet again making clear the other major influence on Boss and the origin of daseinanalysis, namely, Hindu philosophy, which he experienced while he was teaching psychiatry in India in the late 1950s and learning practices that he would continue to follow for the rest of his life.

In his Berkeley lecture listeners heard again from Boss that it was not until 1963 that, while on vacation together in Taormina, Boss and Heidegger had the conversations that eventually led to Heidegger's all-important lecture in honor of Ludwig Binswanger on October 30, 1965, in Amriswil, first published in 1984 as *Zur Frage nach der*

Concluding Note

Bestimmung der Sache des Denkens [*On the Question about the Determination of the Matter of Thinking*].[546] 'Many years later, in 1984, I recollected one day in my study the literal translation of the famous word *Da-sein*' recorded in the Taormina conversation text as '*der Hüter der Lichtung, des Ereignisses* [the guardian of luminance, of eventuality]'.[547] The point of the recollection was that 'at that moment, the mailman arrived with a small book by Martin Heidegger.' It was, of course, *The Question about the Determination of the Matter of Thinking*, that had recently been published. In it is the admission of the major shift in Heidegger's understanding that had been initiated in him by Boss during the years of the Zollikon seminars when Heidegger was in his mid-seventies.

The closing lines of the address are on technicity and *Gelassenheit*. They constitute a fitting conclusion to this review of the major themes of daseinanalysis, its theory and practice, and sources:

> The spirit [*Geist*] of technology consists in the belief that everything is connected with everything else by causal, measurable relations, and that only what can be precisely measured is considered to be really real [*wirklich*]. Heidegger was far from wanting to abolish technology. He fought only against seeing this way as being the only possible way. Such an absolutism would destroy all that is human in humankind. He stressed simply that the full maturity of human beings will only be reached if humans achieve a calmness with regard to the givens [*Gelassenheit zu den Dinge*] of our world, if they do not stay addicted to them, but can let go of them at any time and at the same time stay wide open to the mystery [*Geheimnis*] behind all that is.[548]

The greater freedom of the analysand to realize his ownmost possibilities – to realize they are *there* and, unbeknownst to him have been there all along, and to actualize them to the greatest extent possible – is the goal of daseinanalytic therapy and is in the hands of the analysand himself. The *Stimmung* or atmosphere supporting the pursuit of that goal – *Gelassenheit* – is the gift the analyst hands him to facilitate that realization.

Concluding Note

To an outside observer when we see someone closing a door it is impossible to tell whether he is leaving somewhere or going somewhere. In a trivial sense, of course, he is doing both, but as we have learned from Heidegger, for the human being action is motivated, not caused. That being the case, when we see movement in the life of the analysand he is always going somewhere. His *Aufenthalt* or sojourn originates in the future and is determined by where he is going, not where he has been. He is not pushed along from behind, as causal theories of behavior and experience such as psychoanalysis have proposed, but is motivated by having somewhere to go. This *Stimmung* is beautifully captured by the poet Theodore Roethke in his villanelle 'The Waking'.[549]

Concluding Note

I wake to sleep, and take my waking slow.
I feel my fate in what I cannot fear.
I learn by going where I have to go.

We think by feeling. What is there to know?
I hear my being dance from ear to ear.
I wake to sleep, and take my waking slow.

Of those so close beside me, which are you?
God bless the Ground! I shall walk softly there,
And learn by going where I have to go.

Light takes the Tree; but who can tell us how?
The lowly worm climbs up a winding stair;
I wake to sleep, and take my waking slow.

Great Nature has another thing to do
To you and me; so take the lively air,
And, lovely, learn by going where to go.

This shaking keeps me steady. I should know.
What falls away is always. And is near.
I wake to sleep, and take my waking slow.
I learn by going where I have to go.

As an approach to therapy, daseinanalysis has already accomplished a great deal. It has exposed the previously unacknowledged roots of psychotherapy and its handmaiden, Western psychiatry, in natural science. But it has also begun to sink its own roots in the rich ground of Martin Heidegger's fundamental ontology and the Vedanta tradition of Eastern philosophy.

I have argued that, in due course, daseinanalysis will offer what Western psychiatry and psychotherapy have been unable to provide. Its ascendancy will not occur overnight, of course, and its guidance will be challenged by institutional power and remnants of thinking carried over from our beginnings in Western philosophy that persist despite our vigilance about the seductiveness of technicity. It will grow like a body, slowly, but eventually it will reach its full maturity and height. Taking a step not attempted before or making a new beginning are possible only if we are on track for becoming more human, which is in each the therapeutic goal of daseinanalysis. We never take a step without also setting out.

Boss made a radical beginning for a new kind of therapeutic practice and like the preceding introduction and review of daseinanalytic thinking and the therapeutic practice based on it, the following bibliography is workbook material meant to be a

Concluding Note

guide for the further study of his contribution and that of his colleagues and second- and third- generation daseinanalysts.

2024 marks the 40th anniversary of the movement's journal, *Daseinsanalyse*, In the coming years, it is to be hoped, much of the content of the yearbook will become available in English where there is now a German text. Moreover, critical editions of Boss's books and a volume of his most important papers are planned, many made available for the first time in English translations. If the following annotated bibliography is of value to that project, it will have served its purpose.

Acknowledgements

I want to thank colleagues in the worldwide daseinanalytic community for their now half-century-long preservation of the tradition of practice instituted by Medard Boss. They have been hard at work throughout Europe and in Brazil. The publication of the present volume this year coincides with the 40th anniversary of the yearbook *Daseinsanalyse*, edited by my close friend and co-founder of the American Daseinsanalytic Institute, Tamás Fazekas, to whom I offer many thanks for his support. Finally, there is special gratitude for the meticulous editing eye of Rhone D'Errico, who devoted his valuable time to proofreading the final manuscript.

New York
July 2024

Bibliography[550]

I. BOOKS

1. *Körperliches Kranksein als Folge seelischer Gleichgewichtsstörungen* (Bern: Huber, 1940; 6th ed. 1978).
   [Physical illness as a result of psychological imbalance] {1940c}
   [Swedish translation: *Själsharmoni och hälsa* (Stockholm: Natur und Kultur, 1944)]
   [Japanese translation: *Shinshin igaku nyūmon* (Tokyo: Misuzu Shobo, 1959, 1966)]
2. *Die Bedeutung der Psychologie für die menschlichen Lebens- und Arbeitsgemeinschaften* (Thalwil-Zürich: Oesch, 1943; 3rd ed. 1950).
   [The significance of psychology for human relationships and community life] {1943}
3. *Die Gestalt der Ehe und ihre Zerfallsformen. Ein Beitrag zur Psychopathologie der menschlichen Gemeinschaftsbildungen* (Bern: Huber, 1944).
   [The character of marriage and its forms of disintegration. A contribution to the psychopathology of the formation of human community life] {1944b}
4. *Sinn und Gehalt der sexuellen Perversionen. Ein daseinsanalytischer Beitrag zur Psychopathologie des Phänomens der Liebe* (Bern: Huber, 1947; 2nd revised and expanded ed., 1952, which contains a new 'Vorwort [Preface]'; Munich: Kindler, 3rd, further revised and expanded ed., 1966, which contains a new 'Vorwort [Preface] (9-13)' and an important 'Nachwort [Postscript]' (174-182); 4th ed., Frankfurt: Fisher, 1984; 2017).
   [Meaning and content of sexual perversions. An existential analytic contribution to the psychopathology of the phenomenon of love] {1947}
   [English translation: *Meaning and Content of Sexual Perversions. A Daseinsanalytic Approach to the Psychopathology of the Phenomenon of Love* (New York: Grune and Stratton, 1949).] (Lise Lewis Abell)
   [The 'Preface' for the 'second edition', that is, the edition published in English translation two years after the book was first published, is far more detailed than what would appear in the actual second edition of the German volume as its 'Vorwort'. It is decidedly directed to a post-War American audience who had become familiar with Sartre's literary-philosophical movement known as Existentialism from which Boss wants to distance himself.]
   [Japanese translation: *Seiteki tōsaku: Ren'ai no seishin byōrigaku* (Tokyo: Misuzu Shobo, 1957, 1998)]
   [Italian translations: *Senso e contenuto delle perversioni sessuali* (Milan: Sugor, 1962); *Perversioni sessuali: significati e contenuti* (Milan: Vivarium, 1998)]
   [Russian translation: Moscow: Moscow State Publisher, 1965] [not verified]
5. *Der Traum und seine Auslegung* (Bern: Huber, 1953; 2nd ed., Munich: Kindler, 1974).
   [The analysis of dreams] {1953d}
   [English translation: *The Analysis of Dreams* (New York: Philosophical Library, 1958).] (Arnold J. Pomerans)
   [Japanese translation: *Yume : Sono gensonzai bunseki* (Tokyo: Misuzu Shobo, 1970)]

Bibliography

6. *Einführung in die psychosomatische Medizin* (Bern: Huber, 1954). A revised, expanded version of the book reflecting the ongoing influence of Heidegger, especially the discussions of the body in the Zollikon seminars, was published as *Praxis der Psychosomatik. Krankheit und Lebensschicksal* [*Practice of Psychosomatics. Illness and Personal Fate*] (Bern: Benteli, 1978). See {1978c}.
[*Introduction to psychosomatic medicine*] {1954a}
[French translation: *Introduction à la médicine psychosomatique* (Paris: Presses Universitaires, 1959)]
[*Introduction to psychosomatic medicine*].
7. *Psychoanalyse und Daseinsanalytik* (Bern: Huber, 1957; 2nd ed., Munich: Kindler 1980; Frankfurt: Fischer 2017 [digital]).
[*Psychoanalysis and Daseinsanalysis*] {1957a}
[English translation: Psychoanalysis and Daseinsanalysis (New York: Basic Books, 1963; 2nd ed., New York: Dacapo Press, 1982)] (Ludwig B. Lefebre; Elsa Lehman and Mary Hottinger-Mackie)
[Dutch translation: *Psychoanalyse en daseinsanalyse* (Utrecht: Bijleveld, 1958)]
[Spanish translation: *Psicoánalisis y analítica existential* (Madrid: Javier Morata, 1958)]
[Japanese translation: *Seishin bunseki to gensonzai bunsekiron* (Tokyo: Misuzu Shobo, 1962)]
[Italian translation: *Psicoanalisi e analitica esistenziale* (Rome: Astrolabio, 1973)]
[French translation: *Psychanalyse et Analytique du* Dasein (Paris: Vrin, 2007)]
8. *Indienfahrt eines Psychiaters* (Pfullingen: Neske, 1959; 2nd ed., Freiburg: Herder, 1966 (abridged version); 3rd ed., Bern: Huber, 1976; 4th, expanded and illustrated ed., Bern: Huber 1987; 5th ed., Bern: Huber, 2006). The final chapter of the English translation, 'Eastern Wisdom and Western Psychotherapy' (184-192), was reprinted in John Welwood (ed.), *The Meeting of the Ways* (New York: Schocken, 1979), 183-191.
[*A psychiatrist discovers India*] {1959a}
[English translation: A Psychiatrist Discovers India (London: Wolff, 1965).] (Henry A. Frey)
[Swedish translation: *Indisk visdom och modern psykiatrie* (Stockholm: Natur och Kultur, 1967)]
[French translation: *Un psychiatre en Inde* (Paris: Fayard, 1971)]
[Japanese translation: *Tōyō no eichi to seiō no shinri ryōhō: seishin igakusha no indo kikō* (Tokyo: Misuzu Shobo, 1972)]
[An important postscript was added to the 3rd edition (261-263). The 4th edition includes 'After Thirty Years. Preface to *Indian Journey of a Psychiatrist* (4th Edition)' [1987], in *Review of Existential Psychology and Psychiatry* 27(1-3), 2002/2003, 33-36. Reprinted as a monograph by K. Hoeller (ed.), *The Heidegger-Boss Relationship* (Seattle: Review of Existential Psychology and Psychiatry, 2008), 33-36. See {2002/2003b}.]
9. *Lebensangst, Schuldgefühle und psychotherapeutische Befreiung* (Bern: Huber, 1962; 2nd ed., 1965).
[Anxiety, guilt and psychotherapeutic liberation] {1962c}
[English translation: 'Anxiety, Guilt and Psychotherapeutic Liberation', in Review of Existential Psychology and Psychiatry 2(3), 1962, 173-195 [REPP]. Reprinted in K. Hoeller (ed.), Readings in Existential Psychology and Psychiatry (Seattle: Review of Existential Psychology and Psychiatry, 1990), 71-92]. (B)
[Portuguese translation: *Angústia, culpa e libertação*, 1971; 1975 (São Paulo: Livraria duas Cidades)]
[Japanese translation: *Fuan no seishin ryoho* (Kyoto: Daigoshobo, 2000)]
10. *Grundriß der Medizin. Ansätze zu einer phänomenologischen Physiologie, Psychologie, Pathologie, Therapie und zu einer daseinsgemäßen Präventiv-Medizin in der modernen Industrie-Gesellschaft* (Bern: Huber, 1971; 2nd, expanded ed., 1975; 3rd ed., 1999, with a ‚Preface' by Marianne Boss; new title beginning with 2nd ed.: *Grundriß der Medizin und*

Bibliography

Psychologie. Ansätze zu einer phänomenologischen Physiologie, Psychologie, Pathologie, Therapie und zu einer daseinsgemäßen Präventiv-Medizin in der modernen Industrie-Gesellschaft].
[Existential foundations of medicine and psychology] {1971a}
[English translation: Existential Foundations of Medicine and Psychology (New York: Jason Aronson, 1979)] (Stephen Conway and Anne Cleaves) [The translation is based on the 2nd edition.]
[Czech translation: Nárys medicíny a psychologie (Bratislava: ObNV, 1985)]

11. 'Es träumte mir vergangene Nacht...': Sehübungen im Bereiche des Träumens und Beispiele für praktische Anwendung eines neuen Traumverständnisses (Bern: Huber, 1975; 2nd ed. 1991).
['I dreamt last night...': A new approach to the revelations of dreaming – and its uses in psychotherapy] {1975b}
[English translation: 'I dreamt last night...': A New Approach to the Revelations of Dreaming – and Its Uses in Psychotherapy (New York: Gardner Press, 1977; 2nd ed., 1988)] (Stephen Conway)
[Portuguese translation: Na noite passada eu sonhei... (Sao Paulo: Ed. Summus, 1979)]
[French translation: Il m'est venu en rêve... (Paris: Presses Universitaires, 1989)]
[Croatian translation: Novo tumacenje snova ... (Zagreb: Naprijed, 1985; 2001)]
[Czech translation: Vcera v noci se mi zdálo ... (Prague: Grada, 1994; 2001; Triton, 2002)]

12. Von der Psychoanalyse zur Daseinsanalyse. Wege zu einem neuen Selbstverständnis (Vienna: Europaverlag, 1979).
[From psychoanalysis to daseinsanalysis. Paths to a new self-understanding] {1979c}
[Selected papers (1937-1977).]

Contents:
'Die Grundprinzipien der Schizophrenietherapie im historischen Rückblick' [1937]: 11-53. {1937}
'Individuelle Vorbehandlung zur kollektiven Arbeitstherapie bei schweren, chronischen Schizophrenen' [1938]: 55-70. {1938a}
'Über drei Kategorien vermeidbarer Mißerfolge in der ärztlichen Allgemeinpraxis' [1939]: 71-93. {1939}
'Alte und neue Schocktherapien und Schocktherapeuten' [1941]: 95-103. {1941d}
'Die Möglichkeiten und Grenzen der Psychotherapie' [1948]: 105-121. {1948b}
'Vom Weg und Ziel der tiefenpsychologischen Therapie' [1948]: 123-144. {1948a}
'Beitrag zur daseinsanalytischen Fundierung des psychiatrischen Denkens' [1951]: 145-150. {1951b}
'Die Bedeutung der Daseinsanalyse für die Psychologie und die Psychiatrie' [1952]: 151-160. {1952b}
'Psychoanalyse eines Sadisten' [1953]: 151-160. {1953f}
'Die Psychotherapie des praktischen Arztes' [1959]: 187-202. {1959c}
'Einem Therapeuten wird sein bio-psychologischer Star gestochen [A Therapist Has His Biopsychological Cataracts Removed]' [1953/1957] – [Source given as a combination of an adaptation of 'Martin Heidegger und die Ärzte' [1959, 276-290] and material from the first chapter of what Boss cites as Psychoanalysis and Daseins-Analysis, 'A Patient Who Taught the Author to See and Think Differently' the English 'translation' (1963) of the first edition of his Psychoanalyse und Daseinsanalytik [1957]: 203-244. See 'The Role of Psychotherapy in Schizophrenia' which is preparatory for the opening chapter of Psychoanalysis and Daseinsanalysis (1963) (given as Psychoanalysis and Daseins-Analysis).]
'Daseinsanalytische Bemerkungen zu Freuds Vorstellung des 'Unbewußten' [1960/61]: 245-266. {1960/1961a}
'Die Bedeutung der Daseinsanalyse für die psychoanalytische Praxis' [1960/61]: 267-285. {1960/1961b}

Bibliography

'Begegnung in der Psychotherapie' [1964] – [Source given as 'Vortragsmanuskript' [1965]; but see 'Begegnung in der Psychotherapie', in *Psychotherapy and Psychosomatics* 13(5), 1965, 332-341]: 287-294. {1965d}

'Die sexuellen Perversionen in phänomenologischer Sicht' [1972] – [Source given as 'Vortragsmanuskript; Erstveröffentlichung'] [There is reference in several bibliographies to 'Die sexuellen Perversionen als mitmenschliche Phänomene' as a paper published in *Sozialklinische Studien über Mental Health in der heutigen Gesellschaft* (Tokyo) 4, 1972, but this has not been verified.]: 295-308. {N/A}

'Beispiele für den Einfluß einer Psychotherapie auf die religiöse Einstellung von Analysanden': [1966]: 309-325. {1966b}

'Modell und Antimodell in der psychosomatischen Medizin' [1967]: 327-346. {1967b}

'Schizophrenes Kranksein im Lichte einer daseinsanalytischen Phänomenologie' [1975]: 347-372. {1975c}

'Sexualität und Psychotherapie' [1978] [Source given as 'Vortragsmanuskript; Erstveröffentlichung'; an article by the same title, however, appeared in *Psychosomatische Medizin* 8(2), 1978, 118-128.]: 373-386. {1979d}

'Sigmund Freud und die naturwissenschaftliche Denkmethode' [1973]: 387-404. {1973c}

'Die psychosomatische Medizin und das Kausalitätsprinzip' [1974]: 405-422 {1974}

'Psychotherapie und Wissenschaft' [1974] [Source given as 'Vortragsmanuskript; Erstveröffentlichung']. [Manuscript of a presentation given December 12, 1974, at a meeting of the Society for Psychotherapy, Bern]: 423-442. {1979e}

'Das Träumen und das Geträumte in daseinsanalytischer Sicht' [1975] [Excerpts from *Es träumte mir vergangene Nacht...* (Bern: Huber, 1975; 2nd ed. 1991)]: 443-468. {1975b}

'Der psychotherapeutische Prozeß' [1977] [Source given as 'Vortragsmanuskript; Erstveröffentlichung [Lecture manuscript; first publication].' But see 'Der psychotherapeutische Prozeß', in M. Boss, G. Condrau and A. Hicklin (eds.), *Leiben und Leben. Beiträge zur Psychosomatik und Psychotherapie* (Bern: Benteli, 1977), 233-346, where it had been first published]: 469-476 {1977c}

'Die Ontogenese des Menschen – aus der Sicht des Daseinsanalytikers' [1977]: 477-482. {1977a}

13. *Von der Spannweite der Seele. Ausgewählte Vorträge und Aufsätze aus den Anwendungsbereichen des daseinsanalytischen Menschenverständnisses* (Bern: Benteli, 1982).
[*On the wingspan of the soul. Selected presentations and essays from areas of application of the existential analytic understanding of man*] {1982b}
[Selected papers (1974-1982).]

Contents:

'Ist die Psychotherapie rational oder rationell?' [Also published as 'Das Irrationale in der psychotherapeutischen Behandlung'] [1977]: 9-27. {1979b}

'Der korrespondierende Wandel von Gesellschaftsqualität und Neurosenformer im XX.Jahrhundert' [1974]: 28-45. {1977k}

'Angst und christliches Vertrauen' [Also published as 'Angst und Gelassenheit im daseinsanalytischer Sicht'] [1981]: 46-60. {1981f}

'Sprache und Angst im technifizierten Zeitalter' [1981]. [Originally given as 'Vom Geiste der Technik' as a contribution to the 9th Zürcher Gespräche, June 8, 1981, on the theme 'Sprache und Angst in einer technifizierten Welt [Speech and Anxiety in an Engineered World]']: 61-68. {1982k}

'Begegnung und Auseinandersetzung mit sich selbst in der Schuld und im Gewissen' [1981]: 69-97. {1981d}

'Gewähren und Versagen in der Psychotherapie' [1978]: 98-110. {1982f}

'Das Konzept des Widerstandes in der Daseinsanalyse (in Zusammenarbeit mit Alice Holzhey-Kunz)' [1981]: 111-131. {1981c}

Bibliography

'Das Unbewußte – was ist es?' [1981]: 132-150. {1981b}
'Triebwelt und Personalisation' [1981]: 151-172. {1981e}
'Der Einstieg der 'Daseinsanalytik' in das Denken der Ärtze' [1981]. [Original version of a text published with Gion Condrau as 'Die Weiterentwicklung der Daseinsanalyse nach Ludwig Binswanger.']: 173-181. {1982h}
'Abriss der Psychotherapie – Entwicklung im 20.Jahrhundert.' [German keynote address given at the annual meeting of the Swiss Society of Psychiatry and the Swiss Association of Psychotherapists on October 26, 1980. Abridged French translation under the title 'Exposé sur le developpement de la psychothérapie au XX siècle [Lecture on the development of psychotherapy in the 20th century],' in *Archives Suisse de Neurologie, Neurochirurgie et de Psychiatrie* 128(2), 1981, 183-196] [1980]: 182-198. {1982i}
'Die Bedeutung Martin Heideggers für die Arbeit mit leidenden Menschen und für das Selbstverständnis der Psychotherapie' [1981]: 199-210. {1982j}
'Dank an Martin Heidegger – Ein Hinweis auf seine Zollikoner Seminare' [1977]: 211-225. {1977d}

II. EDITED BOOK

14. Martin Heidegger, *Zollikoner Seminare. Protokolle–Gespräche–Briefe* (Frankfurt: Klostermann, 1987; 2nd ed., 1994; 3rd ed., 2006). Contains 'Freundesbrief' of October 5, 1969, as the editor's 'Schlußwort' to the volume. [See note to 'Martin Heidegger's Zollikon Seminars', 7 (below).]
    [Martin Heidegger, *Zollikon Seminars: Protocols—Conversations—Letters* (ed.)] {1987a}
    [English translation: *Zollikon Seminars: Protocols—Conversations—Letters* (Evanston: Northwestern University Press, 2001)] (Franz Mayr and Richard Askay)
    [Italian translation: *Seminari di Zollikon* (Naples: Guida, 1987)]
    [Japanese translation: *Tsuorikōn zemināru* (Tokyo: Misuzu Shobo, 1991, 1997)]
    [Spanish translation: *Seminarios de Zollikon protocolos, diálogos, cartas* (Michoacán: Red Utopia, 2007)]
    [French translation: *Séminaires de Zürich* (Paris: Presses Universitaires, 2010)]
    [Korean translation: 졸리콘 세미나 (2016)]
    [Portuguese translation: *Seminários de Zollikon* (Sao Paulo: Editora Vozes, 2001; 3rd rev. ed., 2017)]
    [Russian translation: *Tsollikonovskie seminary: komentarii i interpretatsii: sbornik nauchnykh rabot* (Minsk: Logvinaŭ, 2017)].
    [Note: The Heidegger *Gesamtausgabe* (Frankfurt: Klosterman, 2018) edition (*GA* 89, edited by Peter Trawny) contains reprints of the seminar protocols included in Boss (1987) and Heidegger's notes for the seminars.]

III. CO-EDITED BOOKS

15. *Third International Congress for [Medical] Psychotherapy* [Zürich 1954] (M. Boss, H. Fierz and B. Stokvis, eds.) (Basel: Karger, 1955). Also published as *Acta Psychotherapeutica, Psychosomatica et Orthopaedagogica*, Volume 3 (Basel: Karger, 1955).
    [*Third international congress for [medical] psychotherapy*] {1955a}
    [The theme of the conference was transference. The conference included presentations by Karl Graf Dürckheim, Kurt Goldstein, Daniel Lagache and Ramon Sarró. At this conference, Ludwig Binswanger presented a paper on *Daseinsanalyse* and psychotherapy.]

16. *Leiben und Leben. Beiträge zur Psychosomatik und Psychotherapie* (M. Boss, G. Condrau and A. Hicklin, eds.) (Bern: Benteli, 1977).
    [*Being alive and living life. Contributions to psychosomatics and psychotherapy*] {1977f} Selected papers (1955-1979).

    Contents:
    'Die psychosomatische Medizin in Nöten' [1955]: 11-18. {1955b}
    'Die notwendige Revolution im ärztlichen Denken' [1970]: 19-36. {1970a}
    'Das Verhältnis von Leib und Seele im Lichte der Daseinsanalytik' [1976]. Originally published as 'Das Leib-Seele-Problem im Lichte der Daseinsanalyse', in *Psychosomatische Medizin* 6(3-4), 1976, 106-128 [1976]: 37-70. {1976e}
    [G. Condrau: 'Philosophisch-wissenschaftliches Menschenverständnis und ärtzliches Handeln in daseinanalytischer Sicht'] [1977]: 71-78.
    [G. Condrau: 'Psychosomatik und Psychotherapie' – I. 'Die Grundlagen einer psychosomatischen Medizin' (81-131); II. Möglichkeiten und Grenzen der Psychotherapie psychosomatsicher Krankheiten' (131-210)] [1977]: 79-210.
    [G. Condrau: 'Psychotherapie und Krankenlassen'] [1977]: 211-226.
    'Die daseinsgemäße Betrachtungsweise und die psychotherapeutische Beeinflußbarkeit menschlicher Körperleiden' [1977]: 227-232. {1977b}
    'Der psychotherapeutische Prozeß: [1977]. Reprinted in *Von der Psychoanalyse zur Daseinsanalyse. Wege zu einem neuen Selbstverständnis* (Vienna: Europaverlag, 1979), 469-476: 233-246. {1977c}
    [A. Hicklin: 'Die gesellschaftspolitische Bedeutung der psychosomatischen Medizin'] [1977]: 246-26.
    [A. Hicklin: 'Die Therapie einer jungen Frau mit schweren neurotishcen und psychosomatishcen Störungen'] [1977]: 261-338.

IV. CHAPTERS IN BOOKS

17. 'Indications et effets de la cure de sommeil', in *Comptes rendus. Congrès des médecins alienistes et neurologistes de pays de la langue française* [XXXIX, July 22-28, 1935] (Paris: Masson, 1936), 1-4.
    [Indications [for] and effects of the sleep cure] {1936}
18. 'Zusammenfassung und Schußwort [der wissenschaftlichen Kongreß-Arbeit]', in M. Boss, H. Fierz and B. Stokvis (eds.), *Third International Congress for Medical Psychotherapy* [Zürich 1954] (Basel: Karger, 1955), 272-278.
    [Summary and closing remarks] [Schlußsitzung (closing session), July 24, 1954] {1955c}
19. 'Psychotherapeutischer Beitrag zur Schizophrenielehre', in *Second International Congress of Psychiatry* (Basel: Karger, 1957), Volume 3, 254-259.
    [Psychotherapeutic contribution to the theory of schizophrenia] {1957c}
20. 'Martin Heidegger und die Ärzte', in G. Neske (ed.), *Martin Heidegger zum 70. Geburtstag* (Neske: Pfullingen, 1959), 276-290. Adapted version printed in *Von der Psychoanalyse zur Daseinsanalyse. Wege zu einem neuen Selbstverständnis* (Vienna: Europaverlag, 1979), 203-244.
    [Martin Heidegger and the doctors] {1959b}
21. 'Warum verhält sich der Mensch überhaupt sozial?', in *Proceedings of the Third World Congress of Psychiatry* [Montreal, June 9, 1961] (Montreal: McGill University Press, 1961), Volume 1, 228-233.
    [What makes us behave at all socially?] {1961b}
    [English translation: 'What Makes Us Behave at All Socially?', in Review of Existential Psychology and Psychiatry 4(1), 1964, 53-68]. (B)

Bibliography

22. 'Psychosomatics and Existentialism', in Proceedings of the Third World Congress of Psychiatry [Montreal, June 4-10, 1961] (Montreal: McGill University Press, 1961), Volume 3, 277-280. (B)
[Psychosomatics and existentialism] {1961a}
23. 'Vorwort' to Carlos Seguín, *Der Artz und sein Patient* (Bern: Huber, 1965), 7-18. Translated from the Spanish by Marian von Castelberg. See 1965d.
[Introduction [to Carlos Alberto Seguín, *Love and psychotherapy. The psychotherapeutic eros*]] {1965e}
[English translation: 'Introduction' to Carlos Alberto Seguín, Love and Psychotherapy. The Psychotherapeutic Eros (New York: Libra, 1965), v-xiv.] (B)
24. 'Entmythologisierung der psychosomatischen Medizin', in J. Lassner (ed.), *Hypnosis and Psychosomatic Medicine* (New York: Springer, 1967), 35-53. Reprinted in *Zeitschrift für klinische Psychologie und Psychotherapie* 25(2), 1977, 136-151.
[Demythologization of psychosomatic medicine] {1967a}
25. 'Foreword' [1970] to Govind Kaul, Govind Amrit (Bombay: Prithwinath Niranjannath Pandit, 1975), 1-2.
[Foreword to *Govind Amrit*. Letter to J. M. Kayande, November 23, 1970] {1975e}
26. 'Tribute to Martin Heidegger', in Richard Wisser (ed.), Martin Heidegger in Conversation, New Delhi: Arnold-Heinemann, 1977, 9-11. The text is based on Martin Heidegger im Gespräch, Freiburg: Alber, 1970, 20-22. Translated by B. Srinivasa Murthy.
[Medard Boss (Tribute to Martin Heidegger)] {1970c}
27. 'Medard Boss', in L. Pongratz (ed.), *Psychotherapie in Selbstdarstellungen* (Bern: Huber, 1973), 71-106.
[Medard Boss] {1973a}
[English translation: 'Medard Boss', Existential Analysis 30(1), 2019, 169-198.] (Miles Groth)
28. 'Solitude et communauté', in G. Balandier (ed.), *Solitude et Communication. Rencontres Internationales de Genève* (Neuchatel: Edition de la Baconnière, 1975), 47-68. [The French translation of Boss's German text was made by M. Bernard Rordorf, 'reviewed by the author'.]
[Solitude and community] {1975a}
[Portuguese translation: 'Solidao e comunidade', in *Daseinsanalyse* (Sao Paulo) 2, 1976, 25-45].
[German translation: 'Einsamkeit und Gemeinschaft', in *Daseinsanalyse* 1(1) (Zürich), 1984, 6-22.
29. 'Flight from Death – Mere Survival; and Flight into Death – Suicide', in B. Wolman (ed.), Between Survival and Suicide (New York: Gardner Press, 1976), 1-24. (B)
[Flight from death – mere survival; and flight into death – suicide] {1976b}
30. 'Das Träumen und das Geträumte in daseinsanalytischer Sicht', in R. Battegay and A. Trenkel (eds.), *Der Traum* (Bern: Huber, 1976), 71-93. Reprinted in *Von der Psychoanalyse zur Daseinsanalyse. Wege zu einem neuen Selbstverständnis* (Vienna: Europaverlag, 1979), 443-468. Includes excerpts from *Es träumte mir vergangene Nacht...* (Bern: Huber, 1975; 2nd ed. 1991).
[Dreaming and the dreamed in the daseinsanalytic way of seeing] {1976a}
[English translation: 'Dreaming and the Dreamed in the Daseinsanalytic Way of Seeing', in Soundings 60(3), 1977, 235-263.] (Tom Cook)
31. 'Der korrespondierende Wandel von Gesellschaftsqualität und Neurosenformen im 20.Jahrhundert', in G. Condrau and A. Hicklin (eds.), *Individuum, Familie, Gesellschaft im Spannungsfeld zwischen Zwang und Freiheit* [*Weiterentwicklung der Psychoanalyse und ihrer Anwendungen 6*] (Zürich: Vandenhoeck and Ruprecht, 1977), 153-167. Reprinted in *Von der Spannweite der Seele. Ausgewählte Vorträge und Aufsätze aus den Anwendungsbereichen des daseinsanalytischen Menschenverständnisses* (Bern: Benteli, 1982), 28-45.

Bibliography

[Lecture given at the fifth International Forum for Psychoanalysis (1974) in Zürich.]
[Corresponding changes in the quality of social life and the forms of neurosis in the twentieth century] {1977k}

32. 'Die Ontogenese des Menschen – aus der Sicht des Daseinsanalytikers', in G. Condrau and A. Hicklin (eds.), *Das Werden des Menschen* (Bern: Benteli, 1977), 105-119. Reprinted in *Von der Psychoanalyse zur Daseinsanalyse. Wege zu einem neuen Selbstverständnis* (Vienna: Europaverlag, 1979), 477-482.
[The ontogenesis of man ... from the perspective of the daseinsanalyst] {1977a}

33. 'Die daseinsgemäße Betrachtungsweise und die psychotherapeutische Beeinflußbarkeit menschlicher Körperleiden', in M. Boss, G. Condrau, and A. Hicklin (eds.), *Leiben und Leben. Beiträge zur Psychosomatik und Psychotherapie* (Bern: Benteli, 1977), 227-232.
[The existential approach and psychotherapeutic suggestibility in human physical ailments] {1977b}

34. 'Der psychotherapeutische Prozeß', in M. Boss, G. Condrau, and A. Hicklin (eds.), *Leiben und Leben. Beiträge zur Psychosomatik und Psychotherapie* (Bern: Benteli, 1977), 233-246. Reprinted in *Von der Psychoanalyse zur Daseinsanalyse. Wege zu einem neuen Selbstverständnis* (Vienna: Europaverlag, 1979), 469-476.
[The psychotherapeutic process] {1977c}

35. 'Dank an Martin Heidegger – Ein Hinweis auf seine Zollikoner Seminare', in G. Neske (ed.), *Erinnerung an Martin Heidegger* (Pfullingen: Neske, 1977), 31-45. Reprinted in *Von der Spannweite der Seele. Ausgewählte Vorträge und Aufsätze aus den Anwendungsbereichen des daseinsanalytischen Menschenverständnisses* (Bern: Benteli, 1982), 211-225.
[In an editors' note (Thomas Lynaugh and Keith Hoeller) to the translation we read: 'In an agreement between Boss and Heidegger, nothing else of the Zollikon Seminars will be published until after their deaths. At that time, the protocols of the Zollikon Seminars will go to the Heidegger Archives in Marbach, West Germany.' Nevertheless, the protocols plus conversations between Boss and Heidegger and excerpts of letters from Heidegger were published in 1987. The translator, Brian Kenny, was at the time of publication of this first introduction to American readers of the Zollikon seminars Ludwig Binswanger's head of the Bellevue Sanatorium (Kreuzlingen), having succeeded Ludwig Binswanger. Binswanger had overseen the hospital from 1911-1956. Kenny was the last director of the asylum, which closed in 1980.]
[Martin Heidegger's Zollikon seminars] {1977d}
[English translation: 'Martin Heidegger's Zollikon Seminars', in Review of Existential Psychology and Psychiatry 16(1-3), 1978-79, 7-20.] (Brian Kenny)

36. 'Existential Analysis (Daseinsanalyse)', in B. Wolman (ed.), International Encyclopedia of Psychiatry, Psychology, Psychoanalysis and Neurology (New York: Aesculapius, 1977), Volume 4, 395-400. (B)
[Existential analysis (*Daseinsanalyse*)] {1977e}

37. 'Widersprochener Widerspruch', in G. Condrau and A. Hicklin (eds.), *Der Mensch: Gegenstand der Naturwissenschaft?* (Bern: Benteli, 1978), 41-50.
[Contradiction contradicted] {1978a}

38. 'Das Sein zum Tode in tiefenpsychologischer Sicht', in G. Condrau (ed.), *Transzendenz, Imagination und Kreativität* [*Die Psychologie des 20.Jahrhunderts*, Volume 15] (Zürich: Kindler, 1979), 454-463.
[Being-towards-death from the perspective of depth psychology] {1979a}

39. 'Das Irrationale in der psychotherapeutischen Behandlung', in G. Condrau (ed.), *Transzendenz, Imagination und Kreativität.* [*Die Psychologie des 20.Jahrhunderts*, Volume 15] (Zürich: Kindler, 1979), 687-696. Reprinted as ‚Ist die Psychotherpie rational order rationell?', in *Von der Spannweite der Seele. Ausgewählte Vorträge und Aufsätze aus den Anwendungsbereichen des daseinsanalytischen Menschenverständnisses*

Bibliography

(Bern: Benteli, 1982), pp, 9-27. In the sources note, the essay is represented as an 'unpublished contribution' and noted as 'first given as a paper at the Daseinsanalytischen Institut für Psychotherapie und Psychosomatik (Medard Boss Stiftung), April 28, 1977.'
[Is psychotherapy rational or rationalistic?] {1979b}
[English translation: 'Is Psychotherapy Rational or Rationalistic?' in Review of Existential Psychology and Psychiatry 19(2-3), 1984-85, 115-127.] (E. S. Goodstein)

40. 'Martin Heidegger und seine Bedeutung für die gesellschaftliche Evolution', in A. Hicklin (ed.), *Wandel und Tradition. Verharren und Verändern: Gestaltende Kräfte im Menschen und in menschlichen Gesellschaft* [*Change and Tradition. Persistence and Change: Formative Processes in Man and Human Society*] (Bern: Benteli, 1980), 111-129.
[Martin Heidegger and his significance for the evolution of society] {1980a}

41. 'Begegnung und Auseinandersetzung mit sich selbst in der Schuld und im Gewissen', in R. Battegay (ed.), *Herausforderung und Begegnung in der Psychiatrie* [*Festschrift zum 60.Geburtstag von G. Benedetti*] (Bern: Huber, 1981), 54-60. Reprinted in *Von der Spannweite der Seele. Ausgewählte Vorträge und Aufsätze aus den Anwendungsbereichen des daseinsanalytischen Menschenverständnisses* (Bern: Benteli, 1982), 69-97.
[Encounter and self-confrontation in guilt and in conscience] {1981d}

42. 'Triebwelt und Personalisation', in F. Böckle (ed.), *Christlicher Glaube in moderner Welt* [Volume 6] (Freiburg: Herder, 1981), 8-27. Reprinted in *Von der Spannweite der Seele. Ausgewählte Vorträge und Aufsätze aus den Anwendungsbereichen des daseinsanalytischen Menschenverständnisses* (Bern: Benteli, 1982), 151-172.
[This paper includes a version of an excerpt from what would appear in the *Zollikoner Seminare* of an exchange between Boss and Heidegger in a discussion of 'Zum Wollen, Wünschen, Hängen, Drang [On Willing, Wishing, Propensity, Urge]' in Taormina, April 24-May 4, 1963: *Zollikoner Seminare. Protokolle–Gespräche–Briefe* (Frankfurt: Klostermann, 1987, 218-219) [= *Zollikon Seminars: Protocols–Conversations–Letters* (Evanston: Northwestern University Press, 2001), 173-174]. Cf. *GA 89 Zollikoner Seminare*, 76 (Heidegger's note on *Drang*).]
[The world of drives and personalization] {1981e}
[Spanish translation: 'Mundo pulsional y personalizacíon', in H. Döring (ed.), *Experiencia de la contingencia y pregunta por el sentido* (Madrid, SM, 1985)]

43. 'Angst und Gelassenheit im daseinsanalytischer Sicht', in H. Döring and F.-X. Kaufmann (eds.), *Kontingenz und Sinnfrage* [*Christlicher Glaube in moderner Welt* (Volume 9)] (Freiburg: Herder, 1981), 69-85. Reprinted as 'Angst und christliche Vertrauen', in *Von der Spannweite der Seele. Ausgewählte Vorträge und Aufsätze aus den Anwendungsbereichen des daseinsanalytischen Menschenverständnisses* (Bern: Benteli, 1982), 46-60.
[Anxiety and composure from the existential analytic perspective] {1981f}

44. 'Wirklichkeit als das Sich-Entbergen von Seiendem', in E. Grassi and H. Schmale (eds.), *Das Gespräch als Ereignis* (Munich: Fink, 1982), 99-108.
[Contribution to the seventh Zürcher Gespräche, May 9-11, 1980, on the theme 'Rationales Denken – der einzige (wissenschaftliche) Zugang zur Wirklichkeit [Rational Thinking – the Only (Scientific) Approach to Actuality]']
[Actuality as the self-revelation of what is there] {1982c}

45. 'A Phenomenological Approach to Sexual Perversions', in A. de Koning and F. Jenner (eds.), Phenomenology and Psychiatry (New York: Academic Press, 1982), 85-95. (B)
[A phenomenological approach to sexual perversions] {1982d}

46. 'Interpretaçao daseinsanalítica dos sonhos', in G. Lopes (ed.), *Progressos en terapeutica psiquiátrica* (Porto: Biblioteca do Hospital do Conde de Ferreira, 1982), 335-346.
[The existential analytic interpretation of dreams] {1982e}

47. 'Anstöße Martin Heideggers für eine andere Psychiatrie' [1989], in H.-H. Gander (ed.), *Von Heidegger her. Wirkungen in Philosophie – Kunst – Medizin. Meßkirchner Vorträge* (Frankfurt: Klostermann, 1991), 125-140.
   [Martin Heidegger's initiatives for a different kind of psychiatry] {1991}
48. 'Preface to the American Translation of Martin Heidegger's Zollikon Seminars' [1990], in Martin Heidegger, Zollikon Seminars. Protocols – Conversations – Letters (Evanston: Northwestern University Press, 2001), ix-xii. (B)
   [The text is dated Spring 1989. Boss died on December 21, 1990 before completing the preface. His widow, Marianne Boss-Linsmayer, completed it. According to the translators, it contains a few sentences from her preface to the second German edition (1994) and some concluding words that pertain to the English translation (xi-xii).] See {1969} and {1987a}.
   [Preface [to the American Translation of Martin Heidegger's *Zollikon Seminars*]] {2001}

V. JOURNAL ARTICLES

49. 'Zur Frage der erbbiologischen Bedeutung des Memoihols', in *Monatschrift für Psychiatrie und Neurologie* 72, 1929, 264-292.
   [On the question of the evolutionary biological significance of alcohol] {1929}
50. 'Psychologisch-charakterologische Untersuchungen bei antisozialen Psychopathen mit Hilfe des Rorschach'schen Formdeutversuches', in *Zeitschrfit für gesamte Neurologie und Psychiatrie* 133, 1931, 544-575.
   [Psychological and characterological investigations of antisocial psychopaths using the Rorschach Inkblot Test] {1931}
51. 'Halluzinationen *in statu nascendi*', in *Schweizer Archive für Neurologie und Psychiatrie* 32(2), 1933, 1- 4.
   [Hallucinations in process of formation] {1933}
52. 'Die psychischen Energieverschiebungen im Verlaufe eines schizophrenen Schubes', in *Schweizer Archive für Neurologie und Psychiatrie* 36(1), 1935, 58-62.
   [Psychic energy displacements in the course of a schizophrenic episode] {1935a}
53. 'Die psychische Dynamik der Schlafkur bei Schizophrenien', in *Schweizer Archive für Neurologie und Psychiatrie* 36(2), 1935, 209-220.
   [The psychodynamics of the sleep cure in schizophrenics] {1935b}
54. 'Die Grundprinzipien der Schizophrenietherapie im historischen Rückblick', in *Zeitschrfit für gesamte Neurologie und Psychiatrie* 157(3), 1937, 358-392. Reprinted in *Von der Psychoanalyse zur Daseinsanalyse. Wege zu einem neuen Selbstverständnis* (Vienna: Europaverlag, 1979), pp.11-53.
   [Historical review of the fundamental principles of the therapy of schizophrenia] {1937}
55. 'Individuelle Vorbehandlung zur kollektiven Arbeitstherapie bei schweren, chronischen Schizophrenen', in *Schweizer Archive für Neurologie und Psychiatrie* 62(1), 1938, 15-26. Reprinted in *Von der Psychoanalyse zur Daseinsanalyse. Wege zu einem neuen Selbstverständnis* (Vienna: Europaverlag, 1979), 55-70.
   [Preparation of individuals with severe chronic schizophrenia for group occupational therapy] {1938a}
56. 'Psychopathologie des Traumes bei schizophrenen und organischen Psychosen', in *Zeitschrfit für gesamte Neurologie und Psychiatrie* 162(3), 1938, 459-494.
   [The psychopathology of dreams in schizophrenic and organic psychoses] {1938b}
   [English translation: 'The Psychopathology of Dreams in Schizophrenia and Organic Psychoses', in Manfred DeMartino (ed.), *Dreams and Personality Dynamics* (Springfield: Charles Thomas, 1959), 156-175] (Peter Rabe)

Bibliography

57. 'Über drei Kategorien vermeidbarer Mißerfolge in der ärztlichen Allgemeinpraxis', in *Schweizerische medizinische Wochenschrift* 69, 1939, # 26, 602-607. Reprinted in *Von der Psychoanalyse zur Daseinsanalyse. Wege zu einem neuen Selbstverständnis* (Vienna: Europaverlag, 1979), 71-93.
    [On three categories of avoidable failures in general medical practice] {1939}
58. 'Kleine und große Psychotherapie', in *Schweizerische medizinische Wochenschrift* 70(6), 1940, 113-126.
    [Brief and intensive psychotherapy] {1940a}
59. 'Über die geheimen Mühsale seelischen Gesundseins und ihre Linderung', in *Gesundheit und Wohlfahrt* 9/10, 1940, 581-587.
    [On the hidden challenges to psychological well-being and their mitigation] {1940b}
60. 'Die funktionellen Schlafstörungen in der Schizophrenie', in *Schweizerische medizinische Wochenschrift* 71(12), 1941, 390- 391.
    [Functional disturbances of sleep in schizophrenia] {1941a}
61. 'Nahrungsmittelrationierung und Volkspsychologie', in *Gesundheit und Wohlfahrt* 11, 1941, 1-8.
    [Food rationing and popular psychology] {1941b}
62. 'Psychohygiene in vorderer Linie (Militärpsychiatrie)', in *Schweizerische medizinische Wochenschrift* 71(23), 1941, 707-711.
    [Psychological health on the front lines (military psychiatry)] {1941c}
63. 'Alte und neue Schocktherapien und Schocktherapeuten', in *Zeitschrfit für gesamte Neurologie und Psychiatrie* 173(5), 1941, 776-782. Reprinted in *Von der Psychoanalyse zur Daseinsanalyse. Wege zu einem neuen Selbstverständnis* (Vienna: Europaverlag, 1979), 95-103.
    [Early and recent electroshock therapies and electroshock therapists] {1941d}
64. 'Die Funktion der psychiatrischen Beratungsstelle in den selbständigen Heereseinheiten', in *Vierteljahresschrift für Schweizerische Sanitätsoffiziere* 21(2), 1944, 85-90.
    [The function of the psychiatric counseling center in independent army units] {1944a}
65. '*Enuresis nocturna*', in *Schweizerische medizinische Wochenschrift* 75(14), 1945, 293-305.
    [Bed-wetting] {1945}
66. 'Vom Weg und Ziel der tiefenpsychologischen Therapie', in *Psyche* 1(3), 1948, 321-339. Reprinted in *Von der Psychoanalyse zur Daseinsanalyse. Wege zu einem neuen Selbstverständnis* (Vienna: Europaverlag, 1979), 123-144.
    [The method and goal of depth-psychological therapy] {1948a}
67. 'Die Möglichkeiten und Grenzen der Psychotherapie', in *Schweizerische Zeitschrift für Psychologie und ihre Anwendungen* 7(4), 1948, 252-268. Reprinted as 'Möglichkeiten und Grenzen der Psychotherapie', in *Von der Psychoanalyse zur Daseinsanalyse. Wege zu einem neuen Selbstverständnis* (Vienna: Europaverlag, 1979), 105-121.
    [Text of a presentation given at a meeting of the Swiss Society for Psychiatry (Zürich) on November 22, 1947.]
    [The possibilities and limits of psychotherapy] {1948b}
68. 'Die Blutdruckkrankheiten als menschliches Problem', in *Psyche* 2(4), 1949, 499-517.
    [Blood pressure ailments as a human problem] {1949a}
69. 'Die Grundlagen einer psychosomatischen Medizin', in *Schweizerische medizinische Wochenschrift* 79(50), 1949, 1203-1208.
    [Fundamentals of psychosomatic medicine] {1949b}
70. 'Erwiderung. Zum Bericht über mein Referat auf der 66. Wanderversammlung der südwestdeutschen Psychiater und Neurologen in Badenweiler', in *Psyche* 4(7), 1950, 394-400. Reprinted as 'Erwiderung. Zum Bericht über mein Referat auf der 66. Wanderversammlung der südwestdeutschen Psychiater und Neurologen in Badenweiler', in F. Töpfer (ed.), *Verstümmung oder Selbstverwirklichung? Die Boss-Mitscherlich-Kontroverse* (Olton: Walter Verlag, 1981; Stuttgart: Bad Cannstatt, 2012), 19-28.

[Reply to the report on my presentation given at the sixth gathering of Southwest German psychiatrists and neurologists held in Badenweiler [June 2-3, 1950].] {1950a}

71. 'Die neuesten Fortschritte auf dem Gebiete der Psychoanalyse', in *Studium Generale. Zeitschrift für interdisziplinäre Studien* 3(6), 1950, 303-308.
[Latest advances in the field of psychoanalysis] {1950b}

72. ['Schlußwort'] to 'Rundfragen über ein Referat auf der 66. Wanderversammlung der südwestdeutschen Psychiater und Neurologen in Badenweiler', in *Psyche* 4(11), 1951, 634-640. Reprinted in F. Töpfer (ed.), *Verstümmung oder Selbstverwirklichung? Die Boss-Mitscherlich-Kontroverse* (Olton: Walter Verlag, 1981; Stuttgart: Bad Cannstatt, 2012), 95-104.
[Closing remarks on the survey on the report of my paper given at the sixty-sixth gathering of Southwest German psychiatrists and neurologists held in Badenweiler] {1951a}

73. 'Beitrag zur daseinsanalytischen Fundierung des psychiatrischen Denkens', in *Schweizer Archive für Neurologie und Psychiatrie* 67(1), 1951, 15-19. Reprinted in *Von der Psychoanalyse zur Daseinsanalyse. Wege zu einem neuen Selbstverständnis* (Vienna: Europaverlag, 1979), 145-150.
[Contribution on the existential analytic foundation of psychiatric thinking] {1951b}

74. 'Erfahrungen mit dem neuen Schlafmittel 'Plexonal' (Sandoz)', in *Praxis* 40(33), 1951, 679-683.
[Experiences with the hypnotic Plexonal [Scopolamine] (Sandoz)] {1951c}

75. 'Mensch und Technik in der heutigen Medizin', in *Schweizerische medizinische Wochenschrift* 82(25), 1952, 653-657.
[In a prefatory remark to the article, the editors of the journal wrote: 'In sending us his article, Dr. Boss wrote: 'Perhaps it would be possible to add editorially that during the years 1932-33 I was in training at the Berlin Psychoanalytic Institute and there I did supervised analytic work with Karen Horney. From her I received my first impulses which led me to overcome mechanistic thinking and to replace it with a holistic view which since has developed into my *daseins*-analytic concept.']
[Mechanistic and holistic thinking in modern medicine] {1952a}
[English translation: 'Mechanistic and Holistic Thinking in Modern Medicine', in American Journal of Psychoanalysis 14(1), 1954, 48-54.] (B)

76. 'Die Bedeutung der Daseinsanalyse für die Psychologie und die Psychiatrie', in *Psyche* 6(3), 1952/53, 178-186. Reprinted in *Von der Psychoanalyse zur Daseinsanalyse. Wege zu einem neuen Selbstverständnis* (Vienna: Europaverlag, 1979), 151-160.
[The significance of daseinanalysis for psychology and psychiatry] {1952b}

77. 'Über Herkunft und Wesen des tiefenpsychologischen Archetypus-Begriffes', in *Psyche* (10), 1953, 584-597.
[On the origin and essence of the depth-psychological concept of the archetype] {1953a}

78. Antwort: 'Wie soll eine Frigidität in der Praxis beurteilt und behandelt werden?' in *Deutsche medizinische Wochenschrift* 78(45), 1953, 1573-1574.
[Reply to: How should frigidity be evaluated and treated in practice?] {1953b}
[Italian translation: 'Come considerare e trattare la frigidità?' in *Medicina Psicosomatica* 1, 1956, 9-12].

79. 'Reglementierung der Tätigkeit nicht-ärztlicher Psychologen', in *Schweizerische Ärzte-Zeitung* 34, 1953, 272-275.
[Regulation of the activity of non-medical psychologists] {1953c}

80. 'Grundsätzliches zur Wissenschaftlichkeit der Traumbedeutung', in *Schweizerische Zeitschrift für Psychologie und ihre Anwendungen* 13(2), 1954, 128-135.
[Basics of the scientific nature of dream interpretation] {1954b}

81. 'Die psychosomatische Medizin in Nöten', in *Medizin Heute* 4(4), 1955, 185-187. Reprinted in M. Boss, G. Condrau and A. Hicklin (eds.), *Leiben und Leben. Beiträge zur Psychosomatik und Psychotherapie* (Bern: Benteli, 1977), 11-18.

Bibliography

[The text in *Leiben und Leben* is a slightly 'corrected' version of the original publication. See *Leiben und Leben*, 339.]
[Psychosomatic medicine in distress] {1955b}

82. 'Moreno's 'Existentialism, Daseinsanalyse and Psychodrama': A Discussion', *International Journal of Sociometry and Sociatry* 1, 1956, 111-113. (B)
[Moreno's 'Existentialism, daseinanalyse and psychodrama': A discussion] {1956a}

83. 'Daseinsanalytik und Psychotherapie. Über die Grenzen der Psychoanalyse', in *Deutsche Universitätszeitung* 11(23-24), 1956, 17-19.
['Daseinsanalysis' and psychotherapy] {1956b}
[English translation: 'Daseinsanalysis' and Psychotherapy', in J. Masserman and J. L. Moreno (eds.), *Progress in Psychotherapy*. Volume II. *Anxiety and Therapy* (New York: Grune and Stratton, 1957), 156-161. Reprinted in H. Ruitenbeek (ed.) *Psychoanalysis and Existential Philosophy* (New York: Dutton, 1962), 81-89.] (B)

84. 'Wirkungsweise und Indikation der Psychotherapie', in *Schweizerische medizinische Wochenschrift* 87(6), 1957, 128-133.
[The mechanism of action and indication for psychotherapy] {1957b}
[Italian translation: 'Modo d'agire e indicazioni della psicoterapia', in *Medicina Psicosomatica* 3(1), 1958, 3-17].

85. 'Zusammenfassung und Schlußwort [zum internationalen Symposium über die Psychotherapie der Schizophrenie]', in *Acta psychotherapeutica et Psychosomatica et Orthopaedagogica* 5(2-4), 1957, 352-359.
[Summary and closing remarks at the first international symposium on the psychotherapy of schizophrenia] {1957d}

86. 'The Role of Psychotherapy in Schizophrenia', in *Indian Journal of Psychiatry* (Poona) 1(1), 1958, 4-12. (B)
[Paper read at the annual meeting of the Indian Psychiatric Society at Poona in February 1958 during the second of Boss's two visits to India (1956, 1958). The paper is essentially the first chapter of *Psychoanalyse und Daseinsanalytik* that had just been published.]
[The role of psychotherapy in schizophrenia.] {1958}

87. 'Die Psychotherapie des praktischen Arztes', in *Schweizerische medizinische Wochenschrift* 89, 1959, #51, 1336-1341. Reprinted in *Von der Psychoanalyse zur Daseinsanalyse. Wege zu einem neuen Selbstverständnis* (Vienna: Europaverlag, 1979), 187-202.
[Lecture given on October 20, 1959, for the medical continuing education week of the medical faculty of the University of Zürich.]
[Psychotherapy for the practicing physician] {1959c}

88. 'Kleine und große Psychotherapie der essentiellen Hypertoniker', in *Acta Psychosomatica* 3, 1959, 9-40.
[The journal article was taken up by Geigy AG, the Swiss pharmaceutical house, and printed as a pamphlet *Acta Psychosomatica*, one of the *Documenta Geigy* series.]
[Brief and intensive psychotherapy for essential hypertension] {1959d}
[French translation: 'Petite' Psychothérapie et 'Grande' Psychothérapie des Hypertendus Essentiels (Basel: Geigy, 1959].

89. 'Psicoanálisis y análisis del 'dasein', in *Revista de Psiquiatría y Psicología médica de Europa y América Latina* 4(1), 1959, 20-26
[Psychoanalysis and the analysis of 'dasein'] {1959e}
[French translation: 'Psychanalyse et analyse du 'dasein', in *Acta Psychotherapeutica et Psychosomatica* 8(3), 1960, 161-171]

90. 'Große Psychotherapie der psychosomatischen Krankheiten', in *Schweizerische medizinische Wochenschrift* 90(8), 1960, 173-177.
[The intensive psychotherapy of psychosomatic diseases] {1960a}

91. 'Das Ich? Die Motivation?' in *Schweizerische Zeitschrift für Psychologie und ihre Anwendungen* 19(4), 1960, 299-306.

Bibliography

[Paper read at a symposium on 'The Ego in Human Motivation' at the sixteenth International Congress of Psychology, Bonn, August 2, 1960.]
[Ego? Motivation?] [The ego? Human motivation?] {1960b}
[English translation: 'Ego? Motivation?' in *Journal of Existentialism* 1(3), 1960, 275-283. Reprinted as 'The Ego? Human Motivation?' in *Acta Psychologica* 19, 1961, 217-222.] (B)
[French translation: 'Le problème du moi dans la motivation', in *L'évolution Psychiatrique* 25(4), 1960, 481-489]

92. 'Daseinsanalytische Bemerkungen zu Freuds Vorstellung des 'Unbewußten', in *Zeitschrift für psychosomatische Medizin* 7(2), January-March 1960-61, 130-141.
[Existential analytic remarks on Freud's concept of the 'unconscious'] {1960/1961a}

93. 'Die Bedeutung der Daseinsanalyse für die psychoanalytische Praxis', in *Zeitschrift für psychosomatische Medizin* 7(3), April-June 1961, 162-171.
[As noted, this is the German text of chapters 7 and 8 of *Psychoanalysis and Daseinsanalysis*. Boss considered it to be important enough to be reprinted in his anthology *Von der Psychoanalyse zur Daseinsanalyse. Wege zu einem neuen Selbstverständnis* (Vienna: Europaverlag, 1979), 267-285.]
[The significance of existential analysis for psychoanalytic practice] {1960/1961b}

94. 'Outline of the Analysis of Dasein', in *Philosophical Bulletin. Viśva Tattvajñāna Mandira Quarterly* 1(1), 1962, 49-64. (B)
[Outline of the analysis of dasein] {1962a}

95. 'The Conception of Man in Natural Science and Daseinsanalysis', in *Comprehensive Psychiatry* 3(4), August 1962, 193-214. (H.A. Frey)
[The conception of man in natural science and daseinsanalysis] {1962b}

96. 'Gedanken über eine schizophrene Halluzination', in *Schweizer Archive für Neurologie und Psychiatrie* 91(1), 1963, 87-95.
[Thoughts on a schizophrenic hallucination] {1963}

97. 'Presidential Address at the Opening Session [of the VIth International Congress of Medical Psychotherapy, August 24-29, 1964]', in *Psychotherapy and Psychosomatics* 13(1-3), 1965, xi-xii. Also published in the *Proceedings of the VIth International Congress of Psychotherapy* [London], Basel: Karger, 1965, Part I, xi-xii. (B)
[Presidential address at the opening session [of the VIth International Congress of Medical Psychotherapy, August 24-29, 1964].] {1965a}

98. 'Presidential Address at the Closing Session [of the VIth International Congress of Medical Psychotherapy, August 24-29, 1964]', in *Psychotherapy and Psychosomatics* 13(1-3), 1965, 246-248. Also published in the *Proceedings of the VIth International Congress of Psychotherapy* [London], Basel: Karger, 1965, Part I, 246-248. (B)
[Presidential address at the closing session [of the VIth International Congress of Medical Psychotherapy, August 24-29, 1964].] {1965b}

99. 'Discussion of Paper by J. Ruesch [August 24-29, 1964, London],' in *Psychotherapy and Psychosomatics* 13(1-3), 1965, 82-86. (B)
[Discussion of paper by J. Ruesch] {1965c}

100. 'Begegnung in der Psychotherapie', in *Psychotherapy and Psychosomatics* 13(5), 1965, 332-341. Reprinted in *Von der Psychoanalyse zur Daseinsanalyse. Wege zu einem neuen Selbstverständnis* (Vienna: Europaverlag, 1979), 287-294. [Source given as 'Vortragsmanuskript [manuscript of a presentation]'].
[Encounter in psychotherapy] {1965d}
[English translation: 'Medard Boss on 'Encounter in Psychotherapy', in *Daseinsanalyse* 37, 2021, 31-48.] (Miles Groth)

101. 'Cinco lecciones de introduccion a la analitica del dasein', in *Cuadernos de Psiquiatría* 3(4), 1966, 17-38.
[Text based on a lecture series given during a 4-week period at the University of Buenos Aires and University of Mendoza as an invited guest of the Argentine government.]
[Five introductory lectures on the analytics of existence] {1966a}

Bibliography

102. 'Beispiele für den Einfluß einer Psychotherapie auf die religiöse Einstellung von Analysanden', in *Theologia practica. Zeitschrift für Praktische Theologie und Religionspädagogik* 1(3), 1966, 222-234. Reprinted in *Von der Psychoanalyse zur Daseinsanalyse. Wege zu einem neuen Selbstverständnis* (Vienna: Europaverlag, 1979), 309-325, and as 'Der Einfluß der Daseinsanalyse auf die Religiosität der Analysanden', in G. Condrau (ed.), *Transzendenz, Imagination und Kreativität* [*Die Psychologie des 20.Jahrhunderts*, Volume 15] (Zürich: Kindler, 1979), 321-329.
   [Examples of the influence of psychotherapy on the religious attitude of the analysand] {1966b}
103. 'Modell und Antimodell in der psychosomatischen Medizin', in *Therapeutische Umschau* 24, #12, 1967, 536-545. Reprinted in *Von der Psychoanalyse zur Daseinsanalyse. Wege zu einem neuen Selbstverständnis* (Vienna: Europaverlag, 1979), 327-346.
   [Reply to a paper by F. Meerwein, 'Psychosomatische Modellvorstellung' (May 27, 1967, Zürich University Psychiatric Clinic), in *Therapeutische Umschau* 24, 1967, 343-351.]
   [Model and countermodel in psychosomatic medicine] {1967b}
104. 'Psychosomatische Störungen und Organneurosen – Erkentnisse heutiger Psychotherapie', in *Universitas* 22, 1967, 1163-1172.
   [Psychosomatic disorders and organ neuroses – findings of contemporary psychotherapy] {1967d}
105. 'A Conversation with Medard Boss, or the Evolution of Psychoanalysis [Mary Harrington Hall]', in *Psychology Today* 2(7), December 1968, 58-65.
   [A conversation with Medard Boss, or the evolution of psychoanalysis] {1968a}
106. 'Der Mensch – Gegenstand wissenschaftlicher', in *Psychosomatische Medizin* 1(1-2), 1968-69, 1-4.
   [Man – an object of science] {1968/1969}
107. 'Freundesbrief', in *Neue Zürcher Zeitung*, 606 October 5, 1969, 52. Reprinted as the editor's 'Schlußwort' to Martin Heidegger, *Zollikoner Seminare. Protokolle – Gespräche – Briefe*, Frankfurt: Klostermann, 1987, 363-369.
   ['Afterword' to Martin Heidegger, *Zollikon Seminars: Protocols – Conversations – Letters*] {1969}
   [English translation: 'Afterword', Martin Heidegger, *Zollikon Seminars: Protocols—Conversations—Letters* (Evanston: Northwestern University Press, 2001), 293-297.] (Franz Mayr and Richard Askay)
108. 'Die notwendige Revolution im ärztlichen Denken', in *Therapeutische Umschau* 27(12), 1970, 783-790. Reprinted in M. Boss, G. Condrau and A. Hicklin (eds.), *Leiben und Leben. Beiträge zur Psychosomatik und Psychotherapie* (Bern: Benteli, 1977), 19-36.
   [The text in *Leiben und Leben* is a slightly 'corrected' version of the original publication. See *Leiben und Leben. Beiträge zur Psychosomatik und Psychotherapie* (Bern: Benteli, 1977), 339.]
   [A needed revolution in medical thinking] {1970a}
109. 'Die notwendige Revolution der Weltanschauung', in *Journal der Reisehochschule Zürich und des Reisehochschulclubs Zürichs* 10, 1971, 1-22. Reprinted in A. Gloor (ed.), *Die Zukunft im Angriff. Die Schweiz auf dem Weg ins 21.Jahrhunderts* (Frauenfeld: Huber, 1971), p. 11-47.
   [A needed revolution in worldview] {1971b}
110. 'The Training of the Future Psychotherapist. Improvement of Psychiatric Services and Teaching Programs', in *Indian Journal of Psychiatry* [Poona] 15, 1972, 4-14. (B)
   [The training of the future psychotherapist. Improvement of psychiatric services and teaching programs] {1972a}
111. 'Sturmzeichen in der Psychologie und Psychiatrie. Epilog zu einem revolutionären Internationalen Psychotherapeuten-Kongress', in *Psychotherapy and Psychosomatics* 20(1-2), 1972, 92-106.
   [Concluding remarks to the eighth International Congress on Psychotherapy held in Milan, August 25-29, 1970.

Bibliography

Pier Francesco Galli (1931-) was the President of the congress, the theme of which was 'Psychotherapy and the Human Sciences'. Also presenting at the conference were Gaetano Benedetti, Bruno Bettelheim, Harold Kelman, Raymond Battegay, Heinrich-Karl Fierz and Erna Hoch.]
[Warning signs of a storm in psychology and psychiatry. Epilogue to a revolutionary international congress on psychotherapy] {1972b} (See also {1972c})

112. 'Arzt und Tod. Ein daseinsanalytischer Versuch' [1971], in *Psychosomatische Medizin* 4, 1972, 2-12.
[Presentation given December 5, 1971, during a weekend meeting of medical students in Zürich.]
[The physician and death. An existential analytic investigation] {1972c}
[Portuguese translation: 'O Médico e a Morte. Um Ensaio Analítico-Existencial', in *Angústia, culpa e libertação: ensaios de psicanálise existancial* (Saõ Paulo: Livraria Duas Cidades, 1975), 67-77. Also contains a translation of 'Sturmzeichen in der Psychologie und Psychiatrie. Epilog zu einem revolutionären Internationalen Psychotherapeuten-Kongress', in *Psychotherapy and Psychosomatics* 20(1-2), 1972, 92-106.] (See {1972b})

113. 'Die Bedeutung der Daseinsanalyse für die Psychiatrie, dargestellt aufgrund der Behandlung einer schizophrenen Psychose', in *Therapeutische Umschau* 30(1), 1973, 5-11.
[The significance of daseinanalysis for psychiatry illustrated by the treatment of a schizophrenic psychosis] {1973b}

114. 'Sigmund Freud und die naturwissenschaftliche Denkmethode', in *Hexagon* 1(1), 1973, 1-7 and 1(2), 1973, 1-6. Reprinted in *Von der Psychoanalyse zur Daseinsanalyse. Wege zu einem neuen Selbstverständnis* (Vienna: Europaverlag, 1979), 387-404.
[Sigmund Freud and the natural scientific method of thinking] {1973c}

115. 'Die psychosomatische Medizin und das Kausalitätsprinzip', in *Hexagon* 2(2), 1974, 8-18. Reprinted in *Von der Psychoanalyse zur Daseinsanalyse. Wege zu einem neuen Selbstverständnis* (Vienna: Europaverlag, 1979), 405-422.
[Psycho-somatic medicine and the principle of causality] {1974}

116. 'El 'estar enfermo' del esquizofrénico entendido desde el analise existencial', in *Acta Psiquiatrica-Psicologica América Latina* 21(1), 1975, 6-24.
[The schizophrenic's 'being ill' understood in terms of existential analysis] {1975c}
[Portuguese translation: 'O modo de ser esquizofrenico à luz de uma fenomenologia daseinanalítica', in *Revista de Associação Médica Brasileira Daseinsanalyse* 3, 1977, 5-28].
[German translation: 'Schizophrenes Kranksein im Lichte einer daseinsanalytischen Phänomenologie', in *Therapeutische Umschau* 33(7), 1976, 452-464. Reprinted in *Von der Psychoanalyse zur Daseinsanalyse. Wege zu einem neuen Selbstverständnis* (Vienna: Europaverlag, 1979), 347-372.]

117. 'Cultura e psicoterapia', in *Daseinsanalyse* (Sao Paulo) 2, 1976, 25-44.
[Culture and psychotherapy] {1976c}

118. 'Das Leib-Seele-Problem im Lichte der Daseinsanalyse', in *Psychosomatische Medizin* 6(3-4), 1976, 106-128. Reprinted as 'Das Verhältnis von Leib und Seele im Lichte der Daseinsanalytik', in M. Boss, G. Condrau, G. and A. Hicklin (eds), *Leiben und Leben. Beiträge zur Psychosomatik und Psychotherapie* (Bern: Benteli, 1977), 37-70.
[Based on a lecture evidently given in Japan in the Fall of 1974. At one point Boss refers to Koichi Tsujimura.]
[The mind-body problem in light of daseinsanalysis] {1976e}
[Japanese translation, in Y. Masatoshi (ed.), *Martin Heidegger-Festschrift* (Tokyo: Risosha) 1, 1975, 120-143.]

119. 'Mit dem Terror leben', in *Rheinische Post* 144, June 25, 1977, p. 8.
[Living with terror] {1977i}

120. 'Erziehung Ja oder Nein?' in *Neue Zürcher Zeitung* 216, September 15, 1977, p. 46.
[Lecture given at the Zurich Girls School in March 1977.]
[Education – Yes or no?] {1977g}

Bibliography

121. 'Neid entfacht Terror. Das Phänomen menschlicher Gewalttätigkeit', in *Darmstädter Echo* 180, August 6, 1977, 37-38.
    [Envy triggers terror. The phenomenon of human violence] {1977h}
122. 'Der neue Wandel der Neurosen-Erkenntnisse der Psychotherapie', in *Universitas* 33(10), 1978, 1023-1030.
    [Current changes in the identification of the neuroses in psychotherapy] {1978b}
123. 'Sexualität und Psychotherapie', in *Psychosomatische Medizin* 8(2), 1978, 118-128. Reprinted in *Von der Psychoanalyse zur Daseinsanalyse. Wege zu einem neuen Selbstverständnis* (Vienna: Europaverlag, 1979), 373-386.
    [Sexuality and psychotherapy] {1979d}
124. 'Die sexuellen Perversionen in phänomenologischer Sicht' [1972]. In *Von der Psychoanalyse zur Daseinsanalyse. Wege zu einem neuen Selbstverständnis* (Vienna: Europaverlag, 1979), 295-308.
    [Source given in *Von der Psychoanalyse zur Daseinsanalyse. Wege zu einem neuen Selbstverständnis* (Vienna: Europaverlag, 1979), p. 491, as 'Vortragsmanuskript; Erstveröffentlichung' [Lecture manuscript; first publication]. The text appears on pages 295-308 of the anthology. There is a reference in several bibliographies to 'Die sexuellen Perversionen als mitmenschliche Phänomene [The Sexual Perversions as an Interpersonal Phenomenon]' as a paper published in a journal *Sozialklinische Studien über Mental Health in der heutigen Gesellschaft* (Tokyo) 4, 1972, but this has not been attested.]
    [The sexual perversions from a phenomenological perspective] {1979f}
125. 'Psychotherapie und Wissenschaft' [1974]. In *Von der Psychoanalyse zur Daseinsanalyse. Wege zu einem neuen Selbstverständnis* (Vienna: Europaverlag, 1979), 423-441.
    [Manuscript of a presentation given December 12, 1974, at a meeting of the Society for Psychotherapy, Bern.]
    [Psychotherapy and science] {1979e}
126. 'Das Träumen. Ein Therapeuticum magnum', in *Hexagon Roche* 8(1), 1980, 15-24.
    [Dreaming. A great healing] {1980b}
    [Portuguese translation: 'Sonhar e psicoterapia [Dreaming and psychotherapy]', *Revista de Associação Brasiliera de Daseinanalyse* (São Paulo) 6, 1985, 90-109]
127. 'Träume. Unsere zweite Existenz', in *Musik und Medizin* 8, 1981, 17-35.
    [Dreams. Our second life] {1981a}
128. 'O inconsciente. Que è isso?' in *Tempo Psicanalítico* (Rio de Janeiro) 4(1), 1981, 28-40.
    [The unconscious – What is it?] {1981b}
    [English translation: 'The Unconscious – What Is It?' in *Review of Existential Psychology and Psychiatry* 20(1-3), 1986-1987, 237-249. Reprinted in K. Hoeller (ed.), *Readings in Existential Psychology and Psychiatry* (Seattle: Review of Existential Psychology and Psychiatry, 1990), 237-249.] (E. S. Goodstein)
    [German translation: 'Das Unbewußte – was ist es?' in *Von der Spannweite der Seele. Ausgewählte Vorträge und Aufsätze aus den Anwendungsbereichen des daseinsanalytischen Menschenverständnisses* (Bern: Huber, 1982), 132-150].
129. 'Die Entwicklung der Psychotherapie im 20.Jahrhundert', in *Neue Zürcher Zeitung* 79, May 4, 1981, 69-70.
    [The development of psychotherapy in the twentieth century] {1981g}
130. 'Sprache und Angst in einer technifizierten Welt [Language and Anxiety in an engineered World]', in *Von der Spannweite der Seele. Ausgewählte Vorträge und Aufsätze aus den Anwendungsbereichen des daseinsanalytischen Menschenverständnisses* (Bern: Benteli, 1982), 61-68.
    [Given as 'On the Spirit of Technicity' as a contribution to the ninth Zürcher Gespräche, June 6-8, 1981, on the theme 'Sprache und Angst in einer technifizierten Welt [Language and Anxiety in an Engineered World]'.
    [Language and anxiety in an engineered world] {1982k}

Bibliography

131. 'Die normale Angst', in *Neue Zürcher Zeitung* 271, November 20, 1982, p. 37.
     [First given as a lecture on August 17, 1982, in Rio de Janeiro, Brazil, at an International Forum on Anxiety.]
     [Normal anxiety.] {1982a}
132. 'Gewähren und Versagen in der in der Psychotherapie', in *Von der Spannweite der Seele. Ausgewählte Vorträge und Aufsätze aus den Anwendungsbereichen des daseinsanalytischen Menschenverständnisses*, Bern: Benteli, 1982, 98-110.
     [The essay is represented in the sources notes as a heretofore 'unpublished contribution'. Lecture given at the annual gathering of the Swiss Medical Society for Psychotherapy, Bern, November 11, 1978.]
     [Permitting and abstaining in psychotherapy] {1982f}
133. 'Abriss der Psychotherapie – Entwicklung im 20.Jahrhundert [Outline of the Development of Psychotherapy in the 20th Century]', in *Von der Spannweite der Seele. Ausgewählte Vorträge und Aufsätze aus den Anwendungsbereichen des daseinsanalytischen Menschenverständnisses*, 1982, 182-198. Abridged French translation published under the title 'Exposé sur le developpement de la psychothérapie au XX siècle [Lecture on the development of psychotherapy in the 20th century]', in *Archives Suisse de Neurologie, Neurochirurgie et de Psychiatrie* 128(2), 1981, 183-196. Reprinted as 'Développement de la psychothérapie au 20e siècle', in *Psychiatrie Française* 14(3), 1983, 7-26. A revised version had been prepared for publication in the *Neue Zürcher Zeitung* 79, May 4, 1981, 69-70.
     [Keynote address given at the annual meeting of the Swiss Society of Psychiatry and the Swiss Association of Psychotherapists on October 26, 1980.]
     [Outline of the development of psychotherapy in the twentieth century] {1982i}
134. 'Die Magie der psychosomatische Medizin', in *Psychosomatische Medizin* 11(4) 1982, 189-197.
     [The magic of psychosomatic medicine] {1982g}
135. 'Die Bedeutung Martin Heideggers für die Arbeit mit leidenden Menschen und für das Selbstverständnis der Psychotherapie', in *Von der Spannweite der Seele. Ausgewählte Vorträge und Aufsätze aus den Anwendungsbereichen des daseinsanalytischen Menschenverständnisses* (Bern: Benteli, 1982), 199-210.
     [The significance of Martin Heidegger for work with suffering people and for the self-understanding of psychotherapy] {1982j}
136. 'Zur Frage des sogenannten 'Stresses', in *Zeitschrift der Klassisch Homöopathie* 27(4), 1983, 167-170.
     [The question of so-called 'stress'] {1983}
137. 'Gedanken zu Valerie Gampers Referat. An ihrer Sprache sollt ihr sie erkennen', in *Daseinsanalyse* 1(1), 1984, 58-65.
     [Thoughts on Valeria Gamper's presentation, 'By their language shall you know them'] {1984a}
138. 'Die Bedrängnis des Daseins', in *Rheinische Post* 303, December 31, 1984, p. 2.
     [The pressure of existence] {1984b}
139. 'Psychosomatische Medizin? Wissenschaft oder Magie?' in *Daseinsanalyse* 2(2), 1985, 107-119.
     [Based on a lecture given at the University of Hamburg, May 9, 1984]
     [Psychosomatic medicine. Science or magic?] {1985}
140. 'Nach dreißig Jahren', introductory essay for *Indienfahrt eines Psychiaters* [1959] (4th ed.) (Bern: Huber, 1987), 6-10.
     ['After Thirty Years': Preface to *A Psychiatrist Discovers India* (4th ed., 1987)] {2002/2003b}
     English translation: 'After Thirty Years: Preface to A Psychiatrist Discovers India' (4th edition, 1987), in *Review of Existential Psychology and Psychiatry* 27 (1-3), 2002/2003, 33-36. Reprinted as a monograph by K. Hoeller (ed.), *The Heidegger-Boss Relationship* (Seattle: Review of Existential Psychology and Psychiatry, 2008). (Michael Eldred)

141. 'Woraus besteht der Mensch, wenn er träumt, und wo ist er dann?' in *Festschrift aus Anlass der Verleihung des Dr. Margrit Egnér Preises zum Thema 'Der Traum'* (Zürich: Dr. Margrit Egnér Stiftung, 1988, 16-25) and in *Daseinsanalyse* 6(3), 1989, 149-160. [Dedicated to Gion Condrau for his seventieth birthday. An English version of the paper was read at the University of Portland in 1989]
[What does a human being consist in when he dreams, and where is he then?] {1988c}
English translation: "What Does a Human Being Consist in When He Dreams, and Where Is He Then?", in *Daseinsanalyse* 40(2024), 121-133.
142. 'Recent Considerations in Daseinsanalysis', in *The Humanistic Psychologist* 16(1), 1988, 210-230.
[Recent considerations in daseinsanalysis] {1988a} (B)
143. 'An Encounter with Medard Boss', in *The Humanistic Psychologist* 16(1), 1988, 24-57.
[An encounter with Medard Boss] {1988b}(B)
144. 'Martin Heidegger Applied to Psychiatry and the Modern World' [1989], in *Review of Existential Psychology and Psychiatry* 27(1-3), 2002/2003, 23-31. Reprinted as a monograph by K. Hoeller (ed.), *The Heidegger-Boss Relationship* (Seattle: Review of Existential Psychology and Psychiatry, 2008), 23-31. (Michael Eldred)
[Lecture given at the Applied Heidegger Conference, September 8-10, 1989, at the University of California, Berkeley. It is said to have been translated by Michael Eldred for the Hoeller volume but was likely given in English by Boss.]
[Martin Heidegger applied to psychiatry and the modern world] {2002/2003c}
145. 'Daseinsanalytische Bemerkungen zum Wesen der Freudschen Psychoanalyse', in *Daseinsanalyse* 7(3), 1990, 167-173.
[Daseinsanalytic remarks on the essence of Freudian psychoanalysis] {1990}

VI. CO-AUTHORED CONTRIBUTIONS

146. With H. Fierz and A. Maeder. 'Herkunft und Wesen des Archetypus-Begriffes. Ein Diskussion', in *Psyche* 7(3), 1953, 217-240.
[Origin and nature of the concept of the archetype. A discussion] {1953e}
147. With G. Benedetti. 'Psychoanalyse eines Sadisten', in *Psyche* 7(1), 1953/54, 241-263. Reprinted in *Von der Psychoanalyse zur Daseinsanalyse. Wege zu einem neuen Selbstverständnis* (Vienna: Europaverlag, 1979), 161-186.
[An English 'summary by authors' is given (p. 263)]
  [Psychoanalysis of a sadist] {1953f}
[English translation: 'Psychoanalysis of a Sadist', in *Samiksa. Journal of the Indian Psychoanalytical Society* 7(1), 1953, 18-38. (B)
[Czech translation: *Analyza Jednoho Sadisty* (Prague: Kabinet psychoterapie Psychiatrické kliniky fak. vseobec. lékařství, 1989)]
148. With G. Condrau. 'Existential Psychoanalysis', in B. Wolman (ed.), *Psychoanalytic Techniques* (New York: Basic Books, 1967), 443-467. (B)
[Existential psychoanalysis] {1967c}
149. With G. Condrau. 'Existential Analysis', in J. G. Howells (ed.), *Modern Perspectives in World Psychiatry* (London: Oliver & Boyd, 1968), 488-518. (B)
[Existential analysis] {1968b}
150. With G. Condrau. 'Daseinsanalysis', in W. Sahakian (ed.), *Psychopathology Today. Experimentation, Theory and Research* (Itasca: Peacock, 1970), 567-575. This is an excerpt (505-518) from 'Existential Analysis', in J. G. Howells (ed.), *Modern Perspectives in World Psychiatry* (London: Oliver & Boyd, 1968), 488-518. (B)
[Daseinsanalysis] {1970b}

Bibliography

151. With A. Hicklin. 'Daseinsanalyse', in R. Arnold, W. Eysenck, H. Jürgen and R. Meili (eds.), *Lexikon der Psychologie* [Volume I], Freiberg: Herder, 1971, p. 347.
[Daseinsanalysis] {1971c}
152. With G. Condrau. 'Die Daseinsanalyse in der Zürcher Psychiatrie von heute. Rückblick und Ausblick', in *Schweizer Archive der Neurologie, Neurochirurgie und Psychiatrie* 112(1), 1973, 21-30.
[Daseinsanalysis in today's psychiatry in Zürich] {1973d}
153. With G. Condrau. 'Analyse existentielle (Daseinsanalyse)', in *Encyclopédie médico-chirurgicale* [Volume 5], Paris: Elsevier, 1975, 55-60. Reprinted as 'Análisi existencial – Daseinsanalyse – Como a Daseinsanalyse entrou na Psiquiatria [Existential Analysis – Daseinsanalyse – How Daseinsanalysis Became a Part of Psychiatry]', in *Daseinsanalyse* (Sao Paulo) 2, 1976, pp.5-23.
[Existential analysis (Daseinsanalysis)] {1975d}
154. With B. Kenny. 'Phenomenological or Daseinsanalytic Approach [to Dreams]', in J. Fosshage and C. Loew (eds.), *Dream Interpretation. A Comparative Study* (New York: SP Scientific Books, 1978; rev. ed., New York: PMA Publishing Corporation, 1987, 149-189). (B)
[The phenomenological or existential analytic approach [to dreams]] {1978d}
155. With G. Condrau. 'Die Weiterentwicklung der Daseinsanalyse nach Ludwig Binswanger', in U. Peters (ed.), *Die Psychologie des 20.Jahrhunderts*. Volume 10, *Ergebnisse für die Medizin* (Zürich: Kindler, 1980), 728-739. The original version 'Der Einstieg der 'Daseinsanalytik' in das Denkens der Artzte [The Introduction of the 'Analytics of Existence' to the Thinking of the Physician]', in *Von der Spannweite der Seele. Ausgewählte Vorträge und Aufsätze aus den Anwendungsbereichen des daseinsanalytischen Menschenverständnisses*, Bern: Benteli, 1982, 173-181.
[The further development of Ludwig Binswanger's daseinsanalysis] {1980c}
156. With A. Holzhey-Kunz. 'Das Phänomen des Widerstandes in der Daseinsanalyse', in H. Petzold (ed.), *Widerstand – ein strittiges Konzept in der Psychotherapie* (Paderborn: Jungfermann, 1981), 173-189. Reprinted as 'Das Konzept des Widerstandes in der Daseinsanalyse' in *Von der Spannweite der Seele. Ausgewählte Vorträge und Aufsätze aus den Anwendungsbereichen des daseinsanalytischen Menschenverständnisses* (Bern: Benteli, 1982), 111-131.
[The phenomenon of resistance in daseinsanalysis] {1981c}
157. With G. Condrau. 'Der Einstieg der 'Daseinsanalytik' in das Denkens der Ärzte', in *Von der Spannweite des Denkens. Ausgewählte Vorträge und Aufsätze aus den Anwendungsbereichen des daseinsanalytischen Menschenverständnisses* (Bern: Benteli, 1982), 173-181.
[Original version of a 'heavily modified' text first published as 'Die Weiterentwicklung der Daseinsanalyse nach Ludwig Binswanger [The Further Development of Daseinsanalysis after Ludwig Binswanger]', published in U. Peters (ed.), *Die Psychologie des 20.Jahrhunderts*. Volume 10, *Ergebnisse für die Medizin* (Zürich: Kindler, 1980), 728-739.]
[The introduction of the analytics of *Dasein* into the thinking of the physician] {1982h}
158. With D. Rhee. 'Dialogue Between Prof. Medard Boss and Prof. Dongshick Rhee' [June 12 and June 15, 1976], in 精神治療 [*Psychotherapy*] (Seoul) 6, 1996, 30-43.
[Transcribed from audio tape recordings of two interviews online at: http://taopsychotherapy.org/rhee/02_en_sub_view.php?no=15&rno=&page=1&search1=&search2=&table_mode=rhee_papers and http://www.taopsychotherapy.org/rhee/02_en_sub_view.php?no=14&rno=&page=1&search1=&search2=&table_mode=rhee_papers. They are also available at https://docs.google.com/document/d/1Fla6E1ZVs4NquehiWa1N NKcWPUcaFtO4jV3e1t71KXo/edit]
[Dialogue between Prof. Medard Boss and Prof. Dongshick Rhee] {1996}

VII. MISCELLANEOUS

A. CORRESPONDENCE

159. Letters to Erna M. Hoch (1960). Erna M. Hoch, *Sources and Resources. A Western Psychiatrist's Search for Meaning in the Ancient Indian Scriptures* (Zürich: Rüegger, 1991): 'Messenger between East and West', 251-253 [March 12, 1960], 263 and 281 [April 10, 1960], and 282 [May 22, 1960]. (Erna Hoch)
    [Three letters from Boss to Erna Hoch are published in Hoch's collected papers, *Sources and Resources. A Western Psychiatrist's Search for Meaning in the Ancient Indian Scriptures*. All three date from the spring of 1960.]
    [Letters to Erna M. Hoch] {1960c}
160. Letter to Heidegger [of January 12, 1960] (1960), in *Review of Existential Psychology and Psychiatry* 27(1-3), 2002/2003, 37-39. Reprinted as a monograph by K. Hoeller (ed.), *The Heidegger-Boss Relationship* (Seattle: Review of Existential Psychology and Psychiatry, 2008), 37-39. (Eva Mader)
    [Letter to Heidegger [of January 12, 1960]] {2002/2003a}

B. AUDIOVISUAL MATERIALS

161. 'Ein neues Traumverständnis und seine praktisch-therapeutischen Anwendungsmöglichkeiten' [1976], in *Sonderedition anläßlich der 50. Lindauer Psychotherapiewoche 2000: Bedeutende Vorträge aus den Jahren 1970-1996* (Schwarzach: Auditorium Verlag, 2001).
    [Audio recording]
    [A new understanding of dreams and its possibilities in practical therapeutic application]
    {1976d}
162. 'Daseinsanalyse' [1988].
    [Video interview with Boss conducted by Ludwig Pongratz for the University of Würzburg series on *Humanistische Psychologie*. The video includes a taped analytic session with a young man. Two tapes were made: the first, one hour in length, contains the interview with Boss. The second is the full forty-minute session [*Behandlungsstunde*]. The videos were produced by Tellux Film, Munich.
    [Daseinanalysis] {1988d}

VIII. UNPUBLISHED PAPERS (NO MS AVAILABLE)

163. 'La psychoanalyse de Freud et l'analyse existentielle de Heidegger [Freud's Psychoanalysis and Heidegger's Daseinsanalysis]'. Paper read at the fourth International Congress on Psychotherapy, September 1-6, 1958, Barcelona. The theme of the conference was 'Daseinsanalysis and Psychotherapy'.
164. 'Der Traum und seine Bedeutung. Zwei Traumbilder [The Dream and Its Meaning. Two Dream Images]'. Contribution to third Zürcher Gespräche, January 20-23, 1978. The theme was 'Rationale und bildhafte Sprache [Rational and Figurative Speech]'.
165. 'Wo bleibt Gott in der Psychotherapie? Wo bleibt die Psychotherapie in Gott? [Where Is God in Psychotherapy? Where Is Psychotherapy in God?]' Contribution to the twelfth Zürcher Gespräche, October 22-24, 1982. The theme was 'Verlorene Natur, Religion, Persönlichkeit – der Mensch von Heute [Abandoned Nature, Religion, Personhood – the Man of Today]'.

Bibliography

166. 'Ist menschliche Schuld psychotherapeutisch heilbar? [Is Human Guilt Curable with Psychotherapy?]' Lecture given at the Katholische Akademie Freiburg, June 3, 1984.
'*Daseinsanalyse* and the Encounter between East and West'. Lecture given at thirteenth annual Congress for International Federation for Psychotherapy, Opatija, Croatia [Yugoslavia], October 6-12, 1985. The theme of the conference was 'Health for All by the Year 2000'.

Appendix

Awards and Recognition

1959 Honorary Member, Indian Psychiatric Society (Lucknow).
1962 Corresponding Member, Royal College of Psychiatrists of Great Britain (London).
1967 Honorary President, International Federation for Medical Psychotherapy (Zürich).
1969 Honorary Member, Swiss Medical Society for Psychotherapy (Zürich).
1971 Recipient, Great Therapist Award, American Psychological Association (Washington).
1971 Honorary Member, Swiss Society of Psychosomatic Medicine (Zürich).
1972 Honorary Member, Ibero-Latin American Psychiatric Society (Buenos Aires).
1975 Honorary President, Brazilian Association of Existential Analysis (Sao Paulo).
1982 Honorary Guest, Twelfth International Congress of Psychotherapy (Rio de Janeiro).
1985 Honorary President, Swiss Society for Daseinsanalysis (Zürich).
1988 Recipient, Margrit Egnér Institute Prize (University of Zürich).

Notes

1. *Diagnostic and Statistical Manual of Psychological Disorders [5-TR]*, Washington: American Psychiatric Association, 2022.
2. The many forms of psychotherapy and counseling share a view of the human being based on natural science, from the 'hard' sciences (physics, chemistry, biology) to the social sciences (sociology, anthropology) and the *Geisteswissenschaften* (sciences of the spirit or so-called human sciences). Psychology holds the ambiguous position of being somewhat natural and somewhat social science, and, for some, somewhat human science. Some psychologies allow a place for the mind understood in various senses of the term while others, such as behaviorism, do not. Some have retained a place for the soul (for example, logotherapy). Still others have attempted to introduce non-Western spiritual practices into the mix. By contrast, daseinanalysis begins with a view of the human being as existing, that is, prior to any conceptual division into mind (psyche) and body (soma), a view introduced only recently into Western philosophy by René Descartes in the middle of the seventeenth century.
3. This introduction is intended for the beginning student of daseinanalysis and will be used for individuals who are candidates for the certificate program offered by the American Daseinsanalytic Institute to accompany its introductory seminar. It is my hope, however, that it will also gain wider interest.
4. Frederick Crews, *Skeptical Engagements*, New York: Oxford University Press, 1986, 18. See also his summative critique, *Freud. The Making of an Illusion*, New York: Picador, 2017.
5. Jonathan Shedler, 'Where Is the Evidence for Evidence-based Therapy?' *Psychiatric Clinics of North America* 41, 2018, 319-329, where cure is defined as based on *reports of patients who say they got well and stayed well* (324). Shedler has been very careful to examine the methods of gathering data and their statistical manipulation. He concludes that inflated reports of the success of certain modalities may be traced back to flaws in sampling the patient population (most patients are not counted), the myth of the 'control group', and fudging the data, with claims, for example, that CBT is successful for 22% of those who undergo it being vastly exaggerated. Shedler has been studying the literature reporting on efficacy and evidence-based psychotherapy since the early 1990s.
6. The obvious, more than embarrassing, comparison with 'the world's oldest profession' is unavoidable.
7. While we hope the medical doctor has a good bedside manner, it is not essential. All the same, evoking in the patient a sense of reassurance, based on the impression that a disease has been identified and is understood well enough in order for the physician to offer an informed opinion to the patient about the status of the latter's health and to advise him to take advantage of the best range of treatments available. The word 'patient' is correct here, since one willingly *undergoes* (from the Latin *patio*, to undergo) treatment in the care of a physician. One willingly takes a passive stance with respect to the physician's agency. The social graces are suspended in the clinical setting, where we undress for the doctor and stretch out on his examination table in complete trusting vulnerability. We allow ourselves to be touched (palpated, percussed) in ways and places to which otherwise

Notes

only a parent or 'intimate' is given access. We may expose our most 'private' parts for examination. In the surgical suite, we allow ourselves to be rendered unaware and unable to remember what is being done to us. The commonly used intravenous anesthetic Propofol (known familiarly among surgeons, anesthesiologists and nurses as 'milk of amnesia') and other anesthetics allow the surgeon and his team to undertake often drastically invasive procedures without frightening the patient, who does not register what is happening and forms no memories of it. Above all, we trust that the doctor is not motivated by any personal interest in us. He does not see our body as an object of aesthetic appreciation, least of all as a sexual object. We may as well remain nameless. Indeed, in a busy emergency room, one hears talk of 'the possible fracture in bed 3' or 'the acute abdomen in bed 6'.

8   Quoted in Jan van den Berg, *Op het Scherp van de Snede* [*On the Cutting Edge*], Kapellen: Pelckmans, 2013, 81.

9   It is clear that all conversation includes a non-verbal atmosphere. This has puzzled those who have studied psychotherapy more perhaps than the obvious power of any verbal exchange, even when taking into consideration variables such as tone of voice and 'body language'. Apart from this nuance, however, another level of engagement with the patient is assumed that is difficult to describe. Freud, who had an interest in telepathy, described it as communication between the Unconscious of the analyst and the Unconscious of the analysand. It has been related to the presence of the analyst, his personality and even charisma. These mysterious media of communication have been named and touted as essential for 'effective psychotherapy', but little is understood about them. The patient thus reports responding to a certain *sense* or *feeling* that is conveyed by the psychotherapist. In an optimal therapeutic situation, the patient's own *sense* or *feeling* is said to resonate with that of the therapist. There is then, as it were, a harmony between two 'tones'. Boss described this in terms of an intuitive sense that has about it features of something 'sensorially hinted [*spurenhaft-sensoriellem*], perhaps even of [an] extrasensory [*extrasensoriellem*]' nature. See 'Is Psychotherapy Rational or Rationalistic?' {1979b}, 122. References {/} throughout refer to the Chronological Listing of Boss's works.

10 We will soon take a close look at the term *Dasein*. For now, it is best to think of it as denoting the global whole of human *being* as existing, that is, as *being* in the world, keeping in mind that *human* being is unique among every other sort of being.

11 Let us not forget that there was a time not long ago when after someone who was ill had been treated by a physician but could not pay the fee in coin of the realm, a physician was compensated in eggs or chickens or labor instead of cash or a third-party payment. The original Hippocratic oath required that the physician treat the person first and then worry about compensation. Following revisions in the oath beginning in 1964, today when attempting to arrange a consultation with a doctor, the prospective patient must first make his way past the medical office gatekeeper, who first asks 'What insurance do you have?' If you have none or none that is accepted by the physician, you must sign a document agreeing to pay out of pocket for the visit or go elsewhere, places that for the most part are subsidized by the government. Arriving unconscious or incoherent in critical condition at an emergency room is an exception to such preliminary negotiating about payment, but eventually someone must fork over fees. Private hospital setting costs have soared, since they are operated to make a profit and include having made the hospital's facilities and support staff available to those who cannot pay 'out of pocket' or provide 'third-party reimbursement'.

12 In a sense, *each therapist is his own modality or approach*. After Sigmund Freud, there were Carl Gustav Jung (analytical psychology) and Alfred Adler (individual psychology), Fritz Perls (Gestalt therapy) and Viktor Frankl (logotherapy), and so on. While we by convention refer to someone practicing according to the theory and techniques of practice of, say, Jung, as Jungians, there was only one Jungian, just as there had been only one

Notes

Freudian. This suggestion will be roundly ridiculed, but I believe it is warranted. On the other hand, as an approach and not a technique daseinanalysts can claim a certain uniformity of practice. There are many daseinanalysts.

13 The seal of confidentiality of the confessional is absolutely inviolable. The priest is governed by canon law, but the mental health professional is now overseen by civil law, which varies from state to state, country to country. That said, we know that the Hippocratic oath has become optional in some places for those who are licensed to practice medicine. Canon law in the Roman Catholic Church regarding the confessional has been fixed since the eleventh century and is worldwide. Confession is an element of one of the seven sacraments of the Church, in this case that of penance or the sacrament of reconciliation. The status of absolute privacy in communications between doctors and healthcare providers and their patients is indeterminate in many jurisdictions. This becomes important when the issue, for example, of suicidal ideation or threat is in the foreground.

14 The university has not served daseinanalysis as an institutional locus of shared interest and activity. Instead, the first daseinanalytic institute was formed in Zurich in 1970 as a free-standing entity modeled on psychoanalytic institutes. An International Federation of Daseinsanalysis (IFDA) was formed twenty years later which oversees the roughly the half-dozen institutes in Europe and the Americas.

15 It bears recalling that the Latin *doctor* means teacher.

16 I have decided that we can do with a simple noun 'daseinanalysis' to denote the practice described in these pages. There is no need for retaining the German possessive 's' or the practice of capitalizing nouns in German. More important, this translation of *Daseinsanalyse* was Boss's preference in his last completed bit of writing, the 'Preface' to the American translation of Martin Heidegger's *Zollikoner Seminare*. See *Zollikon Seminars*, Evanston: Northwestern University Press, 2001, ix. There hyphenated the term: 'da-seinanalysis'. The traditional translation ('daseinsanalysis') appears in the name of the American Daseinanalytic Institute (ADI) in order to be in conformity with the international organization (IFDA) that oversees the various institutes worldwide. The ADI website retains that usage for the same reason (daseinsanalysis.org).

17 *Freud/Binswanger Correspondence* [1992], New York: Other Press, 2003, xx. Fichtner reports that the term first appears in Binswanger's diary in an entry dated September 11, 1943 (VIII, 30). Wyrsch is said to have devised the term to distinguish it from Heidegger's *Daseinsanalytik* (analytics of existence) with which it nonetheless continued to be confused. Fichtner refers to Roland Kuhn's 'Erinnerungen an Ludwig Binswanger [Recollections of Ludwig Binswanger]', *Der Psychiater Dr. med. Ludwig Binswanger und das Sanatorium Bellevue. Beiträge zur Ortsgeschichte [The Psychiatrist Ludwig Binswanger, MD and the Bellevue Sanatorium. Contributions to the History of the Place]*, Kreuzlingen: Vereinigung Heimatsmuseum 21, 7-14. Binswanger first met Martin Heidegger on January 24, 1929, in Frankfurt, at a meeting of the Kant Society where Heidegger gave a lecture entitled 'Philosophische Anthropologie und Metaphysik des Daseins [Philosophical Anthropology and the Metaphysics of Dasein]' (*GA* 80.1, 213-251). (All references are to the *Gesamtausgabe* edition [= *GA*] of Heidegger's works (Klostermann 1975-). Binswanger noted in his diary: 'Met with [Kurt] Reitzler (1882-1955) and Heidegger and others' after the lecture. He also recorded that he first read Heidegger in April 1928, together with his son who was then only nineteen years old. Binswanger refers in print to Heidegger's influence on his thinking as early as 1930 in his paper 'Traum und Existenz [Dream and Existence]', where he writes about Heidegger's *Daseinsanalytik*. See *Dream and Existence*, New York: Humanities Press, 1993, first published in an English translation in the *Review of Existential Psychology and Psychiatry* 19(1), 1984-1985, 81-105, and as a special edition of the journal in 1986. The English publication famously includes an introduction to the essay by Michel Foucault, 'Dream, Imagination, and Existence' [1953] (30-78), which Foucault had written for

Notes

a French translation by Jacqueline Verdeaux of Binswanger's essay published as *Le rêve et l'existence*, Paris: Descleé de Brouwer, 1954, 8-128. See Binswanger's tribute to Wyrsch in *Psychiatrie et Neurologie* 143(6), 1962, 369-378.

18 See, for example, Emmy van Deurzen *et al.* (eds.), *Wiley Handbook of Existential Therapy*, New York: John Wiley, 2019, 29-126. There we read of 'Daseinsanalytic Psychotherapy' and three modifications of it: hermeneutic daseinsanalysis, humanistic-relational daseinsanalysis and short-term daseinsanalysis. There is only one international oversight organization associated with this tradition and it is the International Federation of Daseinsanalysis (IFDA). There are no such organizations associated with the three named modifications of Boss's 'Daseinanalytic Psychotherapy'. For an earlier account of hermeneutic daseinanalysis, see Alice Holzhey-Kunz, *Daseinsanalysis*, London: Free Association Books, 2014. The authoritative *Handbook* speaks of daseinanalysis as 'the first systematic approach to existential psychotherapy' (33), based on Sigmund Freud's 'pre-ontological understanding of human being', with 'all psychoanalysis [understood] as hermeneutic, a quest for meaning' (36). This is said to line up with Martin Heidegger's 'hermeneutic phenomenology' (38). See the author's review of the *Handbook* in *Existential Analysis* 31(1), 2020, pp. 199-203.

19 In what follows, I will often give the German equivalent of a word so that the reader may have a point of reference for further study. The reader is welcome to simply ignore the interpolations, but often there will be a play on certain related German words that is not evident without considering the original German.

20 Heidegger traces his usage of *Analytik* to Kant's critical philosophy, but it may also hearken back to Aristotle's analytics, the prior and posterior (the *proteros* or beforehand and the *husteros* or afterward) analytics of his *organon*.

21 I suggest translating *Existenzial* with 'existentive' to distinguish this technical term found in Heidegger from other usages of 'existential'.

22 GA 2, 56. This can yield the English sentence 'The essence of existence is in its existence,' since both *Dasein* and *Existenz* can be translated with 'existence'. To avoid what appears in such an English rendering to be saying that the essence of something is itself, the first translators of Heidegger's book did not translate *Dasein* and translated *Existenz* with 'existence'. In Heidegger's later philosophy the term *Existenz* all but disappears. In the meantime, he traced the word *Existenz* to its source in the Latin *eksistere*, which means 'to stand out into'. Some translators adopted the English adjective 'ecstatic' to describe the *temporal* essence of *Dasein*. This word, however, derives from the Greek *ekstatikos* (via the Latin *ekstasis*), which has the meaning of 'being beside oneself' or dissociated. Heidegger's understanding of the 'standing out into' of *Existenz* has to do with time, to be precise, making time for … and not with some sort of spatial extension. Thus, the problematic but basic statement quoted quite clearly says that 'the essence of existence is in its standing out into the world in the sense of making time for things.' It also makes sense to render *Existenz* with 'existing' with the verbal sense of the participial gerund *Existieren* (existing). Thus we might also translate Heidegger's famous saying as follows: 'The essence of existence lies in its existing.' This makes sense, since, for Heidegger, only *Dasein* exists. *Dasein* never *is* until the moment of its death. For this reason, it is understandable that, for Heidegger, *Dasein* is to be understood pre-eminently with respect to its existentive mortality [*Sein zum Tode*], its being-towards-death, where death is the one possibility that has no further possibilities. To say 'a given human being *is* not' may sound nonsensical until the ontological difference explained earlier and Heidegger's technical use of the word *Dasein* are taken into account. Another possible translation of *eksistere* that captures the sense of *Existenz* Heidegger has in mind is 'reach', which means both to stretch out for (to reach for a glass) and to succeed in getting to what is extended toward (to reach my destination). The English word 'reach' is related to the Middle Low German *reiken* (to hold out, give, extend over or extend to) and *reichen* (reach). A reason why Heidegger abandoned the term *Existenz* was because of what

Notes

came to be its association with the notion of *Existenz* in Karl Jaspers' *Existenzphilosophie*. See *Existenzphilosophie*, Berlin: de Gruyter, 1938.

23 According to theologians, the *summum ens* of the Judaeo-Christian is also a 'Who' (capitalized). Heidegger rejects this status for God, since for theologians God is a being that *is*. The predicate of existence in the ordinary sense (for those who believe) applies to God as it does to all lower beings. It may be that God is both a 'What' and a 'Who'. This is a problem for theologians to work out. Heidegger cautions that calling a human being a 'who' rather than a 'what' does not at all eliminate the problem since, in doing so, the human being is understood as a 'subject [*suiectum*]'.

24 From this point on we will use the term '*Dasein*' (the German noun, italicized) rather than 'existence' to call attention to its technical meaning which lies at the basis of what makes daseinanalysis different from psychoanalysis and the variety of other forms of psychotherapy.

25 For an appraisal of the status of psychoanalysis as a form of psychotherapy and other forms of psychotherapy that preceded or were contemporaneous with psychoanalysis, see Frederick Crews, *Freud. The Making of an Illusion*, New York: Picador, 2017.

26 Before inventing psychoanalysis, Freud had tried to work out what has been called his 'Project for a Scientific Psychology' [1895], which is framed in terms of neuron-like entities and quanta of energy. See *The Standard Edition of the Complete Psychological Works of Sigmund Freud* [= *SE*] London: Hogarth, 1950: *SE* I, 281-391. Recent research in the neurosciences has led to some attempts to formulate just such an account (neuropsychoanalysis). See, for example, Mark Solms and Oliver Turnbull, *Brain and the Inner World: An Introduction to the Neuroscience of Subjective Experience*, New York: Routledge, 2002.

27 On the criteria of science, see Karl Popper, *Objective Knowledge*, Oxford: Oxford University Press, 1979, and *Conjectures and Refutations*, London: Routledge, 1989.

28 In the States initially only psychiatrists were admitted to psychoanalytic institutes affiliated with Freud's international association. The same pattern occurred in Europe and the United Kingdom, although a few exceptions were made. For example, the editor and principal translator of *SE*, James Strachey (1887-1967), held only a bachelor's degree from Cambridge. The theorist of ego psychology, Erik Erikson (1902-1994), had no university degree whatsoever. Anna Freud (1895-1982), Freud's daughter, trained as an elementary school teacher. Oskar Pfister (1873-1956) was a Lutheran minister. Lou Andreas Salomé (1861-1937), who was also close with Friedrich Nietzsche and Rainer Maria Rilke, completed only one year of university education at the University of Zurich. All, however, practiced as renowned psychoanalysts by virtue of having been in analysis with Freud. Later, M. Masud R. Khan (1924-1989) came from a background in the humanities. The best known of the early lay analysts was Theodore Reik (1888-1969), who had been accused of quackery, that is, posing as a medical doctor. Having arrived in New York from Austria in 1938, Reik was refused full membership in the New York Psychoanalytic Association, which had been founded in 1911, because he was not a medical doctor. He had earned a PhD in psychology at the University of Vienna with a dissertation on Flaubert. In response, Reik founded the first lay psychoanalytic institute, the National Psychological Association for Psychoanalysis (NPAP), in 1948. In response to Reik's case, Freud published an essay on the question of lay psychoanalysis and concluded that non-medical candidates were perfectly acceptable for institute training and that, in fact, a medical education and psychiatric specialization might in some cases even be a hindrance to successful work as a psychoanalyst. At the very least, he concluded, a medical background was not necessary for the prospective psychoanalyst. See Sigmund Freud, *The Question of Lay Analysis* [1926], *SE* XX, 177-258. This is also true for daseinanalysts. At least four lay psychoanalytic institutes in New York owe their origins to individuals who were trained at NPAP. The author was in training at one of them. Lay analysts came to form a group segregated from the psychiatric psychoanalysts and their

institutes. They struggled for equal status among psychiatrists (especially access to the prescription pad) as providers of psychotherapy as a form of medical treatment, but the battle lost momentum as socialized medicine was instituted in the States and most psychotherapy came to be carried out by clinical *psychologists* (a legally protected title) and a variety of other licensed counselors, rather than by psychiatrists.

29 Given what we know about the way they worked, a number of American psychiatrists and psychoanalysts were in effect daseinanalysts. Their contributions appeared in several journals that began publishing around 1960, especially the *Review of Existential Psychology and Psychiatry*. Outside of the States, three of the most remarkable therapists of our time, Wilfred Bion (1897-1979), Jan van den Berg (1914-2012) and R. D. Laing (1927-1989), were in effect daseinanalysts, even though they did not mention the term in any of their publications. It was the author's good fortune to have worked with the American psychoanalyst Robert J. Gaukler (1924-1984). Like Laing, Bion and van den Berg, while he would not have identified himself as a daseinanalyst, Gaukler was one in practice. The author's lineage as a daseinanalyst can be traced to his experiences in analysis and supervision with Gaukler.

30 *Psychiatric Quarterly* 31(1-4), 1957, 203-227 and 417-444. The *Psychiatric Quarterly* is the second oldest psychiatry journal published in the United States after the *American Journal of Psychiatry*, which was established in 1921 (first published in 1844 as the *Journal of Insanity*). The *Quarterly* was established in 1915 as the *State Hospital Quarterly*. Kahn was a German-born psychiatrist whose *Habilitation* in Munich was supervised in part by Emil Kraepelin (1856-1926). Kahn taught at Yale University from 1930-1951, spent several years (1946-1951) in Switzerland in close contact with Binswanger, Boss, Roland Kuhn (1912-2005) and other representatives of the then innovative form of psychotherapy known as *Daseinsanalyse*, and then returned to the States where he taught at Baylor College of Medicine (1951-1973), during which time he wrote his appraisal. It is ironic that psychiatry's most feared and respected critic, Thomas Szasz, published the first of his papers to appear in the *Psychiatric Quarterly* in the same volume as Kahn's essay. In it Szasz presents 'A Critical Analysis of the Fundamental Aspects of Psychical Research' (96-108). His contribution would be followed four years later by the seminal paper, 'The Myth of Mental Illness', the *American Psychologist* 15, 1960, 113-118.

31 'Appraisal of Existential Analysis', 203.

32 For the record, it is pronounced / däzɪn/ (dah-zyne), with equal emphasis placed on both syllables.

33 Ludwig Binswanger: *Über Ideenflucht [On the Flight of Ideas]* (1933), *Grundformern und Erkenntnis menschlichen Daseins [Basic Forms and Knowledge of Human Existence]* (1942), *Daseinsanalytik und Psychiatrie [Analytics of Dasein and Psychiatry]* (1951), and *Drei Formen missglückten Daseins. Verstiegenheit Verschrobenheit Manieriertheit [Three Forms of Existential Failure. Eccentricity Quirkiness Manneredness]* (1956) (dedicated to Heidegger), three case histories (Ellen West [1945], Jürg Zünd [1947] and Lola Voss [1949]), and 'Symptom und Zeit [Symptom and Time]' [1951]; Medard Boss: *Sinn und Gehalt Sexueller Perversionen [Meaning and Content of Sexual Perversions]* (1947), *Der Traum und seine Auslegung [The Dream and Its Interpretation]* } (1953d), *Einführung in die Psychosomatische Medizin [Introduction to Psychosomatic Medicine]* (1954a), and *Psychoanalyse und Daseinsanalytik [Psychoanalysis and Daseinsanalysis]* (1957a); Roland Kuhn: 'Mordversuch eines depressiven Fetischisten und Sodomisten an einer Dirne [Attempted Murder of a Prostitute by a Depressive Fetishist and Sodomite]' (1948), 'Daseinsanalyse im psychotherapeutischen Gespräch [Daseinsanalysis in Psychotherapeutic Conversation]' (1951), 'Zur Daseinsanalyse der Anorexia nervosa [On the Daseinsanalysis of *anorexia mentalis*]' (1951, 1953) (Kahn gives the title as 'On the Daseinsanalysis of *anorexia nervosa*'), 'Zur Daseinsstruktur einer Neurose [On the Structure of Existence of a Neurosis]' (1954), and 'Der Mensch in der Zwiesprache des

Notes

Kranken mit seinem Artzte und das Problem der Übertragung [The Human Being in the Dialogue between a Patient and His Doctor and the Problem of Transference]' (1955).

34 Walter Kaufmann, *Existentialism from Dostoevsky to Sartre*, New York: Meridian Books, 1956 (2nd, expanded edition, 1975). Among the writers included in Kaufmann's anthology, Kierkegaard (1813-1855) holds pride of place as the first 'Existentialist'.

35 Heidegger's interest in psychiatry was stimulated by his contacts with both Binswanger and Boss. According to Herbert Spiegelberg, it is in the series of papers by Roland Kuhn (1940-1944) on the interpretation of masks in the Rorschach test that 'first references to Heidegger and Binswanger's *Daseinsanalyse*' occur. Herbert Spiegelberg, *Phenomenology in Psychology and Psychiatry*, Evanston: Northwestern University Press, 1972. 105.

36 'Appraisal of Existential Analysis', 207.

37 See *GA* 2, 16. Throughout his article, when Kahn quotes from the three authors whose work he is reviewing, he gives the original German in footnotes but does not specify the work of the author cited. In this case, Kahn also misquotes Heidegger in *Sein und Zeit* in the second sentence of the first passage referred to, and the translation is problematic. At this point in his 'appraisal' just what to do with the word '*Dasein*' becomes critical, but it is not adequately dealt with. Here is the text as it is found in *Sein und Zeit*: '*Das Dasein ist ein Seiendes, das nicht nur unter anderem Seienden vorkommt. Es ist vielmehr dadurch ontisch ausgezeichnet, daß es in seinem Sein zu seinem Sein um dieses Sein selbst geht.*' Heidegger uses the verb *vorkommen*, which means 'to happen' or 'to occur'. Rendering *vorkommt* with 'exists' here introduces unnecessary confusion, given that the words '*Dasein*' and '*Existenz*' are also translated with 'existence'. Also, Heidegger uses the verb *auszeichen* ('distinguish from'), not *kennzeichen* ('identify as' or 'be known as'), as Kahn has it. Finally, Kahn omits the word *ontisch* and does not preserve Heidegger's emphasis on the separable prefix *um-* in *umgehen* (used in the text with the prefix *um-* separated). A more accurate translation of the passage might be: '*Dasein* [left untranslated] is a being which does not merely occur among other beings. It is instead ontically better distinguished [from other beings] as a being that in its be[-ing] is concerned *about* [geht … um] this very be[-ing] itself.' The verb *umgehen* has been variously translated as 'to be an *issue* for' (*Being and Time*, Macquarrie/Robinson [trs.], New York: Harper and Row, 1962, 67) and, as in Kahn, 'being concerned *about*' (*Being and Time*, Stambaugh [tr.] Albany: SUNY Press, 1996, 97; rev. ed. Schmidt [tr.] Albany: SUNY Press, 2010, 101). Neither translation, however, does justice to Heidegger's usage in this critical passage. The construction *gehen um* is perhaps best rendered as 'go about', as in 'I go about my business'. Using the verb *umgehen* allows Heidegger to avoid the verb *sein* (to be), which would require him to say (in German) that *Dasein* 'is'. *Dasein* precisely *is* not; unlike every other being, it *exists*. It 'goes *about*' its be[-ing] (*Sein*). This is the point of Heidegger's fundamental ontology, to show that *Dasein* is remarkable in that it goes about its be[-ing] rather than being something determinate that repeats habits of behavior. It has to do with nothing other than its very be[-ing] itself. My translating *Sein* with be[-ing] may seem odd at first, but I think it is helpful. It avoids 'Being' (a rendering of *Sein*, the nominalized infinitive of the verb *sein*) which is then just a capitalized letter away from 'being', which has been the usual translation of *ein Seiendes* ('a being'), that is, an *instance* of *all that there is* or simply *what there is* (*das Seiende*) (*not* 'beings'). With 'be[-ing]' as the translation of *Sein* we can see that the noun is based on *sein* as a *transitive* verb comparable, say, to taking an infinitive such as *leben* ('to live') and nominalizing it to *Leben* (living) or *denken* ('to think'), nominalized as *Denken* (thinking). My construction 'be[-ing]' would be pronounced 'be' (/bē/) but written as given. We would then speak of the 'be[-ing]' [*Sein*] of what there is (*des Seiendes*). Recall that the verb '*sein*' was, in fact, '*seien*', the 'e' of the suffix denoting the formation of an infinitive, '-en', having dropped out in the development of German. Heidegger's later practice of writing *Seyn* was to distinguish the nominalized transitive verb *seyn* from *Sein*, which refers to the tradition of Western metaphysics in which *sein* is an intransitive verb. This challenging distinction is

not merely orthographic. '*Seyn*' denotes the possibility -- the *may be* -- of any givenness of *Sein* understood historically. In a later comment on *sein*, we will see that from the outset in *Being and Time*, the crucial term is the present participle *seiend*. See the epigraph to this work taken from the *Sophist* (*GA* 2, 2). The present participle [*Mittelwort*] of the verb *participates* in both the verb [*Zeitwort*] and the noun [*Hauptwort*], in this case *sein* and *Seiendes* in the expression 'Das Sein des Seiendes' (the *be*[ing] of what there is. The nominalization of the verb '*sein*' has hidden its uniqueness. Heidegger would argue that this is the legacy of metaphysics.

38 This sentence appears a few lines later in Heidegger's text. In *GA* 2, marginal notes to copies of the book are included. In *GA* 2, two words in the sentence are glossed (footnotes '^b' and '^c'): 'Das^b Sein selbst, zu dem^c das Dasein sich so oder so verhalten kann und immer irgendwie verhält, nennen wir '*Existenz*'.' For ^b: 'Dasjenige [that]'; for ^c: 'als seinem eigenen [as its own]'. Since Kahn will say that both quotations sound 'strange' and require clarification, it is also worth pausing to consider the sentence a bit further. Macquarrie/Robinson (*Being and Time* [1962], 32) translate: 'That kind of Being towards which Dasein can comport itself in one way or another, and always does comport itself somehow, we call '*existence*'.' Stambaugh/Schmidt (*Being and Time* [1996/2010, 10/11]) write: 'We shall call the very being to which Dasein can relate in one way or another, and somehow always does relate, *existence*.' Macquarrie/Robinson retain the word 'existence' in scare quotes (as Heidegger does), but Stambaugh/Schmidt do not. The word is italicized in the original, which all translations observe. Kahn does not observe either of these important details, however. With Heidegger's glosses in mind, the meaning of the sentence would seem to be: 'That being itself to which existence [as intrinsic to what is its own] can comport itself one way or another, and always does comport itself, we call '*a way of living*'.' Some may question my translation of *Existenz* here. It is justified, however, given just how puzzling the sentence is. As we have seen, '*Existenz*' can also be translated with 'existence', but in a crucial passage in *Sein und Zeit* that we have already visited ('*Das Wesen des Daseins liegt in seiner Existenz*') doing so leads to problems. There follows the possibility of translating the sentence as 'The essence of existence lies in its way of living.' In *Being and Time*, I would argue, *Existenz* is probably best understood as 'a way of living' or 'way of comportment', as the suggested translation reflects. The point of all this seeming linguistic nitpicking is in fact a matter of teasing out nuance to make clear that each actualization of *Dasein* is unique as a way of living, so that *Existenz* indicates an indeterminate number of actualizations of *Dasein*'s possibilities [*Daseiende*], each of which, as Heidegger says, has the character of mineness (*Jemeinigkeit*) – one of Heidegger's existentives in the analytics of *Dasein*. Kahn's discussion of forms of the verb *sein* does nothing to shine any light on its sense, however. The context of the passages quoted from *Sein und Zeit* is important and may help shed some light on what is under discussion here. The three sentences are from section §4 ('The *Ontic* Priority of the Question of Being') in which the terms '*Dasein*' and '*Existenz*' are first defined (hence the scare quotes around '*Existenz*'). Highlighted, Heidegger suggests that *Existenz* is of central importance in understanding the structure of *Dasein*. The etymology of *sei*, the root word of both *Sein* and *Seiende*, leads back to the proto-Indo-European *wesana*, from *h'wes* – to dwell, reside at, stay over, stay on. This in turn leads to etymological connections with the root for the English 'be', namely, '*bhū*' (or '*bhévô*'), and '*beon*', and their relation to the Greek , the root of the all-important Greek noun . It is easy to hear the close connection between '*bhū*' and . Moreover, each of the sciences (< *sciens* as a form of expertise or know-how) is a distinct sort of *Existenz* (mathematical or psychological, for example) and a concomitant style of orientation to and comportment toward the things of the world. Given his relation to *be*[-ing], only man does in fact *comport* himself to other beings. This is different than behaving as a reaction to stimuli. Another critical word in the sentence quoted is '*Seinsart*', which here means 'a mode of *be*[-ing]'. The word is rich in connotative meaning as a mode or way or fashion of

Notes

be[-ing] [*Sein*], where the 'of' is understood in both the subjective genitive and objective genitive senses. Each *Existenz*, then, is both *of* (emanating from) be[-ing] and *about* (directed towards) be[-ing]. As such, it is in each case of the essence of *Dasein* in its *Existenz*. It is not indifferent to things (as inorganic beings are) or merely instinctually reactive to things (as animals and perhaps plants are), nor is comportment God's way in our lives given his omnipotent influence on things. In the context of the sentence cited by Kahn, Heidegger introduces the key terms of his ontological analysis (*Dasein* and *Existenz*), but he does this from a given *ontic* perspective, that is, from the perspective of that of a particular living, breathing human being with a particular interest or comportment, a given *Existenz*. Then there is, finally, a bit more to say about the word *Sein* in the sentence cited by Kahn that we have been lingering on. Here Heidegger says that *Existenz* and *das Sein selbst* (be[-ing] itself) are somehow ontologically indistinguishable, inasmuch as *Sein* denotes that alone to which *Dasein* comports itself, whether as mathematician or biologist, psychiatrist or psychologist. In other words, the ontic comportment of *Dasein* differs but it is ontologically always in comportment toward be[-ing] in its varying *Existenz*. Essential to his argument is that 'scientific research is not the only and not the closest [*nächste*] possible *Seinsart* of this being (man). This distinction [*Auszeichnung*] has to be made visible for the first time. At this point, the discussion must [necessarily only] anticipate [*vorgreifen*] the following [discussions] and for the first time in fact revealing analyses' (*GA* 2, 16). Heidegger's concern will therefore turn next to explicating a mode of be[ing] human that is precisely not that of one of the sciences. Another, more intimate ('nearer') way or mode of comportment toward what there is to be revealed and that is the average everyday activity of the simple man or woman at work. At *this* point, however, it is only 'formally indicated'.

39 As we have seen, the expression 'human existence' for *Dasein* is redundant since, for Heidegger, only the human being exists. Heidegger does not have in mind the ordinary philosophical sense of *Dasein* (as found, for example, in Kant) as a predicate of a given entity, one that indicates that the entity is real, not imaginary. Further along in the paragraph of Kahn's 'appraisal' we are soon in a hopeless confusion of terms, with the word 'existence' standing in for both '*Dasein*' and '*Sein*'. It is not the case, as he says, that 'the sentence just quoted ... may be quite understandable now, although at first sight it may have looked odd.' What holds for the third sentence from *Being and Time* just discussed (see previous note) must be said about the 'clarifications' of '*sein*' and '*Seiend*', which does not make anything clearer. So, too, for a note to the word '*Dasein*' (208, n. 14), where Kahn writes: 'The German word *Dasein*, noun with capital 'D', is generally used in the German language to denote existence or life. Heidegger uses *Dasein* with the special meaning mentioned. So do his followers, although, at a closer view, not all of them really mean exactly what Heidegger does. Writers who are not existentially oriented usually take the word in its general meaning. The use of the word *Dasein* is no certification of existentialism.' Finally, to suggest 'existent' (having the quality of existing) for *das Seiende* conflates the distinction between what there is (*das Seiende*) and an instance of what there is (*ein Seiendes*). See the following note.

40 I will point out only a few more problems with Kahn's comments on the verb *sein* in relation to the notions of *Dasein* (existence) and *Existenz* (standing out into be[-ing] and existing as a way of life or comportment). The preceding notes have covered some of the same territory. I belabor the linguistic issues since for an English-speaking psychiatrist first reading about *Daseinssanalyse* Kahn's 'appraisal' was not at all helpful. There is, as we have seen, the noun *das Seiende*, with the definite article, which is a collective noun (like 'cattle') and means 'what there is'. It has often been translated as 'beings', but, as such, there is the sense of a countable, determinable plurality of entities (for example, how many cows there might be in a herd of cattle), which is not what Heidegger has in mind. There is also *ein Seiendes* (with the indefinite article), which denotes 'a being', an instance of all that there is (*das Seiende*). Such an instance might be a pebble, a tree, a horse, or God – or the human

being. Given these two usages of *Seiende* we can speak in an abstract, general sense of what there is (reality) (*das Seiende*) or an example or instance of what there is (*ein Seiendes*), respectively. Finally, further difficulties arise because the distinction between (1) *Dasein* as a predicate (ontic) and (2) Heidegger's usage of *Dasein* as a *terminus technicus* (ontological) is lost again and again in Kahn's discussion.

41 GA 2, 76.
42 GA 2, 487.
43 *Zollikon Seminars* (1987a), 8-35.
44 Kahn reviews two of Binswanger's books and five articles published between 1933 and 1951. These include Binswanger's *Über Ideenflucht* [*On the Flight of Ideas*] (1933), *Grundformen und Erkenntnis menschliches Daseins* [*Basic Forms and Cognition of Human Existence*] (1942), three case studies (Ellen West [1945], Jürg Zünd [1947] and Lola Voss [1949]), and two journal articles ('Symptom und Zeit [Symptom and Time]' [1951] and 'Daseinsanalytik und Psychiatrie [Analytics of Dasein and Psychiatry]' [1951]). Neither of Binswanger's major works has been translated. Two of the case histories have been translated: 'Lola Voss' (in Ludwig Binswanger, *Being-in-the World*, New York: Harper and Row, 1963, 266-341) and 'Ellen West' (in Rollo May, Ernest Angel and Henri F. Ellenberger [eds.], *Existence. A New Dimension in Psychiatry and Psychology*, New York: Simon and Schuster, 1958, 237-364).
45 'Appraisal of Existential Analysis', 212, n. 38 and 215, nn. 49-50.
46 'Appraisal of Existential Analysis', 216.
47 'Appraisal of Existential Analysis', 219.
48 'Appraisal of Existential Analysis', 417.
49 Kahn was evidently not familiar with the second, expanded edition of the book on perversions, which appeared in 1953. Nor does he advise the reader of the English translation of Boss's book, which had appeared in 1949. Boss's first book on dreaming was not translated into English until 1958 and the book on psychosomatic medicine has never appeared in an English version in either of its editions. Boss's first major book on daseinanalysis, *Psychoanalyse und Daseinsanalytik*, appeared the same year as Kahn's 'appraisal' and is discussed in its 'Postscript'.
50 A relation between *Leib* (the lived body) and *leiben* (to happen) is only orthographic since the words derive from different roots. The title of a collection of papers on psychosomatics co-edited by Boss with two colleagues, *Leiben und Leben* (1977f), is a colloquial expression that is exhortative as well as descriptive, ranging from meaning 'in the flesh' to 'As I live and breathe!' It is suggestive of living life to the fullest and being all that one can be, 'being who you are'. The resonances with "Warum eigentlich nicht?' and Augustine's *volo ut sis* resound.
51 'An Appraisal of Existential Analysis', 419.
52 'An Appraisal of Existential Analysis', 427.
53 Roland Kuhn, 'Daseinsananlyse eines Falles von Schizophrenie [Daseinsanalysis of a Case of Schizophrenia]', *Monatschrift für Psychiatrie und Neurologie* 112(5-6), 1946, 233-257.
54 Other papers by Kuhn left out of consideration include 'Daseinsanalyse im psychotherapeutischen Gespräch [Daseinsanalysis in Psychotherapeutic Conversation]', *Schweizer Archiv für Neurologie, Neurochirurgie und Psychiatrie* 67, 1951, 52-60; 'Daseinsanalytische Studie über die Bedeutung von Grenzen im Wahn [Daseinsanalytic Study of the Meaning of Boundaries in Delusion]', *Monatschrift für Psychiatrie und Neurologie* 124 (4-6), 1952, 354-383; and 'The Attempted Murder of a Prostitute', which appeared in Rollo May et al. [eds.], *Existence*, 365-425.
55 Kuhn's findings were published in English in 'The Treatment of Depressive States with G 22355 (imipramine hydrochloride)', *American Journal of Psychiatry* 115(5), 1958, 459-464. The paper was first read by Kuhn at Galesburg State Hospital near Chicago on May 19, 1958.
56 'An Appraisal of Existential Analysis', 428.
57 'An Appraisal of Existential Analysis', 431.
58 'An Appraisal of Existential Analysis', 431.

59 'An Appraisal of Existential Analysis', 434.
60 'An Appraisal of Existential Analysis', 436.
61 Kahn quotes *Einführung in die psychosomatische Medizin*, 212. The book is dedicated to Heidegger, 'dem unermüdlichen Lehrer und gütigen Freund in Dankbarkeit [with gratitude to a tireless teacher and kind friend].'
62 'An Appraisal of Existential Analysis', 437.
63 'Psychotherapeutic eros has to go even somewhat beyond Christian humility [*christliche Demut*] in its selflessness and overcoming of the self [*Selbstüberwindung*] insofar as it must not even intervene [*eingreifen*] in the interest of the therapist's *own* God and seek to guide the partner's life accordingly.' 'Anxiety, Guilt, and Psychotherapeutic Liberation' (1962c), 192. See also 'Examples of the Influence of Psychotherapy on the Religious Attitude of the Analysand' (1966b), where Boss suggests that as a result of daseinanalysis some patients found the harsher demands of their religious commitments had been eased. On psychotherapeutic eros, see the discussion devoted to it in Chapter 5.
64 'An Appraisal of Existential Analysis', 438.
65 'An Appraisal of Existential Analysis', 439.
66 'An Appraisal of Existential Analysis', 440.
67 Martin Heidegger, *Being and Time*, New York: Harper and Row, 1962, §§ 23-24 and *passim*.
68 It should be noted that in this 'Postscript' Kahn overlooked several papers published by Boss in 1956-1957: 'Daseinsanalytik und Psychotherapie. Über die Grenzen der Psychoanalyse [Analytics of Dasein and Psychotherapy. On the Limits of Psychoanalysis]', *Deutsche Universitätszeitung* 11(23-24), 1956, 17-19; 'Wirkungsweise und Indikation der Psychotherapie [The Mechanism of Action and Indication for Psychotherapy]', in *Schweizerische medizinische Wochenschrift* 87(6), 1957, 128-133; and the 'Zusammenfassung und Schlußwort zum internationalen Symposium über die Psychotherapie der Schizophrenie [Summary and closing remarks at the international symposium on the psychotherapy of schizophrenia]', in *Acta psychotherapeutica et Psychosomatica et Orthopaedagogica* 5(2-4), 1957, 352-359.
69 'An Appraisal of Existential Analysis', 442.
70 'An Appraisal of Existential Analysis', 442. See *Psychoanalyse und Daseinsanalytik*, 56, and 'Der Einklang von psychoanalytishcer Praxis und daseinsanalytischem Menschenverständnis [The Harmony of Psychoanalytic Practice and the Daseinsanalytic Understanding of Man]', 75-87 (Chapter 6 of the German original). See the English translation of the chapter in *Psychoanalysis and Daseinsanalysis*, 61-74.
71 'An Appraisal of Existential Analysis', 442-443.
72 'An Appraisal of Existential Analysis', 443.
73 Other works published by Kuhn were overlooked by Kahn. See his 'Ludwig Binswanger', *Bodensee Zeitschrift* 5(6), 1956, 81-83; Über die Ausbildung zum Spezialart für Psychiatrie [*On Training as a Specialist in Psychiatry*], Zurich: Orell Füssli, 1956; *Ludwig Binswanger*, Amriswil: Bodensee Verlag, 1956; Über psychiatrische Hygiene [*On Psychiatric Hygiene*], Münsterlingen: Thurgauischer Hilfverein für Gemütskranke, 1956; 'Beitrag zum Problem der Lärmempfindlichkeit [Contribution to the Problem of Noise Sensitivity]', *Zeitschrift für Präventivmedizin* 2(1-2), 1957, 300-302; 'Griesinger's Auffassung der psychischen Krankheiten und seine Bedeutung für die weitere Entwicklung der Psychiatrie [Griesinger's Conception of Mental Illness and Its Significance for the Further Development of Psychiatry]', in Alfred Glaus (ed.), *Beiträge zur Geschichte der Psychiatrie und Hirnanatomie* [*Contributions of the History of Psychiatry and Brain Anatomy*], Basel: Karger, 1957, 41-67; 'The Treatment of Depressive States with an iminodibenzyl derivative ('Tofranil')', *Schweizerische Medizinische Wochenschrift* 87(35-36), 1957, 1135-1140; 'Zum Problem der ganzheitlichen Betrachtung in der Medizin [On the Problem of the Holistic View in Medicine]', *Schweizerische medizinische Jahrbuch*, Basel: Schwabe, 1957, 53-63. That same year other publications of Binswanger appeared to which Kahn did not have access: *Der*

Notes

Mensch in der Psychiatrie [*The Human Being in Psychiatry*], Pfullingen: Neske, 1957, and *Schizophrenie*, Pfullingen: Neske, 1957. There was also Binswanger's history of Bellevue, his family's hospital on Lake Constance (Bodensee), *Zur Geschichte der Heilanstadt Bellevue in Kreuzlingen 1857-1957* [*On the History of the Bellevue Sanatorium in Kreuzlingen 1857-1957*], Kreuzlingen: Bodan, 1957.

74 *Psychiatric Quarterly* 24(2), 1950, 417. The reviewer, who is not identified, quotes generously from Oskar Diethelm's introduction to the book (vii-viii). Diethelm identifies Boss as 'a leader in the Swiss psychoanalytic group' who 'found in the *Daseinsanalyse* of Martin Heidegger certain philosophically-adequate concepts for some of the limitations of psychoanalytic theories' which led to the formulation of 'a broad concept of personality with equal attention to subjective experiencing and manifestations that can be demonstrated objectively…. *Daseinsanalyse* is based on the assumption that one must try to understand a person's being; i.e. experiencing in the here and now as well as in the past.' The reviewer 'believes that there will be others like himself who will wonder just what these daseinsanalytic conceptions really are.' Quoting Boss in his 'Preface', that 'the German *Daseinsanalyse* translates readily to *existential analysis*' (x), he concludes that 'after reading the book, your reviewer found himself in a confused daseinsanalytic state.' The reader will find the most helpful comments on the topic of the distinction between *Daseinsanalytik* (analytics of existence) and *Daseinsanalyse* (analysis of existence) in Herbert Spiegelberg, *Phenomenology in Psychology and Psychiatry*, Evanston: Northwestern University Press, 1972, in his article 'Medard Boss: Phenomenological *Daseinsanalytik*' (333-342): 'The term *Daseinsanalytik*, in contrast to *Daseinsanalyse* (*Daseinsanalysis*), as used in the English version of Boss's basic work of 1957, indicates some of the difficulties in interpreting this new type of existential analysis. The word *Analytik* forms part of the German title, where it makes clear the difference between Boss's complete allegiance to Heidegger's existential analytics in *Being and Time* and Binswanger's *Daseinsanalyse*, which is based on a much freer understanding of the early Heidegger, if not a misunderstanding, however productive, of his intentions. The exclusive use of *Daseinsanalysis* for both is apt to conceal the difference between the two phenomenologies of *Dasein*. The price of leaving the title [of the chapter on Boss] even more Germanic than in Boss's book title seems to me worth paying here' (333). Spiegelberg is misleading only in identifying Daseinsanalysis as a species of 'existential analysis'. However, he may be credited with having drawn attention in print to the Zollikon Seminars (1987a), perhaps for the first time, when he cited Boss's 'Letter to a Friend', published in 1969 on the occasion of Heidegger's eightieth birthday in the *Neue Zürcher Zeitung* (October 5, 1969, 5). The letter was later published as Boss's 'Afterword' to the volume, *Zollikon Seminars* (1987a), 293-297. See also Spiegelberg's chapter on Ludwig Binswanger, 'Phenomenological Anthropology (*Daseinsanalyse*)' (193-232): 'The most appropriate title for [Binswanger's] contribution is still the *untranslatable* [emphasis added] term *Daseinsanalyse*, which according to Roland Kuhn was first suggested by Jakob Wyrsch but was adopted by Binswanger himself in the forties. Binswanger was thinking of the phrase 'phenomenological anthropology', and in the present context that may be preferable as a less mystifying label for his enterprise' (193-194). Spiegelberg accurately reflects Binswanger's intention, which was to derive an anthropology (in the Kantian sense) from Heidegger's *Daseinsanalytik* found in *Sein und Zeit*. In a note to the word 'untranslatable' for '*Daseinsanalyse*' Spiegelberg adds: 'I call it untranslatable because it is too closely connected with Heidegger's conception of human existence to be safely rendered by the vague term "existential analysis".' Later, writing on Binswanger's 'Heideggerian Phase', Spiegelberg notes: 'For Binswanger, Heidegger had simply added another dimension to Husserl's phenomenology as the basis for what he was to call *Daseinsanalyse*. Binswanger himself admitted later that his interpretation and utilization of Heidegger's enterprise for a new *anthropology* [emphasis added] was based on a misunderstanding but, in fact, a 'productive' misunderstanding, as Hans Kunz (1924-1982)

Notes

had called it before, of Heidegger's *Daseinsanalytik*, the attempt to use the ontological structure of human existence as the privileged access to an interpretation of the meaning of Being as such' (204). With his usual incisiveness, Spiegelberg makes clear that 'what Binswanger took out of *Being and Time* were mostly motifs from the first section, the preparatory analysis of everyday existence.... Only comparatively little of the 'fundamental analysis' of *Dasein* in Heidegger's second section seems to have permeated Binswanger's creative interpretation....' (205). According to Spiegelberg, who had access to Binswanger's private papers thanks to the latter's son, Wolfgang, Binswanger and Heidegger, who had both attended the gymnasium in Constance, met several times, in Freiburg, Constance, Kreuzlingen and, on October 30, 1965, in Amriswil, where Heidegger gave a talk on the occasion of Binswanger's eighty-fifth birthday. The lecture was eventually published as 'Zur Frage nach der Bestimmung der Sache des Denkens [On the Question of the Determination of the Matter of Thinking]'. See *GA* 16, 620-633. As we will see, it is an extremely important paper in revealing a major change in Heidegger's understanding of *Dasein* and the *Lichtung* of *Sein*. Binswanger's son showed Spiegelberg a packet of thirty-five letters between Binswanger and Heidegger which Spiegelberg characterizes as 'fascinating pieces' (205). On questions of the translation of the term '*Dasein*', Spiegelberg is, once again, more helpful than nearly anyone writing on Heidegger and daseinanalysis at the time or since: 'The difficulties of rendering the German *Dasein* satisfactorily are so well known that they need not be restated here. The crux of the matter is that Heidegger has loaded the harmless German word *Dasein*, and especially the element of '*Da*' (there), which is neither here (*hier*) nor there (*dort*), with so many new connotations that *not only a literal rendering but also a complete substitution is apt to break down* [emphasis added] under this load. An artificial word like 'there-being', coined by William J. Richardson [which Richardson capitalized as 'There-being'], at least gives warning of this difficulty. 'Existence', especially in quotes, might do properly interpreted, but the use of the untranslated German *Dasein* is still the safest way to give notice to the new connotations' (220). Finally, there are Spiegelberg's specific comments on the difference between the *Daseinanalytik* of Heidegger's *Being and Time* and the form of *therapy* known as *Daseinsanalyse*. Here we find the essential distinction on the basis of which we may understand the shift from Binswanger's psychiatric *Daseinsanalyse* to Boss' therapeutic daseinanalysis: 'Thus [for Binswanger] the science of man as mentally sick presupposes *Daseinsanalytik* just as pathology presupposes general biology, *Daseinsanalytik* being understood as insight into the a priori structure or *Seinsverfassung* [constitution of being] of human being in general. On this ground floor rests *Dasaeinsanalyse* as the empirical-phenomenological investigation of definite modes or *Gestalten* of *Dasein*. Therapy forms a second story above pathology' (229-230). Binswanger's understanding of Heidegger's contribution is that of the medical doctor, for whom tissue pathology and the functioning of the organism is based on knowledge of anatomy and physiology. To the latter (which he terms 'biology'), Spiegelberg says, corresponds Heidegger's structure of *Dasein* which he describes as the 'investigation of definite modes or *Gestalten* [forms] of *Dasein*'. Here Spiegelberg articulates exactly the problem with Binswanger's recourse to Heidegger to provide an anthropological norm as it were with respect to which the psychopathologist (psychiatrist) judges the mental wellness or illness of a patient. Of course, Heidegger's *Daseinsanalytik* is not descriptive of an ontic norm but rather of the ontological structure of *Dasein*. On Spiegelberg's reading, what Binswanger terms 'modes or *Gestalten* of *Dasein*' are rather the mutually equiprimordial *Existenziale* (existentives or existentials) of *Dasein: Sorge* [caring about things], *Fürsorge* [caring about the other], *Verstehen* [understanding], *Verfallenheit* [distraction], *Geworfenheit* [givenness], *Angst* [anxiety], *Rede* [talk], and the rest. Binswanger took the existentives as a fixed ensemble of modes or forms of the ontic actualization of *Dasein* and assembled a philosophical anthropology from them. But there is no implicit anthropology in *Being and Time*. Thus, that 'Binswanger modified Heidegger's implicit anthropology significantly... and applied his *Daseinsanalyse*' to the study of patients reflects a basic misunderstanding. Spiegelberg concludes his chapter on Binswanger, saying that '*Daseinsanalyse* would have been impossible without phenomenological philosophy. But its validity does not depend on it' (230). Here he is reflecting on his own principal interest, which is the place of phenomenology in psychology and psychiatry as it unfolded after Husserl. For our purposes, the point is that in the end Binswanger's psychiatric *Daseinsanalyse* was not about the therapeutic possibilities arising from an understanding of Heidegger's *Daseinsanalytik* but rather only about a way of understanding a given individual's *behavior* and *experience* on the basis of an ontic reading of Heidegger's *Daseinsanalytik*. Here he proceeds as a doctor should. The question of the therapeutic value of Heidegger's *Daseinsanalytik*, however, would be the concern of Boss's therapeutic *Daseinsanalyse*.

75 *Psychiatric Quarterly* 31(1-4), 570. The reviewer, who is not identified, provides a parenthetic translation of *Psychoanalyse und Daseinsanalytik* as 'Psychoanalysis and Existential Analytics', which is correct. He writes that 'after a brief review of Freud's and Jung's theories and those of their students and followers, Prof. Boss devotes the rest of his discussion to Martin Heidegger's theories and their application to psychoanalysis'. The reviewer suggests that Heidegger is 'merely an extension and development of [the] earlier works [of Freud and Jung]', that 'the Existential analytic technique is... far more scientific than that of its predecessors, and thereby permits a better insight into the mental make-up of the human being', and that, for Boss, the technique 'is one of the best tools that the analyst can use in his work. In German-speaking circles, where Heidegger is better known as a philosopher than a psychologist, this book should make for a new evaluation of his work.' The reviewer thus labels Heidegger a psychologist. Nothing could be farther from the truth, of course, since Heidegger's work, from *Sein und Zeit* to the *Zollikon Seminars*, was in critical contrast to psychology. Nor does Boss present a 'technique' in his book. As we will see, the English book *Psychoanalysis and Daseinsanalysis* is not really a translation of *Psychoanalyse und Daseinsanalytik*. Here a few examples of how the books differ may be in order. The chapter 'Abriß der Daseinsanalytik [Outline of the Analytics of *Dasein*]' is Chapter 5 of the German. This becomes Chapter 2, 'Outline of Analysis of *Dasein*', in the English. Only in the English version, however, do we read at the beginning of Chapter 3, 'The Most Common Misunderstandings about Analysis of *Dasein*', that 'a summary of a philosopher's life work amounts at best to an incomplete sketch of his understanding of man and mankind. If we have successfully traced the way of thinking of analysis of *Dasein* (albeit modestly), much must be owed to Martin Heidegger's untiring personal help in compiling the foregoing summary' (49). We therefore reasonably conclude that sometime in the mid-1950s Heidegger went over the manuscript of the original German text of what became the 'Outline' chapter. On the other hand, he may not have seen it until the years between 1957 and 1963 when Boss was preparing the English version. These questions will be answered only when we have access to the complete correspondence between the two men. What we have in print of Heidegger's letters to Boss (*SZ* 297-362/237-291) is heavily redacted. There is no mention in them of Heidegger working on such an 'outline' with Boss.

76 *Psychiatric Quarterly* 34(3), 1960, 495-504. Citing an unpublished paper by Boss given in French in September 1958 at an International Congress of Psychotherapy in Barcelona ('La psychoanalyse de Freud et l'analyse existentielle de Heidegger'), Boss is reported to have quoted Heidegger on '*l'homme clairière de l'existence* [man the clearing of existence]'. Thomas Hora's article is still well worth reading since it recounts basic principles of daseinanalysis as Boss viewed and practiced it. Hora, who was psychiatrist and psychoanalyst, writes: 'To think in terms of 'techniques' of psychotherapy, or of 'doing' psychotherapy is... a mistake.... Man is not a 'case', and psychotherapy cannot be 'done'.... [To think this way] is based on lack of understanding of existence as an event. The idea of 'managing' or of the 'handling of' cases in psychotherapy represents an objectification which

violates the essence of man as an existential phenomenon.... The psychotherapeutic process is a segment of life. Life is an event. Life is happening to man. *Existence is reflected in man somewhat in the way light becomes visible while passing through a translucent medium* [emphasis added]. Medard Boss in quoting Heidegger speaks of '*l'homme clairière de l'existence* [man the clearing of existence]'. Man experiences existence. He does not cause it to be.... Psychotherapy, like life itself, is an event in time. Therefore, one can only talk about a process of psychotherapy, or the *way of psychotherapy*, as the Taoist sages spoke of the 'Way or Tao of Life' (495-496). Hora's intuition about the nearness of daseinanalysis to this Eastern tradition was keenly on target.

77 *Psychiatric Quarterly* 41(1), 1965, 173-174. Once again, the reviewer is not identified. It is an interesting piece in making the observation for psychiatrists that 'as phenomenologic[al] psychiatry superseded analytic methods, the older, speculative type of practitioner has been forced to the wall by his ignorance not only of behaviorism but more especially physics, and particularly biochemistry. There has been a rush to patch up antiquated training by the frantic study of drug house releases, the memorization of a few popular, chemical formulae, and the ordering of laboratory tests. Such an approach bespeaks the mentality of a technician. The modern phenomenologic[al] approach to psychiatry was predictable because of the inadequacy of its theoretical precedent. It was logically inevitable. Just as past events in psychiatry were predictable philosophically, the alternative to the development of the technician's mentality can also be anticipated – if one is adequately informed, philosophically speaking.' One wishes that many psychiatrists had paid closer attention to this unknown reviewer's observation that Heidegger's 'phenomenologic[al] approach' provides an antidote to the trends in psychiatry that at the time were leading to the hegemony of psychopharmacology, mediated by 'the mentality of the technician'. The readers of this review were told that '*Dasein* may be translated as 'the being which is man'.

78 *American Journal of Psychiatry* 137(8), 1980, 1001-1003 (reviewed by Leston L. Havens). Originally published in 1971, the English translation is based on the second edition (1973) of the book. (Details on the volume and most of Boss's publications are surveyed in Part III of the present volume.) Havens' review is fairly extensive and notable for several observations. 'Every disorder, from a broken leg to schizophrenia [that a doctor encounters] is described from the existential viewpoint in its impact on human freedom, by which is meant one's ability to relate fully to the world or, in Boss's language, to have access to the modes of being in the world.... Descriptions of pathology are descriptions of impingements on these modes, and the therapist's responsibility, whether as surgeon or psychiatrist, is to place himself or herself with the patient in the task of restoring human freedom' (1002). This accurately reflects the perspective of therapeutic daseinanalysis. 'The first goal of the existential healer is to see the world from the patient's point of view' (1002). This is the goal claimed by many existential analysts but, as all therapists know, though it is a much desired goal, it is in principle not possible. One can never know the experience of another, including his or her perspective on the world. Havens' comment about the efficacy of existential analysis by comparison with the two other forces in psychology, psychoanalysis and behaviorism, loses its force by in effect mistaking Boss's daseinanalytic approach for one of the humanistic (so-called 'third force') modes: 'Psychoanalytic and behaviorist treatments may be effective, but Boss implies this is because both provide the brittle patient with an ally against uncertainty. The existential claim, which I have seen sustained enough not to dismiss it, is that the same result can be achieved more fully and directly by allying with the patient in his world view and then helping him gradually to modify it' (1002). The reviewer's reading of Boss leads him to offer that 'the existential view is curiously like the medical view. Both see the patient as impinged upon: in the medical view, by bacteria, viruses, cancers; in the existential view, by these and, as well, other people, social systems, etc.' (1002). Havens' criticism of the 'tone' of Boss's book is difficult to

accept. He writes: 'The tone of the book is polemical, at times cranky, and repetitious.... Boss's presentation of existential work suffers from the same tone. He does not speak well of even the existentialists. Indeed, he cannot speak of many at all. (The American reader will miss any reference to May, Fromm, Rogers, or Kohut.) Most readers, I suspect, will deplore the 'only I know' attitude so epidemic on the present sectarian scene' (1002). Placing Boss within the 'existentialist' tradition, Havens claims that 'existential writings often have a flat, broad quality, for all their occasional rising to poetry and philosophy, that does fit the uneven terrain of actual clinical work. I write this appreciating that Boss's own clinical work probably does not imitate his conceptualizations. It is very hard to write accurately of clinical work' (1003). Havens is on target in saying that one does not and cannot get a sense of how a therapist works by reading his accounts of technique or case studies. This can be accomplished only by seeing him at work first-hand. That Boss's prose 'rises to poetry and philosophy' is not a limitation but likely gives us a sense of how he expressed himself when he worked with analysands. There is rare footage of Boss in a daseinanalytic session with a young medical student. See (1988d).

79 Hendrik Ruitenbeek (ed.), *Psychoanalysis and Existential Philosophy*, New York: Dutton, 1962, 188-253.

80 It is worth repeating that, with a few exceptions, from its beginnings in the States, psychoanalysis was practiced only by psychiatrists. The few who were not such as Theodore Reik and Erik Erikson had emigrated to the States from Europe. As 'lay' psychoanalysts became more common, however, meetings of medically- and non-medically-trained individuals who worked as daseinanalysts became more common. Their shared allegiance to daseinanalysis was perhaps more faithful than that of their psychoanalyst colleagues, medical and lay, to each other. It was not until 2021 that the first daseinanalytic institute (ADI) opened in the States, founded by the author and Tamás Fazekas, a Viennese pediatrician and daseinanalyst. It is unique in having been co-founded by a lay psychoanalyst turned daseinanalyst and a daseinanalyst who also practices medicine, albeit not psychiatry.

81 For a period of time, the *Review* was associated with Division 24 of the American Psychological Association (now the Society for Theoretical and Philosophical Psychology, founded in 1962), which has independently published the *Journal of Theoretical and Philosophical Psychology* since 1993. Several other journals were published for brief periods of time directed to psychiatrists interested in 'existential analysis': *Existential Inquiries* (1959-1960, Rollo May, ed.), *Journal of Existential Psychiatry* (1960-1964, Jordan Sher, ed.; the journal of the American Orthoanalytic Association), and *Existential Psychiatry*, also known as the *Journal of Existentialism* (1964-1968). *Existential Inquiries* was superseded by the *Review of Existential Psychology and Psychiatry* (1961-2003).

82 Rollo May, Ernest Angel and Henri F. Ellenberger (eds.), *Existence. A New Dimension in Psychiatry and Psychology*, New York: Simon and Schuster, 1958.

83 *Existence*, vii.

84 *Existence*, 4, 41, 119, 269.

85 *Existence*, 4.

86 In 1951, Boss published a paper on the psychiatric use of a hypnotic Scopolamine (Plexonal) at a time when the first of the new so-called psychotropics were being used. See 'Erfahrungen mit dem neuen Schlafmittel 'Plexonal' (Sandoz) [Experiences with the Hypnotic Plexonal (Sandoz)]' (1951c). He also contributed articles to Geigy Pharmaceutical's journal *Hexagon* ((1973c), (1974), (1980b)). That said, Boss was certain that chemical substances could not be psychotropic ('mind-changing') 'agents', since having abandoned the notion of the psyche clearly there was nothing to change. Moreover, inert chemical compounds cannot *act* on the existing human being.

87 It is misleading to refer to Medard Boss's therapeutic daseinanalysis as 'daseinsanalytic psychotherapy', as we find in the Wiley *Handbook of Existential Therapy*, New York: John

Wiley, 2019, 43 ff. Similarly, references to psychopathology remain grounded on the medical model, which Boss abandoned. While Boss used the word 'psychotherapy' in his lectures and papers until the end, in those same texts he explained that daseinanalysis rejected the notion of the psyche. His Grundriß (ground plan or layout) for a new approach to medicine and psychology was intended to base them on the analytics of *Dasein* rather than the natural science model of the *animal rationale*. Just as, for Freud, psychoanalysis was really not the province of medicine, for Boss, daseinanalysis was not a form of psychiatric practice. It was not subsumed by the science of clinical psychology. The inherent *contradiction* of being a physician and a daseinanalyst was never fully expressed by Boss, but I am convinced that, as his letter to Kayande (1975e) made very clear, when he listened to analysands, he was not attending to them as a physician. Given the lingering ambiguities just outlined, it is not at all surprising to read in the Wiley *Handbook* that there is a 'lack of consensus about what daseinsanalytic psychotherapy is, its purposes and aims, how it proceeds' (72). On the other hand, it is very plain from what he wrote just what daseinanalysis was for Medard Boss and what it is for daseinanalysts practicing today. That there are 'three contemporary approaches to daseinsanalytic practice' which 'differ considerably' from each other (72-80) contests the view that there is only one therapeutic daseinanalysis deveoped by Boss. 'Hermeneutic daseinsanalysis', 'humanistic, relational daseinsanalysis' and 'short-term daseinsanalytic therapy' belong among the existential therapies, but they are not orthodox therapeutic daseinanalysis as represented and discussed here. The 'hermeneutic daseinsanalysis' of Holzhey-Kunz (traced back to the 'early Heidegger', Kierkegaard and Sartre [73]) and Perikles Kastrinidis's 'short-term daseinsanalytic therapy' (traced back to the psychiatrist Habib Davanloo's 'intensive short-term dynamic psychotherapy' [ISTDP] [77]) were evidently created in reaction to what was perceived as an insufficient sensitivity by Boss to the psychiatric patient's psychic 'suffering'. In both as in psychoanalysis hidden meanings are to be disclosed by interpretations. Erik Craig's 'humanistic, relational daseinsanalysis' is derived from the 'relationship therapy' of Clark Moustakas and the work of the 'existential psychoanalyst', Paul Stern, and influenced by attachment theory and Eastern religious practices (75-77). All three 'approaches to daseinsanalytic psychotherapy' make generous reference to the Heidegger of *Being and Time* (1927). While Holzhey-Kunz and Kastrinidis draw on the 'early Heidegger', Craig admits to having been influenced more by the 'later Heidegger', which followed what has been termed a turning-back [*Kehre*] of his thinking about the relation of being [*Sein*] and being there [*Da-sein*] originally essayed in the fundamental ontology of *Being and Time*. The famous *Kehre* is documented by Heidegger's essay (1949) of the same name. See *GA 79*, 68-77.

88 *Zollikon Seminars* (1987a), 216. See also Boss's definitive comments on the unintelligibility of the psyche in *Existential Foundations of Medicine and Psychology* (1971a): 'It is necessary to explode the traditional notions of an encapsulated psyche with its enclosed field of consciousness to understand human being-in-the-world, and it should be clear by now that to do so is a main goal of this existential foundation of medicine' (135); 'Human behavior cannot be comprehended in terms of a boxlike psyche nor as a similarly constituted ego, consciousness, subjectivity, or person. Where, in human behavior, may we find even a trace of the actual presence of such a psychic capsule? And we have yet to see a demonstration of the actual existence of intrapsychic mental representations of reality or of quantitatively measurable drives. The conception of human experience as a series of physiochemical reactions that relay impressions from the sense organs to that mysterious psychic capsule is such a misconstruction that, if it were so, we would be a miserable species with no inkling that there is an outside world. To know and comprehend the outside world the person, who is not a passive receptacle, must literally grasp it and he can do this only by extending into that world in whose immediate vicinity he already is.' (225); 'We have shown there is no evidence for the actual presence in people of the kind of internality represented in the container concepts of ego, consciousness, psyche, subject, or person. Instead, human beings are inherently engaged in relatedness to whatever

phenomena address them from their locations in the human world and exist as these perceiving and responding relationships' (271).
89 *Zollikon Seminars* (1987a), 4.
90 *Zollikon Seminars* (1987a), 201.
91 'Das Leib-Seele-Problem im Lichte der Daseinsanalyse' (1976e), 57. Reprinted as 'Das Verhältnis von Leib und Seele im Lichte der Daseinsanalytik', in M. Boss, G. Condrau, G. and A. Hicklin (eds), *Leiben und Leben. Beiträge zur Psychosomatik und Psychotherapie* (Bern: Benteli, 1977), pp. 37-70, the text is evidently based on a lecture given in Japan in the Fall of 1974, since at one point Boss refers to Koichi Tsujimura.
92 *Zollikon Seminars* (1987a), 297. The expression appeared in Boss's open 'letter to a friend' published in a Swiss newspaper on October 5, 1969, which is now the 'Afterword' of the *Zollikon Seminars*. See (1969).
93 *Zollikon Seminars* (1987a), 198. In American psychiatry, the term has officially disappeared, but for different reasons *Psychosomatics. The Journal of the Academy of Psychosomatic Medicine* ended its twenty-seven-year career in 1987, renamed *The Journal of Consultation-Liaison Psychiatry*. In October 2017, the American Board of Psychiatry and Neurology voted to eliminate the subspecialty psychosomatic medicine, to be replaced by the subspecialty consultative-liaison psychiatry, effective 2018.
94 The theme of the Fourth Congress, held in Barcelona, in 1958, on 'Daseinsanalysis and Psychotherapy', featured a paper by Medard Boss which has not been published, 'La psychoanalyse de Freud et l'analyse existentielle de Heidegger [Freud's Psychoanalysis and Heidegger's Daseinsanalysis]'. Boss had hosted the previous congress in Zurich, in 1954, on 'Transference in Psychotherapy'. The professionalization of psychotherapy is dealt with in an excellent monograph by Gerhard Heim, published as a supplement to the journal *Psychotherapy and Psychosomatics* 79, 2010, 1-90.
95 The Foundation eventually came to be known as the Blanton-Peale Institute and Counseling Center and continues to provide outpatient psychoanalytically oriented psychotherapy. As a state-accredited mental health care provider, it accepts most insurance and, in 2022, charged $90.00 out-of-pocket for an hour of counseling for individuals without insurance. Elsewhere in New York, the few remaining psychiatrists who have trained as psychoanalysts may charge as much as $350.00 for a 45-minute hour, which is usually billed to private insurance.
96 Together they published books such as *Faith Is the Answer* [1940] (rev. ed.), New York: Prentice-Hall, 1950, and *The Art of Real Happiness*, New York: Prentice-Hall, 1950. Peale's book *The Power of Positive Thinking*, New York: Prentice-Hall, 1952, was an American national best seller and has been in print for seventy years. Resonating with Freud's early interest in hypnosis, Peale's practices have been compared to self-hypnosis.
97 In some countries, psychotropic medications may be prescribed only by psychiatrists. In the States, these drugs are generously offered by primary care physicians.
98 As noted earlier, in a prefatory remark to the publication of 'Mensch and Technik in der heutigen Medizin' (1952a), however, the editors of the *Schweizerische medizine Wochenschrift* tell us that Boss had written to them that 'perhaps it would be possible editorially to add that during the years 1932-33 I was in training at the Berlin Psychoanalytic Institute and there I did supervised analytic with Karen Horney. From her I received my first impulses which led me to overcome mechanistic thinking and to replace it with a holistic view which since has developed into my *daseins*-analytic concept.'
99 *GA* 64, 118.
100 Eugène Minkowski (1885-1972), *Lived Time* [1933], Evanston: Northwestern University Press, 1970.
101 The history of the units of time and time pieces is fascinating. The earliest clocks from the twelfth century did not mark the second, but only longer units, even though the second as a unit had been identified at the turn of eleventh century as calculated with reference to

Notes

the lunar cycle. Highly sophisticated mechanical devices now calculate chronometrically in terms of milliseconds and nanoseconds imperceptible to the human senses.

102 I prefer the term 'existentive' to 'existential' in order to avoid confusion with other usages of the word 'existential'.
103 See *Sein und Zeit*, GA 2, 73.
104 German reserves the word *Körper* for the body considered as an organism or animate physical entity. Like a cat, for example, the human being has a *Körper* but, as *Dasein*, it *exists* as its *Leib* (lived body).
105 GA 12, 10 ff. Cf. *GA 9*, 72.
106 See 'Das Phänomen des Widerstandes in der Daseinsanalyse', a paper co-authored with Alice Holzhey-Kunz. (1981c).
107 *Zollikon Seminars*, 4.
108 GA 2, 163.
109 'An Encounter with Medard Boss' (1988b), 33.
110 *A Psychiatrist Discovers India* (1959a), 191. Kaul told Boss that psychotherapy and psychoanalysis – and what would become daseinanalysis – were only 'preliminary treatments', saying: 'The outward realities of your work will hardly change. For the best thing you can do as a conscientious doctor is quietly to assimilate your Indian experiences. If these have sunk in deeply enough, everything else will follow of itself.' This seems to be just what happened.
111 Charlotte Aigner, 'Vom 'psychotherapeutischen Eros'. Die Existenzialien des Mitseins und der Sorge in besonderer Hinsicht auf die abstinente Haltung in der daseinsanalytischn Psychotherapie [Of 'Psychotherapeutic Eros'. The Existentials of Being-with and Caring about Things in Particular with Regard to the Abstinent Attitude in Daseinsanalytic Psychotherapy]', *Daseinsanalyse* 37, 89-109. Lecture, June 5, 2020, Philosophical Institute of the University of Vienna.
112 Theodore Reik, *Listening with the Third Ear* [1952], New York: Farrar, Straus and Giroux, 1983.
113 René Spitz's famous demonstration of the infant's response to the basic elements of the *Gestalt* of the human face drawn on a piece of cardboard and worn as a mask, with an accompanying movement of the head up and down as eliciting a smile, comes to mind. See *The First Year of Life*, New York: International Universities Press, 1965. In cases of undifferentiated senile dementia, the smile sometimes restores the security of the mother-infant relation with individuals who have lost the ability to communicate verbally. I recall meeting a woman I had known since childhood who no longer recognized her own daughter. She was brought in in a wheelchair and, placed facing each other, I reached for both of her hands, looked her 'straight in the eye', and smiled broadly. She smiled back and there we sat for a good twenty minutes. No words were exchanged. This combination of touch, gaze and smile mediated the *Dasein* to *Dasein* relation I have tried to describe in these pages.
114 A note on note-taking is in order here, since it has often been pointed out that the placement of the analyst out of sight of the analysand allows for the analyst to record thoughts on paper without annoying the analysand. In our time, note-taking is often done by psychotherapists meeting *vis-á-vis* using a laptop. This practice is discouraged in daseinanalysis even when out of sight of the analysand. After having completed my 'training' as a psychoanalyst, which required keeping detailed process notes, and having prepared to practice as a daseinanalyst, I stopped taking notes entirely during a session other than jotting down a telephone number, the spelling of a name or, in recent years, an email address. Note-taking is a distraction from listening. Written accounts of reports of past experiences by the analysand, observations about his behavior, and any associations one might have as an analyst to what is said might be of interest for *later* reflection, but they are superfluous to the therapeutic endeavor and interrupt steady, 'evenly suspended' listening. Taking notes draws the analyst's attention away from the present-making of the analysand with which the analyst endeavors to be in harmony to the greatest extent possible.

Notes

115 There will always be unanticipated situations in which the *responsibility* for the therapeutic setting and encounter requires the analyst to intervene. After all, the analyst is hosting the analysand for a span of clock time in a physical space for which he pays and has oversight. Such interventions are qualitatively different, however, from interventions such as changing the topic, offering interpretations about the causes of current behavior, and giving advice.

116 'Gewähren und Versagen in der Psychotherapie' (1982f), 108. The Swiss genetic epistemologist, Jean Piaget (1896-1980), identified stages of cognitive development, the last of which he termed formal operational thinking, or the capacity to think about thoughts (metacognition) which he believed every human being reached. The stage is said to begin around age eleven and has usually been completed by age sixteen. Piaget eventually concluded, however, that in some individuals it is never attained. This would be the sort of individual referred to here. Jean Piaget and Bärbel Inhelder, *The Psychology of the Child* [1966], New York: Basic Books, 1969, 130-160.

117 'Das Konzept des Widerstandes in der Daseinsanalyse' (1981c), 115-116. The essay begins with the well-known statement: 'Daseinanalysis itself is not anything more than a purified [geläuterte] psychoanalysis' (111).

118 'Das Konzept des Widerstandes in der Daseinsanalyse' (1981c), 116.

119 The sense of *Sache* here is of 'matter' (as in 'the matter at hand'), but also 'what matters' as in Husserl's slogan on the approach of phenomenology, 'to the things themselves [zu den Sachen selbst]', that is, 'to what matters'.

120 'Das Konzept des Widerstandes in der Daseinsanalyse' (1981c), 116.

121 'Das Konzept des Widerstandes in der Daseinsanalyse' (1981c), 118.

122 'Das Konzept des Widerstandes in der Daseinsanalyse' (1981c), 118-119.

123 'Das Konzept des Widerstandes in der Daseinsanalyse' (1981c), 119.

124 'Medard Boss on 'Encounter in Psychotherapy' (1965d), 34.

125 'Medard Boss on 'Encounter in Psychotherapy' (1965d), 35.

126 'Medard Boss on 'Encounter in Psychotherapy' (1965d), 38. See Martin Buber [1923], *I and Thou*, New York: Scribner, 1970.

127 Text appearing in braces {/} appears only in the Italian publication of the lecture.

128 'Medard Boss on 'Encounter in Psychotherapy' (1965d), 41.

129 'Encounter in Psychotherapy' (1965d), 41-42.

130 'Medard Boss on 'Encounter in Psychotherapy' (1965d), 43.

131 'Medard Boss on 'Encounter in Psychotherapy' (1965d), 43-44.

132 'Medard Boss on 'Encounter in Psychotherapy' (1965d), 47. The terms translate Heidegger's *Nähe* (closeness) and *Ferne* (distance) which refer to the degree of therapeutic intimacy between analyst and analysand.

133 'Medard Boss on 'Encounter in Psychotherapy' (1965d), 47.

134 Quoted in Jan van den Berg, *Op het Scherp van de Snede* [*On the Cutting Edge*], Kapellen: Pelckmans, 2013, 81.

135 Friedrich Hölderlin, 'Friedensfeier [Celebration of Peace]'. The context of the clause is important:

Man has learned much since morning,
For we are a conversation, and we listen
To one another, but soon we'll be song.
And the picture of time, which the great spirit unfolds,
Lies as a sign before us, indicating that a covenant
Between himself and others, himself and other powers, exists.

[*Viel hat von Morgen an,
Seit ein Gespräch wir sind und hören voneinander,*

Notes

Erfahren der Mensch; bald sind wir aber Gesang.
Und das Zeitbild, das der große Geist entfaltet,
Ein Zeichen liegts vor uns, dass zwischen ihm und andern
Ein Bündnis zwischen ihm und andern Mächten ist.]

The translation is by James Mitchell: https://holderlinpoems.com/index.html.
136 In English in the original.
137 Boss's image reminds one of tennis, but a match in which only one partner ever puts the ball into play. This also nicely resonates with Boss's reference to Freud's characterization of the analytic setting as a playground [*Tummelplatz*] to test out new ways of talking, behaving and feeling.
138 'Das Konzept des Widerstandes in der Daseinsanalyse' (1981c), 122-123.
139 'Das Konzept des Widerstandes in der Daseinsanalyse' (1981c), 123-124.
140 'Das Konzept des Widerstandes in der Daseinsanalyse' (1981c), 125.
141 'Das Konzept des Widerstandes in der Daseinsanalyse' (1981c), 126.
142 See *Existential Foundations of Medicine and Psychology* (1971a), 279-280.
143 The American psychologist Abraham Maslow (1908-1970) made self-actualization the pinnacle of the human being's hierarchy of needs. See *Toward a Psychology of Being*, Princeton: van Nostrand, 1962. Carl Rogers' (1902-1987) person-centered psychotherapy made self-actualization its goal. See *On Becoming a Person*, London: Constable, 1961.
144 'Das Konzept des Widerstandes in der Daseinsanalyse'(1981c), 127. Boss's wit is present in this text, for example, in his allusions to 'loose relationships' and the requirement that the analyst 'is hardly allowed to fool around'.
145 'Das Konzept des Widerstandes in der Daseinsanalyse' (1981c), 128.
146 'Anxiety, Guilt, and Psychotherapeutic Liberation' (1962c), 56.
147 He cites Seguín as having established at the medical school of the Universidad Nacional Mayor de San Marcos, in Lima, Peru, a version of medical training that 'should serve as an example for a revision of medical training in Europe and North America, where an all too materialistically-bound tradition still hampers the necessary development of a truly human medicine,' one that Boss was working out in his soon to be published *Grundriß* for medicine and psychology. Boss had often met with Seguín at meetings of the International Federation of Medical Psychotherapy, for which Seguín was a council member from 1958 to 1976.
148 'Introduction' (1965e), xiii.
149 'Introduction' (1965e), xiv.
150 'Introduction' to Carlos Alberto Seguín, *Love and Psychotherapy. The Psychotherapeutic Eros*, New York: Libra, 1965, v-xiv. A translator is not named. The text was based on the 'Vorwort' to Carlos Seguín, *Der Artz und sein Patient*, Bern: Huber, 1965, 7-18, a German translation of Seguín's *Amor y Psicoterapia. El Eros Psicoterapéutica*, Buenos Aires: Paidos, 1963, by Marian von Castelberg.
151 *Love and Psychotherapy. The Psychotherapeutic Eros*, New York: Libra, 1969, 113-114.
152 'Anxiety, Guilt and Psychotherapeutic Liberation' (1962c), 192.
153 See, for example, *The Myth of Mental Illness* [1961] (rev. ed.), New York: Harper and Row, 1974.
154 [154]'Anxiety, Guilt and Psychotheraspeutic Liberation' (1962c), 192.
155 *GA* 9, 316.
156 'Anxiety, Guilt and Psychotherapeutic Liberation' (1962c), 192.
157 'Anxiety, Guilt and Psychotherapeutic Liberation' (1962c), 192.
158 *The Analysis of Dreams* (1953d), 150.
159 'Phenomenological or Daseinsanalytic Approach' (1978d), 150.
160 Boss cites the ancient Chinese parable of the dreaming butterfly in both of his dream books: *The Analysis of Dreams* (1953d), 11, and '*I dreamt last night…*' (1975b), 175. Boss's

Notes

version runs as follows: 'I, Tschung-tse, once dreamt I was a butterfly, a butterfly flittering hither and thither. I knew only I was a butterfly, following my butterfly whims. I knew not that I was human. Suddenly, I awoke. I lay there. I – once more 'myself'. Now I do not know: was I then a man who dreamt he was a butterfly, or am I now a butterfly dreaming I am a man?' The parable appears at the end of Chapter Two, 'Discussion on Making All Things Equal', in the Burton Watson edition of *The Complete Works of Chuang Tzu*, New York: Columbia University Press, 1968, 49: 'Once Chuang Chou dreamt he was a butterfly, a butterfly flitting and fluttering around, happy with himself and doing as he pleased. He didn't know he was Chuang Chou. Suddenly he woke up and there he was, solid and unmistakable Chuang Chou. But he didn't know if he was Chuang Chou who had dreamt he was a butterfly, or a butterfly dreaming he was Chuang Chou. Between Chuang Chou and a butterfly there must be *some* distinction! This is called the Transformation of Things.'

161 Boss refers to Pascal *Pensées* [1670], # 386. He also cites Schopenhauer (who was much influenced by Eastern thought), *Die Welt als Wille und Vorstellung* [*The World as Will and Representation*] [1818], Volume 1, New York: Dover, §5.

162 'Phenomenological or Daseinsanalytic Approach' (1978d), 154.

163 The famous dream of the chemist August Kekulé (1829-1896), quoted by Freud, is a good example. Puzzling about the chemical configuration of benzene, in a reverie or dream the chemist saw a snake biting its tail (the *ouroboros* of alchemy). He realized that a compound compound could be represented by a circular and not only a linear configuration.

164 'Phenomenological or Daseinsanalytic Approach' (1978d), 159.

165 'Phenomenological or Daseinsanalytic Approach' (1978d), 187.

166 'Phenomenological or Daseinsanalytic Approach' (1978d), 187.

167 'Phenomenological or Daseinsanalytic Approach' (1978d), 160.

168 There is, for example, Freud's famous paper on the 'Dream of the Three Caskets [*Das Motiv des Kätschenwahl*]' [1913] based on his reading of Shakespeare's *The Merchant of Venice*, where the caskets (boxes) are symbolic of women, in this case three sisters. *SE* XII, 291-301.

169 'Phenomenological or Daseinsanalytic Approach' (1978d), 162.

170 'Warum denn eigentlich *nicht*?' See *Grundriß der Medizin und Psychologie* (1971a), 564. See also *Existential Foundations of Medicine and Psychology* (1971a), 279, and *Psychoanalysis and Daseinsanalysis* (1957a), 248-249.

171 See the concluding section of Medard Boss's *Grundriß der Medizin und Psychologie* [*Existential Foundations of Medicine and Psychology*] (1971a), 564.

172 ADI is recognized by the International Federation of Daseinsanalysis (IFDA). ADI is not affiliated with the American Psychological Association (APA), the American Psychoanalytic Association (APsA), or the American Psychiatric Association (APA). European institutes are certified by the European Association for Psychotherapy (EAP). The Brazilian daseinanalytic institute (ABD) is governed by a different set of general guidelines for the practice of psychotherapy than that found in Europe. It marked its 50th anniversary in 2024.

173 Traditionally, *Lehranalyse* has been rendered as 'training analysis'. For a recent historical account of supervision in classic psychoanalysis, see C. Edward Watkins Jr., 'The Beginnings of Psychoanalytic Supervision: The Crucial Role of Max Eitingon', *The American Journal of Psychoanalysis* 73, 2013, 254-270.

174 It is notable that in the States, for programs leading to the PhD in clinical psychology or the PsyD degree no such experience is required and is, at most, optional. That is also the case for preparation in psychiatry. The teaching analysis is unique to psychoanalysis and daseinanalysis.

175 For the public, the coveted title 'Dr.' invariably reminds most of the *medical* doctor. Those who consult someone with an earned MD, PhD, PsyD, or DSW degree have expectations based on their experiences with their family doctor, primary care physician, or general practitioner. Only the DD – Doctor of Divinity – defers to the title of 'Pastor', a title like 'Father' or 'Rabbi', that comes with ordination.

Notes

176 As recounted earlier, the clearest exposition of the differences between the psychiatric *Daseinsanalyse* of Binswanger and Boss's therapeutic daseinanalysis is still Herbert Spiegelberg, *Phenomenology in Psychology and Psychiatry*, Evanston: Northwestern University Press, 1972, in his articles 'Medard Boss (1903-[1990]): Phenomenological *Daseinsanalytik*' (333-342) and 'Ludwig Binswanger (1881-1966): Phenomenological Anthropology (*Daseinsanalyse*)' (193-232).

177 'Da-seinanalysis' was Boss's final (1990) preferred 'American translation' of the German term *Daseinsanalyse*. See the 'Preface' to *Zollikon Seminars* {1987a}, ix. I have adopted Boss's practice throughout (unhyphenated) unless quoting published sources, most of which opted for 'Daseinsanalysis' (capitalized).

178 The author saw to publication a second edition of Gion Condrau's *Martin Heidegger's Impact on Psychotherapy*, London: Free Association Books, 2021, which was first published in 1998. A volume of Boss's essential papers, most of them in their first English translation, is being prepared, as is an anthology of papers by other daseinanalysts drawn from issues of the yearbook *Daseinsanalyse*.

179 But see Urte Paulat, *Medard Boss und die Daseinsanalyse – ein Diaglog zwischen Medizin und Philosophie im 20. Jahrhundert*, Marburg: Tectum, 2001, for a biographical study.

180 A more detailed account of his background and development written by the Boss himself will be presented in Part III, Section I.

181 Boss contributed to five Zürcher Gespräche: (1) July 1-7, 1977 [second conference, on 'Der Herrschaftsanspruch der Wissenshcaft auf Welterklärung [The Claim of Science to an Explanation of the World]'] [No MS title given]; (2) January 20-23, 1978 [third conference, on 'Rationale und bildhafte Sprache [Rational and Figurative Language]': 'Der Traum und seine Bedeutung. Zwei Traumbilder [The Dream and Its Interpretation. Two Dream Images]'] [No MS. Unpublished]; (3) May 9-11, 1980 [seventh conference, on 'Rationale Denken – der einzige (wissenschaftliche) Zugang zur Wirklichkeit [Rational Thinking – The Only (Scientific) Approach to Reality]': 'Wirklichkeit als das Sich-Entbergen von Seiendem [Reality as the Unhiding of What There Is]'] {1982c}; (4) June 6-8, 1981 [ninth conference, on 'Sprache und Angst in einer technifizierten Welt [Language and Anxiety in an Engineered World]': 'Vom Geiste der Technik [On the Spirit of Technology],' published as 'Sprache und Angst in einer technifizierten Welt [Language and Anxiety in an Engineered World]'] {1982k}; (5) October 22-24, 1982 [twelfth conference, on 'Verlorene Natur, Religion, Persönlichkeit – der Mensch von heute? [Doomed Nature, Religion, Personality – Today's Man?]': 'Wo bleibt Gott in der Psychotherapie? Wo bleibt die Psychotherapie in Gott? [Where Is God in Psychotherapy? Where Is Psychotherapy in God?]'] [No MS. Unpublished]. These meetings brought together psychiatrists and public officials to discuss relevant contemporary themes of general social and political interest.

182 Three books were substantially revised. One was the for the most part thoroughly reworked translation of *Psychoanalyse und Daseinsanalytik* {1957a}, which appeared as *Psychoanalysis and Daseinsanalysis* in 1963. Two were revised and expanded texts: *Einführung in die psychosomatische Medizin* {1954a}, which was later reissued as *Praxis der Psychosomatik. Krankheit und Lebensschicksal* {1978c}, and *Grundriß der Medizin* {1971a}, revised and published as *Grundriß der Medizin und Psychologie* in 1975.

183 These contributions range from peer-reviewed journals to newspaper articles, a few of which are of substantial interest and value. Some are written for fellow physicians and psychotherapists, others for a general audience.

184 Currently, among his works, only the Boss edition of Heidegger's *Zollikon Seminars* {1987a} is in print in English. Two of Boss's books are still in print in German: *Sinn und Gehalt der sexuellen Perversionen. Ein daseinsanalytischer Beitrag zur Psychopathologie des Phänomens der Liebe* {1947} and a digital version of *Psychoanalyse und Daseinsanalytik* {1957a}. Boss's edition of *Zollikoner Seminare* {1987a} also remains in print although the *Gesamtausgabe* edition, prepared by Peter Trawny (*GA* 89, 2018) has superseded it. The

latter is especially important for containing hundreds of pages of notes Heidegger prepared for the seminars. Apart from the notes and protocols, it contains only one of the 'Conversations' included in Boss's edition. Several seminars not accounted for in the Boss edition are included in *GA* 89.
185 *Zollikon Seminars*, 235-291.
186 The author has given the attention due this figure in the history of therapeutic daseinanalysis in a two-part paper 'Messenger Between East and West. Erna Hoch, Martin Heidegger, and the Beginnings of Daseinanalysis', in *Existential Analysis* 35(1), 163-186, and 35(2),forthcoming 2024.
187 Letters (1947-1971) contained in Part III of Boss's edition of Martin Heidegger's *Zollikon Seminars* (1987a) are not listed separately here. Several other letters from Boss will be published in the near future: an important letter, dated September 18, 1960, to the American psychoanalyst, Leslie Farber, regarding a possible visit to the United States by Martin Heidegger in 1961, letters to Boss's training analyst, Hans Behn-Eschenburg, from 1931, and a letter to the Italian psychoanalyst, Emilio Servadio from 1954.
188 The second book on dreaming life, '*I dreamt last night...*' (1975b), is dedicated to his second wife – the first edition (1975) to 'Marian', the second (1991) to 'Marianne' (evidently corrected by Mrs. Boss-Linsmayer).
189 This volume has inspired two papers by the author, 'Medard Boss and Martin Heidegger. The Existential Analyst as 'a Western Kind of *rishi*'', *Review of Existential Psychology and Psychiatry* 27(1-3), 2008, 43-60, and 'Heidegger and Boss's India. On Encounter in Daseinanalysis', *Daseinsanalyse* 38, 2022, 26-44.
190 'Medard Boss' (1973a). In 1988, Ludwig Pongratz interviewed Boss in connection with a series on 'humanistic psychology' coordinated by the University of Würzburg. The interview is supplemented by an extended recording of Boss working with an analysand. See (1988d). This is a remarkable document, especially in showing the setting in which Boss worked and his conversational style. A transcript of the interview and the analytic session is being prepared and should be considered to be among the most important pedagogic sources we have on daseinanalytic practice. Next there is 'A Conversation with Medard Boss, Or the Evolution of Psychoanalysis', with Mary Harrington Hall (1968a). Finally, there is 'An Encounter with Medard Boss', from 1988, which is based on interviews with Erik Craig (1988b). Boss's 'Foreword' to Govid Kaul, *Govind Amrit,* Bombay: Prithwinath Niranjannath Pandit, 1975, is also very valuable as a personal reflection on the influence on Boss of Eastern thought. It is a letter from 1970 to the editor of Kaul's book.
191 'Medard Boss', in Ludwig Pongratz (ed.), *Psychotherapie in Selbstdarstellungen*, Bern: Huber, 1973, 71-106. English translation, 'Medard Boss', *Existential Analysis* 30(1), 2019, 169-198**,** by the author. Other therapists represented in the anthology included Alfred Adler, Karl Graf von Dürckheim and Viktor Frankl. See (1973a).
192 I have not been able to locate the passage in Freud that Boss is quoting. He may be paraphrasing Freud.
193 Ludwig Binswanger, 'Freuds Auffassung des Menschen im Lichte der Anthropologie', *Nederlandsch Tijdschrift voor Psychologie* 4, 1936, 5-6. Translated as 'Freud's Conception of Man in the Light of Anthropology', in *Being-in-the-World: Selected papers of Ludwig Binswanger*, New York: Basic Books, 1963, 149-181.
194 *Introductory Lectures on Psychoanalysis* [1917]. *The Standard Edition of the Complete Psychological Works of Sigmund Freud* [hereafter *SE*], London: Hogarth, XV, 67: 'On our view the phenomena that are perceived must yield in importance to trends which are only hypothetical.' Boss would often quote this line.
195 Boss refers to the seventh edition. See *GA* 2, 162-164.
196 Sigmund Freud, *Papers on Technique* (1911-1915) [1914], in *SE* XII, 89-171.
197 These terms are taken from a passage in Heidegger's *Sein und Zeit*. See *GA* 2, 163. The distinction is fundamental for the entire discussion of daseinanalysis. The difference

concerns a kind caring about the other that intervenes and takes over for the other (much as parents and doctors do), thus relieving the other of responsibility for what he does, and a caring about the other that makes way, perhaps for the first time, for the other to see himself as existing, as *Da-sein*, free in his ontological *be*-[ing] as caring about things [*Sorge*]. The latter 'position' or 'disposition' is Taoist: the most effective action is precisely non-action. It seems to me that Boss did not see the full implications of Heidegger's insights as long as he remained a doctor 'at heart', one whose business it is to intervene (albeit while above all 'doing no harm'), to do something. However, way-making caring about the other is the essence of daseinanalysis, which is to the greatest extent possible precisely non-interventional. See my *After Psychotherapy*, New York: ENI Press, 2017. I present the text and my own rendering. Readers may also consult *Being and Time*, Macquarrie/Robinson [trs.], 158-159, and Stambaugh [tr.], 114-115; (rev. ed.) Schmidt [tr.], 118-119:

Die Fürsorge hat hinsichtlich ihrer positiven Modi zwei extreme Möglichkeiten. Sie kann dem Anderen die »Sorge« gleichsam abnehmen und im Besorgen sich an seine Stelle setzen, für ihn einspringen. Diese Fürsorge übernimmt das, was zu besorgen ist, für den Anderen. Dieser wird dabei aus seiner Stelle geworfen, er tritt zurück, um nachträglich das Besorgte als fertig Verfügbares zu übernehmen, bzw. sich ganz davon zu entlasten. In solcher Fürsorge kann der Andere zum Abhängigen und Beherrschten werden, mag diese Herrschaft auch eine stillschweigende sein und dem Beherrschten verborgen bleiben. Diese einspringende, die »Sorge« abnehmende Fürsorge bestimmt das Miteinandersein in weitem Umfang, und sie betrifft zumeist das Besorgen des Zuhandenen. Ihr gegenüber besteht die Möglichkeit einer Fürsorge, die für den Anderen nicht so sehr einspringt, als daß sie ihm in seinem existenziellen Seinkönnen vorausspringt, nicht um ihm die »Sorge« abzunehmen, sondern erst eigentlich als solche zurückzugeben. Diese Fürsorge, die wesentlich die eigentliche Sorge – das heißt die Existenz des Anderen betrifft und nicht ein Was, das er besorgt, verhilft dem Anderen dazu, in seiner Sorge sich durchsichtig und für sie frei zu werden.

[With regard to its positive modes, caring about the other has two extreme possibilities. It can, as it were, take 'care' [caring about things] away from the other and put itself in its place in caring about the other; it can intervene for him. This caring about the other takes over for the other what he is to care about. Thus forced from his position, he [the other] steps back so that afterwards he can either take over what has been taken care of as an already done deal, or disburden himself of it completely. In such caring about the other, the other can become one who is dependent and controlled, even though this control may be tacit and remain hidden from him. This intervening, 'care'-removing kind of caring about the other to a great extent determines [everyday] togetherness, and for the most part it concerns caring about what is at our disposal. In contrast to this, there is also the possibility of a kind of caring about the other that does not so much intervene on behalf of the other as make way for him in his existential capacity to be, not in order to take away his 'care' [caring about things] but instead to essentially restore it to him as such for the first time. This kind of caring about the other which actually concerns real care, [that is, concerns] the way of life of the other and not a 'what' that one cares about, in that way helps the other to become transparent to himself in his caring about things and to become free for it.]

198 I have not been able to determine the text to which Boss is referring here.
199 The text in Pongratz does not show where the following quotation ends. Most likely, however, given Boss's style, this quotation or paraphrase of Heidegger in conversation ends with the paragraph as printed. One would expect the sentences to appear

somewhere in the *Zollikoner Seminare* (1987a) or the *Grundriß* (1971a), but these seem to be unique reports of Heidegger's comments to Boss not found in either text. See also the next quotation attributed to Heidegger. I again quote the passage in its entirety:

> Das Wort Transzendenz hat bei mir nie und nimmer einen Überstieg des Menschen zu den Dingen der Welt, zum einzelnen Seienden gemeint. Vielmehr habe ich unter Transzendenz immer nur die Beziehung des menschlichen Daseins zum Sein als solchem und im verbalen Sinne dieses Wortes gemeint. Dabei ist der Bezug menschlichen Existierens zu diesem Sein als solchem einzigartig. Menschliches Dasein verhält sich zum Sein als solchem so, daß es nicht anderes ist als ein wahrhaftiges Existieren, ein Ek-stare im wörtlichsten Sinne. Der Mensch ek-sistiert nämlich als das Aus-stehen eines allen Menschen gemeinsamen Welt-Offenheitsbereiches, der aus Vernehmen-können der Anwesenheit alles Begegnenden und aus Ansprechbar-Sein für die Bedeutsamkeiten und Verweisungszusammenhänge des Anwesenden besteht. Dank solcher Grundnatur menschlichen Existierens bildet dieses die Erscheinungs- und Entfaltungsstätte alles dessen, was ist und zu sein hat, das heißt: alles dessen, was Sein als solches aus sich aufgehen und in den vom menschlichen Existieren gebildeten Weltoffenheitsbereich hinein als einzelnes Seiendes anwesen läßt. Nur in solcher Sicht wird die berüchtigte Subjekt-Objekt-Spaltung nicht bloß durch ein rätselhaftes subjektivistisches Transzendieren scheinbar überbrückt; vielmehr kann die cartesianische Vorstellung von einer Kluft zwischen einer res cogitans und den res extensae schon gar nicht mehr aufkommen.

The key word is *Überstieg* (surpass, literally, step out of to a higher position) which, for Binswanger, means a removal of the subject form his subjectivity and thus a separation of man from himself that is necessary to allow contact with things outside of him. For Heidegger, however, transcendence does not imply an initial separation that requires a subsequent meeting and joining, but points to the primordial relation [*Beziehung*] between existence [*Dasein*] and being [*Sein*], 'understood in the verbal sense of the word.' For Binswanger, transcendence implies a subject-object split, which Heidegger denies is primary. Instead, *Dasein* is understood to be *transcending* in its very nature.

200 See *Indienfahrt eines Psychiaters* (1959a).
201 By 1959, two of Boss's books had been translated into Japanese and two into English. At this time seven of Boss's books have been translated into Japanese and seven into English.
202 This may not be entirely accurate, since Heidegger had been exposed to Taoism even before writing *Sein und Zeit*. His source was very likely Martin Buber. On 'Eastern' influences discerned in Heidegger's works, see G. Parkes (ed.), *Heidegger and Asian Thought*, Honolulu: University of Hawaii Press, 1987; H. W. Petzet, *Encounters and Dialogues with Martin Heidegger, 1929-1976*, Chicago: University of Chicago Press, 1983; R. May, *Heidegger's Hidden Sources. East Asian Influences on His Work*, London: Routledge, 1996. Revised edition, *Heideggers verborgene Quellen: Sein Werk unter chinesischem und japanischem Einfluss*, Wiesbaden: Harrassowitz, 2014; L. Ma, *Heidegger on East-West Dialogue: Anticipating the Event*, New York: Routledge, 2008; and L. Ma, *Heidegger on Eastern/Asian Thought*, Cambridge: Cambridge University Press, 2024.
203 This is a key term in Boss's phenomenology of *Dasein*. It is best translated as the 'ability to take in' what is confronting the existing person, but it also has the senses of seeing, as in 'getting' the significances of something encountering the given *Dasein*.
204 My, how times have changed. As noted earlier, Heidegger was to have accompanied Boss on one of his visits to lecture in the States. Leslie Farber's invitation for Heidegger to speak at the Washington School of Psychiatry in 1961 was scuttled by comments about the significance of Heidegger's time as rector of the University of Freiburg beginning in 1933 and whatever connections he had with National Socialism then and later in his

Notes

Überlegungen (considerations), published generically as 'the black notebooks (*GA* 94-102, 2014-2021). Heidegger was 'disinvited', which elicited from Boss a letter to Farber, dated September 18, 1960, in defense of Heidegger's reputation. It was said that Heidegger was ill in 1961 and could not have made his first and likely only visit to the States.

205 'A Conversation with Medard Boss, or the Evolution of Psychoanalysis' (1968a) in *Psychology Today* 2(7), December 1968, 58-65.

206 See also Boss's letter to Marvin Farber, referenced earlier, dated September 18, 1960 (unpublished).

207 'A Conversation with Medard Boss' (1968a), 62.

208 Sigmund Freud, 'Preface' [1925] to August Aichhorn, *Wayward Youth*, in *SE* XIX, 271-276. Freud's expression is *unmögliche Berufen*. The noun *Beruf* can be translated as both 'profession' and 'calling'. See *Verwahrloste Jugend* [*Neglected Youth*], Leipzig: Internationaler Psychoanalytischer Verlag, 1925, 3. The title of the English volume as translated is misleading. A minor classic, worth reading today more than ever, the translation was based on the second German edition (1931) of Aichhorn's book. It was translated by a committee of seven.

209 'A Conversation with Medard Boss' (1968a), 63.

210 'A Conversation with Medard Boss' (1968a), 63.

211 'A Conversation with Medard Boss' (1968a), 64.

212 For Heidegger, the history of Western metaphysics is nothing but a prolonged fool's errand to somehow link two sorts of hypothetical reality and to explain one in terms of the other. The dualism begins with Plato (the world of the cave and the sunlit world above) and continues through Kant and Descartes, whose physical *materia* and psychic *materia* name the dualism at the source of natural science. A clue as to just how problematic such a distinction has been from the start, we note only that the West had to wait a few centuries for the discoveries of quantum physics to make it clear that matter and energy cannot be distinguished from one another. If we allow that 'matter' covers *res extensa* and physical *materia* (the physical world) and 'energy' covers *res cogitans* and psychic *materia* (the psychological world), given doubts about the sort of that led Descartes to his revolutionary hypothesis which these findings compel us to reconsider, we must conclude that, in principle, one is not justified in differentiating between matters physical and matters psychological. As Boss points out, Freud realized this but found it expedient and necessary to postulate it in order to justify his theory. But *the res cogitans* was never something discovered like the pineal gland. It was merely postulated. Distinguishing a set number of non-material psychological functions (consciousness, perception, memory, thinking, conation) has been arbitrary.

213 *Sinn und Gehalt der sexuellen Perversionen. Ein daseinsanalytischer Beitrag zur Psychopathologie des Phänomens der Liebe* [*Meaning and Content of Sexual Perversions. A Daseinsanalytic Contribution to the Psychopathologie of the Phenomenon of Love*] (1947).

214 Boss published a paper on the theme with his younger colleague and psychiatrist in supervision, Gaetano Benedetti, 'Psychoanalyse eines Sadisten' (1953f). Many years later he published 'A Phenomenological Approach to Sexual Perversions', in A. de Koning and F. Jenner (eds.), *Phenomenology and Psychiatry*, New York: Academic Press, 1982, 85-95. See (1982d), discussed below.

215 Five years later, the diagnostic category 'homosexuality' was voted out by the American Psychiatric Association, replaced by notions of 'gender dysphoria' and 'gender identity disorder', and there would be no more talk of the phenomenon.

216 'A Conversation with Medard Boss' (1968a), 64.

217 Boss discusses three cases of same-sex attraction (two female, one male) in his book on the perversions. He may have had the male homosexual discussed there in mind when talking about those who 'deteriorate in a schizophrenic way' and 'and can exist as men only through another man'. See 'A Psychotic Homosexual Man', in *Meaning and Content of*

Notes

Sexual Perversions (1947), 120-125. There we read about Josef Wernle, who experienced a psychotic episode following the completion of his grammar school examinations and again after sitting for medical school entrance examinations at about age eighteen to nineteen. Just before this, however, Josef had fallen in love with his female cousin and for the first time felt that the world was more real and colorful in its detail. A year into the relationship, the sexual passion for her was so overwhelming that he was exhausted by any contacts, sexual or otherwise, with the young woman. In response to this, he quite spontaneously fell in love with a man three years younger, with whom he felt 'blissfully happy'. He found the sexual relationship with a man to be 'much more stable'. He did not recall having had any earlier erotic feelings toward another male. He told Boss that in a love affair with a man 'there is no danger of losing oneself; on the contrary, even one's 'manhood' can be found in the partner, because he too is a man. One can collect oneself within the male partner, one can restore one's self instead of being emptied out, as had happened before with the girl. Indeed, he felt himself grow much stronger in this love for the male friend and this showed up in a complete remission of his disease. 'Through the love of my cousin I had become completely empty and barren, now my male friend replenishes my masculine strength'; 'Together with him I am a complete man; women do not exist any more for me in this world.'" The ensuing schizophrenic process, says Boss, 'depleted his masculinity' and 'much of his own male feelings 'had run out." As a result, 'he suddenly and for the first time in his life felt driven to 'open himself' to a certain form of homosexual love. He described most vividly how in this homosexual love he succeeded in experiencing at least half of the fullness of existence.' With the woman, he had to expend his energy to achieve the 'semi fullness' he subsequently could experience with another male. What had been depleting with a female was fulfilling with a male. Boss found in any relationship both spiritually male and spiritually female components. This held for the full range of relationships, from those that are sexual to those found in a 'normal 'asexual' friendship between two men or two women.' Thus, as in heterosexual relationships, in a homosexual relationship and in nonsexual bonds of friendship, there are echoes of the *yin* and *yang*, the yielding and the leading. There can be no relationship in which one of the two partners does not first take the initiative and the other responds, one calls and other replies. This is an inevitability and for this reason Boss can refer to it as spiritual [*geistig*], that is, having its source in the spirit [*Geist*] and the soul [*Seele*], not in the genitally sexed body of the individual.

218 Where the sexual (genital) component is missing, these tendencies nevertheless remain. That is, there is more to masculinity than phallic genital sexuality in the male and more to femininity than clitoral excitation and vaginal receptivity. In a sexual relationship between a male and a female, each is able to experience the world of male masculinity and female femininity, respectively, in the perfomance of the other-sex partner. The male homosexual is unusual in needing to find his own masculinity in an experience with another male. There are also examples of homosexuals who find the imitated other-sex features of a same-sex partner attractive. Thus a female may find a masculine female exciting. She is attracted to the masculine, but not in a male. Another female homosexual may find in her same-sex partner a rich source of femininity. There are many forms of homosexuality in each sex. Boss's understanding of the case of the schizophrenic male homosexual and of the 'neurotic' male homosexual assumes limited experience of masculinity in each. Boss's case examples of other paraphilias in the 1947 volume are worth consulting. There he discusses sadomasochism, voyeurism, exhibitionism, coprophilia and fetishism (now considered to be 'paraphilic disorders') and kleptomania (now classified as a 'disruptive, impulse-control and conduct disorder').

219 'A Conversation with Medard Boss' (1968a), 64.

220 'A Conversation with Medard Boss' (1968a), 65. It is not clear to what Boss might have been referring here. We do know that he was completing the text of the first edition of his *magnum opus* (1971a).

Notes

221 'Foreword' [1970] {1975a} to Govind Kaul, Go*vind Amrit*, Bombay: Prithwinath Niranjannath Pandit, 1975, 1-2. The book by Govind Kaul is available online. See https://archive.org/details/GovindAmritKashmiriSwamiGovindKoul/page/n13/mode/2up.
222 'Foreword' to *Govind Amrit*. [Letter to J. M. Kayande, November 23, 1970] {1975e}, 1-2.
223 I have looked into the topic in several publications: 'Medard Boss and Martin Heidegger. The Existential Analyst as 'a Western kind of *rishi*'', in *Review of Existential Psychology and Psychiatry* 27 (1-3), 2008, 43-60; *Medard Boss and the Promise of Therapy. The Beginnings of Daseinsanalysis*, London: Free Association Books, 2020, 99-122; and 'Heidegger and Boss's India. On Encounter in Daseinanalysis', *Daseinsanalyse* 38, 2022, 26-44.
224 'An Encounter with Medard Boss' {1988b}, *The Humanistic Psychologist* 16(1), 1988, 24-57.
225 It is possible that there are letters from the last five years of Heidegger's life that were not represented in the 1987 edition of Heidegger's book Boss was editing. As noted, this was a special book in that it was originally not to have been published until both men had died. It was also not officially part of the *Collected Edition*, thirty volumes of which had already appeared before 1987.
226 'An Encounter with Medard Boss' {1988b}, 50, n. 2.
227 'An Encounter with Medard Boss' {1988b}, 26.
228 'An Encounter with Medard Boss' {1988b}, 27.
229 'An Encounter with Medard Boss' {1988b}, 27.
230 'An Encounter with Medard Boss' {1988b}, 31.
231 The theme of luminance is related to the Hindu notion of *chit*. See *A Psychiatrist Discovers India* {1959a}, 128-129.
232 'An Encounter with Medard Boss' {1988b}, 34. Boss was then only twenty-two years of age. Freud was sixty-nine. Boss marks this encounter with Freud as the beginning of his psychoanalytic training, which continued with Hans Behn-Eschenburg (1893-1934) in Zürich and later with Karen Horney (1885-1952) as his training and supervising analyst at the Berlin Psychoanalytic Institute. He mentions that his wife, Gertrud Wissler, was also in analysis with Horney at that time. Other senior analysts with whom Boss worked were Otto Fenichel (1897-1946), Hanns Sachs (1881-1947) and Harald Schultz-Hencke (1892-1953). He also worked in the hospital setting with Eugen Bleuler (1857-1939) and Carl Gustav Jung (1875-1961) in Zürich. Finally, Boss mentions his experience with Wilhelm Reich (1897-1957) at the Berlin Psychoanalytic Institute in the 1920s, with Kurt Goldstein (1878-1965) at the Frankfurt Institute for Research into the Consequences of Brain Injuries, and for six months in London at the National Hospital for Nervous Diseases in weekly analytic sessions with Ernest Jones (1879-1958). Also mentioned are Manfred Bleuler (1903-1984) and Gustav Bally (1883-1966), with whom he worked at the Burghölzli Hospital. The reminiscences of Jung, with whom Boss met along with other psychiatrists at bi-weekly study sessions for ten years, are especially interesting (35-37). The ten years with Jung overlapped with the time Boss first met Heidegger. Finally, Boss recalls having eulogized Jung at the Third World Congress of Psychiatry in Montreal (June 4-10). Jung died on June 9 while the conference was being held.
233 Marguerite Sèchehaye (1887-1964), *Symbolic Realization* [1947], New York: International Universities Press, 1951, recounts the Swiss psychotherapist's work for seven years with Luisa Düss, whom she eventually adopted. The details of the procedures of Boss's work with 'Regula Zürcher' are also quite remarkable.
234 'An Encounter with Medard Boss' {1988b}, 32-33.
235 See, for example, 'A Patient Who Taught the Author to See and Think Differently', the opening chapter of *Psychoanalysis and Daseinsanalysis* {1957a}, 5-27. The material discussed there had its origins in material from the early 1950s.
236 See 'Is Psychotherapy Rational or Rationalistic?' (1979b), 122.
237 'An Encounter with Medard Boss' {1988b}, 32-33.

238 'An Encounter with Medard Boss' (1988b), 34. In a note, Craig refers to passages in *Existential Foundations of Medicine and Psychology* (9-10) on the matter of Heidegger's reactions to Freud's papers on therapeutic practice, which evidently 'made him feel more conciliatory' toward Freud. By contrast, the metapsychological works 'made him literally feel ill.'

239 'An Encounter with Medard Boss' (1988b), 36. Boss mentions Gion Condrau (1919-2006) and Alois Hicklin (1931-) and Perikles Kastrinidis (1946-) as stewards of the Zürich institute. Boss also cites with approval daseinsanalytic institutes in Jerusalem, São Paulo and India.

240 Boss may have had in mind Karin Schoeller-von Haslingen, 'Gedanken zu Werken von Paul Klee und Edvard Munch aus der daseinsanalytischen Sicht Martin Heideggers [Thoughts on Works by Paul Klee and Edvard Munch from the Daseinsanalytic Perspective of Martin Heidegger],' *Daseinsanalyse* 3(1), 23-34.

241 'An Encounter with Medard Boss' (1988b), 38.

242 'An Encounter with Medard Boss' (1988b), 40.

243 'An Encounter with Medard Boss' (1988b), 40-41.

244 'An Encounter with Medard Boss' (1988b), 41. In a note to the word 'mind', Craig reminds the reader that Boss's usage does not denote an apparatus but rather has as its referent 'the observable fact of human 'consciousness' itself, to the 'luminating realm' as which we primarily exist as human beings'. Here Craig cross-references Heidegger on *Lichtung* (luminance) in *Being and Time*, Macquarrie/Robinson, 171. Making 'human 'consciousness' (even in scare quotes) equivalent to the 'luminating realm [*Lichtungsbereich*]' is, unfortunately, potentially misleading with its implied connection with Husserl's phenomenology, which postulates consciousness but leaves it unexplained. The idea of having Boss 'in mind' while in St. Moritz means to say that both St. Moritz and Zollikon are comprehended by the expansiveness of the bodiliness (*Leiblichkeit*) of *Dasein*.

245 'An Encounter with Medard Boss' (1988b), 41-42.

246 'An Encounter with Medard Boss' (1988b), 43.

247 See the *Letter on 'Humanism'* [1946], *GA* 9, 331. It is worth remembering that, for Heidegger, calling on the human being for such stewardship is nothing initiated by the human being. It is given by *be*[-ing] [*es gibt Sein*].

248 'An Encounter with Medard Boss' (1988b), 43.

249 'An Encounter with Medard Boss' (1988b), 43.

250 See 'Begegnung in der Psychotherapie' (1965d).

251 'An Encounter with Medard Boss' (1988b), 43. The sentence elicited a note by Craig, which refers to Helmut Thomä, 'Sigmund Freud: Ein Daseinsanalytiker?' *Psyche* 12(12), 1959, 881-890. Craig adds: 'This is one of the proudest claims of daseinsanalysis: to have understood the fundamentals of psychoanalytic practice better than psychoanalysis itself, even better than its founder, Freud' (55, n. 29).

252 'An Encounter with Medard Boss' (1988b), 44.

253 'An Encounter with Medard Boss' (1988b), 47.

254 'Dialogue Between Prof. Medard Boss and Prof. Dongshick Rhee' [June 12 and June 15, 1976] (1996), in 精神治 [*Psychotherapy*] (Seoul) 6, 1996, 30-43. Transcribed from audio tape recordings of two interviews online at: https://sites.google.com/view/gemenetzis/βιβλιοθηκη/ψυχοθεραπεια/medard-boss/dialogue-between-prof-medard-boss-and-prof-dongshick-rhee.

255 See *Psychotherapeutic Approaches to Schizophrenic Psychoses: Past, Present and Future*, New York: Routledge, 2009, 200.

256 See in connection with these dialogues Rhee's 'The Tao, Psychoanalysis and Existential Thought', in *Psychotherapy and Psychosomatics* 53, 1990, 21-27. Rhee's article was published the year Boss died.

257 A translator for the English text is not named. In a few cases, it seems that whoever was speaking was misidentified by Rhee. I have silently corrected for these oversights and for

Notes

misspellings. I believe I have not introduced any errors of sense in doing so, but the reader should compare my edited version to the website texts and the Korean original. What appears between brackets is either an interpolation made by the transcriber of the audio tapes (for example, a quick comment during a longer speech by the other interlocutor or a translator's gloss) or my own connective or corrective tissue, introduced to make the text readable. Even with that, some passages do not seem to make sense. Rhee was said to be fluent in English and German, as was Boss. I have bolded what are for this reader the most stimulating observations made by these two very different psychiatrists.

258 Erik Craig has reported on Rhee's ideas in 'Tao Psychotherapy: Introducing a New Approach to Humanistic Practice', *The Humanistic Psychologist* 35(2), 2007, 109-133.

259 Others have played important roles in what we know as daseinanalysis, beginning with Ludwig Binswanger. Distinguishing Boss's therapeutic daseinanalysis from Binswanger's psychiatric *Daseinsanalyse* and its related psychopathology worked out against the background of a philosophical anthropology ostensibly based on Heidegger's fundamental ontology, we do not discuss his publications in any detail here. For this, we recommend the reader to Alice Holzhey-Kunz, *Daseinsanaysis*, London: Free Associations Books, 2014, and papers by the author cited in her book. The great deal of material published by Gion Condrau should also be mentioned, but limitations of space make a full discussion of these books impossible. See, however, *Angst und Schuld als Grundprobleme der Psychotherapie* [*Anxiety and Guilt as Fundamental Problems of Psychotherapy*], Bern: Huber, 1962; *Daseinsanalytische Psychotherapie* [*Daseinsanalysis and Psychotherapy*], Bern: Huber, 1963; *Die Daseinsanalyse von Medard Boss und ihre Bedeutung für die Psychiatire* [*Medard Boss's Daseinsanalysis and Its Significance for Psychiatry*], Bern: Huber, 1965; *Psychosomatik und Frauenheilkunde* [*Psychosomatics and Gynecology*], Bern: Huber, 1965; *Einführung in die Psychotherapie* [*Introduction to Psychotherapy*], Olton: Walter, 1970; *Medard Boss zum siebzigsten Geburtstag* [*Medard Boss on His seventieth Birthday*], Bern: Huber, 1973; *Medizinische Psychologie* [*Medical Psychology*], Zurich: Kindler, 1975; *Der Januskopf des Fortschritts* [*The Janus Head of Progress*], Bern: Benteli, 1976; *Aufbruch in die Freiheit* [*Awakening to Freedom*], Bern: Benteli, 1977; *Transzendenz, Imagination und Kreativität: Religion, Parapsycholoige, Literatur und Kunst* [*Transcendence, Imagination and Creativity, Religion, Parapsychology, Literature and Art*], Zurich: Kindler, 1979 (contains Boss (1979a)); *Fordern, Auffordern, Herausfordern: Thesen fu r eine humane christliche Politik* [*Require, Demand, Challenge. Theses for a Christian Politics*], Bern: Benteli, 1979; *Transzendenz und Religion* [*Transcendence and Religion*], Weinheim: Beltz, 1982; *Psychologie der Kultur* [*Psychology of Culture*], Weinheim: Beltz, 1982; *Der Mensch und sein Tod. certa moriendi condicio* [*Man and His Death: The Certain Condition of Dying*], Zurich: Benziger, 1984; 'Daseinsanalytic psychotherapy', *Psychiatry and Phenomenology* [fourth Annual Symposium, Simon Silverman Phenomenology Center]Pittsburgh: Duquesne University, 1987, 63-77; *Daseinsanalyse. Philosophisch-anthropologische Grundlagen* [*Daseinsanalysis. Philosophicoa-anthropological Foundations*], Dettelbach: Röll, 1989; *Daseinsanalyse* [*Daseinanalysis*], Bern: Huber, 1989; *Depression. Medizinische, kulturelle und anthropologische Aspekte* [*Depression. Medical, Cultural and Anthropological Aspects*], Basel: Karger, 1989; *Sigmund Freud and Martin Heidegger. Daseinsanalytische Neurosenlehre und Psychotherapie* [*Sigmund Freud and Martin Heidegger. Daseinsanalytic Theory of Neurosis and Psychotherapy*], Bern: Huber, 1992; *Phänomenologie und psychotherapeutische Praxis*, Basel: Karger, 1995; *Ama et fac quod vis. Gion Condrau zum 80. Geburtstag* Erlenbach (*Love and Do as You Will. Gion Condrau for His eightieth Birthday*), [self-published], 1999; and *Martin Heidegger's Impact on Psychotherapy*, New York: Mosaic, 1998; rev. ed. 2022. See also *Leiben und Leben*, which Condrau co-edited with Boss and Alois Hickin, Bern: Benteli, 1977, contains Boss (1955b), (1955b), (1970a)), (1976d), (1977b), and (1977c), and *Das Werden des Menschen* [*Becoming Human*], edited by Condrau and Hicklin, Bern: Benteli, 1977, which contains Boss (1977a).

Mention should also be made of Alois Hicklin: *Der Mensch zwischen Gestern und Morgen* [*Man Between Yesterday and Tomorrow*], Bern: Benteli, 1978; *Wandel und Tradition. Verharren und Verändern: Gestaltende Kräfte im Menschen und in menschlichen Gesellschaft* [*Change and Tradition. Persistence and Change: Formative Processes in Man and Human Society*], Bern: Benteli, 1980, which contains Boss (1977a)); *Begegnung und Beziehung* [*Encounter and Relation*], Bern: Benteli, 1982; and *Das menschliche Gesicht der Angst* [*The Human Face of Anxiety*], Zurich: Kreuz, 1989. Finally, marking its fortieth anniversary of publication in 2024, is the journal *Daseinsanalyse*, which to date contains nearly 600 papers by more than 200 authors. The most notable figures represented include Wolfgang Blankenburg, István Fehér, Hans-Dieter Förster, Carlos Freire, Valeria Gamper, Konstantin Gemenetzis, Thanasis Georgas, Holger Helting, Erna Hoch, Uta Jaenicke, Perikles Kastrinidis, Bin Kimura, Ania Padrutt, Hanspeter Padrutt, Günther Pöltner, Hansjörg Reck, Gerlinde Schopf, Hubertus Tellenbach, Friedrich-Wilhelm von Herrmann, Detlev von Uslar, Helmut Vetter, Johannes Vorlaufer, Aleš Wotruba, Augustinus Wucherer-Huldenfeld and Dieter Wyss. The most represented topics are psychosomatics, dreaming life and the relation between daseinanalysis and Heidegger's thought.

260 *Meaning and Content of Sexual Perversions. A Daseinsanalytic Approach to the Psychopathology of the Phenomenon of Love* [1947] (New York: Grune and Stratton, 1949), ix-xiii.

261 'Beitrag zur daseinsanalytischen Fundierung des psychiatrischen Denkens' (1951b) *Schweizer Archive für Neurologie und Psychiatrie* 67(1), 1951, 15-19. Reprinted in *Von der Psychoanalyse zur Daseinsanalyse. Wege zu einem neuen Selbstverständnis* (Vienna: Europaverlag, 1979), 145-150.

262 'Beitrag zur daseinsanalytischen Fundierung des psychiatrischen Denkens' (1951b), 145.

263 'Beitrag zur daseinsanalytischen Fundierung des psychiatrischen Denkens' (1951b), 147-148.

264 Heidegger's 'Zur Erörterung der Gelassenheit. Aus einem Feldweggespräch über das Denken' was not published until 1959, but it is likely that Boss knew of the 1944-45 text from Heidegger himself. See *GA* 13, 37-74, and *Discourse on Thinking*, New York: Harper and Row, 1966, 58-90.

265 The verb *hüten* has the double sense of 'being on the lookout for' and 'looking out for' or 'tending to'. *Dasein* is on 'guard duty' for the truth of being, as it were, and when such truth appears it is inevitably responsible for 'watching out for' it in the sense of protecting it from being distorted. The German word is closely related to the English 'heed' in the sense of 'being attentive to' as when we speak of 'taking heed' of what someone points out. The sense of careful attentiveness to what 'shows up' of its own, but only insofar as there is the luminating effect [*Wirkung*] of existence [*Dasein*], is shared by both words. Providing shelter or protection for the truth of being is, for Boss (as he had learned from Heidegger), an irrevocable responsibility of being human. Restoration of this obligation follows from the freeing up of – the analysis – the analysand's *Dasein*.

266 In music, there has always been an association between certain tones and certain colors. This was explored in the notion of the tone colors [*Klangfarben*] of Heidegger's contemporary, Arnold Schoenberg (1874-1951), and in the mystical notions held by the Russian composer Alexander Scriabin (1872-1915). We also speak of colors as having a certain tone.

267 The German verb *erschließen* (open up) is built on the verb *schließen*, which means 'to close'. The sense is that what there is [*das Seiende*] was hidden away as it were and but is now dis-closed. There is in Heidegger also the sense of *erschließen* as an unlocking the meaning of a mystery or saying [*Sagen*] which provides a 'way in' or access to what is puzzling.

268 'Die Bedeutung der Daseinsanalyse für die Psychologie und die Psychiatrie' (1952b), *Psyche* 6 (3), 1952/53, 178-186. Reprinted in *Von der Psychoanalyse zur Daseinsanalyse. Wege zu einem neuen Selbstverständnis* (Vienna: Europaverlag, 1979), 151-160.

Notes

269 'The Significance of Daseinsanalysis for Psychology and Psychiatry' (1952b), in *Von der Psychoanalyse zur Daseinsanalyse. Wege zu einem neuen Selbstverständnis* (Vienna: Europaverlag, 1979), 151.
270 'Daseinsanalytik und Psychotherapie. Über die Grenzen der Psychoanalyse' (1948b), *Deutsche Universitätszeitung* 11 (2324), 1956, 17-19. English translation: "Daseinsanalysis' and Psychotherapy', in J. Masserman and J. L. Moreno (eds.), *Progress in Psychotherapy.* Volume II. *Anxiety and Therapy*, New York: Grune and Stratton, 1957, 156-161. Reprinted in H. Ruitenbeek (ed.) *Psychoanalysis and Existential Philosophy*, New York: Dutton, 1962, 81-89. Translation by Medard Boss.
271 *Psychoanalysis and Existential Philosophy*, viii.
272 As recently as 2019, the two terms continue to be associated. See Alexander Batthyány (ed.), *Logotherapy and Existential Analysis,* Basel: Springer Switzerland, 2016, the first volume of proceedings of the Viktor Frankl Institute in Vienna. *The Wiley Handbook of Existential Therapy*, New York: John Wiley, 2019, devotes a sizable section (305-403) to 'Logotherapy and Existential Analysis'.
273 Frankl first used the term '*Logotherapie*' in 1926 to distinguish his approach from *Psychoanalyse* and only in 1939 began to refer to it as *Existenzanalyse*. He eventually settled on the former as the name of his approach.
274 Rollo May, Ernest Angel and Henri F. Ellenberger (eds.), *Existence. A New Dimension in Psychiatry and Psychology*, New York: Simon and Schuster, 1958. The British journal *Existential Analysis* has published since 1990, but its predecessors date back to the journal series first called *Existential Inquiries*, founded by Rollo May in 1959, and the *Review of Existential Psychology and Psychiatry*, which published from 1961-2002.
275 *Psychoanalysis and Existential Philosophy*, 85.
276 *Psychoanalysis and Existential Philosophy*, 84.
277 GA 2, 158-159: 'Auf dem Grunde dieses *mithaften* In-der-Welt-seins ist die Welt je schon immer die, die ich mit den Anderen teile. Die Welt des Daseins ist *Mitwelt.* Das In-Sein ist *Mitsein* mit Anderen. Das innerweltliche Ansichsein dieser ist *Mitdasein* [On the basis of this *with-like* being-in-the-world, the world is always one I share with others. The world of existence is a *with-world*. Being-in is *being-with* others. The inner-worldly being-in-itself of others is *existing-with*].' The verb *teilt* used with the preposition *mit* suggests the verb *mitteilen*, which can mean to disclose or intimate (hint at) with the associated nuance of intimacy. Heidegger's emphasized neologism *mithaft* really requires a neologism of its own such as 'withly' to modify the nominalized verbal expression *In-der-Welt-sein* (being-in-the-world). There is, however, the verb *mithaften* to consider here, which suggests 'being in this together' (as in 'We're all in this together!'), that is, as our being jointly and collectively responsible for the appearance of things in the world. Heidegger's analysis of being-in [*In-sein*] is essential background for the discussion, as is further elucidation of the existentive *Mitsein*. All of this was very likely lost on most readers.
278 Boss will often refer to this expression from Freud's second paper on technique, 'Remembering, Repeating and Working-through' [1914]. See Sigmund Freud, *SE* XII, 154.
279 *Psychoanalysis and Existential Philosophy*, 86.
280 *Psychoanalysis and Existential Philosophy*, 87.
281 *Psychoanalysis and Existential Philosophy*, 87-88.
282 'Das Ich? Die Motivation?' (1960b), *Schweizerische Zeitschrift für Psychologie und ihre Anwendungen* (4), 1960, 299-306. Originally a read at a symposium on 'The Ego in Human Motivation' at the sixteenth International Congress of Psychology, Bonn, August 2, 1960. French translation: 'Le problème du moi dans la motivation', in *L'évolution Psychiatrique* 25 (4), 1960, 481-489. English translation: 'Ego? Motivation?' in *Journal of Existentialism* (3), 1960, 275-283. Reprinted as 'The Ego? Human Motivation?' in *Acta Psychologica* 19, 1961, 217-222. Translation by Medard Boss.

Notes

283 The issues were numbered sequentially, with 1(3) as #4. Boss was on the journal's international editorial board along with David Cooper (1931-1986), Viktor Frankl (1905-1997), whose 'Beyond Self-Actualization and Self-Expression' was the lead article of the journal, Eugène Minkowski (1885-1972) and Ramo Sarró (1900-1993). In the States, the founding editor, Jordan Scher, was assisted by, among others, the Heidegger scholar William Barrett (1913-1992), and psychotherapists Harold Kelman (1906-1977), Jacob Moreno (1889-1974), Carl Rogers (1902-1987), and Erwin Straus (1891-1975). The 'epigraph' of the journal was, in Hebrew, the expression from Exodus 3:14: 'אֶהְיֶה אֲשֶׁר אֶהְיֶה [ἐγώ εἰμι ὁ ὤν, I am who am].' The term 'ontoanalysis' is an attempt at denoting a form of analysis based on the 'fundamental ontology [*Fundamentalontologie*]' of *Dasein* in Heidegger. It may also refer to the analysis of *seiend* (be-ing), Heidegger's translation of the Greek ὄν. See *GA* 2, 2.

284 Congresses on psychology as a discipline were sponsored by the International Union of Psychological Science. This one was chaired by Wolfgang Metzger (1899-1979). The first congress, which met in Paris in 1889, the year Heidegger was born, was arranged by Freud's mentor, Jean-Martin Charcot (1825-1893). Its most recent meeting was in 2018 in Prague.

285 'Ego? Motivation?' (1960b), 275.

286 'Ego? Motivation?' (1960b), 281.

287 'Ego? Motivation?' (1960b), 275.

288 'Ego? Motivation?' (1960b), 279. James Strachey's choice of 'agency' for '*Instanz*' was intended to be understood in a sense as 'similar to that in which the word occurs in the phrase 'a Court of First Instance' and this 'by analogy with tribunals or authorities which judge what may or may now pass.' Jean Laplanche and Jean Baptiste Pontalis, *The Language of Psychoanalysis*, London: Hogarth, 1973, 16. For Strachey's note, see *SE* IV, 537. Other languages preserve some form of '*Instanz*'. Those who had read Freud were used to 'agency' (as 'id', 'ego', 'superego') or 'system' (Pcs., Ucs., Cs.) and may have been thrown by Boss's use of '*Instanz*'.

289 See, for example, Heinz Hartmann, *Ego Psychology and Problem of Adaptation* [1939], New York: International Universities Press, 1958.

290 'Ego? Motivation?' (1960b), 280.

291 'Ego? Motivation?' (1960b), 280-281.

292 'Ego? Motivation?' (1960b), 281-282.

293 'Ego? Motivation?' (1960b), 282. Those familiar with Husserl's notion of intentionality as the structure of consciousness might be reminded of it here. To say that things confront or encounter us does not require consciousness, however. The original involvement with things of encounter makes possible something like talk of an intentional relation between consciousness and its object in the first place. It was Heidegger's critique of intentionality that marked his departure from the latter's phenomenology to his more fundamental hermeneutic phenomenology.

294 Speaking from a position within academic psychology, twenty-five years later Sigmund Koch (1917-1996) would also deliver a strong blow against psychology in *A Century of Psychology as a Science*, New York: McGraw-Hill, 1985. This followed seven volumes of studies of the entire range of the 'areas' of psychology since the first laboratory for the study of psychological phenomena and life was established in 1879 by Wilhelm Wundt (1832-1920). See Ralph Norman Haber, 'Perception: A One-hundred-year Perspective', 250-281. The conclusion was that nothing had been learned about perception. This was verdict with respect to the other functions and structures of the psyche.

295 'Outline of the Analysis of Dasein' (1962a), *Philosophical Bulletin. Viśva Tattvajñāna Mandira Quarterly* 1(1), 1962, 49-64. Written in English by Boss.

296 *GA* 2, 68, 418; 23, 307-314, 345, 403, 441, 485.

297 'Outline of the Analysis of Dasein' (1962a), 50.

298 'Outline of the Analysis of Dasein' (1962a), 50.

299 'Outline of the Analysis of Dasein' (1962a), 52.

Notes

300 Thomas Nagel, *The View from Nowhere*, London: Oxford University Press, 1986.
301 Jean Piaget and Bärbel Inhelder, *The Psychology of the Child* [1966], New York: Basic Books, 1969, 130-160.
302 'Outline of the Analysis of Dasein' (1962a), 53.
303 It is remarkable that the meaning of the adjective *hell* on which the noun is based refers to auditory resounding brightness of tone that is clear and pure.
304 'Outline of the Analysis of Dasein' (1962a), 56-57.
305 'Outline of the Analysis of Dasein' (1962a), 60.
306 'Outline of the Analysis of Dasein' (1962a), 60-61.
307 *Lebensangst, Schuldgefühle und psychotherapeutische Befreiung*, Bern: Huber, 1962 (2nd ed., 1965) (1962c). English translation: 'Anxiety, Guilt and Psychotherapeutic Liberation', *Review of Existential Psychology and Psychiatry* 2(3), 1962, 173, 195. Reprinted in K. Hoeller (ed.), *Readings in Existential Psychology and Psychiatry*, Seattle: Review of Existential Psychology and Psychiatry, 1990, 71-92. Translation by Medard Boss. I have modified the translation in many quoted passages.
308 The published text appeared in the second volume of the *Review*, which had been established only the year before, edited by Adrian van Kaam, then at Duquesne University. The first issues were printed in the Netherlands, van Kaam's home country. Boss was on its editorial board from the start. Its contributors were a distinguished group, including Ludwig Binswanger (1881-1966), Leslie Farber (1912-1981), Michel Foucault (1926-1984), Viktor Frankl (1905-1997), Julia Kristeva (b. 1941), Jacques Lacan (1901-1981), R. D. Laing (1927-1989), Rollo May (1909-1994), Maurice Merleau-Ponty (1908-1961), William J. Richardson (1920-2016), Carl Rogers (1902-1987), Paul Tillich (1886-1965), Thomas Szasz (1920-2012) and Jan van den Berg (1914-2012).
309 *Lebensangst, Schuldgefühle und psychotherapeutische Befreiung* (1962c), 12.
310 'Anxiety, Guilt and Psychotherapeutic Liberation' (1962c), 173, note.
311 'Vorwort', *Lebensangst, Schuldgefühle und psychotherapeutische Befreiung* (1962c), 9.
312 'Vorwort', *Lebensangst, Schuldgefühle und psychotherapeutische Befreiung* (1962c), 10.
313 'Vorwort', *Lebensangst, Schuldgefühle und psychotherapeutische Befreiung* (1962c), 11.
314 'Anxiety, Guilt and Psychotherapeutic Liberation' (1962c), 173.
315 'Anxiety, Guilt and Psychotherapeutic Liberation' (1962c), 174.
316 'Anxiety, Guilt and Psychotherapeutic Liberation' (1962c), 177.
317 *Sinnfrei* can also mean 'senseless' or 'pointless'. The point is, however, that not being attuned to the world of meaning, therapists will miss or overlook it in their patients.
318 The English version adds the final clause 'and quite neutral as to meaningful values'.
319 Here Boss refers to the later Freud's view of a primal death instinct (Thanatos) that is in constant battle with an equally powerful life force (Eros). See *Beyond the Pleasure Principle* [1920], *SE* XVIII, 1-64.
320 The German edition has the additional modifier '*nachweisbar*'. *Lebensangst, Schuldgefühle und therapetische Befreiung* (1962c), 23.
321 In the German text, Boss says that neither the 'that' nor the 'why' of earlier appearing events [*Erscheinende*] can be held to account for what appears later in life as distressing conditions.
322 'Anxiety, Guilt and Psychotherapeutic Liberation' (1962c), 177 (translation modified).
323 'Anxiety, Guilt and Psychotherapeutic Liberation' (1962c), 178.
324 'Anxiety, Guilt and Psychotherapeutic Liberation' (1962c), 178.
325 'Anxiety, Guilt and Psychotherapeutic Liberation' (1962c), 179. We can safely replace 'Analysis of Dasein' with 'daseinanalysis'.
326 'Anxiety, Guilt and Therapeutic Liberation' (1962c), 186. The German text varies considerably in important details. See *Angst, Schuldgefühl und psychotherapeutische Befreiung* (1962c), 45.
327 Here the English version as translated by Boss is illuminating: 'Anxiety when experienced in its deepest meaning ... bursts asunder all subjectified, psychologized anxiousness ...

and opens up the way of love toward the boundless origin of things that not longer merely *is*, that is *beyond* the dichotomy of being and non-being.' The very distinction between being and non-being, which brings into relief what *is*, is here sublated. Possibility implies nothing about what will come to pass versus what will not come to pass. 'Anxiety, Guilt and Therapeutic Liberation' (1962c), 186.

328 *GA* 2, 51-52: 'Höher als die Wirklichkeit steht die *Möglichkeit*'.

329 The discussion is in the section 'Von der Überwindung der Schuldenlast [On Overcoming the Burden of Guilt]' (1962c), 46. The term *Schuldenlast* is perhaps better rendered with 'weight of guilt', implying a permanent burden one always bears or carries that does not change.

330 Boss had recently taken up the theme of socialization in 'Warum verhält sich der Mensch überhaupt Sozial?' (1961b).

331 'Anxiety, Guilt and Psychotherapeutic Liberation' (1962c), 187.

332 'Vielmehr hielten wir uns alle miteinander von Angebinn an schon draußen auf, im ganzen Spielraum dieses Hörsaales anwesend, angespannt in die Offenheit dieses Hörsaales anwesend, ausgespannt in die Offenheit dieses uns erschlossen, gelichteten Weltbereiches und im Verstehen uns darin gemeinsam Begegnenden.' *Lebensangst, Schuldgefühle und therapeutische Befreiung* (1962c), 48-49.

333 The phrase *zum Vorschein kommen* means 'to come to light' in the sense that we say that something previously not known of is discovered or revealed and comes to known *of*. There is the sense that whatever comes to be known *of* was there all along but had lacked what is necessary for it to be revealed, exposed, uncovered and, so, known *about*.

334 'Anxiety, Guilt and Psychotherapeutic Liberation' (1962c), 188.

335 *GA* 2, 268. In a note to this passage, Heidegger refers to the all-important lecture from July 1924 on the concept of time. See *GA* 64, 107-125. In considering what conscience means in terms of the analytics of existence, it must be understood as having nothing to do with a voice that regularly reminds us, for example, to stay in line and behave, which Freud thought was the voice of the father that had been internalized and comes to mind when one is tempted to be 'bad'.

336 *Angst, Schuldgefühle und psychotherapeutische Befreiung* (1962c), 52.

337 *Angst, Schuldgefühle und psychotherapeutische Befreiung* (1962c), 56-57.

338 'Timing' is everything, both for the analyst and the analysand. It is the time of καιρός, the opportune moment.

339 *Psychoanalyse und Daseinsanalytik* (1957a) Bern: Huber, 1957 (2nd ed.), Munich: Kindler 1980; Frankfurt: Fischer 2017 [digital]. English translation: *Psychoanalysis and Daseinsanalysis*, New York: Basic Books, 1963; 2nd ed., New York: Dacapo Press, 1982. Translation by Ludwig B. Lefebre, Elsa Lehman and Mary Hottinger-Mackie.

340 For a detailed discussion of the two works, see the author's *Medard Boss and the Promise of Therapy*, London: Free Association Books, 2020, 52-60.

341 'Daseinsanalytische Bemerkungen zu Freuds Vorstellung des 'Unbewußten' (1960/1961a), *Zeitschrift für psychosomatische Medizin* 7, 1960-61, 130-141, and 'Die Bedeutung der Daseinsanalyse für die psychoanalytische Praxis' (1960/1961b), *Zeitschrift für psychosomatische Medizin* 7, 1960-61, 162-171.

342 *Psychoanalysis and Daseinsanalysis* (1957a), v.

343 *Psychoanalysis and Daseinsanalysis* (1957a), v. Boss writes of 'dozens of letters that had to be exchanged [with Lefebre] in order to crystallize all the questions about the Daseinsanalytic approach.' Only chapter 4 of the English is more or less equivalent to chapter 6 of the German. The new material was written in German, which needed translating. Lefebre was a psychotherapist in California who had been Boss's student in Zürich. Although Lefebre is the only translator named on the title page and in standard bibliographic sources, in fact much of the case material (about sixty pages in all of the 285 pages of the book) was translated by Elsa Lehman, MD (chapters 1, 7, 11 and 20) and

Notes

Mary-Hottinger Mackie (chapter 11, as co-translator with Lehman). Elsa Lehman was a New York psychiatrist who taught at the Cornell University New York Hospital School of Nursing. Mary Hottinger-Mackie was a translator who taught English at the University of Zürich. The opening chapter on 'Dr. Cobling' is given as translated by Lehman. Boss's report on the patient in an Indian journal does not give an alias. See (1958). Nor does the text in 'Heidegger und die Ärzte' (1959b). I have the impression that Boss prepared a fresh version of the case for the publication or returned to an earlier, perhaps his original case report that became the basis for the Lehman translation.

344 Suspicions of antisemitism and reports of Heidegger's involvement with National Socialism led to an exchange of letters between Boss and Farber, and Heidegger never visited the States. In a letter of August 10, 1960, Heidegger wrote to Boss: 'I thank you for your detailed letter with the description of the plan to work with you in Washington for three weeks. All this sounds tempting [*Alles klingt verlockend*]. On the whole, I am inclined to take a chance on it. *One* major difficulty is my very poor command of *English*. I cannot speak the language at all and can barely understand spoken English. Through translation everything gets changed [*verwandelt*] and becomes wearisome [*langwierig*]. My way of thinking and the phenomenological approach will probably still be strange [*fremd*] over there ....' Four months later, he would write to Boss: 'Once again I have to apologize from my heart that I canceled my planned trip to Washington, and with such late notice, that is, only after you went through all the trouble of preparation. Of course, I knew that *Nietzsche* [the two-volume set published in 1960] would keep me very busy until next year, but I did not think that I would have much additional work to do. I would not have been able to prepare for the trip sufficiently. Furthermore, in the end the looming specter of American publicity [*heraufsteigende Gespenst der amerikanische Publicity*] deterred me.' *Zollikon Seminars* (1987a), 255-256. As noted, I have located the correspondence between Farber and Boss from September 1960, in which Boss defends Heidegger against reservations Farber had expressed about Heidegger's visit. Boss eventually said that illness prevented Heidegger from making the trip. That seems not to be the case, however. Heidegger's reference to 'publicity' may indicate that he had heard from someone about the kerfuffle. One might have expected that if the problem was known to anyone in the States, it would have been known to Hannah Arendt, but there is nothing in her published correspondence about it, although Arendt wrote to Heidegger in October 1960.

345 *Psychoanalysis and Daseinsanalysis* (1957a), 49. Earlier in the 'Outline' chapter, Boss tells us that he 'has had a great many discussions and has exchanged many letters with Heidegger concerning possible English translations' of key terms. *Psychoanalysis and Daseinsanalysis* (1957a), 36, n. 4. It is not clear that their exchanges were all that helpful, however, given Heidegger's limited familiarity with English. Boss then quotes from one of those letters from Heidegger: 'The suggestion to translate (a) *das Seiende* or *Seiendes* as 'being' or 'particular being', (b) *Seiendheit*, in the sense of the mode of being of a specific species of things or living beings, as 'being-ness' (lower case), and (c) *Seyn*, as such, as 'Being-ness' (capitalized) seems best. To be sure, in the sufficient distinction between (b) and (c) the whole road of my thinking is concealed, insofar as one follows its progression through the essence of metaphysics. It is probably not accidental that the 'ontological difference' cannot be adequately stated in either English or French.' Some of Lefebre's stated translation decisions did not reflect these suggestions (see *Psychoanalysis and Daseinsanalysis* (1957a), 31). On the term *Daseinsanalyse*, see the translator's note, *Psychoanalysis and Daseinsanalysis* (1957a), 2-3

346 *Psychoanalysis and Daseinsanalysis* (1957a), 230-231.
347 *Psychoanalysis and Daseinsanalysis* (1957a), 235.
348 *Psychoanalysis and Daseinsanalysis* (1957a), 234.
349 *Psychoanalysis and Daseinsanalysis* (1957a), 243.
350 *Psychoanalysis and Daseinsanalysis* (1957a), 245.

351 We have already remarked on Marguerite Sèchehaye's (1887-1964) remarkable *Symbolic Realization*, New York: International Universities Press, 1951, first published in French in 1947 with Boss's publisher, Hans Huber. In the case of 'Renée' (Louisa Düss), Sèchehaye worked with the eighteen-year-old for ten years and eventually adopted her. In turn, Düss became a psychoanalyst. Together, the two produced *Renée. Autobiography of a Schizophrenic Girl* [1950], New York: Grune and Stratton, 1951.
352 *Psychoanalysis and Daseinsanalysis* (1957a), 248.
353 *Psychoanalysis and Daseinsanalysis* (1957a), 284.
354 *Psychoanalysis and Daseinsanalysis* (1957a), 284. Here Boss alludes to what Heidegger will later refer to as the fourfold [*Geviert*] that brings to a point of intersection the spatial (horizontal and vertical) and the temporal (what is limited by a beginning and an end and is mortal, and what has neither a beginning nor an end and is divine). See, for example, 'Das Ding' [1949], *GA* 7, 165-187.
355 *The Review of Metaphysics* 17(3), 1964, 475. There is a single sentence without comment by an unnamed reviewer.
356 *American Sociological Review* 28(5), 1963, 831-832. Reviewed by Edward Tiryakian. A Harvard sociologist, the reviewer was the most sympathetic of Boss's reviewers. He groups Heidegger with John Malthus, Charles Darwin and Karl Marx as being a figure outside of the social sciences whose work, the 'seminal philosophical treatise' *Being and Time*, has the potential for playing a 'catalytic role' in theory development and research for sociology and psychology much as had *The Origin of Species* or *Capital*. He characterizes Heidegger's perspective as 'existential-phenomenological', one at the center of which is *Dasein*, 'human existence seen as a spatial-temporal mode of being intrinsically related to and involved in man's worldly situation'. It is significant that he cites as examples of psychiatrists and psychotherapists influenced by Heidegger, Ludwig Binswanger, Eugène Minkowski and Viktor Frankl, and R. D. Laing, in Europe and the United Kingdom, and Rollo May, Clemens Benda, Frieda Fromm-Reichmann, John Rosen and Carl Rogers in the States. All are said to belong to the 'phenomenological-existential movement', none of whose members, however, could agree on an 'orthodox' approach. As a result, 'existential psychiatry has a variety of named modalities: 'existential analysis', [']logotherapy', 'existential psychotherapy', etc.' This leads Tiryakian to Boss, whom he describes as 'a distinguished Swiss psychiatrist who presents in *Psychoanalysis and Daseinsanalysis* his own 'Daseinsanalysis' approach to clinical psychology.' He distinguishes Boss from Binswanger, who had been identified as a representative of 'existential analysis' in May's *Existence*. The review says that Boss's book is not, like *Existence*, 'an overview of existential psychiatry', but rather an attempt at 'making a comprehensive contrast between the cardinal notions of Freudian psychology and those of existential psychology.' He sees that Boss is interested in recognizing the greatness of Freud as a guide for therapists even while dispensing with the Viennese neurologist's theoretical apparatus. Tiryakian is spot on in noting that 'Boss gives much attention to the clinical situation relating patient and analyst and a Dasein analyst's approach to this role differs from a Freudian analyst's.' He recommends the book to sociologists, for whom 'this book is a worthwhile initial contact with the phenomenological-existential perspective on personality. It will either whet the appetite or dull the taste for further readings in this new horizon.' The review concludes: 'What I wish to suggest, briefly, is that existential analysis may well turn out to be as fruitful a frame of reference common to psychology and sociology as, say, functionalism has been to sociology and anthropology (in fact, I would argue that existential and functional analysis themselves have some common denominators).' The comparison seems not to be apt, but the reviewer was correct in suggesting that 'the acceptance of existential or Daseinsanalysis will not be easy in academic circles, any more than the acceptance of psychoanalysis was less than two generations ago, but it should prove to be as rewarding in the development of our field.' Tiryakian makes the important point that it took two generations to come to terms with

psychoanalysis, which was initially thought to be a bit of quackery. This may well be the fate of daseinanalysis in its renaissance.

357 *British Journal of Psychiatry* 110, #468, September 1964, 738. Reviewed along with Ludwig Binswanger's *Being-in-the-World,* New York: Basic Books, 1963, Frank Fish was not at all sympathetic, claiming that, influenced by Heidegger and existentialism, Boss 'seems concerned to do away with an objective world. If, however, there is no real world which can be used as a yardstick to measure our own and our patients' psychic reality, then it is difficult to find any reason for practicing psychotherapy, or for that matter any branch of medicine.' Clearly also not a fan of psychoanalysis, the reviewer suggests that 'all Boss appears to have done is to reformulate psychoanalytic ideas in a more incomprehensible jargon. Some of his interpretations are even more far-fetched than the usual psychoanalytic ones.' Fish nevertheless encouraged his colleagues to read the book: 'Despite all objections, there is no doubt that Professor Boss has written an interesting and persuasive account of daseinsanalysis, which should be read by everyone interested in psychotherapy and psychopathology.'

358 *Canadian Journal of Psychiatry* 9(4), 1964, 362-363. Like the other reviewer who was a psychiatrist, Dimitrije Pivnicki was less than encouraging. Of the author, he says at the outset: 'Medard Boss is a convert to existentialism and as such seems to be emotionally involved in everything he says.' He speaks of Boss's 'fascinating language and picturesque style' as being a result of having abandoned 'the cold, objective style of science and its disciplined concentration on facts.' Pivnicki is critical of Boss's suggestions that there can be a 'harmonization of psychoanalytic practice and existential philosophy' and that it is possible to 'make a strict separation between psychoanalytic theory and its practice'. Most important, he points to an earlier attempt by the German psychiatrist Alfred Storch (1888-1962) to do what Boss has done. He likely had in mind Storch's *Die Welt der beginnenden Schizophrenie und die archaische Welt: ein existenzial-analytischer Versuch* [*The World of Incipient Schizophrenia and the Archaic World: An Existential-analytic Study*], Berlin: Springer, 1930. If that is the case, it is worth bearing in mind that Storch had much the same misunderstanding of Heidegger's *Daseinsanalytik* as did Binswanger. The reviewer doubtfully points to Boss's claim that Freud was 'actually only an 'unconscious' existential analyst', so that 'the psychoanalytic approach and practice of Freud have always been a Daseinsanalytic understanding'. Pivnicki is familiar with the original German version of the book, whose 'charm, impressiveness and suggestibility' he suggests have been lost in translation. However, given that only a few pages of *Psychoanalyse und Daseinsanalytik* were translated for the 'enlargement' of 'the rather slim and small monograph', the reviewer evidently did not take a close look at both books. Pivnicki spends more time on Heidegger than the other reviewers do, beginning with a reference to Boss's attention to Heidegger's original vocabulary. Pivnicki has in mind the sections in which he identifies Boss speculating on the etymology of words such as '*Dasein*', '*Sein*', '*das Seiende*'. The reviewer is skeptical of attention to the sources of words, comparing it to a species of Gnosticism: 'Words given a great halo around their trivial everyday meaning consequently acquire the impression of transcending the mundane and passing into the realm of truth. This is a dangerous and highly uncertain procedure,' he continues. He is concerned that such a book as Boss has written is probably accessible only to German-speaking readers who would 'get' the sense of basic words Boss is ostensibly using to transmit information about a technique to future generations of practitioners. 'Can the firm convictions of Medard Boss really be transmitted through the 'rational' framework of his book' if, the reviewer seems to be suggesting, what is to be transmitted is not rational? Pivnicki raises several stinging questions: 'Could we improve psychotherapy and our understanding of man by studying [his book]? Has Medard Boss explained what were the ways and means through which his patients have improved and become better? Does he really believe that he was successful in telling us that secret?' He concludes that he is 'afraid that he [Boss] has only

Notes

given us one more radical proof that the success of psychotherapy, to a great degree, depends on the convictions, enthusiasm and charm, if we may say, of the therapist, charm emanating from him and influencing his patients, helping them to take the road to improvement.' The review is worth considering in some detail for its comments on Heidegger. Pivnicki wants the prospective reader to consider that given Boss's acknowledgement of Heidegger's 'detailed discussions with the author ... Heidegger himself has never written, as far as we know, one word about what he feels, and what he does not [feel] about the application of his philosophy to Medicine in general and to Psychiatry in particular.' Of course, as Boss reports in the preface to the first German edition of the *Zollikon Seminars*: 'Only much later did I discover the most important motive for Heidegger's prompt answer to my first letter [1946]. From the beginning, as he himself once admitted, Heidegger had set great hope on an association with a doctor who had a seemingly extensive understanding of his thought. He saw the possibility that his philosophical insights would not be confined merely to the philosopher's quarters but also might benefit many more people, especially people in need of help [*hilfsbedürfigten Menschen*].' See *Zollikon Seminars* (1987a), xvii. Cf. 237 for an excerpt from the letter. The excerpt from the 1947 letter reveals that Boss had informed Heidegger about his *Habilitation* thesis, which would be published as *Sinn und Gehalt der sexuellen Perversionen* (1947). In addition, the year *Psychoanalysis and Daseinsanalysis* was published, Heidegger wrote to Boss on the occasion of the psychiatrist's sixtieth birthday with 'one word' about his hopes for the possible contribution to the 'helping profession [*helfenden Beruf*]' that his thought might provide. See *Zollikon Seminars* (1987a), 264. The review ends with the observation: 'It remains to be seen how much of the Boss 'system' will influence the coming generation of psychotherapists and how much he will become the founder of a new school and consequently isolate himself. It is difficult to foresee great success from this attempt.' This was not of much encouragement to Canadian psychiatrists and others who read the review. 'On the other hand his words have an inflammatory power, power to provoke controversy and disturb comfortable stagnations, and through that to promote discussion, at times in a most spirited way. This is useful.' Pivnicki (1918-2007) lived long enough to see publication of the *Zollikon Seminars* and would have had an opportunity to look back on his appraisal of Boss's work twenty-three years earlier.

359 'Existential Psychoanalysis', in B. Wolman (ed.), *Psychoanalytic Techniques*, New York: Basic Books, 1967, 443-467. Written in English.

360 Two sections of Jean-Paul Sartre's *L'Être et le Néant*, Paris: Gallimard, 1943, were published in an English translation by Hazel Barnes as *Existential Psychoanalysis*, New York: Philosophical Library, 1953. They were a teaser for the publication of the book in its entirety in 1956. The parts of *Being and Nothingness* published as *Existential Psychoanalysis* are: Part IV (ii, I-III): *Faire et avoir* (Doing and Having) – (I) *La psychanalyse existentielle* (Existential Psychoanalysis) (II) *Faire et avoir: La possession* ('Doing' and 'Having': Possession), (III) *De la qualité comme révélatrice de l'être* (Quality as a Revelation of Being), and Part I (ii, I-III): *La mauvaise foi* (Bad Faith) – (I) *Mauvaise foi et mensonge* (Bad Faith and Falsehood), (II) *Les conduites de mauvaise foi* (Patterns of Bad Faith), (III) *La 'foi' de la mauvaise foi* (The 'Faith' of Bad Faith). I have used Barnes's translation of the headings. A new translation by Sarah Richmond has only recently been published (New York: Washington Square Press, 2021). *Existential Psychoanalysis* was widely reviewed in philosophy journals (*Philosophy and Phenomenological Research, Ethics, The British Journal of Philosophy of Science, The Journal of Philosophy*) and journals in the social sciences (*Phylon (1940-1956), The Southwestern Social Science Quarterly*), but not in journals of psychoanalysis, so that psychoanalysts were likely unaware that such a form of psychoanalysis had been named. A later English edition of *Existential Analysis* (Chicago: Henry Regnery, 1962) contains an important introduction by Rollo May. May addresses the misleading nature of the title of this extract from Sartre's larger work: 'The name *Existential*

Notes

Psychoanalysis suggests that Sartre will offer an alternative form of psychoanalysis. This he neither does nor seeks to do; indeed, he rightly acknowledges that *a genuine existential psychoanalysis can not yet be formulated or written* [emphasis added] ... He indicates [however] ... in what direction an existential psychoanalysis might be developed.' See Rollo May, 'Introduction' to Jean-Paul Sartre, *Existential Psychoanalysis*, 9. May points out Sartre's rejection of the Freudian Unconscious, but for different reasons than Boss does, acknowledging that 'Sartre is in the general line of the phenomenological psychologists and psychiatrists such as [Kurt] Goldstein, [Ludwig] Binswanger and Boss.' He repeats his disclaimer at the end of the Introduction, that Sartre's "psychoanalysis' is not supposed to be a worked-out new form of technical analysis' (17). As it happens, this did not prevent Sartre from 'practicing' existential psychoanalysis with individuals, even though he had no experience as an analysand and no preparation or training as a psychotherapist of any sort, let alone as a psychoanalyst. He wrote to the French psychoanalyst and friend, Jean-Bertrand Pontalis (1924-2013) about his work as an existential psychoanalyst. See Hazel Rowley, *Tête-à-Tête. The Tumultuous Lives & Loves of Simone de Beauvoir & Jean-Paul Sartre*, New York: HarperCollins, 2005, 311.
361 'Existential Psychoanalysis' (1967c), 443.
362 After the introductory sentence and in line with the title of Boss's 1963 book, the authors commit to the term 'Daseinsanalysis' (capitalized) for their 'existential psychoanalysis'. These details may seem to be pedantic and yet it is important to be aware of such historical details to appreciate the confusion of tongues around matters 'existential' that persists.
363 In addition to the Boss-Condrau chapter, which was the last of 'The Non-Freudian Techniques' (preceded by chapters on Alfred Adler's 'individual psychology', Karen Horney's 'holistic approach', and Sullivan's 'interpersonal approach'), the volume covered 'The [Orthodox] Freudian Technique', 'Freudians and Neo-Freudians' (represented by Sándor Ferenczi, Melanie Klein, Franz Alexander and Thomas French, and John Rosen, as well as Wolman's own 'interactional psychoanalysis', and contributions by Hyman Spotnitz and Martin Grotjahn), and 'Special Techniques' ('psychoanalytic psychotherapy', 'psychoanalytically oriented group psychotherapy', and 'hypnoanalysis'). It was a textbook of *techniques* by heavyweights in the psychoanalytic movement during the peak of its influence in the States. We learn that Wolman 'consulted' with Anna Freud, Edward Glover, M. Masud R. Khan, Sándor Rado, Bertram Lewin and Mark Kanzer – all major figures in orthodox Freudian psychoanalysis – to determine which approaches should be included in the handbook.
364 'Existential Psychoanalysis' (1967c), 444.
365 The following year, another important anthology, edited by J. G. Howells, was published to which Boss and Condrau contributed. There the approach was referred to throughout as 'existential analysis'. See (1968b), reviewed next. Only in 1970 was the term 'Daseinsanalysis' used in a reprint of part of the text of the Howells anthology.
366 'Existential Psychoanalysis' (1967c), 445.
367 'Existential Psychoanalysis' (1967c), 444-445.
368 'Existential Psychoanalysis' (1967c), 447.
369 'Existential Psychoanalysis' (1967c), 447.
370 Here, with his reference to an outdoor playground [*Spielplatz*], Boss suggests an alternative to Freud's *Tummelplatz* (usually an indoor play area).
371 'Existential Psychoanalysis' (1967c), 448.
372 On the problem of (and with) empathy, see *Zollikon Seminars* (1987a), 111, 162. The term *Empathie* was a neologism that appeared on the scene only in 1895 in philosophy and was adopted by American psychologists only in the mid-1940s. OED q.v. 'empathy'.
373 In German, 'perception' is '*Wahrnehmung*', that is, taking to be (*nehmen*) true (*wahr*) or what is actually the case.

Notes

374 'Existential Psychoanalysis' (1967c), 449.
375 'Existential Psychoanalysis' (1967c), 450-451.
376 'Existential Psychoanalysis' (1967c), 450. See also 'Das Phänomen des Widerstandes in der Daseinsanalyse [The Phenomenon of Resistance in Daseinsanalysis]' (1981c).
377 'Existential Psychoanalysis' (1967c), 450-451.
378 Sigmund Freud, 'A Note on the Unconscious in Psycho-Analysis' [1912], *SE* XII, 255. 'Um dieser Tatsache Rechnung zu tragen, sind wir zu der Annahme genötigt, daß die Vorstellung auch während der Zwischenzeit in unserem Geiste gegenwärtig gewesen sei, wenn sie auch im Bewußtsein latent blieb. In welcher Gestalt sie aber existiert haben kann, während sie im Seelenleben gegenwärtig und im Bewußtsein latent war, darüber können wir keine Vermutungen aufstellen.' The paper was originally written in English by Freud and later translated into German by Hanns Sachs. The text published in the *Standard Edition* is a version prepared by James Strachey. The key term is 'latent', which is, of course, in Freud's psychology of dreams the state of the dream thoughts [*Gedanken*]. On the connections between knowing, consciousness and the Unconscious that are evident in German, but not in English, we note that '*bewußt* (conscious)' is a form of the verb *wissen* (to know), specifically a modification of the past participle of the verb – '*gewußt*' – which refers to current knowing *of* something. What is *bewußt* is both currently known *of* and also present to and in one's awareness. What is *unbewußt* (unconscious), then, is known *of* but not present to and in one's awareness. In this state it is *as if* were not known.
379 The phenomenology of Edmund Husserl (1959-1938), Freud's contemporary, attempted to render intelligible the structure of consciousness in relation to the objects it is conscious of, something that Freud's metapsychology could not do. Both simply postulate consciousness without making clear what it is. Notice that, for Freud, consciousness (literally, being conscious [*Bewußtsein*]) is a faculty attributed to human beings (as to animals), whereas, as a location in the psychic apparatus, the Unconscious [*Unbewußt*] is the reification of a state, namely, a not awake [*bewußt*] state. Considered as a state, unconsciousness [*Unbewußtsein*] means simply not being awake. The latter term is used only three times by Freud in relation to his notion of the location of a system in his model of the psychic apparatus. This is likely because talk about 'a consciousness' (*ein Bewußtsein*, as a *state*) and 'an Unconscious' (*ein Unbewußt*, as a *location*, a *container*, and contents of the container) introduces serious categorical confusion. Framing discussion of the latter in terms of psychodynamics does not solve the problem. Just what 'a Consciousness' could mean is problematic, since it is not, like the Unconscious, a location. It is precisely here that the difficulty with the notion of consciousness arises for Freud. As Boss points out, it is simply taken over from Gustav Fechner (1801-1887), who spoke in terms of 'psychic localities' and layers, as it were, of psychic activity. However, *metaphorically* localizing Consciousness and then suggesting that something is to be found 'below' [*unter*] it (namely, the Subconscious [*Unterbewußt*]) simply does not fly. Nor does substituting the not-conscious (*unbewußt*) for the below-conscious (*unterbewußt*) without reconceiving a state as a location or a location as a state. Freud explicitly rejects the terms Subconscious [*Unterbewußte*] and subconsciousness [*Unterbewußtsein*]. He does this in order to distinguish between what is psychical [*psychisch*] and what is conscious [*bewußt*], which leaves him contrasting a location and a state. Finally, what is *unbewußt* refers to contents that are not in conscious awareness (i.e., known of but not in awareness), but what is designated as *unterbewußt* would seem to imply a second consciousness found at a lower level of layered functions. For discussion of this issue, see *The Language of Psychoanalysis*, 'Subconscious, Subconsciousness' qv. (430-431).
380 'Existential Psychoanalysis' (1967c), 454.
381 The allusion here is to Freud's paper 'Remembering, Repeating and Working Through' [1914]. *SE* XII, 145-157. This is the second of Freud's papers on 'further recommendations on the technique of psycho-analysis'.

382 'Existential Psychoanalysis' (1967c), 458.
383 'Existential Psychoanalysis' (1967c), 458.
384 'Existential Psychoanalysis' (1967c), 459.
385 'Existential Psychoanalysis' (1967c), 461.
386 'Existential Psychoanalysis' (1967c), 462.
387 Freud actually writes of a patient whose *compulsion to repeat* is given free reign in 'die Tummelplatz [of the transference] ... sich in fast völliger Freiheit zu entfalten [ist].' *SE* XII, 154.
388 'Existential Psychoanalysis' (1967c), 466-467.
389 'Existential Analysis' (1968b), in J. G. Howells (ed.), *Modern Perspectives in World Psychiatry*, London: Oliver & Boyd, 1968, 488-518.
390 Delay and Deniker were among the first to experiment with the use of Thorazine (chlorpromazine) among hospitalized patients in the early 1950s. They came under fire, however, for not having had proper consent from patients. They also experimented with LSD and other hallucinogens in the treatment of in-patient schizophrenics. Student protests in 1968 related to the 'antipsychiatry movement' challenged Delay's use of 'chemical straightjackets' and physically forced him out of his office and practice as a psychiatrist. Around this time a number of psychiatrists, including the daseinsanalyst, Roland Kuhn, were also charged with unethical practices in the use of the then new psychotropic medications.
391 Rollo May, Ernest Angel and Henri F. Ellenberger (eds.), *Existence. A New Dimension in Psychiatry and Psychology*, New York: Simon and Schuster, 1958.
392 See, for example, *Two Essays on Analytical Psychology*, Princeton: Bollingen, 1967. The *Collected Works* in the Bollingen edition had begun in 1953.
393 Ludwig Binswanger, *Grundformen und Erkenntnis menschlichen Daseins* (2nd ed.), Zurich: Niehans, 1953, 449.
394 *GA* 9, 324-325. *Pathmarks*, New York: Cambridge University Press, 1998, 246-247.
395 *GA* 2, 56: 'Das 'Wesen' des Daseins liegt in seiner Existenz.' – 'The 'essence' of being there [*da*] lies in its standing out into the open.' Here we have perhaps the most telling 'translation' of this key sentence in *Sein und Zeit*.
396 'Existential Analysis' (1968b), 494.
397 'Existential Analysis' (1968b), 497.
398 'Existential Analysis' (1968b), 497.
399 'Existential Analysis' (1968b), 498.
400 See, for example, *Die Kunst und der Raum* [1969], *GA* 13, 203-210, and passages in the *Zollikon Seminars* (1987a), 8-17, 28-35.
401 'Existential Analysis' (1968b), 499. The authors add that understanding 'things as what they are naturally includes the possibility of also misunderstanding them.... Even in such a mistaken perception, there still is understanding of something as something, though an erroneous one.' It is the 'as-structure' as Heidegger terms it in *Being and Time* that is crucial here. See *GA* 2, 198-213. A fascinating example from daseinanalytic practice is of a man whose perception of the body was fundamentally altered by having early on mistaken the back of a man's body as the front. Curious interests, erotic fantasies and preferences regarding his own body and that of all males made sense and lost their fascination when that fundamental misunderstanding was realized by him.
402 'Existential Analysis' (1968b), 502.
403 As noted, word of the seminars was first given in 1977 in a tribute to Heidegger, *Erinnerung an Martin Heidegger*, Pfullingen: Neske, 1977, pp. 31-45. The "teaser" text was translated into English that same year.
404 *Grundriß der Medizin. Ansätze zu einer phänomenologischen Physiologie, Psychologie, Pathologie, Therapie und zu einer daseinsgemäßen Präventiv-Medizin in der modernen Industrie-Gesellschaft*, Bern: Huber, 1971 (2nd, expanded ed., 1975; 3rd ed., 1999, with a 'Preface' by Marianne Boss) (1971a). We recall again that a new title was used beginning with

second edition, *Grundriß der Medizin und Psychologie. Ansätze zu einer phänomenologischen Physiologie, Psychologie, Pathologie, Therapie und zu einer daseinsgemäßen Präventiv Medizin in der modernen Industrie-Gesellschaft*. English translation: *Existential Foundations of Medicine and Psychology*, New York: Jason Aronson, 1979. Translation by Stephen Conway and Anne Cleaves of the second edition. A more faithful translation of the title would be *Outline of Medicine and Psychology: Approaches to Phenomenological Physiology, Psychology, Pathology and Therapy, and an Existential Preventative Medicine*.

405 See my article 'Medicine and Dasein-therapy. Medard Boss and the Beginnings of a Human Therapeutics', *Free Associations. Psychoanalysis and Culture, Media, Groups, Politics*, #46, September 2019, 108-135.

406 *Existential Foundations of Medicine and Psychology* (1971a), xxiii.

407 *Existential Foundations of Medicine and Psychology* (1971a), xxiii-xxiv.

408 *Existential Foundations of Medicine and Psychology* (1971a), xxv.

409 *Existential Foundations of Medicine and Psychology* (1971a), xvii.

410 See *GA 42* (1988), first published in 1971, the year the *Grundriß* was first published.

411 'Der psychotherapeutische Prozeß', in M. Boss, G. Condrau, and A. Hicklin (eds.), *Leiben und Leben. Beiträge zur Psychosomatik und Psychotherapie*, Bern: Benteli, 1977, 233-246 (1977c). Reprinted in *Von der Psychoanalyse zur Daseinsanalyse. Wege zu einem neuen Selbstverständnis* (1979c), Vienna: Europaverlag, 1979, 469-476. Quotations are from the text in *Leiben und Leben*.

412 'Der psychotherapeutische Prozeß' (1977c), 235.

413 'Der psychotherapeutische Prozeß' (1977c), 236.

414 Here Boss is contrasting the well-studied philosophical and theological problem of immanence [*Immanenz*] and transcendence [*Transzendenz*], while playing on the literal meaning of 'transcend' (*übersteigen* [German] and *transcendere* [Latin]). It is important to recall that for Heidegger *Dasein* is *transcendens* proper.

415 'Der psychotherapeutische Prozeß' (1977c), 240.

416 'Der psychotherapeutische Prozeß' (1977c), 241.

417 'Der psychotherapeutische Prozeß' (1977c), 245.

418 'Der psychotherapeutische Prozeß' (1977c), 245-246.

419 The author had the privilege of presenting a discussion of the major ideas of this paper on October 18, 2023, in Belo Horizonte, Brazil, at an annual conference on existential psychotherapy hosted by the faculty of the Department of Psychology at the Federal University of Minais Gerais. The paper, 'Freedom and the Irrational in Psychotherapy', will be published in a Portuguese translation. The epigraph for the present volume is from Boss's paper. See (1982b), 22.

420 See especially 'Begegnung in der Psychotherapie', *Psychotherapy and Psychosomatics* 13(5), 1965, pp. 332-341. Reprinted in *Von der Psychoanalyse zur Daseinsanalyse. Wege zu einem neuen Selbstverständnis*, Vienna: Europaverlag, 1979, 287-294.

421 'Begegnung und Auseinandersetzung mit sich selbst in der Schuld und im Gewissen' (1981d), in R. Battegay (ed.), *Herausforderung und Begegnung in der Psychiatrie [Festschrift zum 60. Geburtstag von G. Benedetti]*, Bern: Hans Huber, 1981, 54-60. Reprinted in *Von der Spannweite der Seele. Ausgewählte Vorträge und Aufsätze aus den Anwendungsbereichen des daseinsanalytischen Menschenverständnisses* (1982b), Bern: Benteli, 1982, 69-97.

422 'Begegnung und Auseinandersetzung mit sich selbst in der Schuld und im Gewissen' (1981d), 69.

423 'Begegnung und Auseinandersetzung mit sich selbst in der Schuld und im Gewissen' (1981d), 75-76.

424 The play on *Gebirge* (*Ge-birge*) and *Gewissen* (*Ge-wissen*) is taken from Heidegger. The prefix *ge-* indicates that certain matters have taken place and are already in place. In the case of a mountain range, it is that a group of individual mountains manifest as one

Notes

sprawling entity; in the case of conscience, it is knowledge of the great variety of possibilities open to a given existence, manifesting as one capability or 'know-how' in the serial actualization of individual possibilities. The Latin *conscientia* captures this sense: con- (being with) + *scientia* (understanding how to do something and in a certain way). The term 'science' refers to a certain *kind* and *way* of knowing, namely, grasping things as objects as a subject and subjecting them to control. Heidegger's point is that before there can be what psychologists have termed consciousness in the sense as a mental function, there is this knowing awareness of one's possibilities.

425 'Begegnung und Auseinandersetzung mit sich selbst in der Schuld und im Gewissen' (1981d), 82.

426 'Begegnung und Auseinandersetzung mit sich selbst in der Schuld und im Gewissen' (1981d), 82.

427 The objections are that, understood daseinsanalytically, conscience (1) does not apply to specific instances; (2) cannot provide an exhaustive account of its content, which moral philosophy would require; (3) reflects conformity to what 'the Establishment' (*das Man*) currently sees as 'good' and 'bad'; and (4) is a 'purely theoretical' and 'purely academic' undertaking and therefore has no real applicability to social problems or in the therapeutic setting. Boss' replies can be summarized as reminding the critics that (1) they misunderstand the meaning of 'world'; (2) human being is ever-changing (indeed, that the human being never 'is' something, but exists) as it is modified by one's innumerable, successive choices; (3) the focus of the approach is not on specific isolated behaviors (as if such could be singled out and examined as though they were worldless specimens) but rather on how the person lives his life [*Existenz*]; and, finally, (4) that 'there is no thinking about 'being [*Sein*]' as such and in itself without also considering human being there [*Da-sein*] and its being [ontologically] indebted.' The critics responded to in the case of (4) failed to see the givenness of existence.

428 'Begegnung und Auseinandersetzung mit sich selbst in der Schuld und im Gewissen' (1981d), 95.

429 'Die normale Angst' (1982a) in *Neue Zürcher Zeitung* 271, November 20, 1982, 37.

430 'Gewähren und Versagen in der in der Psychotherapie' (1982f), in *Von der Spannweite der Seele. Ausgewählte Vorträge und Aufsätze aus den Anwendungsbereichen des daseinsanalytischen Menschenverständnisses* (1982b), Bern: Benteli, 1982, 98-110. The essay is represented in the notes on sources as a heretofore 'unpublished contribution'.

431 Boss will contrast the Freudian technique said to be based on complete abstinence with *Gewährungstherapien* (permissive therapies). The terms based on *gewähren* (in effect, 'to allow') play with the notions of giving permission for and giving free play to what is emerging.

432 'But even if Freud would turn over in his grave in view of such actions, this would not be the slightest proof that his technique of abstention is therapeutically superior to such 'group therapies', whose methods I tend to call those of 'instant satisfaction' [in English]. One can, however, make the matter easy for oneself by looking down from the pedestal of Freud's pure, orthodox teaching with contempt for the new permissive therapies [*Gewährungstherapien*] and condemning them as cures which served only the resistance [*Widerstand*] of the sick person to help himself. Therefore they could not possibly lead to a recovery [*Heilung*] in the sense of leading to autonomous, free individuality [*Persönlichkeit*].' Boss notes that in his practice, as one who both worked with patients and prepared other daseinanalysts, he has had ample opportunity to look more closely at how the analysand's perception of what is going on in the analytic process affects it. Finally, he takes into consideration how very different the social climate was a half-century after he had experienced first-hand Freud's way of working. We face a similar problem now a half-century after the beginnings of daseinanalysis, namely, a very different world.

433 'Gewähren und Versagen in der Psychotherapie' (1982f), 107.

Notes

434 'Gewähren und Versagen in der Psychotherapie' (1982f), 109-110.
435 'Recent Considerations in Daseinsanalysis' (1988b), *The Humanistic Psychologist* 16(1), 1988, 210-230.
436 The issue of *The Humanistic Psychologist* in which this and 'An Encounter with Medard Boss' (1988b) appears includes a number of photographs that had not been available to the general public before. In addition to several informal portraits of Boss, there are 'Martin Heidegger and Medard Boss on the *Feldweg*, Meßkirch 1963', 'Swami Govind Kaul, Boss's Teacher in India in the Kashmir Valley', 'Medard Boss in 'Heidegger's Chair' in the Zollikon seminar room, August 10, 1965', 'Eric Craig and Medard Boss in Boss's Library/Waiting Room, August 1987', 'Medard Boss, age 26, as a Young psychiatrist during his early 'psychoanalytic years', 'Medard Boss, age 5', 'Medard Boss, age 35, as a captain in the medical corps of the Swiss Army', 'A painting by Medard Boss: 'A Portrait of Human Suffering', 'Self-portrait by Medard Boss', 'A Painting by Medard Boss: 'A peasant's farm (*Anwesen*)', 'Martin Heidegger and Medard Boss in the Zollikon seminar room, 1965', 'Martin Heidegger in the Zollikon seminar room, 1965', 'Medard Boss and Martin Heidegger on the *Feldweg* looking toward Meßkirch (Heidegger's birthplace), 1963', 'Gion Condrau outside his chalet in Flims, March 1987', 'Gion Condrau, Medard Boss and Alois Hicklin in front of The Daseinsanalytic Institute, May 1987', 'An Institute seminar: Alois Hicklin, Medard Boss, Andre Thali, Gion Condrau, May 6, 1987', and 'Medard Boss in his analyst chair, August 26, 1987'.
437 'Recent Considerations in Daseinsanalysis' (1988a), 68-69.
438 'Recent Considerations in Daseinsanalysis' (1988a), 69.
439 In a note (74, n. 9), Boss stresses that primordial freedom is not something a person 'possesses': 'We do not really possess such fundamental characteristics [of freedom] but rather we exist *as* them. It is all too easy to slip into the habit of thinking that first there is a *Da-sein* and then this *Da-sein* 'takes possession' of its basic traits [*existentialia*]. In Sanskrit and Hindi there is no word for the idea of possession! Even if you buy something in India there is no way to say that you possess it but only that you are *close to it*. There is no way to say 'this belongs to me' but only that 'I am close to it'.'
440 'Recent Considerations in Daseinsanalysis' (1988a), 70.
441 'Recent Considerations in Daseinsanalysis' (1988a), 70.
442 'Recent Considerations in Daseinsanalysis' (1988a), 70-71.
443 'Recent Considerations in Daseinsanalysis' (1988a), 71.
444 'Recent Considerations in Daseinsanalysis' (1988a), 72.
445 'Recent Considerations in Daseinsanalysis' (1988a), 72.
446 *Indienfahrt eines Psychiaters*, Pfullingen: Neske, 1959; 2nd ed., Freiburg: Herder, 1966 (abridged version); 3rd ed., Bern: Huber, 1976; 4th, expanded and illustrated ed., Bern: Huber 1987; 5th ed., Bern: Huber, 2006 (1959a). The final chapter of the English translation, 'Eastern Wisdom and Western Psychotherapy' (184-192), was reprinted in John Welwood (ed.), *The Meeting of the Ways,* New York: Schocken, 1979, 183-191. English translation: *A Psychiatrist Discovers India*, London: Wolff, 1965. Translation by Henry A. Frey. An important postscript was added to the third edition (261-263). The fourth edition includes 'After Thirty Years. Preface to *Indian Journey of a Psychiatrist* (fourth Edition)' [1987], *Review of Existential Psychology and Psychiatry* 27(1-3), 2002/2003, 33-36. Reprinted as a monograph by K. Hoeller (ed.), *The Heidegger-Boss Relationship* (Seattle: Review of Existential Psychology and Psychiatry, 2008), 33-36. This, Boss said, was his 'favorite book' of those he published. It is of interest in connection with his work with Heidegger in having been published the year of the lecture the philosopher gave at the Zürich Psychiatric Clinic (September 8, 1959), an event that opened the way to the Zollikon seminars themselves, which began in earnest more than four years later (January 24, 1964) at Boss's home. The English translation, which contains two important references to Heidegger, appeared five years later during the second year of the seminars in 1965. In 1976, the year Heidegger died, Boss added a

Notes

postscript in which he repeated a tribute to Heidegger which, of course, did not make its way into the English translation (1965). The fourth edition of the 'India book', published the same year as Heidegger's *Zollikoner Seminare* (1987a), which Boss edited, contains an important preface. The book he and Heidegger worked on together, the *Grundriß*, was published in 1971, three years after the seminars had wrapped up. The seminars had run a little more than four years, from January 24, 1964 to March 21, 1968. The seminars and added material should be read with the history of the editions of the 'India book' in mind.

447 The author has discussed this book in detail in several publications: 'Medard Boss and Martin Heidegger. The Existential Analyst as 'a Western kind of *rishi*', *Review of Existential Psychology and Psychiatry* 27 (1-3), 2008, 43-60; *Medard Boss and the Promise of Therapy. The Beginnings of Daseinsanalysis*, London: Free Association Books, 2020, 99-122; and 'Heidegger and Boss's India. On Encounter in Daseinanalysis', *Daseinsanalyse* 38, 2022, 26-44.

448 *A Psychiatrist Discovers India* (1959a), 180.

449 *A Psychiatrist Discovers India* (1959a), 128-129, 139. The two important passages were added for the English translation. We will review these below.

450 Hoch published some of Boss's letters from 1960. See (1960c).

451 *Indienfahrt eines Psychiaters* (3rd ed.) (1976) (1959a), 262. These 'realities [*Gegebenheiten*]' are better understood as 'givens'.

452 As we have seen, the word *Lichtung* is central to Heidegger's vocabulary. The senses range from 'clarifying' and 'making clearer', to 'showing up in contrast to what else is nearby'. The references to a forest glade or clearing are common in discussions of the later Heidegger, but the term is first seen in *Being and Time* in connection with discussions of being-in [*In-sein*] and the famous *lumen naturale* human beings were said to be possessed of. See GA 2, 226. The sense of coming to see something as it is (at all, or for the first time, or as it is) is central to Heidegger's phenomenological method. Such first sighting of something is central to daseinanalysis. Boss frequently refers to the basic character of existing as making accommodation for what there is that is encountering us precisely in order for it to be seen in the sense of 'I *see* what you mean', often for the first time. We say a child 'takes it all in' or that an enraptured, awestruck person seeing something remarkable is 'taking it all in'. This is related to the human being's distinctive *Vernehmenkönnen* or ability to take in [*Vernehmen*]. The psychological notion of perception [*Vorstellung*], which has dominated the discussion of such 'getting it' and 'taking it in', is frequently criticized by Boss. There 'taking in' is understood as somehow internalizing something, capturing and removing to an 'inner place' what is 'out there' in the 'real world'. Objects are somehow incorporated by and into a subject, construed as a container-like psyche. The best general translation for *Lichtung* is luminance, but it is important not to forget its other nuances. The German *Licht* and the English *light* have in common the sense of a brightness that refers to what makes something stand out from among other things and come into view. The question will become whether and, if so, how human standing out (ek-sisting) is related to a dawning of [*Aufgehen*] something on the human being, just as things little by little by come into view after the darkness of night. Finally, there is the sense of *light* that refers to a lightening or thinning out or making less dense.

453 *Indienfahrt eines Psychiaters* (3rd ed.) (1959a), 264

454 On what Boss has to say about Indian philosophy, see *A Psychiatrist Discovers India* (1959a), 125-140. Briefly, *Brahman* is primal luminance (perhaps *Urlicht*), which is more fundamental than the luminating [*Lichtende*] of *Dasein*. Boss's mentor, Govind Kaul, traces the word back to *braha*, which is said to mean 'to grow [*wachsen*] and ever more encompass what is unfolding [*immer mehr Aufgehendes umfassen*]'. For *atman* or being human [*Menschsein*] it is perhaps best to think of it as 'but a subphenomenon [*Teilphänomen*] of *Brahman*'. Boss's teacher was clear that *all such terms should not be understood as substantives but always verbally* – like be[ing] [*Sein*]. See *Indienfahrt eines*

Notes

Psychiaters (4th ed., 1979) {1959a}, 170-171. In fact, in this text we read that *Sein* is to be understood verbally, that is, as an action verb (125). Here Indian wisdom and Heideggerian thought converge on an essential point.

455 *A Psychiatrist Discovers India* (1959a), 185.
456 *A Psychiatrist Discovers India* (1959a), 185.
457 The term is taken from Heidegger, who in turn had discovered it in Meister Eckhart. See 'Gelassenheit. Bodenständigkeit im Atomzeitalter [Serenity. Down-to-earthiness in the Atomic Age]' from 1955 (GA 13, 517-529). The essay was translated as 'Memorial Address', in *Discourse on Thinking* [1966], New York: Harper and Row, 1970, 43-57. The term '*Gelassenheit*'ranges over senses including imperturbable equanimity, composure, serenity and a posed calm, to a detachment from things.
458 *A Psychiatrist Discovers India* (1959a), 187.
459 *A Psychiatrist Discovers India* (1959a), 188.
460 *A Psychiatrist Discovers India* (1959a), 189.
461 *A Psychiatrist Discovers India* (1959a), 190.
462 *A Psychiatrist Discovers India* (1959a), 191.
463 *A Psychiatrist Discovers India* (1959a), 191.
464 *A Psychiatrist Discovers India* (1959a), 191.
465 Those who have a copy of the fourth edition of Boss's 'India book' are treated to a series of color photographs that followed the short 'Postscript' to the third edition. While we have a number of portraits of Boss the patrician Swiss physician, only here do we have a glimpse at the world that changed his outlook and opened his eyes to what a genuinely human therapy could be. Apart from photographs of two of the sages with whom he worked, including Govind Kaul in Shrinigar, we see pictured, among others, an eleven-year-old boy who was beginning his apprenticeship as a monk, a yogi priest and a female sage, an Ayurvedic physician treating a boy who has been bitten by a poisonous snake and, most compelling of all in one sense, pictures of Boss' simple bedroom at an ashram in Anandamoyee and the view from a room at another such place in Rishikesh. These are quite different places than, for example, the Hotel Zürichsberg where daseinanalysts from around the world met most recently in 2023.
466 'Nach dreißig Jahren', introductory essay for *Indienfahrt eines Psychiaters* (4th ed.), Bern: Huber, 1987, 6-10 (2002/2003b). English translation: 'After Thirty Years: Preface to *A Psychiatrist Discovers India* (4th ed., 1987)', *Review of Existential Psychology and Psychiatry* 27(1-3), 2002/2003, 33-36. Reprinted as a monograph by K. Hoeller (ed.), *The Heidegger-Boss Relationship,* Seattle: Review of Existential Psychology and Psychiatry, 2008. Translation by Michael Eldred.
467 'Nach dreißig Jahren' (2002/2003b), 6.
468 'After Thirty Years' (2002/2003b), 35.
469 The word appears only twice: (1) first (already noted), in the section on 'being in [*In-sein*]' in the context of a comment on the so-called *lumen naturale*; and (2) second, in the section on curiosity [*Neugier*]: (1) 'The ontically figurative talk of a *lumen naturale* in the human being means nothing other than the existential-ontological structure of this being [*Seiende*], that it *is* by way [*Weise*] of being its there [*sein Da zu sein*]. It is 'enlightened [*erleuchtet*]', means [that it is] luminant [*gelichtet*] in itself *as* being-in-the-world, not by another being [*Seiende*] but rather such that it itself *is* the luminance [*Lichtung*]. Only to an existentially thus illuminated being are extant things [*Vorhandenen*] accessible in the light [*im Licht*] hidden in the darkness.' GA 2, 177. (2) 'In the analysis of the understanding [*Verstehen*] and the disclosure [*Erscholssenheit*] of the there [*Da*] in general, reference was made to the *lumen naturale* and the disclosure of being-in [*In-sein*] was called the luminance [*Lichtung*] of D*asein* in which only something like sight [*Sicht*] becomes possible. With regard to the basic sort of all existential disclosing [*daseinsmäßigen Erschließens*], sight is understanding [*Verstehen*] in the sense of the genuine making one's own

Notes

[*Zueignung*] of what there is [*Seiende*] to which existence [*Dasein*] can relate according to its essential possibilities of being [*Seinsmöglichkeiten*]. *GA* 2, 226. The *Zueignung* Heidegger referred to in the second passage can also mean dedication to what *Dasein* accomplishes.

470 'Zur Frage nach der Bestimmung der Sache des Denkens [On the Question of the Determination of the Matter of Thinking].' *GA* 16, 620-633. As noted earlier, the text originated as a lecture given in Amriswil on October 30, 1965, in honor of Ludwig Binswanger. Boss refers to the essay published as *Zur Frage nach der Bestimmung der Sache des Denkens* (Franz Larese and Jürg Janett, eds.), St. Gallen: Erker, 1984, 19 (= *GA* 16, 631). In the *GA* text, *Dasein* is not hyphenated as it is here (*Da-Sein*). The sentence Heidegger 'quotes' does not appear as such in *Being and Time*. It is an altered version of a sentence from the first passage cited in the previous note where *Lichtung* is used: '[The human being] is 'enlightened [*erleuchtet*]', means [it is] luminant [*gelichtet*] in itself *as* being-in-the-world [that is, as *Dasein*], not [made luminant] by another being [*Seiende*], but rather such that it itself *is* the luminance [*Lichtung*].'

471 'After Thirty Years' (2002/2003b), quoted 35.
472 'After Thirty Years' (2002/2003b), 36.
473 'After Thirty Years' (2002/2003b), 36.
474 'After Thirty Years' (2002/2003b), 36.
475 'Martin Heidegger und die Ärzte', in G. Neske (ed.), *Martin Heidegger zum 70. Geburtstag*, Neske: Pfullingen, 1959, 276-290. Adapted version printed in *Von der Psychoanalyse zur Daseinsanalyse. Wege zu einem neuen Selbstverständnis*, Vienna: Europaverlag, 1979, 203-244.
476 'The Role of Psychotherapy in Schizophrenia' (1958), 11-2. Cf. *Psychoanalysis and Daseinsanalysis* (1957a), 10-11.
477 'Heidegger und die Ärtze' (1959b), 286.
478 'Heidegger und die Ärtze' (1959b), 290.
479 'Tribute to Martin Heidegger', (1970c), in Richard Wisser (ed.), *Martin Heidegger in Conversation*, New Delhi: Arnold-Heinemann, 1977, 9-11. The text is based on *Martin Heidegger im Gespräch*, Freiburg: Alber, 1970, 20-22. The translator is given as B. Srinivasa Murthy.
480 *Zollikon Seminars* (1987a), 293-297.
481 The interview was published along with Boss's tribute as well as similar texts by Carl-Friedrich von Weizäcker (1912-2007), Maurice de Gandillac (1906-2006), Ernst Jünger (1895-1998), Kôichi Tsujimura (1922-2010), Emil Staiger (1908-1987), Leo Gabriel (1902-1987), Karl Löwith (1897-1973), Dolf Sternberger (1907-1989), Heinrich Ott (1929-2013) and Karl Rahner (1905-1984).
482 *Zollikon Seminars* (1987a), 294.
483 'Tribute to Martin Heidegger', (1970c), 10.
484 'Martin Heidegger und seine Bedeutung für die gesellschaftliche Evolution', (1980a), in A. Hicklin (ed.), *Wandel und Tradition. Verharren und Verändern: Gestaltende Kräfte im Menschen und in menschlichen Gesellschaft* [*Change and Tradition. Persistence and Change: Formative Processes in Man and Human Society*], Bern: Benteli, 1980, 111-129.
485 'Martin Heidegger und seine Bedeutung für die gesellschaftliche Evolution' (1980a), 116. He refers to an article by Alois Hicklin due to appear in G. Condrau (ed.), *Transzendenz, Imagination und Kreativität* [*Die Psychologie des 20. Jahrhunderts*, Volume 15] Zürich: Kindler, 1979. He likely had in mind Hicklin's 'Phänomenologie des Gewissens', 446-453.
486 'Martin Heidegger und seine Bedeutung für die gesellschaftliche Evolution' (1980a), 115.
487 'Martin Heidegger und seine Bedeutung für die gesellschaftliche Evolution' (1980a), 120.
488 On this, see the excellent paper by João Augusto Pompéia, 'Pain and Time', in Alfred Denker, Miles Groth, Josef Jenewein and Holger Zaborowski (eds.), *Heidegger-Jahrbuch* 14, 2023, 139-152.
489 In this connection, see also Boss's paper 'Warum verhält sich der Mensch überhaupt sozial? [Why Do Human Beings Behave Socially at All?]' (1962b).

490 'Martin Heidegger und seine Bedeutung für die gesellschaftliche Evolution' (1980a), 125.
491 'Martin Heidegger und seine Bedeutung für die gesellschaftliche Evolution' (1980a), 126.
492 'Die Bedeutung Martin Heideggers für die Arbeit mit leidenden Menschen und für das Selbstverständnis der Psychotherapie' (1982j), in *Von der Spannweite der Seele. Ausgewählte Vorträge und Aufsätze aus den Anwendungsbereichen des daseinsanalytischen Menschenverständnisses* (1982b), Bern: Benteli, 1982, 199-210.
493 The Catholic Academy was established in 1956, having been planned in part by Conrad Gröber (1872-1948), an archbishop of the archdiocese who is remembered for having given the young high school student, Martin Heidegger, a copy of Franz Brentano's (1838-1917) book on Aristotle which inspired the young man to delve deeply into the question about the sense of be[-ing] [*Sein*]. Heidegger was at the time living at Konradihaus in Constance, the seminary where Gröber was rector. The book was a birthday present for Heidegger's 18th birthday in 1907, with the expectation that he would study for the priesthood. Bernhard Welte (1906-1983), who delivered the eulogy at Heidegger's funeral, had been instrumental in establishing the mission of the Academy.
494 'Die Bedeutung Martin Heideggers für die Arbeit mit leidenden Menschen und für das Selbstverständnis der Psychotherapie' (1982j), 201.
495 'Die Bedeutung Martin Heideggers für die Arbeit mit leidenden Menschen und für das Selbstverständnis der Psychotherapie' (1982j), 202.
496 'Die Bedeutung Martin Heideggers für die Arbeit mit leidenden Menschen und für das Selbstverständnis der Psychotherapie' (1982j), 204.
497 'Die Bedeutung Martin Heideggers für die Arbeit mit leidenden Menschen und für das Selbstverständnis der Psychotherapie' (1982j), 209.
498 'Dank an Martin Heidegger–Ein Hinweis auf seine Zollikoner Seminare' (1977d), in G. Neske (ed.), *Erinnerung an Martin Heidegger*, Pfullingen: Neske, 1977, 31-45. Reprinted in *Von der Spannweite der Seele. Ausgewählte Vorträge und Aufsätze aus den Anwendungsbereichen des daseinsanalytischen Menschenverständnisses* (1982b), Bern: Benteli, 1982, 211-225. English translation: 'Martin Heidegger's Zollikon Seminars', *Review of Existential Psychology and Psychiatry* 16(1-3), 1978-79, 7-20. Translation by Brian Kenny. In an editors' (Thomas Lynaugh and Keith Hoeller) note to the translation we read: 'In an agreement between Boss and Heidegger, nothing else of the Zollikon Seminars will be published until after their deaths. At that time, the protocols of the Zollikon Seminars will go to the Heidegger Archives in Marbach, West Germany.' Nevertheless, the protocols plus conversations between Boss and Heidegger and excerpts of letters from Heidegger were published in 1987 thanks to a dispensation granted by Heidegger's younger son, Hermann. The translator, Brian Kenny, was at the time of publication of this first introduction to American readers of the Zollikon seminars head of the Bellevue Sanatorium (Kreuzlingen), having succeeded Ludwig Binswanger. Binswanger had overseen the hospital from 1911-1956. Kenny was the last director of the asylum, which closed in 1980.
499 *Zollikon Seminars* (1987a), 7.
500 'Martin Heidegger's Zollikon Seminars' (1977d), 7.
501 'Martin Heidegger's Zollikon Seminars' (1977d), 9.
502 'Martin Heidegger's Zollikon Seminars' (1977d), 11-12.
503 The parenthetic remark was added for the translation. Since the reminiscence was published in English in 1978-79, it likely appeared around the same time as the issue of the *Review of Existential Psychology and Psychiatry* in which this text appears. At the time of the special issue on Boss in which this translation is found, Boss was on the editorial board of the journal, along with, among others, Leslie Farber, William Richardson and Herbert Spiegelberg, who had proposed publishing the translation (7, editors' introductory note). Boss had been on the board since the journal was founded in 1961.
504 'Martin Heidegger's Zollikon Seminars' (1977d), 14-17. A transcript of the facsimile is given, 18-19.
505 See *Zollikon Seminars* (1987a), 136-143.

Notes

506 At the time of Boss's reminiscence, this was ostensibly the only evidence for the seminars. It is not clear why the scans of the manuscript pages were attributed text to the *Grundriß* (1971a) unless this was part of a very early working manuscript that was greatly transformed in time for publication.
507 Kenny misleadingly translates '*Gegebenheiten*' with 'beings'.
508 Martin Heidegger, *Zollikoner Seminare. Protokolle–Gespräche–Briefe*, Frankfurt: Klostermann, 1987; 2nd ed., 1994; 3rd ed., 2006 (1987a). Contains 'Freundesbrief' of October 5, 1969, as the editor's 'Schlußwort' to the volume. See note to 'Martin Heidegger's Zollikon Seminars' (1977d), 7. English translation: *Zollikon Seminars: Protocols–Conversations–Letters*, Evanston: Northwestern University Press, 2001. Translation by Franz Mayr and Richard Askay. The Heidegger *Gesamtausgabe*, Frankfurt: Klosterman, 2018, edition (GA 89, Peter Trawny, ed.) contains reprints of the seminar protocols included in Boss's edition and Heidegger's notes for the seminars.
509 See (1996).
510 See 'Der Einstieg der Daseinsanalytik in das Denken der Ärzte' (1982h), 181, written with Gion Condrau. Excerpts are taken from sessions held on July 5, 1965 (*Zollikon Seminars* (1987a), 121ff.), November 28, 1965 (*Zollikon Seminars* (1987a), 253), November 29, 1965 (*Zollikon Seminars* (1987a), 254-256), and July 14, 1969 (*Zollikon Seminars* (1987a), 186-187). The texts were reworked in many places after the publication of this contribution before appearing in 1987. One passage (178-179) does not appear in *Zollikoner Seminare*. It is given in the context of a very important statement by Boss that a more adequate appropriation of Heidegger's fundamental ontology and its use as the basic theory of a new pathology and as the basis of a therapy more suitable for human beings [than that offered by Binswanger] was the life task of the author, his co-workers and teachers, among them first G. Condrau. First of all, as Heidegger himself recorded it in writing, after the clarification of the true relation between 'science' and Heidegger's fundamental ontology, all accusations occasionally raised against the 'Boss school' collapse from the outset. It can be neither about a 'circumvention of the scientific problematic alone' nor a 'closer response [*Rückkoppelung*]' to Heidegger's intentions. Finally, [daseinanalysts] strictly refrain from the erroneous distinction which claims that the 'psychiatric daseinsanalysis [*Daseinsanalyse*]' is exclusively concerned with the empirical description and structural clarification of pathological modes of existence [*Daseinsweise*], while Heidegger is concerned with the attempt to clarify 'possible forms [*Formen*]' of Dasein ontologically. It can never be a matter of such a 'transformation' of an ontological approach into an empirical conception and 'methodology' oriented towards concrete [some] human life course [*Lebensverlauf*].'
511 See 'Martin Heidegger's Zollikon Seminars' (1977d), 7 (editor's note). Only in 2018 was the GA edition finally published, edited by Peter Trawny. As noted, it contains extensive notes Heidegger had prepared for each session and the protocols of the seminars. With one exception, the conversations and excerpts from correspondence Boss included in his edition are not included.
512 See (1988c).
513 *Zollikon Seminars* (1987a), 3-4, 188-195, 212-213, 222-224. Trawny includes notes for sessions held in November 1959, and February 3, 1960 at the Burghölzli (*GA 89*, 7-16, 21-61), which Boss does not record. He did not find documentation for the text attributed to Heidegger from September 8, 1959. The texts of notes for seminars on March 10 and 12, 1965, and November 13 and 16, 1966, are reproduced in his edition (*GA 89*, 235-377, 563-577). These do not appear in the Boss edition.
514 'Freundesbrief' (1969), in *Neue Zürcher Zeitung*, 606 October 5, 1969, 52. Reprinted as the editor's 'Schlußwort' to *Zollikoner Seminare* (1987a), 363-369. English translation: 'Afterword', in *Zollikon Seminars* (1987a), 293-297.
515 'Afterword' (1969), 293.
516 'Afterword' (1969), 294.

Notes

517 As for awareness of Heidegger's work in general, it took thirty-five years for *Sein und Zeit* to be translated into English for the first time, and by 1969, when Boss wrote his letter, there was still little Heidegger available in English. Twelve books: *Existence and Being* (1949) (incorporating six essays: 'On the Essence of Truth'; 'What Is Metaphysics?'; 'Postscript' to 'What Is Metaphysics?'; 'Hölderlin and the Essence of Poetry'; Prefatory Remarks to a Repetition of the Address'; 'Remembrance of the Poet'); *The Question of Being* (1958); *What Is Philosophy?* (1958); *An Introduction to Metaphysics* (1959); *Essays in Metaphysics. Identity and Difference* (1960) (two essays: 'The Onto-theological Nature of Metaphysics'; 'The Principle of Identity'); *Kant and the Problem of Metaphysics* (1962); *Being and Time* (1962); *Discourse on Thinking* (1966) (two essays: 'Memorial Address'; 'Conversation on a Country Path about Thinking'); *What Is a Thing?* (1967); *The Piety of Thinking* (1968) (four essays: 'The Problem of a Non-objectifying Thinking and Speaking in Contemporary Theology'; 'Phenomenology and Theology'; 'Review of Ernst Cassirer's *Mythical Thought*'; 'Conversation with Martin Heidegger'); *What Is Called Thinking?* (1968); *The Essence of Reasons* (1969); *Identity and Difference* (1969) (two essays: 'The Onto-theological Constitution of Metaphysics'; 'The Principle of Identity'). There were also twenty articles, short texts and letters: 'The Age of the World View' (1951); 'What Is Metaphysics?' (1956); 'Hölderlin and the Essence of Poetry' (1959); 'On the Essence of Ground' (1962); 'Letter on Humanism' (1962); 'Philosophy – What Is It?' (1962); 'Plato's Doctrine of Truth' (1962); 'Art and Thinking' (1963); 'Eventide on Reichenau' (1963); 'Letter to Alcopley' (1963); letter to Manfred Frings (1964); 'Editor's Foreword' to Edmund Husserl, *The Phenomenology of Inner Time-Consciousness* (1964); 'A Cassirer-Heidegger Seminar' (1964); 'The Origin of the Work of Art' (1965); 'The Self-Assertion of the German University' (1965); '*Curriculum vitae*' (1965); 'The Pathway' (1967); 'Who Is Nietzsche's Zarathustra?' (1967); 'A Letter from Heidegger' (1968); and an excerpt from a letter to Medard Boss (1963).
518 'Afterword' (1969), 294-295.
519 The 2001 translation mistakenly glosses 'being-human' with '*Mensch sein*', which would mean 'to be human'.
520 'Afterword' (1969), 295.
521 'Afterword' (1969), 297.
522 'Preface to the American Translation of Martin Heidegger's *Zollikon Seminars*' [1990], in *Zollikon Seminars* (1987a), ix-xii. Written in English. The text is dated Spring 1989. Boss died on December 21, 1990, before completing the preface.
523 This was an English version of 'Woraus besteht der Mensch, wenn er träumt, und wo ist er dann?' (1988c).
524 Bertolt Brecht (1938), *Collected Poems*, New York: W.W. Norton, 2018, 681.
525 By the end of 1998, Heidegger's book had been translated into Italian (1987) and Japanese (1991).
526 'Anstöße Martin Heideggers für eine andere Psychiatrie' [1989] (1991), in H.-H. Gander (ed.), *Von Heidegger her. Wirkungen in Philosophie – Kunst – Medizin. Meßkirchner Vorträge*, Frankfurt: Klostermann, 1991, 125-140.
527 'Anstöße Martin Heideggers für eine andere Psychiatrie' (1991), 125.
528 The German colloquial phrase '*Leiben und Leben*' as an exclamation can mean 'Be alive and live your life!' 'Be all you can be!' or 'Be who you really are!' It is the title of one of Boss's books, co-edited with two first-generation daseinanalysts, Gion Condrau and Alois Hicklin, published in 1977, on psychosomatics. See (1977f).
529 'Anstöße Martin Heideggers für eine andere Psychiatrie' (1991), 128.
530 'Anstöße Martin Heideggers für eine andere Psychiatrie' (1991), 128.
531 The nominalized verb *Vernehmen* is used in the Zollikon seminars, as here, to denote taking in what is encountering *Dasein*. Translated as 'receiving-perceiving' introduces the notion of perception [*Vorstellung*], which Boss consistently rejects as inexplicable.
532 'Anstöße Martin Heideggers für eine andere Psychiatrie' (1991), 129.
533 'Anstöße Martin Heideggers für eine andere Psychiatrie' (1991), 130.

Notes

534 'Anstöße Martin Heideggers für eine andere Psychiatrie' (1991), 131.
535 Here it is important to recall Heidegger's notion of human temporality or being-temporal understood from the perspective of time as a unity of three 'exstases', that is, ways of standing out into the world (futural, past-reckoning and presentative).
536 'Anstöße Martin Heideggers für eine andere Psychiatrie' (1991), 133.
537 'Anstöße Martin Heideggers für eine andere Psychiatrie' (1991), 133.
538 This is one of the few references to ethics to be found in Boss's writings. The claim that there is an 'original ethics' in Heidegger's fundamental ontology had already been made a few years earlier by the American philosopher John D. Caputo in 'Heidegger's Original Ethics', in *The New Scholasticism* 45(1), 1971, 127-137.
539 'Anstöße Martin Heideggers für eine andere Psychiatrie' (1991), 139.
540 As noted earlier, the term '*Gelassenheit*' is central to the late Heidegger. With origins in Meister Eckhart, it is difficult to translate while preserving its several evocative senses. It has been rendered as 'releasement', which in English has to do with the relaxation of constraints and makes little sense here. For Boss, invoking a disposition of the human being toward things, *Gelassenheit* refers to detachment from them. Heidegger's 'Memorial Address' of 1955 was first published as *Gelassenheit* (1959). See *GA* 16, 517-529. It should be read along with 'Conversations on a Country Path about Thinking' from 1944-45 (*GA* 13, 37-74). The whole passage from which Boss quotes runs as follows: 'We let [*lassen*] technical objects into our daily world and at the same time leave [*lassen*] them outside, i.e., [leave them] to themselves as things that are not absolutes but remain dependent on something higher. I would like to call this attitude of simultaneous yes and no to the technical world with an old word: detachment [*Gelassenheit*] with respect to things. In this attitude we no longer see things only technically.' See *GA* 16, 427.
541 'Gelassenheit', in *GA* 16, 527-528.
542 'Martin Heidegger Applied to Psychiatry and the Modern World' [1989] (2002/2003c), *Review of Existential Psychology and Psychiatry* 27(1-3), 2002/2003, 23-31. Reprinted as a monograph by K. Hoeller (ed.), *The Heidegger-Boss Relationship*, Seattle: Review of Existential Psychology and Psychiatry, 2008, 23-31. Lecture given at the Applied Heidegger Conference, September 8-10, 1989, at the University of California, Berkeley. It is said to have been translated by Michael Eldred for the Hoeller volume but was likely given in English by Boss.
543 *An Informal English Paraphrase of Sections 1-53, with Certain Omissions as Noted* (manuscript, Cambridge: Harvard Divinity School) was undertaken in 1955 by John Wild, Robert J. Trayhern, Cornelius de Deugd and Dreyfus at Harvard. The translation is notable for having rendered *Dasein* with 'transience'. The typed manuscript is held by only a few university libraries.
544 'Martin Heidegger Applied to Psychiatry and the Modern World' (2002/2003c), 28.
545 See *Zollikon Seminare* (1987a), 273. It is not clear what the source of the quotation is.
546 Franz Larese and Jürg Janett (eds.), St. Gallen: Erker, 1984), 19 (= *GA* 16, 631).
547 See *Zollikoner Seminare* (1987a), 223.
548 'Martin Heidegger Applied to Psychiatry and the Modern World' (2002/2003c), 31. Based on his other texts, I have interpolated what I can safely say were Boss's German terms.
549 Theodore Roethke, *Words for the Wind*, Bloomington: Indiana University Press, 1966, 124.
550 I have arranged the items chronologically by genre. It is likely that when a translator is not named for an item it was Boss himself who prepared it. These are marked (**B**). In cooperation with the journal's editor and Marianne Boss-Linsmayer, a first iteration of this bibliography was published as 'An International Bibliography of the Writings of Medard Boss 1929-2002', in *Review of Existential Psychology and Psychiatry* 27(1-3), 2002/2003, 155-171, reprinted in a monograph by K. Hoeller (ed.), *The Heidegger-Boss Relationship* (Seattle: Review of Existential Psychology and Psychiatry, 2008), 155-171. Twenty-nine items could not be located and in one case could not be attested. I have not seen the unpublished papers. The items have been given a date that corresponds to the Chronological Listing {/}.

Index

A

abstaining [Versagen] [n.], 160
acting out [Agieren] [n.], 24, 31, 52, 133–134, 138–139, 142–143, 160, 162
actualization, human [Daseiende] [n.], 4, 238n37
adream [ertäumen] [v.], 56
Allport, Gordon, 32, 150–151
American Daseinsanalytic Institute (ADI), 61–62, 231n3, 233n16, 246n80, 252n172
analysis [Analyse] [n.] (cf. analysis (of dreams) Auslegung), 12–18, 20, 61–65, 92–95, 262, 264n299, 265, 273n398, 278
analysis (of dreams) Auslegung, 12, 59
analytics of Dasein [Daseinsanalytik] [n.], 12, 121, 136, 146, 176, 236n33, 240n44, 241n68, 244n75
animal rationale [n.], 32, 247n87
anxiety [Angst] [n.], 77, 125–126, 128, 130, 159–160, 170, 243n74, 253n181, 261n259, 262, 265n326
appearance [Vorschein] [n.], 129, 155
Arendt, Hannah, 195, 267n344
atmosphere, 28, 42, 48, 80, 134, 186, 201, 232n9
atmosphere, attunement, 28
atmosphere [Stimmung] [n.] (cf. attunement), 28, 201
attunement, 28–29, 40, 57, 115, 123–124, 145, 159
attunement [Stimmung] [n.] (cf. atmosphere), 28, 57, 115, 123
Augustine of Hippo authenticity [Eigentlichkeit] [n.], 29
awaken [erwachen] [n.], 56
awakening [Erwachen] [n.], 56

B

be[-ing], 237–239, 260n247, 280n493
be-ing [seiend] [adj.], 43, 264n283
be[-ing] [Sein] [n.] (cf. Being), 163, 237–239, 260n247, 280n493
Beaufret, Jean, 175
behavior, xii, 18–19, 48, 52–53, 125, 127, 131, 247n88, 250n115, 275n427
behavior [Verhalten] [n.] (cf. comportment), 197
Being, 10–14, 28, 54
being-with, 249, 263n277
being, a [ein Seiendes], 3, 10, 174, 177, 179–180, 188, 192, 235n23, 237, 239–240, 262n265
being, a [ein Seiendes] [n.] (cf. what there is), 239n40, 262n267, 278n469
being-with [Mitsein] [n.] (cf. togetherness), 249n111, 263n277
being, a [n.], existent [adj.], 3, 10–11, 122–123, 179–180, 188, 192, 235n23, 237, 239, 262n265
Being [Sein] [n.] (cf. be[-ing]), xii, 4, 10–11, 92, 96, 114, 170, 200, 260n247, 263n277, 279n470, 282
being-a-self [Selbstsein] [n.], 180
being there [Da-sein] [n.] (cf. existence, There-being), 247n87, 275n427
being there, existence, 29, 198, 247n87, 275n427
being there, There-being, xii, 29, 100, 107, 198, 243n74, 247n87, 273n395, 275n427
being-towards-death [Zein-zum Tode] [n.], 29, 234n22
being-in-the-world [In-der-Welt-sein] [n.], 263n277

Index

Binswanger, Ludwig, 3, 7, 115, 150, 179, 200, 233n17, 261n259, 265n308, 279n470, 280n498
Bleuler, Eugen, 70, 81–82, 84, 94, 98, 149, 259n232
bodiliness [Leiblichkeit] [n.], 11, 13, 30, 54, 116, 123, 189, 260n244
bodily being [Leiblichkeit] [n.], 197
bodily [leiblich] [adj./adv.], 11–12, 20, 196
body, physical [Körper] [n.] (cf. lived body), 11, 20, 114, 129
boredom [Langweiligkeit] [n.], 161
Boss, Medard, xi, xiii, 3, 7, 78–79, 97, 105, 109, 112, 253, 257, 283n550
Brahman, 158, 168–169, 173, 277n454
Braque, Georges, 175
Bultmann, Rudolf calling [Beruf] [n.], 155, 175

C

caring about the other [Fürsorge] [n.], 27, 32–33, 90, 107, 175–176, 243n74, 255n197
    interventional [einspringend] [adj.], 33
    way-making [vorausspringend, vorspringend] [adj.], 33, 90, 175
caring about things (care) [Sorge] [n.], 12, 28–29, 32–33, 90, 255n197
CBT (cognitive-behavioral therapy), 8, 25
Char, René, 175
chit, 259n231
closeness [Nähe] [n.], 37, 40, 123, 250n132
come to pass [wesen] [v.], 52
comportment, xii, 23, 33, 111, 238–239
comportment [Verhalten] [n.] (cf. behavior), 238n38
composure [Gelassenheit] [n.], 33, 53, 197, 278
concealment [Verborgenheit] [n.], 30, 179
Condrau, Gion, 69, 72, 136–137, 145, 276n436, 281n510, 282n528
conscience [Gewissen], 30, 156, 178
conscious [bewußt] [adj.], 141–142, 272
consciousness [Bewußtsein] [n.], 19, 99, 141–142, 272
consideration [Besinnung] [n.], 127, 130

control analysis, 62, 65
conversation [Gespräch] [n.], 46, 153, 236n33, 240n54, 250n135, 279n479
couch [n.], 25, 37–38, 50, 58, 64, 70, 82, 101, 107, 111, 143–144
countertransference [Gegenübertragung] [n.], 24, 133, 160
cura [n.], 12

D

da-seinanalysis [Daseinsanalyse] [n.] (cf. daseinanalysis, Daseinsanalysis), 233n16, 253n177
daseinanalysis, da-seinanalysis, 18, 69, 72, 74, 76, 78, 116–117, 121, 233n16, 259n223, 261n259, 262, 277n447
daseinanalysis [Daseinsanalyse] [n.] (cf. Daseinsanalysis, da-seinanalysis), 3, 9, 12–14, 18, 69, 72, 74, 76, 78, 116–117, 121, 132, 145, 233n16, 243n74, 250n117, 253n176, 254n189, 259n223, 261n259, 262, 277n447
daseinanalysis, Daseinsanalysis, xi–xvi, 3–5, 7–21, 48–54, 56–57, 266, 276n438, 281n510
Daseinsanalysis, da-seinanalysis, 3, 8, 11, 57, 157–158, 163–166, 263n269, 267n345, 281n510
Daseinsanalysis [Daseinsanalyse] [n.] (cf. daseinanalysis, da-seinanalysis), 3, 72, 74–76, 78, 94, 175, 233n16, 236n33, 240n54, 242n74, 253n177, 259n223, 277n447, 281n510
Descartes, René, 19, 102, 231n2
determination [Bestimmung] [n.], 201, 243n74, 279n470
disposition [Befindlichkeit] [n.], 29
distance [Ferne] [n.], 123, 250n132
distraction, 243n74, 249n114
distraction [Verfallenheit] [n.] (cf. lapsing [Verfallen]), 243n74
dreaming life [Träumen] [n.], 30, 54
    analysis (of dreams) [Auslegung] [n.] (cf. analysis [Analyse]), 12–13, 21n160, 70, 74, 251n158
    latent idea, 142
    manifest content, 56
DSM-5-TR (2022), 107, 134, 231n1

Index

E

ego [Ich] [n.], 19, 120, 170, 263n282
Ellis, Albert empathy [n.], 17
encounter [Begegnung] [n.], 23, 31, 41, 72, 111, 124, 156, 262
encountered, what is [Begegnende] [n.], 177, 197–198
encountering [Begegnen] [n.], 44
encountering, what is [Begegnende] [n.], 44, 197–198
environment [Umwelt] [n.], 5, 20
essence [Wesen] [n.], 4, 43, 52, 116, 127, 169, 238, 273n395
event, 18–19, 27, 47–48, 55–56, 69, 79, 82, 102, 125–127, 134, 144, 152, 183, 188, 193, 197, 244n76, 245, 256n202, 265n321, 276
event [Ereignis] [n.] (cf. eventuality), 188
eventuality, 201
eventuality [Ereignis] [n.] (cf. event), 188
existence [Dasein] [n.] (cf. being there, There-being), 2–5, 10–12, 15–18, 44, 117–118, 193, 196–199, 233n17, 234n22, 235n24, 236n33, 237–238, 279, 281n510
existence, There-being, 243n74
existent, an [ein Seiendes] [n.] (cf. being, a [n.], existent [adj.]), 10, 239n39
existent, an [n.], 11
existent [seiend] [adj.] (cf. existent, an [n.]), 10–11, 239n39
existential [existentiell] [adj.], 165
existential [Existenzial] [n.] (cf. existentive), 234n21, 269n358
existential [existenziell] psychoanalysis (Sartre), xi, 3, 7–8, 14, 19–20, 72–75, 100–101, 268, 279n476
existentive, 4, 12, 28–32, 234, 238, 243n74, 249n102, 263n277
existentive [Existenzial] [n.] (cf. existential [n.]), 4, 12, 28–32, 44, 54, 107, 125, 128, 156–157, 263n277, 269n358
  anxiety [Angst] [n.], 77, 125–126, 128, 130, 159–160, 170, 243n74, 253n181, 261n259, 262, 265n326
  being-with [Mitsein] [n.] (cf. togetherness), 249n111, 263n277

caring about the other [Fürsorge] [n.], 27, 32–33, 90, 107, 175–176, 243n74, 255n197
caring about things [Sorge] [n.], 28–29, 32, 130, 243n74, 249n111, 255n197
disposition [Befindlichkeit] [n.], 29
distraction [Verfallenheit] [n.] (cf. lapsing), 243n74
givenness [Geworfenheit] [n.] (cf. givenness [Gegebenheit]), 29, 156, 243n74
indebtedness [Schuld] [n.], 30, 125, 128–129, 156, 178
mineness [Jemeinigkeit] [n.], 238n38
spatiality [Räumlichkeit] [n.], 30, 54, 151, 189
talk [Rede] [n.], 30–31, 38, 153, 243n74
temporality [Zeitlichkeit] [n.], 151, 155
truth [Wahrheit] [n.], 30, 169
understanding [Verstehen] [n.], 16, 29, 43, 114, 171, 243n74, 278
existing [adj.], xii, 4, 10–11, 20, 103, 106, 111, 184, 191, 198–200, 277n452
existing [Existieren] [n.] (cf. existing [adj.]), 28, 32, 43–44, 92, 96, 115, 179–181, 191, 198, 234n22
existing with others [Mitdasein] [n.], 118
existing [vorhanden] [adj.] (cf. extant [adj.]), 25
extant [adj.], 44, 148, 278
extant [vorhanden] [adj.] (cf. existing [adj.]), 148

F

Farber, Leslie, 9, 17, 132, 254n187, 256n204, 265n308, 280n503
Fenichel, Otto, 259n232
Foucault, Michel, 17, 233n17, 265n308
Frankl, Viktor, 117, 124, 145, 232n12, 254n191, 263n272, 264n283, 265n308, 268n356
free association, 39–40, 83, 155, 171, 234n18, 266n340, 274n405, 277n447
freedom [Freiheit] [n.], 44, 170, 261n259
Freud, Sigmund, 3, 70, 76, 82, 88, 136, 188, 254n196, 257n208, 260n251, 261n259, 263n278, 272n378

Index

fundamental ontology
[Fundamentalontologie] [n.],
264n283
fundamental rule [Grundregel] [n.], 39

G

Gadamer, Hans-Georg, 175
givenness [Gegebenheit] [n.] (cf.
givenness [Geworfenheit], realities
[Gegebenheiten]), 156–157, 168, 182
givenness [Geworfenheit] [n.] (cf.
givenness [Gegebenheit]), 29,
243n74
Goldstein, Kurt, 85, 259n232
guilt feelings [Schuldgefühle] [n.], 126

H

Heidegger, Martin:
  analytics of existence
  [Daseinsanalytik] [n.], 4, 12, 14,
  16–17, 60, 233n17, 269n358, 281
  existentatives +
  Existenzialetentatives
  [Existenziale] [n.], 4, 28, 243n74
  fundamental ontology
  [Fundamentalontologie] [n.], 4, 14,
  23, 63, 92, 101, 237, 281n510,
  283n538
  ontological difference, 4, 12, 179,
  234n22, 267n345
  preontological [adj.], 12
Heisenberg, Werner, 175
Hicklin, Alois, 72, 260n239, 262, 276n436,
279n485, 282n528
Hoch, Erna, 71, 172–173, 254n186, 262
Hölderlin, Friedrich, 46, 250n135
homosexuality, 103, 257n215, 258n218
Horney, Karen, 84–85, 248n98, 259n232,
271n363
human being [Mensch] [n.], 11, 155, 191,
198–199, 242, 279n489
human existence, 10–13, 43, 70, 92–94,
96, 100, 104, 106, 109–110, 112, 115, 156,
160, 242n74, 243n74, 268n356
human existence [Existenz] [n.] (cf. way
of life), 10, 96, 125, 160
Husserl, Edmund, 63, 272n379, 282n517
Hyginus, 12

I

id [Es] [n.], 85, 120
idea, perception, 37, 88, 93
idea, representation, 32, 88, 93
idea [Vorstellung] [n.] (cf. perception,
representation), 142
indebtedness [Schuld] [n.], 30, 125,
128–129, 156, 178
India, 34, 70–72, 74, 78–79, 95, 97,
104–106, 249n110, 254n189, 278
intellectual, 9, 56, 88, 91, 96, 99, 116, 118,
169–170, 174, 182, 186
intellectual [geistig] [adj.] (cf. spiritual),
174
International Federation of
Daseinsanalysis (IFDA), 62, 233,
234n18, 252n172
interpretation [Bedeutung] [n.],
253n181
intrapsychic introjection, 57, 115, 175,
247n88

J

Jung, Carl Gustav, 23, 98, 145, 232n12,
259n232
Jünger, Ernst, 175, 279n481

K

Kahn, Eugen Kashmir, 8
Kaul, Govind, 34, 72, 97, 106, 111, 167–168,
171, 276n436, 277n454, 278n465
Kuhn, Roland, 8, 13, 233n17, 236, 237n35,
240n53, 242n74, 273n390

L

Laing, R.D., 18
language [Sprache] [n.], 30–31, 77,
253n181
lapsing [Verfallen]), 30
lapsing [Verfallen] [n.] (cf. distraction),
30
Leibniz, Gottfried Wilhelm, 174
liberation [Befreiung] [n.], 72, 265
light [Lichte] [n.], 44, 86, 130, 254n193
listening [Hören] [n.], 38, 157
lived body, 20, 240n50, 249n104
lived body [Leib] [n.] (cf. body, physical
[Körper]), 20, 240n50, 249n104

Index

love [Liebe] [n.], 131, 257n213
luminance [Lichtung] [n.], 106, 113, 118, 129, 260n244, 277n452, 278, 279n470

M

manifestation [Vorschein] [n.], 40, 43, 93, 114, 129, 155, 174, 242n74, 266n333
May, Rollo, 17–18, 117, 263n274, 265n308, 268n356, 270n360, 271, 273n391
meaning) sight [Sicht] [n.], 239n39
meaning [Sinn] [n.] (cf. sense), 12, 126, 163, 191, 236n33, 257n213
memory [Gedächtnis] [n.], 151
mental, psychic [psychisch], 272n379
mental, psychic [seelisch], 129
mental [seelisch] [adj.] (cf. psychic [seelisch]), 129
Merleau-Ponty, Maurice, 265n308
metaphysics, 4, 14, 157, 168, 233n17, 237–238, 257n212, 267n345, 268n355, 282n517
mineness [Jemeinigkeit] [n.], 238n38
Minkowski, Eugène, 18, 248n100, 264n283, 268n356
mood [Stimmung] [n.] (cf. atmosphere, attunement), 27–28, 57, 115
more human, the [Überich] [n.], 120, 141
motivation [Motivation] [n.], 24, 74, 119, 155, 191, 263n282, 264
mystery [Geheimnis] [n.], 159, 199, 201

N

natural science nature [Natur] [n.], 7, 20, 75, 87, 102, 106, 147

O

object, 20, 32, 54, 58, 75, 93–94, 179, 193, 232n7, 277n452, 283n540
occur [eignen] [v.], 131
ontic [ontisch] [adj.], 4
ontological difference, 4, 12, 179, 234n22, 267n345
ontological [ontologisch] [adj.], 4
open, the [Offen] [n.], 38, 40–41, 44, 49, 110, 153, 157, 171, 180, 273
openness [Offenheit] [n.], 44, 53, 106, 159, 164, 175, 199
organism [Organismus] [n.], 147

P

paraphilia [Perversion] [n.], 12, 17, 70, 73, 77, 236n33, 240n49, 257–258, 262n260
partnership, therapeutic [n.], 63, 105, 140–141, 156, 167
pastoral care [n.], 8, 20–21
people [das Man] [n.], 30, 166
perceiving, 40, 54, 57, 100, 104, 109, 112, 119–120, 122, 166, 282n531
perceiving, seeing, 54
perceiving, taking in, 112, 282n531
perceiving [Vernehmen] [n.] (cf. seeing, taking in), 112, 282n531
perception, representation, 19, 32, 37, 62, 257n212, 264n294, 271n373, 273n401, 275n432, 277n452, 282n531
perception [Vorstellung] [n.] (cf. idea, representation), 277n452, 282n531
perception [Wahrnehmung] [n.] (cf. perceiving), 123, 271n373
permitting [Gewähren] [n.], 160
person [Person] [n.], 19, 43, 52
personality [Personalität] [n.], 53, 119, 125, 129, 253n181, 268n356
phenomenology [Phänomenologie] [n.], 261n259
phenomenon [Phänomen] [n.], 130, 272n376
playground, therapeutic [Tummelplatz] [n.], 51, 53, 131, 251n137, 271n370, 273n387
preontological [adj.], 12
presence [Anwesenheit] [n.], 55, 173–174
present, the [Gegenwart] [n.], 25, 30, 155, 164, 272
projection, 119, 175, 190
psyche [Psyche] [n.], 43
psychiatry [n.], xiv–xvi, 3, 7–8, 10, 13, 17–21, 148–151, 156, 252n174, 276, 277n447, 283n550
psychic [psychisch] [adj.] (cf. mental, psychic [seelisch]), 272n379
psychic [seelisch], 116, 129
psychic [seelisch] [adj.] (cf. mental, psychic [psychisch]), 116, 129, 272n379
psychoanalysis [n.], xi, 3, 7–8, 14, 19–20, 23–25, 271, 272n380, 279n476

psychopathology [Psychopathologie] [n.], 19, 32, 53, 69, 73, 92, 126, 128, 140, 196, 247n87, 253n184, 257n213, 261n259, 262n260, 269n357
psychopharmacology [n.], 245n77
psychosomatics [Psychosomatik] [n.], 72, 94, 261n259
psychotherapeutic eros, 24, 50–52, 75, 131, 139, 241n63, 249n111, 251
psychotherapy, xi–xii, xv–xvi, 7, 14, 17–21, 31–33, 124–127, 245, 246n87, 247n87, 276, 279n476
psychotropic drugs, 18, 21
   chlorpromazine [Thorazine, Largactil], 13, 150, 273n390
   imipramine [Tofranil], 13, 240n55, 241n73
   scopolamine [Plexonal], 74, 150, 246n86

R

realities [Gegebenheiten] [n.], 168, 171, 277n451
Reich, Wilhelm, 84, 259n232
relation [Beziehung] [n.], 24, 256, 262
relationship [Verhältnis] [n.], 25, 192
representation [Vorstellung] [n.] (cf. idea, perception), 252n161
resistance [Widerstand] [n.], 23, 137, 275n432
Rhee, Dongschick, 78, 112, 151, 183
Richardson, William J., 18, 195, 243n74, 265n308
Rogers, Carl, 18, 150, 251n143, 264n283, 265n308, 268n356
Rümke, H.C., xiii, 46

S

Sartre, Jean-Paul, 270n360, 271
schizophrenia, 13, 16, 73–74, 85, 241n68, 245n78, 269n358, 279n476
Sechehaye, Marguerite, 107, 259n233, 268n351
seeing, taking in, 277n452
seeing [Vernehmen] [n.] (cf. perceiving, taking in), 43, 197, 277n452
Seguín, Carlos Alberto, 24, 50, 75, 139, 251n150

sense, xi, xiv–xvi, 3–4, 7, 11–13, 89, 93, 100, 111–120, 261–262, 264n288, 266n333, 283n540
sense [Sinn] [n.] (cf. meaning) sight [Sicht] [n.], 12, 29, 126, 163, 198
soul [Seele] [n.], 7, 72, 114, 147, 258
spatial [räumlich] [adj.], 11, 196
spatiality [Räumlichkeit] [n.], 30, 54, 151, 189
Spiegelberg, Herbert, 237n35, 242n74, 253n176, 280n503
spirit [Geist] [n.], 13, 114, 162, 201, 258
spiritual, 11, 13, 15, 24, 82, 88, 184, 188, 195, 231n2, 258
spiritual [geistig] [adj.] (cf. intellectual), 11, 13, 258
Straus, Irwin, 18, 150, 264n283
subconscious [Unterbewußte] [n.], 272n379
subconsciousness [Unterbewußtsein] [n.], 272n379
subject [Subjekt] [n.], 19, 43, 256
Szasz, Thomas, 18, 52, 236n30, 265n308
Szilasi, Wilhelm, 14

T

taking care of [Besorgen] [n.], 29, 32–33, 177
taking in [Vernehmen] [n.] (cf. perceiving, seeing), 112, 123, 157, 277n452, 282n531
talk [Rede] [n.], 30–31, 38, 153, 243n74
Tanabe, Hajime, 175
tao, 112–113, 195, 245, 260n256, 261n258
teaching analysis [Lehranalyse], 64, 131, 200
technology [Technik] [n.], 192, 253n181
temporality [Zeitlichkeit] [n.], 151, 155
Therapeutae, xv
therapy [n.], xv–xvi, 3, 7–8, 14, 84–85, 92, 94–95, 100–101, 246n87, 278n465, 281n510
   abstaining [Versagen] [n.], 160
   conversation [Gespräch] [n.], 46, 153, 236n33, 240n54, 250n135, 279n479
   encounter [Begegnung] [n.], 23, 31, 41, 72, 156, 262
   liberation [Befreiung] [n.], 72, 265

permitting [Gewähren] [n.], 160
psychotherapeutic eros, 24, 50–52, 75, 131, 251
therapeutic playground [Tummelplatz] [n.], 53, 131, 251n137
There-being [Da-sein] [n.] (cf. being there, existence), 96, 243n74
thinking [Denken] [n.], 77, 173, 201, 237, 262n264, 279n470
thought [Gedanke] [n.], 272
Tillich, Paul, 18, 117, 124, 265n308
togetherness, 24, 29, 118, 153–154, 255n197
togetherness [Mitsein] [n.] (cf. being-with), 29, 118, 153
transference [Übertragung] [n.], 137, 237n33
trauma, 56
Trawny, Peter, 253n184, 281
truth [Wahrheit] [n.], 30, 169

U

unconcealment [Unverborgenheit] [n.], 30, 113
Unconscious, the [das Unbewußt] [n.], 7, 23, 39, 141–142, 232n9, 272n379
unconscious [unbewußt] [adj.], 138, 141–142, 272
unconsciousness [Unbewußtsein] [n.], 272n379
understanding [Verstehen] [n.], 16, 29, 43, 114, 171, 243n74, 278

V

van den Berg, Jan, 18, 117, 232n8, 236n29, 250n134, 265n308
Vedanta, 23, 69, 168, 190, 202
von Gebsattel, Viktor, 18, 150, 176
von Weizäcker, Carl-Friedrich, 175

W

waking life [Wachen] [n.], 54, 58
way of life, 45, 90, 96, 173, 239n40, 255n197
way of life [Existenz] [n.] (cf. human existence), 45, 90, 96, 239n40, 255n197
what there is, 17, 33, 77, 93, 106, 120, 127, 199, 237–239, 277n452, 279
what there is [das Seiende] [n.] (cf. being, a [ein Seiendes]), 106, 199, 237, 239–240, 262n267
world with others [Mitwelt] [n.], 118
world [Welt] [n.], 29, 77, 89, 198, 256, 263n277, 269n358
worldliness [Weltlichkeit] [n.], 29
Wyrsch, Jakob, 3, 242n74

Z

Zollikon seminars, 11, 16, 19, 32, 50, 69–72, 194–195, 201, 270, 280n498, 282